D1555567

Developing Responsive Human Services

New Perspectives About Residential Treatment Organizations

Developing Responsive Human Services

New Perspectives About Residential Treatment Organizations

Jack Thaw
Mansfield Training School,
Connecticut Department of
Mental Retardation, and
University of Connecticut

Anthony J. Cuvo
College of Human Resources
and Rehabilitation Institute,
Southern Illinois University
at Carbondale

with contributions by associates

 LAWRENCE ERLBAUM ASSOCIATES, PUBLISHERS
1986   Hillsdale, New Jersey   London

Lawrence Erlbaum Associates, Inc., Publishers
365 Broadway
Hillsdale, New Jersey 07642

Library of Congress Cataloging-in-Publication Data

Thaw, Jack.
  Developing responsive human services.

  Includes bibliographies and index.
  1. Mental retardation facilities — United States —
Addresses, essays, lectures. 2. Mentally handicapped —
Institutional care — United States — Addresses, essays,
lectures. 3. Mentally handicapped — Government policy —
United States — Addresses, essays, lectures. I. Cuvo,
Anthony J. II. Title. [DNLM: 1. Community Mental
Health Services — organization & administration — United
States. 2. Health Planning — United States. 3. Resi-
dential Facilities — organization & administration —
United States. 4. Social Work — United States.
WM 29 AA1 T3d]
HV3006.A4T55   1986   362.3'85'0973   85-31194
ISBN 0-89859-612-2

Printed in the United States of America
10 9 8 7 6 5 4 3 2 1

To our parents,
David and Gertrude
Joseph and Nancy
and
To our wives and children,
Rebecca and David
Marlene, Lisa, and Joseph

For the opportunity, belief, and perspective

Contents

Acknowledgments

The authors wish to express their appreciation to the several competent and dedicated persons who typed this manuscript and as they did so discovered and corrected numerous oversights and errors: Elaine B. Modean, Emilie M. Philbrick, Shirley N. Wright, Diane M. Connors, Sherry Seibel, Debra Kohrs, Margery Richards, Harriet E. Maiorano, and Elizabeth A. Carlson. A special thanks to Irene M. LaBonte, who, in addition to meeting a whole department's clerical needs, contributed her own time to handle expertly the seemingly endless communications, correspondence, and "need it now" typing demands that tend to accumulate as a large manuscript is developed.

The authors and their contributing associates have spent most, in some cases all, of their professional years working both with mentally handicapped individuals and with the men and women who serve them in residential facilities. This book, at its core, is about the future of these people. To no small extent, its undertaking was inspired by a commitment of direct-care, professional, administrative, and support staff to the clients, a commitment that always seemed to be visible above the turmoil and adversity these organizations came to experience over the past two decades.

Senior Authors

Jack Thaw, Ph.D. • Chief, Psychological Services, Mansfield Training School, Connecticut Department of Mental Retardation; and Assistant Professor of Psychology, University of Connecticut

Anthony J. Cuvo, Ph.D. • Associate Dean, College of Human Resources; and Professor, Behavior Analysis and Therapy, Southern Illinois University at Carbondale

Contributing Associates

George J. Allen, Ph.D. • Professor of Psychology and Director of Clinical Training Program, University of Connecticut

Edward Benjamin, M.S. • Chief, Psychological Services, Southbury Training School, Connecticut Department of Mental Retardation

Laurie Heatherington, Ph.D. • Assistant Professor of Psychology, Williams College

Michael I. Lah, Ph.D. • Counseling Center, Wesleyan University

Roger D. MacNamara, M.Ed. • Former Director, Mansfield Training School, Connecticut Department of Mental Retardation

Gareth D. Thorne, M.A. • Former Commissioner, Connecticut Department of Mental Retardation

Scott F. Wolfe, M.A. • Director, Inservice Training - Region #6, Connecticut Department of Mental Retardation

Preface

For most of the past century, residential treatment facilities for mentally handicapped persons have been sterile, habilitatively inert settings, largely disconnected from the normative currents of American social culture. For most of the past 15–20 years, these conditions have undergone radical reconsideration. In response to more progressive and humanitarian insights about handicapped persons, broad-scale programs of reform were imposed upon the residential facility over a short period of time. Ideological, moral, technological, legislative, judicial, and organizational interventions began to occur and reoccur with increasing velocity, producing a continuous experience of upheaval for most of these agencies in recent years. This magnitude of change is even more pronounced when viewed in contrast with the period of historical motionlessness that preceded it.

It is generally believed that this two-decade attempt at changing the residential facility has achieved disappointing results. Most of these settings, especially the larger ones, are deficient as habilitative treatment centers. Most have been unable to meet the expectations of such grand concepts as normalization, interdisciplinary service, deinstitutionalization, and active treatment; nor have they been able to manage the turbulence in their work environments generated by the demands to do so.

Future roles for residential facilities are now being designed that would alter the size, location, function, indeed the very definition of these settings. Future plans call for residential concepts that are fiercely responsive to the needs of client consumers and continuous with the social, economic, and educational systems of the communities in which they are located. The authors and contributors of this book strongly endorse these ideas but began their work from a different perspective, the compelling reality that past "future concepts" of residential services have failed to produce broad and enduring results despite their moral and clinical worthiness. These disappointments occurred not only in larger, more traditional facilities, but in smaller, community-based programs as well. Much of the thinking in this book develops from the belief that it may now be historically appropriate to examine the *process* through which changeworthy concepts have been applied in residential treatment settings. If this "application process" is treated as a factor independent of the ideas and concepts themselves, one can observe that it has been poorly understood and perhaps mishandled in previous programs of change. As a result, many of those individuals conducting reform as well as those individuals in the receiving environments have been inadequately prepared to manage the process of implementing change.

The development of future-responsive residential treatment settings can be expected to be significantly influenced by errors occurring in the application process. This book focuses extended attention on the norms, values, and practices that govern how reform or change is applied. It considers the potential futures of residential treatment organizations by developing an alternative perspective about the mentality that powered past efforts to create "innovative futures." The intention is to use that perspective to revise what should be considered required organizational and individual competencies for developing and working in future-relevant residential treatment settings.

The book approaches this mission at two levels of focus. First, the authors and contributors provide an analysis of the social, political, and organizational practices that determine how residential facilities and the larger public systems that house them function. Information is presented about all levels of the system from client care operations to the dynamics at the top of the state bureaucracies that administer human service agencies. Four key staff groups (administrators, professionals, supervisors, and direct-care workers) are studied, with particular attention to the problems each has encountered in managing the conditions generated by recent programs of reform. Additionally, the book examines the impact and longer range implications of several specific external forces that have exerted influence on facilities serving mentally handicapped persons: (a) judicial interventions; (b) federally regulated programs such as Title XIX (ICF/MR); (c) labor-management relationships in public human services; (d) technological developments; and (e) changes in public policy.

Translating this information and analysis into practical guidelines for professionals and administrators constitutes the second level of focus. The authors and contributors provide profiles of specific organizational, social, and political competencies that will likely be required of the practitioners who will develop and work in future residential service settings. Among the areas covered are guidelines for the following:

• Coping with the accelerated rates of change and high levels of uncertainty that have come to characterize practitioner work environments in residential facilities
• Overcoming resistance to program interventions by direct-care personnel
• Revising the professional/academic programs that train and supply personnel to work in residential facilities
• Developing inservice training programs responsive to staff needs produced by the effects of recent reform
• Negotiating, conducting, and utilizing systematic evaluation to assist the process of applying program change
• Using policy development as a device for effecting innovation at various levels of the service system.

The contributors to this volume have spent most of their careers working within residential service settings and the systems that surround them. Their collective experience in several facilities and across several state programs numbers well over 100 years and includes tenure at virtually every level of the system from commissioner to client-care worker. Each contribution was prepared specifically for this book and was selected to reflect long-term access to specific situations, forces, or groups that are likely to influence the development and operation of future residential treatment settings for mentally handicapped individuals.

There is one exception to this contributor profile. The final chapter considers the residential treatment facility's encounter with reform as seen by external observers, in this instance a team of independent researchers who conducted a longitudinal evaluation both of program change and the organization's response to the process of independent evaluation itself.

For the reader's clarification, the many planners and providers of change discussed throughout the book variously are referred to as innovators, program specialists, or change interventionists when not identified more precisely. We use these terms interchangeably. It should be apparent that numerous persons in numerous roles internal and external to the residential facility qualify by their activities as planners, providers, or receivers of change. Many individuals qualify in all three categories. Although some writers make distinctions among processes of change, innovation, and reform as these apply to organizations (e.g., Davis, 1973; Thompson, 1976), the purposes of this book do not require it. Thus, these terms also are used interchangeably except when certain interventions are identified more specifically. The clientele of concern are those with developmental disabilities and associated conditions. While this clinical population is still undergoing changes in classification and definition (e.g., Zigler, Balla, & Hodapp, 1984), precise diagnostic distinctions are not crucial to the discussions that follow. Any person who becomes a client in a residential facility for mentally handicapped persons will be exposed, at some level, to the issues considered in this volume regardless of specific diagnostic determination.

In sum, this book is best viewed as a source book on the issues, forces, and people that can be expected to influence the process of developing futures for residential treatment facilities. It is clearly an early effort to address this subject, and it is our hope that these discussions will prompt an expanded interest in the empirical study and overall attention devoted to these matters.

Jack Thaw
Mansfield Depot, Connecticut

Anthony J. Cuvo
Carbondale, Illinois

REFERENCES

Davis, H. R. (1973). Change and innovation. In S. Feldman (Ed.), *The administration of mental health services* (pp. 289–341), Springfield, IL: Charles C. Thomas.

Thompson, V. A. (1976). *Bureaucracy and the modern world.* Morristown, NJ: General Learning Press.

Zigler, E., Balla, D., & Hodapp, R. (1984). On the definition and classification of mental retardation. *American Journal of Mental Deficiency, 89,* 215–230.

Foreword

Those of us interested in the care and habilitation of mentally handicapped persons have seen tremendous advances in technologies for training a wide variety of skills to these individuals. Within the last 25 years our perception of these persons has gone from a view that there was very little that could be done, to accepting the idea that much is possible. The development of programs to teach independent toileting and how to dress, eat independently, and shower has been augmented by more recent research showing that mentally handicapped persons can be trained to use a bus, make change, and shop in a store. Similarly, we have learned that many aggressive and self-injurious behaviors that made these persons very undesirable to others can be changed. Even more recently, the mental health needs of these persons have begun to be recognized, and treatments are beginning to be developed. All these improvements are very positive and have to a large degree revolutionized the field and how we as a society think about handicapped persons.

Technology is most certainly necessary, but the highest quality of life cannot be achieved with an empirically based technique only. This may account for related changes that have occurred but which have interfaced very little with treatment. This area of concern has been referred to as normalization, mainstreaming, deinstitutionalization, and placement in the least restrictive environment. All these terms are synonymous in that they refer to an emphasis on handicapped persons' environment as an important element in overall adjustment. There is no doubt that it is a very crucial element. The institution and its shortcomings have been the central point from which this philosophical and often heated discussion has proceeded. Legal issues have become intertwined with science, as has social advocacy, making this particular issue even more difficult to resolve. Similarly, the advocacy of various professional and parent groups, often using different ideals and beliefs, has resulted in a Tower of Babel effect or at least comparisons between apples and oranges. There are many groups using many types of professional jargon, which often mean appreciably the same thing. But their differences often lead to misunderstanding and disagreement. Obviously, all of us are interested in the welfare of the handicapped. Something needs to be done — but what approach should be taken to resolve the difficulties?

It seems to me that given the central role of the institution in this controversy, it is important to start with an examination of the residential treatment centers and their future. Applying the scientific method, which has proven so helpful in improving quality of life for mentally handicapped persons (as exemplified by the wide variety of skills that have been effectively trained), seems to be a reasonable option here too. Despite the expenditure in money, time, and expertise regarding how to normalize handicapped persons, no books and few articles have appeared that tackle this problem. The current volume meets a very critical need and is in my view an important contribution to the literature. Thaw and Cuvo note that "the process through which changeworthy concepts have been applied in residential settings" deserves systematic review and investigation. I wholeheartedly agree.

The authors, who have had a considerable amount of experience working with residential treatment centers and other agencies that deal with mentally handicapped persons, convincingly describe and thoroughly discuss the various factors that may operate in the residential treatment environment. This book's major strength is the review of many nuts and bolts issues that affect the day-to-day operation of these settings and the factors that can affect efforts to provide the best possible care. Issues such as the impact of unions, management-staff relations, staff burnout and stress, and many other very important but often neglected topics that greatly affect the quality of services and life for clients in these facilities are reviewed. Where possible, research data are brought into the discussion; this has not always been possible, given that this topic has been largely unstudied.

This book is a unique and very important effort. Many of the complexities of service delivery are discussed, as are some possible solutions. But additional study is needed. Heightened awareness of these issues will undoubtedly result in better planning and services for mentally handicapped persons. It is hoped that books such as this one will spur greater professional interest. Without dealing with these problems in more effective ways, the challenge to enhance — and, just as importantly, to maintain — the quality of life for these individuals is unlikely to be met.

Johnny L. Matson, Ph.D.
Professor, Department of Psychology
Louisiana State University

1 Creating Future Responsive Residential Facilities: A Perspective on the Process of Applying Reform

Jack Thaw, Ph.D.

ISSUES AND AGENDA

There may not be an organized form of human service that has undergone a more radical and turbulent experience in the past two decades than the residential facility serving mentally handicapped clients. Across this relatively short span of time, it has been subjected to ideological, moral, technological, legislative, political, judicial, and various humanitarian intrusions of massive scale. Social change of such magnitude is difficult to sort out without some historical distance from the events. Yet the events continue, and designing the futures of residential settings for this clientele remains an active and ambitious enterprise. Thus, it may be useful to risk constructing a perspective about this recent history while still adjacent to it, if such perspective can instruct the process of preparing those futures. The objectives of this volume develop from this possibility.

Future concepts of residential facilities now are fiercely responsive to the needs of client consumers (e.g., Christian, Hannah, & Glahn, 1984). Although many of these ideas are encouraging and have been demonstrated successfully, we should be cautioned that "future concepts" of residential treatment developed in the past have failed to produce broad and enduring habilitative outcomes, as many observers and investigators have pointed out (e.g., Boles & Bible, 1978; Cullari, 1984; George & Baumeister, 1981; Granger, 1972; Landesman-Dwyer, 1981; Reid & Whitman, 1983; Repp & Barton, 1980; Sarason & Doris, 1979). These authors indicate that recent ideas such as unit system organization, smaller residential settings, community-based facilities, and the Standards for Intermediate Care Facilities for the Mentally Retarded (ICF/MR) have been beset with operational and other difficulties despite the worthiness of their client focus.

It is not our intention to force inappropriate comparisons among contemporary notions of residential services or to judge any of them. Instead, we suggest that it may be historically appropriate to raise a different issue—that despite many client-worthy concepts of residential setting and residential treatment, their application has been poorly understood and even mishandled. Most of the reforms in residential systems of service over the past 15 to 20 years have been implemented under conditions of continual change and upheaval powered by the intervention of the social forces noted earlier. In the hurried pursuit of reaching complex and sweeping outcomes under these circumstances, the organizational and personal requirements for managing the process of intense and constant change appear to have been neglected and thus undeveloped. For example, a process of continual change itself characterizes numerous residential facilities, yet many who apply reforms and many who receive them act as if this were not so. This misconception adversely affects the validity of the outcomes of the reforms. Other examples of the deficiencies in the application process are developed in some detail later in this chapter.

These considerations help frame the central premise of this discussion: The development of future-responsive residential settings for mentally handicapped persons must include sophisticated attention to the norms, values, and practices that govern how reform is applied. Such focus is necessary if validity is to be achieved with the available and emerging forms of residential setting. Among many observers of such matters, Toffler (1970) in a societal sense and Michael (1973) in the more restricted study of public agencies have cautioned about the hazards that accrue when the reach of innovative ideas outpaces the grasp that institutions and systems have on testing and managing the applications adequately.

This book attempts to develop and analyze the issues surrounding this premise and provide some recommendations about responding to it. This chapter addresses three questions: (a) What are the potential future roles and functions for residential facilities? (b) Can we develop an alternative perspective about the recent history of reform in residential facilities that can advise the conduct of subsequent efforts? (c) What organizational and interpersonal competencies will be needed by those who will develop and those who will work in future-relevant residential facilities?

It seems necessary to set forth at the outset some definitions and conventions concerning residential facilities and their clientele. A recent national survey (Hauber et al., 1984) reported an array of residential alternatives now available to mentally handicapped people unable to live at home. Residences ranged in size from small (1 to 5 clients) community-based facilities to larger facilities (64 or more clients). Over 58% of client residents still live in the larger settings, and most of these individuals have severe disabilities. The survey also revealed that nearly as many residents live in privately operated facilities (47.2%) as in publicly operated facilities (52.8%).

This book generally is concerned with the larger public residential facilities (PRFs) though the distinction between what is large and what is small may well become blurred in the years ahead. Moreover, it is becoming increasingly apparent that smaller, community-based public and private facilities are confronting issues similar to those that have historically affected PRFs (e.g., Bruininks, Kudla, Wieck, & Hauber, 1980; George & Baumeister, 1981; Landesman-Dwyer, Sackett, & Kleinman, 1980; Slater & Bunyard, 1983). Thus, much of the information presented in this volume should have relevance and significance for the spectrum of residential settings available to mentally handicapped citizens in this country. All these settings meet the definition used by Hauber et al. (1984) for a residential facility: Any living quarter(s) that provide 24-hour, 7 days-a-week responsibility for room, board, and supervision of clients with staff members present at all times when clients are in the residence.

The clientele of concern are those with developmental disabilities due to mental retardation, epilepsy, cerebral palsy, or other neurological condition that originated before the age of 18 and that constitutes a substantial handicap (U.S. Department of Health, Education, and Welfare, 1971). Zigler, Balla, and Hodapp (1984) have proposed a refined definition emphasizing inefficient cognitive functioning and etiology, but they point out that further changes in classification and definition are likely as assessment methods improve. For the discussions in this book, precise diagnostic distinctions are less crucial. Any individual who becomes a client in a residential facility will be exposed, at some level, to the issues considered in this volume regardless of specific diagnostic determination. Throughout the book, the terms *mental handicap, developmental disability,* and *mental retardation* are used interchangeably.

POTENTIAL FUTURES FOR RESIDENTIAL FACILITIES

The dialogue on creating futures for residential facilities has passed rather quickly through a number of stages over the past 20 years. In the 1960s and into the early 1970s, a major focus of reports about residential institutions, especially the larger public ones, was to change and improve them (e.g., Bensberg, 1974; Peck & Cleland, 1966; Roos, 1966). By the start of the 1980s, the subject had become the appropriateness of their very existence, and the discussion was strident (e.g., Ellis et al., 1981; Menolascino & McGee, 1981). Much of the argument about what residential facilities should look like, where they should be located, and what they should do has been offered on ideological and moral grounds. In the 1970s and early 1980s, much of the discourse was conducted in federal courtrooms and legislatures. Among the outcomes of these efforts was the imperative to provide residential settings responsive to the liberty interests and habilitative needs of mentally disabled persons (Cook, 1983).

The clinical and operational questions surrounding this imperative, however, have remained complex (e.g., Begab, 1975; Landesman-Dwyer, 1981) and in any conjectures about the potential futures of residential facilities, should be conceptually distinguished from moral and ideological preferences. Viewed clinically, residential facilities of all sizes and locations have experienced difficulties in producing effective and durable habilitative programs responsive to the developmental needs of clients (e.g., Balla, 1976; Birenbaum & Re, 1979; Butler & Bjaanes, 1977; George & Baumeister, 1981; Intagliata & Willer, 1982; Landesman-Dwyer, 1981; Zigler & Balla, 1977). Although moral arguments have been made for both the inhumanity of institutionalizing any individual (e.g., Roos, 1979) and the inhumanity of deinstitutionalizing individuals with specific kinds and degrees of impairment (e.g., Ellis et al., 1981), the accumulating empirical evidence suggests important clinical questions along different lines. For example, Landesman-Dwyer, Sackett, and Kleinman (1980) found the nature of the social grouping of clients to be a more significant influence on social behavior than such factors as size of facility. Other studies have identified the influential effects of staff members' behavior on clients (e.g., Eyman & Call, 1977; Mayhew, Enyart, & Anderson, 1978; Sutter, Mayeda, Call, Yanagi, & Yee, 1980). The match between individual needs and type of program or environment also has been an important focus (e.g., Begab, 1975; Sundberg, Snowden, & Reynolds, 1978). Comparing client functioning across several deinstitutional studies, Kleinberg and Galligan (1983) concluded that community residential facilities, in contrast to larger, centralized institutions, are more conducive to establishing therapeutic conditions but do not guarantee it. Clinical interventions that teach clients how to utilize an environment emerged as a factor more important than the setting itself.

Despite considerable progress in the development of residential services (e.g., Baroff, 1980; Eyman, Demaine, & Lei, 1979; Rotegard, Hill, & Bruininks, 1983; Thompson & Carey, 1980), many areas of concern about clinical effectiveness remain substantially uninvestigated. Crawford, Aiello, and Thompson (1979) emphasized the need to examine the interaction of client behavioral characteristics with the sociophysical environmental characteristics of residential settings. In her extensive review of the literature on CRFs, Landesman-Dwyer (1981) noted that achieving success with client placements is not equivalent to understanding which features of the residential program are responsible for the results. She called for attempts to predict success involving well-controlled, longitudinal, and multidimensional assessment of both individuals and their treatment environments. The available evidence seems to suggest that the successful habilitation of developmentally disabled individuals in residential treatment settings involves a complex interaction among a variety of factors, including elements of the living space, network of available support services, staff characteristics, the nature of the social grouping, and the profile of needs and abilities presented by the client. Progress in the construction and validation of instruments used to measure these characteristics of residential treatment settings is encouraging (Rotegard, Hill, & Bruininks, 1983). However, until broad scale use of predictions from such instruments can be applied to the planning of residential facilities, achieving clinical and habilitative efficacy may remain a problem of some consequence.

Organizational and operational problems also have accompanied the development of residential alternatives in recent years. Cohen (1975) described a range of practical, logistical, and operational barriers to developing comprehensive services for clients in community residences. Problems in recruitment of qualified personnel, absenteeism, and staff turnover have been reported in several surveys and studies (e.g., Bruininks, et al., 1980; George & Baumeister, 1981; Zaharia & Baumeister, 1978). Inservice training programs in residential facilities have been disappointing (Ziarnik & Bernstein, 1982). Management, supervisory, and funding difficulties have been identified in residential facilities regardless of size and location (e.g., Bruininks et al., 1980; Favell, Favell, Riddle, & Risley, 1984; Reid & Whitman, 1983; Slater & Bunyard, 1983; Tjosvold & Tjosvold, 1983).

Problems also persist at resource and support levels. Eyman and Borthwick (1980), surveying services to 11,000 clients in community and institutional settings, concluded that community resources appear to be insufficient to accommodate all currently institutionalized residents. Bock and Joiner (1982) came to a similar conclusion after matching over 3,000 institutionalized mentally retarded persons with 121 community residential facilities. Janicki, Mayeda, and Epple (1983), investigating the national scope of group home programs, reported significant growth in availability of community living alternatives but cautioned that the country's fiscal climate may cause this growth to abate. In a well-known longitudinal study of community placement, Edgerton and Bercovici (1976) reported a lack of reliable and supportive servies in the community, a deficiency that still existed when the same cohort of clients was contacted again 10 years later (Edgerton, Bollinger, & Herr, 1984).

Some conclusions may be drawn from this body of information that frame the speculations about future residential service systems. Twenty years ago, a family was faced with two choices if it had a mentally handicapped member who could not live at home: (a) a large, primarily custodially oriented institution; or (b) one of the early forms of community-based facilities such as group homes. In many parts of the country, only the first option was available. Monumental improvements over this two choice situation were made in the intervening two decades.

This progress notwithstanding, the residential facility has not been perfected at or near criterion levels of clinical and organizational performance. The events of the past 20 years have led to this point: The moral arguments to prohibit inhuman treatment of mentally handicapped persons in any setting and to require their habilitation have been successfully made and judicially endorsed. It is morally clear that self-contained, custodial, nonhabilitative institutions of any size should be abandoned. It seems clinically, if not morally, required to resist indiscriminate approaches such as small group homes for everyone (Landesman-Dwyer, 1981) in favor of developing residential alternatives that respond to client needs and meaningfully articulate with other forms of consumer service. Future efforts must address the habilitation—environment relationship and the characteristics of the larger social systems (e.g., community, governmental, economic) in which this relationship functions.

Observers speculating about the future of larger residential facilities have incorporated these concerns in their views. Zigler and Balla (1977), pointing to the positive effects that can occur when the boundaries between institution and community are more permeable, seemed to support the notion of a community-responsive institution. Others have called for models of residential facilities continuous with community services (e.g., Clements, 1970; Roos, 1975) or simply as one type of agency in a comprehensive community-oriented continuum of care (e.g., Scheerenberger, 1977). Landesman-Dwyer (1981) recommends discarding concepts like "institution," "community-based residence," and "deinstitutionalization" because they do not convey information about habilitative content. Instead, she suggests developing a useful typology of residential facilities and services.

A forthcoming publication (Rosen & Crissey, in press) takes a bold and creative look at possible future roles for larger residential settings. It incorporates current notions about systems of residential services but broadens the perspective with sophisticated conjectures about contributions uniquely possible in larger settings. Residential facilities are seen as centers for information, research, advocacy, planning, and service coordination fully integrated in a network of community services. Such organizations could amass extensive material resources and expertise and serve as regional training centers for large geographical areas. Client residential services could be provided where needed, based on the specific types of freedoms that could be provided in such settings.

Residential treatment centers could become powerful forces of service provision in such domains as multidisciplinary consultation, development and systematic evaluation of model programs, and staff training. One may wonder whether the considerable problems in staff morale, turnover, and skill deficits in community facilities (e.g., George & Baumeister, 1981; Slater & Bunyard, 1983) could be corrected if these facilities articulated with highly resourced staff training centers designed specifically to prepare personnel for work in CRFs. Present estimates suggest larger numbers of more severely impaired and behaviorally disordered clients moving to community settings. The relatively small staff complement in these facilities may require special training, supervision, and access to behavioral intervention teams that would otherwise be unavailable to a small setting on a continual schedule. Such specialized services, especially for this type of clientele, do not always exist and may never exist in many communities.

The Rosen and Crissey (in press) volume conceptualizes larger residential centers as well planned communities themselves, not merely as residential or work facilities. They believe that concepts of planned communities (e.g., Perloff & Sandberg, 1973) can be applied to residential settings, transforming a facility into a social and vocational community designed for the particular work, recreation, leisure, and social needs of its members. Such a community would convert clients into members, with opportunities, choices, and responsibilities. It could provide its members ease of movement and communication within the community and with other communities. The environment could be designed to provide architectural and cultural continuity between the community and its natural setting, as well as continuity between the community residences and their inhabitants (Reiter & Bryen, in press).

Crissey (in press) provides a different, yet perhaps more compelling, view of what may well be the future for larger centers. Describing the results of the Conference on the Future of Vineland held in March, 1982, she presents a model for the residential facility attached to the full life cycle of consumers and responsive to the circumstances their families are likely to encounter. Crissey argues persuasively that at the family planning, genetic counseling, and early assistance levels of a family's needs, an established residential facility whose function is specifically to serve developmentally disabled individuals and their families would be a central agency preferable to a more generic community service. Noting that the best environment for young handicapped children (i.e., their own families) has undergone major change in recent years (e.g., breakup or separation of nuclear and extended families, increase in single working parent households), she demonstrates that the residential facility could be in the best position to meet the special needs that would develop. For example, short-term nursery or day care services with child care teachers could assist and train parents and at the same time ease the burdens imposed by the family circumstances. Similarly, for children with special medical needs, the residential center could be more closely affiliated with specialized medical practices and research facilities than would the typical community general hospital.

Crissey's (in press) view of the residential facility's role during the school-age period represents at least a partial response to the problems public school systems are experiencing in serving mentally handicapped students (e.g., Sarason & Doris, 1979). For children who, for various reasons, cannot take advantage of public school offerings, whose behavior is so disruptive that they require service beyond what the school can provide, or who require 24-hour service to support the school experience—for these and other special-need situations, the residential center envisioned by Crissey could affiliate with the schools, provide assessment, observational, and treatment resources to teachers, and even offer 24-hour services properly coordinated with the public school program. In this view, the training school of the past, discontinuous in every respect with public school systems, is replaced with a residential center specifically resourced to service and collaborate with the public school program.

For a final illustration of Crissey's (in press) concept, consider the mentally handicapped senior citizens of the future. There is already evidence that they may not have access even to modest support services (e.g., Edgerton, Bollinger, & Herr, 1984). Crissey observes that, despite the preference for single family homes, older nondisabled citizens increasingly are locating in adult complexes and senior residential facilities. These special residential communities, providing social, recreational, religious, and other activities along with some special services, may fulfill the needs of senior mentally handicapped citizens as well. These individuals probably will share with nonhandicapped citizens the particular disabilities and needs that characterize the elderly in our society. With uncertainties about health costs and the capacities of communities to service these citizens, a concept of residential facilities shared by both groups of senior citizens becomes an attractive alternative for those who will not be able to live in single-unit dwellings in the general community or who will not be supported in such residences by the general community.

Conjectures about the potential futures of residential facilities and other forms of service to mentally handicapped persons increasingly should become more sophisticated with time. The Rosen and Crissey (in press) volume presents an informed, creative, and responsible example. Informed estimates about any future conditions, the planning of those futures, and the circumstances that actually evolve all will be affected, to some degree, by social, political, economic, and other forces. In the case of residential facilities and services for mentally handicapped citizens, there is reason to be vigilant and cautious with these forces. Scull (1977) has offered a sobering perspective in this regard. He argues that deinstitutionalization movements have been successful only when they were economically and therefore politically feasible. Historically, according to his analysis, the moral or clinical propriety of such movements was a small factor in their success.

Merges (1982) reviewed New York State's history with community-based residential programs and reports information that supports Scull's (1977) conclusions. The system of community residences was sacrificed in New York in the 1940s as economic, social, and political conditions became less favorable, with the national focus on the war effort and economic readjustment afterwards. Merges cautions that some present conditions (e.g., limited financial resources, dependency on the social context, attitudes, and economic welfare of particular towns or communities) and possible future conditions could exert similar debilitating effects on residential services.

The precipitous change in the role of the United States Department of Justice on behalf of mentally handicapped citizens provides another illustration of these social and political forces. Functioning as a strong ally of plaintiffs in federal deinstitutionalization litigations throughout the 1970s, the United States, through the Department of Justice, in just a few short years nearly reversed its position to argue that community living arrangements for mentally retarded citizens may not be sustained under the U.S. Constitution or federal statutes (*Halderman v. Pennhurst*, 1984).

The proposals for potential futures of residential facilities illustrated earlier, and any others as well, are not the first set of recommendations for revising the future of these institutions. As described earlier, many past "future concepts" failed to reach successful outcomes. Nor is there any indication that the social, political, and economic forces will be restrained in their influence on the process of implementing any new "future concepts." To be sure, it is likely that the transition to new reforms, new concepts, and new futures will engage the same or similar set of individuals, groups, agencies, and field of forces that attended the process of applying previous proposals. Thus, this book examines the application process—the events, conditions, and people that influence how concepts or reforms get introduced and then stabilized in the receiving organization and the system in which it is embedded.

The following section reconsiders the experience of previous reforms in residential facilities and the response of those involved with that process. The intention is to develop an alternative perspective on that history, one that can inform subsequent applications of change. The final section attempts to formulate a tentative profile of some of the organizational and interpersonal requirements that will be needed to achieve valid representations of proposed futures.

A PERSPECTIVE ON RECENT HISTORY

In a literature review of program change in various types of human service organizations, Reppucci and Saunders (1983) concluded that the *lack* of change was the most prevalent condition found. They suggested that the history of such efforts in a given organization may be actively used in the formulation of further planned innovations. The purpose of this section is to inquire why previous efforts to revise and reform residential facilities, particularly PRFs, did not reach satisfactory outcomes. Subsequent chapters in this book address this inquiry in selected contexts. Here the intention is to offer a general analysis of the process through which recent attempts to modernize the role and function of PRFs were conducted.

One can review a journal such as *Mental Retardation* over the 1960s and early 1970s to trace the ideologies and forces that became propellants for change in PRFs: normalization, deinstitutionalization, mainstreaming, developmental model, active treatment, behavior modification, unit management, interdisciplinary systems of service, federal standards, human rights, advocacy, litigation, staff development, management by objective, organizational development, program accountability. These themes emerged not only from ideology, but also from technological and administrative developments, from changes in judicial initiative, from political and media policy and events, and, indeed, from the history of the general society during and preceding those years.

The experiences of the past 20 years for PRFs are better understood in concert with the history of the previous 100 years. Competent reviews of this history have been written (e.g., Crissey, 1975; Kanner, 1964; Scheerenberger, 1982; Wolfensberger, 1969) and should be consulted for a complete context. Concerning data on more recent attempts at innovation, some specific studies have examined individual facilities' responses to major but single interventions such as the introduction of unit systems (e.g., Granger, 1972; Raynes, Bumstead, & Pratt, 1974). There is also an available literature with respect to the effects of behavior modification interventions in institutional settings (e.g., Reppucci & Saunders, 1974; Thompson & Grabowski, 1977; Willems, 1974) and staff development programs (e.g., Bensberg & Barnett, 1966; Boles & Bible, 1978; Thaw, Palmer, & Sulzer-Azaroff, 1977; Ziarnik & Bernstein, 1982). However, hard information on the effects of multiple, system-wide changes over time in PRFs is difficult to find. It is also difficult to gather, as illustrated in Chapter 7 of this volume.

One informative data base that does exist in every facility is the document and paper traffic over time. Memos, directives, internal reports, anecdotal problem logs, policy statements, general notices by administrators, minutes of committees, tables of organization and structure—these and other records are archives that, in their content, volume, frequency, style, and tone, can reveal, among other things, a facility's experience with managing change over an identified period of time. I know of no systematic use of such archives in studying the effects of recent measures of reform in PRFs. However, these archives are easily accumulated (most are public records), and I have done so for a 14-year period in the PRF where I am employed. To a less complete extent, I have accumulated comparable archives for the state system of which this facility is one unit and for a number of other facilities as well. I have also observed and participated in the experiences reflected by the archives in that state and have done so at most levels of the system. Finally, I have observed and consulted in other systems and found comparable circumstances. Some of the impressions presented in this section developed from these archives and experiences. Although this is something less than formal empirical inquiry, it does provide a representative sense of some important factors that governed the process of institutional reform during those years.

In a thorough historical review, Wolfensberger (1969) noted that by 1930 all the beliefs that had motivated the dehumanization of mentally handicapped people for the previous approximately 40 years were recognized as untenable. However, he stressed that for many years after this insight, most large institutions in the United States operated as if these beliefs were still held. Without alternative rationale, relatively void of qualified professionals, and largely without public support, most of these facilities continued to operate for well over a quarter century on the basis of highly unfavorable attitudes and practices toward mentally handicapped people. Wolfensberger describes these conditions as building enormous momentum over the years. It is against this momentum that recent programs of reform must first be considered. The progressive perspectives and ideologies about mentally handicapped people that emerged and became officially endorsed in the 1950s and 1960s were radical, visible departures from those reflected by institutional practices. The contrast, by its very magnitude, caused the goals developed from the new perspective to be impossibly high though congruent with the general expectancy for social change technologies during the 1960s and early 1970s. Similarly, the magnitude of the contrast prompted the urge to get things done in a hurry. Few who worked in PRFs over those years could not sense and feel the rushed, impatient quality to the innovations and reforms introduced.

McClelland (1978) has argued that when this mix of circumstances (i.e., grandiose goals to transform large social problems in a hurry by applying, inappropriately, massive doses of technology) occurred with programs of social reform in the 1960s and 1970s, the efforts often failed miserably. He suggests that these failures were, at least in part, the result of a misdirected emphasis. Large, expensive programs were established to have ''impact''—to do something about the ''alcohol problem,'' the ''poverty problem,'' the ''problem of public residential facilities for the mentally handicapped.'' McClelland distinguishes this type of action from the act of gradually applying modest, but more precisely targeted and evaluated, doses of technology to problems it can solve.

Much of the innovation in PRFs over the past 20 years or so, from large, systemic changes to smaller projects and procedures, seems to have been of the impact variety. For example, many of the reorganizations of services in some facilities were introduced in response to the current vogue of decentralization and unit management concepts. However, those reorganizations often were designed poorly and introduced too rapidly. Unit organization often was layered over jobs already rooted in past practices, with minimal retraining provided to job incumbents. Once in place, the units were supervised improperly with respect to the unit concept itself. Lastly, they tended to remain in operation without adequate evaluation of their real effects on service delivery to clients.

What may be called an internal perspective on innovation in PRFs since the 1960s requires a grasp of what was experienced by those directly affected by it, the clients and particularly the staff at all levels of the organization. Viewed this way, the course of reform may be seen as embracing three related characteristics: (a) preoccupation with outcomes; (b) unmanaged rates of innovative events; and (c) inadequate preparation of persons applying and receiving the innovations. I shall try to demonstrate that where these characteristics have defined the approach to innovation and reform, changeworthy concepts may have been lost to the changing process itself.

Preoccupation with Outcomes

Several years ago, a superintendent of a PRF called a meeting of several members of his professional staff who had just returned from a national conference on major issues and developments in the field of mental retardation. He informed the group that he was going to list what he felt were the five most important changes taking place in the field. He mentioned normalization, deinstitutionalization, unit management, developmental model, and human rights and then said this: "I have all of these things here. Tell me if you heard of any new trend at the conference that we don't have at this facility, and we shall go about getting it."

This chief administrator, aware of the growing scrutiny of PRFs at that time, knew the importance of his facility's being a progressive institution. From his perspective, "having" normalization or unit management programs was an outcome. In some respects "having" a normalization program became the attainment of normalization itself, even if evaluative information suggested a more modest outcome or if such information were absent altogether. It is not that this man was not interested in real service outcomes for clients; to the contrary, he was passionately concerned. Rather, his recognition of the need for change was tied to the presence and absence of discrete situations or programs considered innovative. He saw units of change, not a process of change.

A preoccupation with outcome tends to become concern with acquiring units of change or innovation and having results that confirm that acquisition. It tends to de-emphasize both the process *of* innovation and the effects of a particular innovation on the system that receives it and the people who work the system. Also underemphasized are the requirements it makes for subsequent innovations. A preoccupation with outcome is a bias that fails to anticipate both the broader implications of an innovation and the significance of the process by which the innovation is applied. It promotes a discontinuous view of change. To audit competence at innovation using a discontinuous view, one observes a series or collection of products rather than the developing norms about how the changing process is conducted.

The bias toward outcome is powered by several factors. Recent accountability concepts imposed on PRFs primarily examine program outcomes and products. The political cycles and legislative procedures that influence public services typically are geared to promote and defend results more than means unless the latter are ethically or fiscally improper. The recent class action litigations against many PRFs also have relied heavily on judgments of effects. One can also sense a general historical impatience with social change in the field. Perhaps, after several decades of inactivity, there is a restive desire to minimize the journey from conceiving an idea to implementing it.

Two illustrations support this view. In one facility, a planning group designed an interdisciplinary assessment procedure to replace the practice of having different professions evaluate clients separately. The group prepared a developmental assessment tool that was to be implemented by a team of professionals working together during all phases of the evaluation. Developing the assessment tool, establishing the procedural steps for its use, and providing technical training to those who would be required to use it were seen by the planning group as the thrust of its responsibility. These stages being executed competently, the outcome, an effective interdisciplinary assessment approach, was thought to be secured. A trial run of the procedure by the planning group proved otherwise. Anxieties surfaced about learning new skills and having to perform them in front of colleagues from other disciplines. Whereas the previous assessment practice was a mostly private interaction (and therefore a safe one) between a professional and a client, now there was "competence exposure," and resistance to it emerged. There was also exposure to feedback as the assessment team was encouraged to exchange comments. Questions also arose about any one profession's control over participation in the assessment procedure, a control that was clear under the previous approach. Functions of leading and coordinating the more complex interactions of staff required by interdisciplinary evaluation also had to be problem-solved. Compatibility difficulties among group members, minimized under a profession-by-profession method of assessment, were magnified by the demands of interdisciplinary assessment. Ambiguity about their role on the team became a problem for some professionals. Other problems developed because the target staff (those who would use the new approach) had not designed it. Thus, at the outset, they did not buy into it easily. From their perspective, someone else owned it. They owned their old approach, and they held on to it.

The planning group, operating under severe deadline pressure, nearly decided to overlook these and other "process" problems and simply have the administration put the program in operation following the technical training. Wisely, they chose to respond to the process factors. However it is not uncommon in residential facilities for such a choice to be deferred in favor of a more direct rush to achieve the outcome.

The second illustration involves the use of independent inspectors, or program auditors, as an accountability vehicle. This method is built into the widely adopted Title XIX ICF/MR program. Licensed surveyors, as they are called, periodically visit a facility and examine an array of program, training, and environmental elements to determine if they are in compliance with regulations set forth by the then Department of Health, Education and Welfare and published in the Federal Register in 1974 and revised in the Standards for Intermediate Care Facilities for the Mentally Retarded (1978). Certification and federal financial support of the program or facility are contingent upon compliance.

Despite the many virtues of accountability and independent program auditing procedures, in practice they have the potential to overemphasize outcomes. Typically, surveyors review program records and other documents as required in the regulations. They have less time to observe actual program service over any continuous period of time. In some facilities, this has resulted in an orientation to program choices that fit the documentation requirements better than they do the needs of the clients. The degree to which this occurs varies widely across facilities. In my own facility, the decision to participate in ICF/MR some years ago and the manner in which that participation initially was accomplished illustrate what many employees felt was an excessive submission to the outcome requirement at the expense of developing effective programs in such areas as staff training, treatment evaluation, and interdisciplinary service delivery.

In our case, the outcome state quickly came to mean certified units. The desire of the state government to secure the funding translated, at the facility level, into rapid compliance with certification requirements as reflected principally in reviews of certain prepared documents including the following: approved admission papers for all eligible clients; evaluation reports by the psychologist, nurse, and social worker; one-year service contracts and at least one individual program plan (IPP) for each client; postinstitutional plans; and client activity schedules. Preparing this paper began to govern all other events, including the hiring, orientation, and training of new professionals acquired under the extended funding. Converting our previously centralized and departmentalized system of service into the interdisciplinary model (Crosby, 1976) utilized under ICF/MR also assumed a lower priority. In some instances, so did actual service to clients. Professionals were hired quickly and, along with tenured staff, were rapidly assembled into interdisciplinary teams and put to work evaluating clients and writing service plans. IPPs were written hastily. These were responsive to client needs, most often to simple needs that called for relatively uncomplicated program procedures. The client contract meeting schedules and the various deadlines associated with them forced postponement of both developing an integrated, efficient team process among professionals and providing needed technical and supervisory training. The orientation and transition of direct care staff to ICF/MR and the revisions it created in their job roles also were conducted hurriedly, if at all. This often courted staff resistance to the whole idea of ICF. Nevertheless, these all seemed to be necessary compromises to achieve certification. Unfortunately, they were grievous errors inasmuch as an effective team process and an informed, well-prepared, and supportive direct care staff underbrace the validity of the ICF/MR concept of service.

Certification was accomplished for all designated units, but, so too, were a certain outlook and rhythm of service. The work norms established to reach certification in a hurry carried forward to the cycles of maintaining certification. A strong sensitivity to the ICF/MR accountability demands plus the actual encounters with surveyors and a second team of paper-conscious outside reviewers led to a kind of overindulgence in record keeping. People became very good at paper. Meanwhile, day-to-day events and crises that ordinarily consume time in a 24-hour service setting still kept on occurring, further postponing attention both to the development of the program concept and to the people who were charged with operating it. Another factor was the relatively few new staff resources provided under the formula the state used to enter the ICF/MR program. Although an improvement over past staff-to-client ratios, it was not enough to cope with the requirements of an interdisciplinary service system.

These circumstances all combined to keep the service teams fastened to documentation, accountability schedules, and an enduring experience of trying to keep up with the cycle generated by both. Although some very good client service was provided despite these problems, many exceedingly dedicated clinicians and direct care staff learned more about preparing for and passing accountability checks than they did about developing an interdisciplinary service system. The absence of an effective service system acted in turn, as its own factor in sustaining the preoccupation with certification and paper outcomes. For several years, that system simply did not become good enough to apply ICF/MR accountability procedures to clinical practice without forsaking the latter in pursuit of the former.

The people in both illustrations were implementing innovations. They became preoccupied with an identified outcome state for the innovation to the exclusion of learning *how* to innovate. They reached or achieved outcomes, to be sure. However, especially in the second example, once having reached outcome, they were no better prepared than before for managing the next innovation that would come along. Each new idea, concept, or program was managed in the same way, as if it were the first one they had handled.

Unmanaged Rates of Innovation

In 1978, a chief administrator of a large PRF prepared and distributed several documents to his staff: (a) a statement of goals for the coming year; (b) a table of organization for each major domain of service; and (c) a flow chart of the roles and responsibilities of principal staff. The goal statements were dominated by concerns and issues that had emerged over the previous few months. The table of organization represented a near complete revision of most service structures and functions in the facility. The flow chart was, in effect, a redesign of the job roles and job relationships of most key administrative and clinical staff. In sum, the facility had radically turned over its form in response to a set of needs and responsibilities most of which were not present as compelling issues a short time before. One year later it was to do this again in another major reordering of priorities and organizational structure.

Employees with 20 or 30 years service in a PRF invariably will describe the earlier years of their tenure as less turbulent ones for their facility than the more recent period. This is to be expected and corresponds with the increased activity and change in PRFs over the last decade or so. But after literally hundreds of conversations with long term employees, I have observed a pattern of response that reflects more than an increase in activity. These people, in many ways, seem to be without appropriate reference points for their jobs, their facility, even their clients. It is not that they have failed to respond to changes in the design of their particular jobs; nor is it that they have failed to grasp major changes in thinking about mentally handicapped people. Rather, the difficulty seems more a matter of fatigue with constant revisions in too many important parts of their work lives.

One staff member described his recent job experience this way: "There is too much new stuff coming at me all the time, plus they keep changing the routine things too. I don't know what to pay attention to anymore. I'm tired." Like this employee, many men and women working in PRFs have reached the upper limits of their capacity to respond well to continuous turnovers in the concepts, methods, forms, places, and people associated with their work. Contributing to the dilemma has been the mistaken belief among many of these individuals that each new event or change would be a relatively permanent one. Indeed, those responsible for introducing a particular change often promote this expectation; they believe it themselves and probably are personally invested in its successful outcome.

For many of those exposed repeatedly to the expectancy of permanent changes and the experience that contradicts it, adaptation and identity problems have developed. Their images of their jobs, their facility, even of themselves seem to become invalid after a while, and their work responses do not seem to be anchored in a mission that, to them, has either clarity or reliable direction. In Chapters 3 and 4 we present detailed profiles of two staff groups, client care workers and professionals, who have had these difficulties in many residential facilities.

The issue for the present discussion is that PRFs have, in recent years, been exposed to innovative events at an accelerating rate, and that their capacity to manage these changes effectively has been exceeded in many instances. The rate of change has become a factor of magnitude independent of the events themselves.

Social scientists and other observers have discussed this phenomenon of scale. Bevin (1976) described it as events occurring at so rapid a rate and with so vast a scope that they are impossible to accommodate by past strategies of adaptation. Several authors (e.g., Davis, 1973; Lippitt, 1973; Roos, 1972, 1975) predicted that principal themes in Toffler's (1970) concept of future shock, such as increased levels of transience, novelty, and diversity experienced in shorter and shorter intervals of time, would affect human service systems generally and services to mentally handicapped individuals specifically. Bennis and Slater (1968), Gardner (1963), Thompson (1976), and Toffler (1970), among others, have argued that the traditional bureaucratic structure of most organizations is unsuited to managing rapid change. Most organizations are configured to solve problems and respond to environmental demands that no longer exist. This is true in many PRFs despite philosophies and commitments contrary to the traditions of fixed bureaucratic control.

Three related circumstances in PRFs tend to deepen the problems associated with accelerated rates of change. First, many staff at all levels in the facility probably have not been prepared adequately to anticipate and cope with the rapid turnovers of events in their work lives. The deficiency exists both in technical and interpersonal preparation. It is a significant problem and is considered in more detail later in the discussion.

Second, there is currently a stronger external scrutiny of PRFs than ever before. The large number of recent class action and other litigations against these facilities is but one illustration of that scrutiny. Such conditions make it risky for institution officials and personnel to acknowledge their problems with managing an excessive rate of change even if the problem is perfectly legitimate. The risk exists because this kind of admission is likely to be viewed as an indication of incompetence by opponents or monitors.

The increasing rate of innovative events is more precisely an increasing rate of uncoordinated innovative events, and this constitutes the third factor. Many new programs and procedures of change are single issue matters; that is, their implementation is promoted or required independently of other interventions and without regard to their impact on other interventions. For example, new Affirmative Action policies may call for the preparation and follow through of certain employment initiatives by most departments at the same time that a new labor-management contract may require numerous revisions of personnel procedures also affecting the majority of the facility's departments. Newly developed human rights committees also may be active in several areas of employee performance and require their own procedures for each area of involvement. Although all three of these programs represent interventions in the area of personnel administration that did not exist a few years earlier, and although they may be functionally related to one another at times, they may well be uncoordinated as inputs on certain staff. Thus, supervisors and managers may be forced to respond to the procedural requirements of all three even when they converge on the same set of events. The record systems in some PRFs are informative in this regard for many programs of change. There is often considerable overlap in documentation, and it is not atypical to find certain activities or procedures recorded in several places, each documentation satisfying the conditions of a particular requirement.

It is not difficult to observe specific expressions of a facility's experience with an overstimulation of innovation. Again, the archives of the institution often are quite instructive. In most facilities, there have been dramatic increases in the gathering of information in recent years without a corresponding increase in the sophistication of processing it. Most of the new information is manually collected by facility staff in addition to their regular responsibilities. Unlike many parts of the private and corporate sector, computer assistance at state-of-the-art levels in hardware, software, and personnel is beyond budget limits for most PRFs. Thus, information organization and particularly information processing often can be problematic. At times it can reach overload conditions.

One area where information overload has combined with acceleration of innovative events is the regulation of behavior modification methods. Many agencies and states have adopted formal policies and guidelines (Pollack, 1978; Stolz, 1977), many of which are quite detailed both in procedure and in documentation. In Connecticut, state level policy requires that all facilities serving mentally retarded persons comply with a set of operational guidelines for standardized use of behavioral interventions with clients. There are 115 pages of standards covering 12 major areas of intervention. There are over 150 items of information (definitions, procedural requirements, minimum physical conditions, documentation requirements, etc.) covering the use of time-out interventions alone.

Such a policy, cumbersome and overwhelming by itself, sets in motion other events that further multiply the rate of change. If the policy is to be implemented faithfully, staff must be competent in its technical and administrative procedures. In practice, many are not, and this requires new staff development interventions. Many of the behavioral procedures require technical, human rights, and administrative review and approval before implementation is possible. This calls for the establishment of new committees or new assignments for existing committees. In one Connecticut facility, a new committee for independent technical review of behavioral programs was established. It developed a responsible review process but in so doing generated more required documents, procedures, and meetings for program personnel. With no additional staff resources to assist program professionals with the additional workload, time that otherwise would have been used for service implementation had to be diverted to complying with the review committee's requirements. Thus, well-intended changes responsive to real needs to regulate behavioral interventions came to compete with the delivery of client service itself. A year after the policy went into effect, an informal survey of human rights representatives from each state facility revealed serious problems with responding adequately to the standards. For some facilities, the chain of requirements and innovations descending from the policy itself had become unmanageable.

Similar situations can be found in other domains of activity. In one facility, nearly 60 new personnel procedures were issued over a 4½-year period. Over roughly the same period, 45 new administrative directives were issued, and about 65 administrative policies were developed and implemented. Many of these procedures, directives, and policies addressed complex issues and imposed major changes in function for literally hundreds of people. The directives and policies governing restraint of assaultive and self-injurious clients, for example, required new patterns of communication among several levels of staff plus extensive new methods of review, documentation, and follow-up for every incident in either category of client behavior. When changes are multiplied by hundreds of incidents sometimes over periods of time as short as one month, responding becomes difficult. Placed in context with changes coming from other policies, directives, and procedures, the overall experience with innovative events can be staggering. Each change by itself is justifiable, often critically necessary. Collectively, however, they represent excessive turnovers of novel events that require new responses and new adjustments by large numbers of people over shorter frames of time.

Toffler (1970) has discussed this experience of compression in great depth. He points out that when change is accelerated, more novel, first-time circumstances occur to confront individuals with unfamiliar and irregular conditions that require nonroutine responses. This alters the balance between predictable and unpredictable elements in an individual's life. Decisions tend to be more complex and taxing in unpredictable situations, so that where the novelty ratio is high, the response demands are more severe. To this one must add the effects of transience, another factor considered by Toffler. As noted earlier, many changes are set in place only to become obsolete or to need revision sooner than expected. Kaufman (1971) and Thompson (1976) have indicated that organizational systems cannot adjust well to such short life expectancies for innovations. This is certainly true for PRFs. They are systems that often require considerable effort both to gear up for major changes and to overcome various resistances that occur in response to those changes. However, once changes such as unit management, collective bargaining, or behavior modification policies take hold, they develop a momentum of their own that, in turn, tends to be refractory toward further revision. Sajwaj (1977) has noted this problem with respect to the difficulty of incorporating changes into behavior modification guidelines once the policy enabling the guidelines has been processed through its many phases of formulation and approval. It is cumbersome and time consuming to revise policy in most public human service systems. This is the case generally with many types of innovation in the public service systems in which most PRFs are imbedded. The systems are just not well suited to revise, turn over, and continuously make alterations in quick response to new insights, mandates, or technology.

From the chief administrator down to the entry level direct care worker, one can readily observe Toffler's (1970) factors of compression, novelty, and transience in operation. A few years ago, one PRF superintendent prepared a table organizing the influences on his office that originated outside the facility itself. There were more than 30 entries representing large scale influences (e.g., labor unions, ICF/MR, court actions). Importantly, most of these influences were not present a few years before and most had extensive agendas of activity with his office unrelated to other sources of influence. Because the superintendent had to manage these circumstances without any decline in other areas of responsibility and without any additional resources to his office, his administrative practice experienced significant compression.

The staff development or inservice training department in many PRFs is another place to observe high turnover rates with novel events. Ziarnik and Bernstein (1982) have examined inservice training programs in PRFs. They note the large increase in staff training interventions, but their review raises strong questions about the effectiveness of these efforts and concludes that there is a general lack of clear, long-term results. These authors suggest that the problem lies with the the incorrect application of staff training to situations where skill deficiency may be but one factor among many accounting for performance difficulties. They argue that other factors, such as inadequately reinforcing environments for staff, are often responsible for performance problems.

In many facilities, if one tracks backwards from the failed or modest inservice training outcomes, problems with unmanageable rates of change are likely to be found. Most new changes absorbed by an institution result in new competency requirements in some set of jobs. For example, when collective bargaining is adopted by a public service system, managerial personnel must acquire competency in such things as progressive discipline, grievance hearings, and contract management. When an independent program audit of the facility reports serious deficits in the quality of supervision, it is likely that supervisory competencies will be developed for specific positions so criticized. In these and countless other instances where competency problems occur, the instinct of the organization tends to identify the needed remedy as staff training. Other responses, such as changing the job environments or systematically evaluating the variety of factors that might be related to the visible competency problem, are seemingly too complex and cumbersome for the facility to manage. Indeed, these may be responses it is not competent to make. In contrast, a staff training workshop is an easily graspable response, more suited to the short time frames frequently imposed for correcting the competency deficits. As a result, inservice training departments easily can become overrun with multiple requests to train large numbers of staff in many new skill areas. Workshops are put together and churned out, but meaningful planning, systematic evaluation of outcomes, and longer term follow-up are likely to be casualties to the attempt to keep up with the demand.

Some types of changes are sprawling events that affect numerous areas of activity and set off further changes. A class action litigation and subsequent judicial intervention represents such an event, and there are scores of such actions currently in progress across the country. At a minimum, any litigative action against a PRF will likely increase the organization's experience of compression and accelerate the turnover of novel occurrences. It is not uncommon for hundreds of interrogatories to be exchanged between plaintiff and defense attorneys during the course of the discovery phase of the litigation. Typically, responses to these interrogatories require information that must be gathered by staff in the facility, and they are usually subject to precise deadlines. In extensive litigations, the information gathering may involve hundreds of staff members.

The specific tasks may consume days, weeks, even months. For example, a case analysis of a named plaintiff may require 50 hours or more to complete. If several of these are required, the task becomes enormous. Records of every operation in the facility over the previous 10 years may have to be compiled and analyzed, and current operations may have to be internally audited. Large numbers of expert witnesses may spend hundreds, even thousands, of hours visiting the facility, requiring time with staff at all levels and making further requests of them. Often the requested information is not organized or has not been kept and must be retrieved literally by hand.

All of these tasks are intrusions on the normal routines of care and service. Because these routines cannot be suspended, the litigative activity is compressed into the available time units. Other aspects of litigation compound the problem. Most legal events typically are novel events for the facility. Virtually by definition, these are adversary events as well, often threatening to the staff who must be involved. It is not uncommon for intrusive phases of a large litigation, such as discovery, to continue for several months or more, thus prolonging the facility's experience with compressed, novel, and adversary legal events.

Another signal index of increased and unmanaged rates of change is the committee turnover in a PRF. Little more than a decade ago, a few standing committees handled most of the planning, development, and implementation of services. Currently, as many authors predicted (e.g., Bennis & Slater, 1968; Michael, 1973; Mintzberg, 1981; Toffler, 1970), temporary committees, task forces, and work groups form, reform, and disassemble on a regular basis. They tend to gather around new ideas, problems, or responsibilities, generate activity (e.g., policies, procedures, new job functions, etc.) in that specific domain, and then go out of business. Their members promptly redistribute into other task groups constructed around yet newer ideas, problems, or responsibilities. In my own facility in 1982 more than 20 new committees and task forces were formed in response to a set of needs and changes experienced by the organization. Some of these groups existed for only a few meetings and were no more. Others spawned their own subcommittees and recruited members from various areas in the facility to staff them. All of these groups generated activity that had to be absorbed by the service system. In contrast, I could find only one new committee formed for client services or programming for the year 1971, eleven years earlier.

One can observe similar effects in individual roles. For decades, and in many PRFs, well into the 1970's, the duties of direct care workers were principally hygienic care and custodial management. In but a few years' time, that role has exploded with new responsibilities and competencies. Direct care job roles now normally include competencies in use of client safety restraints, human rights procedures, behavior programming, policy implementation, various paramedical and emergency procedures plus medication side effects, data collection, principles of human development, and a host of other duties. A relatively simple role, at least in skill requisites, quickly has become a complex one. Such role transformations occur in many other positions as well. The extent to which these reflect unmanageable rates of change probably varies with the facility, but it is unlikely that such major alterations in what must be viewed as the foundation role in the service system, the direct care role, have occurred without difficulty, as several authors have noted (e.g., Bogdan, Taylor, deGrandpre, & Haynes, 1974; Kaufman, 1971; Roos, 1975).

Another problem associated with unmanaged rates of change concerns the interventions designed to cope with them. In one sense, the test for such interventions is whether they control the rate of change and direct progress, or contribute further to the accumulation of novel, transient, and compressed experience. Wedel (1976) has reviewed the use of matrix organization as an approach to managing high change environments. The matrix organization is essentially a project structure developed and managed around specific goals or tasks. Arrangements of staff and management in projects are often temporary. Specific management approaches frequently are associated with matrix organization: Planning, programming, budgeting systems (PPBS); program evaluation review technique (PERT); critical path method (CPM); management by objectives (MBO); and organizational development (OD).

Good results have been reported with the use of matrix approaches in public human services (e.g., Beckhard, 1974; Gray, 1974), yet these are innovations themselves subject to the same outcome and rate problems already discussed. Therefore, administrations that adopt matrix organization, MBO, OD, or any other approach to manage high rates of change must do so carefully. This means that staff, especially managers and supervisors, must be well trained in these methods. This may take time, as will a correct program of implementation. Likert's (1961) conclusions are instructive in this regard. His field experiments on introducing participative management methods in several private organizations indicated that 3 or 4 years would be necessary to develop the application of this approach. He believed that in organizations with more than 200 employees an additional 5 years would be required to shift to full-scale application. He cautioned that the process cannot be hurried, which could be a problem in contemporary PRFs. This kind of time simply is not available, nor do most PRFs have a 3- to 8-year perspective for such interventions. Like other interventions, change management methods are likely to be imposed and pushed into operation hurriedly. However, the organization still will need to adjust to them as they would to any other innovations. Thus, if the planning, introduction, and use of approaches such as matrix organization are not conducted wisely, it is possible that, rather than providing some effective control in high change environments, they may well contribute to the overload.

Signs of this paradox can be observed in certain institutions. A feeling or pressure develops that the organization should be coping better with changes, that it should be employing change management strategies. Much like the superintendent who wanted to "have" normalization and unit programs, administrators become preoccupied with the outcome state, in this case "having" programs of organizational development, MBO, PERT, or matrix management. Before too long, the organization is struggling to cope with the remedies for its difficulties with managing change.

There are countless other situations and events that illustrate the presence of unmanaged rates of change. Their nature will vary with the individual facility and the forces propelling the changes. Each event that accelerates the rate of change presents a problem in adaptation for some individuals, larger groups of staff and clients, possibly the organization as a whole. Although many units of change are manageable through an institution's available resources, there do appear to be upper limits to the adaptive capacity. As these limits are approached and exceeded, the facility risks losing control over the reforms it is committed or required to make.

The dilemmas of early attempts to initiate reform in relatively dormant state institutions have been described by several authors (e.g., Rappaport, Chinsky, & Cowen, 1971; Saper, 1975; Thompson & Grabowski, 1972). Most of these efforts occurred in the 1960s and early 1970s, the earliest phase of the period under discussion. The problem at that time often was inertia—it was difficult to get any change going. A telling image of the effects of excessive change and reform a decade later is provided by an experienced, change-oriented chief administrator of a mid-western facility in a letter to the state's director of programs for developmentally disabled persons:

> . . . The impact of new demands is significant. ICF, collective bargaining, and OSHA have taken their toll on already thin schedules. . . . The demand for increased quality of services and range of these services is escalating. . . . New systems are being imposed upon us monthly, without additional staff. . . . Middle managers and administrators involved in these issues are beginning to burn out. The message seems to be, "make due with what you have, but satisfy everyone." . . . I am becoming paper bound, desk bound, policy bound, procedure bound, while the problems in our residential units continue unabated. . . . Planning has become a lost art; problem solving an ineffective one. One cannot take pride in his products because there is no time to develop them to acceptable standards. . . . This is the state of the art of residential administration to which we have arrived. Crisis administration.

Inadequate Preparation

The third characteristic of this perspective on the course of recent reform efforts in PRFs concerns the preparation of persons applying and receiving those reforms. A general discontinuity between the formal training of certain human service professionals and their subsequent job duties has been reported in the literature (e.g., Light, 1979; Rickard & Clements, 1981; Walker, 1981). Cherniss, Egnatios, and Wacker (1976) have brought attention to the particular failure to prepare professionals for the organizational dynamics of public institutions and negotiating one's way through them. In residential facilities for mentally handicapped individuals, there exists a troubling discontinuity between the formal training or experience of many staff members who design, conduct, and receive innovative programs and what these persons actually encounter in their work. Both providers and receivers of multiple units of change are not adequately equipped to manage the experience.

Although there may be certain kinds of technical training gaps (e.g., professionals hired who have never worked with mentally handicapped clients), the preparation shortfall of concern here is in the deficits in knowledge about and responses to the conditions of high, uncoordinated change, the compression of events, the overemphasis of preset outcomes, and the social and interpersonal working environments these conditions produce over time. Vickers (1963) observed that any change introduced into a system will have numberless and unpredictable repercussions throughout the system. Even when the intent of a change is to render control in only one part of the system, the total system, he argues, is likely to be less predictable than before. Importantly, skills based on the previous arrangement of the system will become depreciated. More than 20 years later, these conclusions seem fresh and relevant to the residential facility.

By producing new and often temporary arrangements of structures, roles, and people, the accelerated rate of reform has created shifting stabilities in the workplace. The skill requirements, mostly technical, that previously served adequately in PRF work settings have become depreciated. They do not, alone, usefully assist individuals in managing the more turbulent and complex circumstances in which they must conduct technical and other duties.

To understand the response requirements for which the preparation has been so poor, it is necessary first to examine more precisely the personal and social effects that can occur in working environments characterized by high levels of continuous, uncoordinated, and compressed change. Certain effects already are known to be associated merely with working in human service environments, even more stable ones. These include increased stress, tedium, and burnout, all of which have been studied and widely discussed in recent years (e.g., Freudenberger, 1975; Greenberg & Valletutti, 1980; Pines & Aronson, 1981). Burnout, for example, is a state of physical, emotional, and attitudinal exhaustion, according to Pines & Aronson (1981). They report research involving 724 workers in 14 mental retardation facilities that reveals high levels of burnout among administrative, professional, and direct care staff. Major correlates of burnout in this sample included such experiences as task overload, conflicting demands in the workplace, administrative hassles (e.g., red tape, communication difficulties), lack of autonomy, and a sense of giving more emotional energy than one receives in return.

The information available clearly indicates a high probable occurrence for stress and burnout in PRFs. Worse, some observers (e.g., Scholom & Perlman, 1979) have suggested that where these conditions exist, they are often neglected. The occurrence and its neglect in PRFs would be serious enough, but a condition of stress and burnout among human service workers does not necessarily require high change, time-compressed environments to happen. The available information suggests that it occurs, in large part, because of the nature of the work and its client-oriented focus (Pines & Aronson, 1981). Thus the effects due specifically to the existence of high levels of uncoordinated, constant, and compressed change would seem to be additional, perhaps separate, consequences.

It does appear that such reactions as the role disorientation described earlier are attributable, at least in part, to high change factors. The rearrangements and workplace instabilities that develop with an unmanaged current of change tend to be viewed or felt by staff as matters of trust, identity, or risk rather than as a legitimate course of reform for the organization. For example, in some innovative programs, especially those with deadline and outcome pressure, ambiguities, uncertainties, and some anxiety among participants are bound to occur. This is to be expected given the complex ecologies of the PRF, the unperfected nature of the program technologies being applied (e.g., Baumeister, 1981), and how little is known about the application process (e.g., Reppucci & Saunders, 1974; Willems, 1974). But these conditions also increase the probability that errors will be made, especially in early phases of the program or when participants simultaneously are involved with other areas of change. The problem that then develops concerns acknowledging the errors. In many organizations, this is a high risk response, one to be avoided. Staff in these circumstances may find it safer to seek quick fix solutions or at least to protect the appearance of knowing what they are doing, even though these actions may be counterproductive to the true success of the program innovation itself.

Another illustration involves distrust. During periods of upheaval, decisions tend to become centralized at the top even in facilities with more decentralized philosophies. Such decisions may uproot or reorganize various individuals or work groups, but under the press of time the decision makers choose to depend on lower level managers or supervisors to deliver the orders and explanations. Not infrequently, the explanations are incomplete, inadvertently edited, and unresponsive to the needs of the uprooted persons, who may be left wondering whether the changes mean their performance has been questioned. Perhaps they are confused about the purpose of a reassignment. Unless the organization has strongly endorsed norms that enable such individuals to share these reactions and obtain constructive feedback in return, the reactions are likely to go unexpressed. After a few instances of this sort of thing, the reactions tend to go underground. In either case, trust in the organization's leaders and choices probably has been set back. Over time, individuals repeatedly exposed to this experience will develop other identifications that may compete with the facility's mission.

Strong, aggressive labor unions, for example, often attract staff disillusioned by what they feel is an unreasonable trend in administrative choice or direction.

It is not that trust failure can't happen in more stable organizations—it can and does because other variables, such as supervisory effectiveness, act independently on its occurrence. The point to be emphasized is that it is more likely to develop in working environments destabilized by high levels of change.

Some reactions and effects can be traced either to the specific preemployment experience of certain individuals or the nature of their formal training. This can be observed in administrative and professional personnel for whom the identities they were trained to embrace in professional schools are not fully adaptive or acceptable in the job environment. We discuss this problem in depth in Chapter 4, but a couple of brief examples are provided here. Many professionals develop an investment, if not an identification, with their technical procedures (e.g., Bucher & Stelling, 1977; Light, 1979). It is a source of respect as well as evidence of their clinical control of services. In the PRF workplace, these individuals must rely on many layers of staff and supervisors across three time shifts each day to handle or mishandle their procedures. Often, they become distressed when the reputation of the procedures, and by extension their own reputation, develop from the actions of this large mix of people. Trained through laboratory practica typically arranged by their professional schools (and thus fairly well controlled and precise applications of technical procedure), these professionals may be unfamiliar with the application experience in more complex, less controllable environments.

Another related illustration is the situation of single profession training and interdisciplinary concepts of practice. Institutional psychologists, speech clinicians, physicians, teachers, and other service providers typically were trained by members of their own profession in settings controlled or directed by that profession. They may have interacted with other disciplines during training, but the exchanges were usually limited, restricted by rules of hierarchy, territory, or tradition. The high level interaction of these groups required in a faithfully executed interdisciplinary practice may contradict or at least confuse the identity acquired from the training experience, necessitating an adjustment for which the organization provides neither time nor guidance.

Identifications, whether developed from a professional school or any other experience, are anchor points that support staff members' images of their work and its fit in the organization. It may also support their view of other staff groups and clients as well. Toffler (1970) suggests that under conditions of rapid and complex change, individuals have to adjust these images in a way that correlates with the pace of change. If they cannot do this, they must reject either the change or their images. Each choice exacts a toll in stress or anxiety. Perhaps more importantly, if the selected image is off course, the individual's responses to various job situations can become inappropriate. One can find many persons working in PRFs, often in key positions, for whom this is valid. In too many instances, the situation often is unacknowledged by the individual and unknown or unsupervised by his or her superiors. We conclude this sampling of effects with a brief look at ambiguity and uncertainty caused by unmanaged and compressed change. All that has been said thus far supports the conclusion that the work settings under discussion will become ambiguous and uncertain at some times, perhaps frequently. Although some low or moderate levels of uncertainty and ambiguity in the work environment may be manageable, even adaptive in relatively stable organizations, there is evidence that high levels of unexpected, unclear conditions, particularly in more turbulent environments, raise serious questions of adaptability for many individuals (LaPorte, 1971). The point at which the uncertainty or ambiguity is no longer bearable will vary and be difficult to pinpoint. We develop this issue further in later chapters, but here consider one case, a facility where many project teams were set in motion to develop a new service approach. A limited range of personnel resources resulted in several persons' having memberships on two or three teams. Goals and purposes also overlapped across groups, and eventually so did the tasks. Despite some efforts at coordination, teams developed products and procedures that contradicted one another in several areas that overlapped. The failure at coordination (due in large part to the short time frame allowed for completion and the presence of other independent sources of change that distracted the principal coordinators) left the project teams to develop a course and momentum of their own. For many individuals with memberships on contradicting teams, it became a self-canceling experience. The recipients of the teams' service products and procedures, those who were to run the services, were, for a while, unable to function at all. In both cases, people were experiencing a kind of disabling mix of uncertain and unclear conditions to which they could not adapt.

There are numerous other related effects produced or aggravated by conditions of high, uncoordinated, and compressed change in residential facilities. Some occur as a function of characteristics or situations present in the individual agencies interacting with these conditions. The contention is that in many of these facilities the response requirements to control and correct these effects are undeveloped.

Perhaps the most disconcerting element of this shortfall is that many individuals experiencing these reactions, their supervisors, and those entrusted with developing and managing the organization's course of reform do not recognize the problem as deriving from the process of change itself. Even if they do, it may not be considered to be a legitimate matter for intervention. Some are unaware of what is happening to them. Many misdiagnose their own situations and those of their colleagues. For example, too many supervisors falsely assess these reactions as performance problems and counsel the supervisee to "correct" the performance. In all these instances, the valid deficits go unnoticed and the needed skills go undeveloped. One way to confirm the existence of these circumstances is to determine if the organization has on staff anybody recruited or assigned specifically to monitor the effects of excessive change on people and to develop corrective responses to the condition. Usually there is no such individual. Those on staff with the best chance and ability to detect the problem and respond to it frequently are assigned to implementing the changes themselves.

The adaptive difficulties of people struggling with too much uncertainty, confusion, and stress, having role identities that are disconfirmed in experience, developing a sense of distrust about the organization or its goals, and feeling at risk when they attempt to respond to these matters are problems that don't easily go away. Collectively they generate a great deal of energy that is expressed inappropriately in committees, among task groups, and at work stations. What seems to be inappropriate is that these problems are expressed as task content rather than as the interpersonal and adaptive difficulties they actually are. Put differently, persons overloaded and spent by conditions of excessive change tend to assert their discontent against the task, the goal, or some procedure rather than address the faltering process. As noted earlier, they often cannot identify the process factors in the first place. Many times it is also true that work group norms to discuss the process (if it is recognized as defective) have not been developed or accepted. Thus, they do not feel permission to bring up the subject. Argyris (1982) has observed this phenomenon in many other types of organizations as well.

The distinction between content and process is important. Schein (1969) has described *process* as the pattern of relationships among people and the perceptions, experiences, and personality factors that influence those relationships. This is separate both from *structural* variables (i.e., those defining the configurations of positions and roles in the organization), and from *content* variables (i.e., those involving the organization's goals and tasks).

When process—the human variables—is disguised or coded as content issues, the working group becomes disabled and the environment is strained. More often than is realized, this occurs when committees, interdiscipinary service teams, even high level administrative task groups reach seemingly impassable differences on content while working under conditions of too much change. A typical scenario might go like this: Points of view on an issue rapidly escalate to locked-in positions. Exchange among participants narrows to judgments and counter-judgments about the merits of each position. Previously developed views about one another's competencies and biases seem to affect much of what is said. The interaction itself may be charted almost as an uninterrupted series of declarative statements, often beginning with "I think . . ." and seldom developing, clarifying, or otherwise pursuing the thoughts of other speakers. When resolution is pursued, the search often is for a content or technical fix. Somehow the group is unable to move beyond this activity and face up to its need to share the uncertainties, fear, and discomfort members may be experiencing and which may be contributing to the strident dialogue. Unless formally prepared to act otherwise, the group may be unable to perform this move; that is, it cannot make a "content-to-process shift."

This failure, where it occurs, is crucial, because the problems of inadequate preparation for managing high change conditions are largely problems of process. The response requirements to which this discussion has referred are process requirements. There is a growing recognition of this dilemma in the public health and mental health fields (e.g., Report of the National Task Force, 1979; Scott & Crosby, 1981), but many organizations have not built process preparation into their management and service practices. As Dyer (1977) and Glaser and Backer (1979) have indicated, doing so is a time-consuming undertaking, and the current state of process technologies applied to public human service settings must be considered to be early, if not primitive. In recent years there have been applications of such process strategies as organizational development to the health care fields (Glaser & Backer, 1979), but few of these efforts have been systematically evaluated (Jerrell & Kouzes, 1982). Attempts to apply such models to more turbulent environments already numbed by excessive change and instability probably are fewer still, since these organizations may be unreceptive to yet another intrusion and too impatient to attend to slower moving, long-range interventions. Further, as Maguire (1970) noted in a review of the literature on change, most models portray change as a novel event interposed between periods of organizational stability. This view is becoming progressively unsuited to the conditions of continuous change that have characterized many PRFs in recent years.

The major problem implicit in all this is how to provide an organizational environment that recognizes the need to revise what is considered required competence in work settings destabilized to various degrees by high rates of change. A corresponding problem concerns the design of interventions to develop those competencies and the means to maintain them at appropriate levels of criteria. ˮ

At present, three aspects of the problem need attention. First, in many facilities these organizational process difficulties and the adaptive deficits they represent are denied or disguised as content issues. Even where appropriately acknowledged, they are often viewed as noise or distraction in the organization rather than as important variables. And even when seen as proper subjects of concern, their priority is typically too low for adequate responses to be made. Some time ago, I conducted a workshop for several PRF professionals working on 10 separate interdisciplinary units in a facility experiencing high rates of change. The workshop's sole objective was to see if participants could recognize their stress, function, and role difficulties on the job as human process issues deriving from conditions of unmanageable change, rather than as the program content matters they had identified as the trouble. Recognition was achieved after some resistance, but the considerable degree of relief that came with the recognition is the point of the illustration. In a curious microcosm, it seemed to reveal the significance of the whole adaptive problem. Noticeable, though probably temporary, relief came with a modest probe at awareness and with no attempt at further corrective intervention. According to these participants, the awareness or recognition barrier would never have been overcome in the normal course of events in their jobs. The content-to-process shift in focus would not have occurred.

The second aspect concerns the competencies themselves. These need to be identified operationally for specific circumstances of change, for specific environments, and for specific people or roles within a given organization. Perhaps the initial competency is the acquisition of an attitude or perspective that accepts the residential facility as a place of accelerated change that will be characterized by continuous instabilities for some time to come. This will not be easy. Many key personnel see their importance as reducing turbulence, having control, and being right. Their identities depend on these functions, as we indicate in later chapters. They will not abandon this for a seemingly more uncomfortable outlook. Yet the competency to accept a broad perspective of uncertainty and instability would permit individuals to accept such things as temporary assignments, nonpermanent innovations, and role confusion. These would become valid expectancies about their jobs. It might also help lower the preoccupation with preset outcome states since these would have to be viewed more tentatively. Finally, if widely held, such a perspective might make it safer to acknowledge error and take constructive risks in the work environment. In the next section of the chapter, this matter of perspectives and competencies is considered more broadly.

The third aspect of the preparation problem involves resource. There is a scarcity of persons in public residential facilities with the training and ability to understand the problems that have been described here and to assist those individuals and groups struggling with it. Right now, we do not intentionally produce or recruit such people, nor do we establish positions to scan for the presence of the problems and to evaluate its impact on operations. Finally, we do not view this subject as a legitimate area of job performance for countless numbers of persons who are assigned to supervise others.

I have attempted to characterize some dimensions of the efforts, roughly over the past 20 years, to modernize the role and function of the public residential facility for mentally handicapped individuals. This analysis is admittedly selective, and many aspects of reform programs have undoubtedly been overlooked. The general contention has been that the application, not the ideas or goals of reform, has gone wrong. The means of implementing change and managing its effects on the system have been maladaptive. This reasoning does not necessarily call for less innovation or support a retreat from any ideologies, concepts, and methods of reform that could be introduced to the PRF. It does, however, require a revised mentality about the application process and the consideration of alternative views about the needed competencies of providers, receivers, and managers of innovating organizations. These issues form the agenda for the remaining discussion of the chapter.

SOME THOUGHTS ON NEEDED COMPETENCIES

This discussion has been organized around three questions about residential facilities. Thus far we have considered two of them: (a) potential futures for these facilities; and (b) an alternative perspective on recent history. In different contexts, the chapters that follow provide further detail on these issues. In this section, I examine the third question, the matter of organizational and interpersonal requirements for those who will develop and those who will work in future-relevant residential facilities.

It is useful to review the themes developed to this point. In a general sense, we have concentrated on certain conditions or factors associated with recent efforts at reforming PRFs. More specifically, the main contention has been that, despite changeworthy concepts and technologies, the changing process itself has been poorly understood and applied. Although units of reform or specific outcomes have been acquired in PRFs, much less has been learned about developing adequate norms, values, and practices to govern how reform is conducted. Similarly, little seems to have been learned about adaptive functioning under the conditions of intense change being encountered by these organizations. New mandates or programs for change seem to be attacked with unimproved expertise about the effects the reforming process itself exerts upon the organization and its people. I have provided a perspective that characterizes the course of many recent reform efforts in three ways: (a) a preoccupation with or bias toward hurriedly achieving preset outcomes; (b) unmanaged rates of continuous change or innovation; and (c) inadequate preparation of providers and receivers of change. These characteristics and the effects they produce are considered to be maladaptive where they occur, inhibiting rather than promoting a sense of validity for the residential facility.

At the heart of it, much of the reforming in PRFs seems to have been governed by a widely held belief that innovating was largely a technical matter—if a new program of change was needed, and if it was supported by good concept and technology, then retooling people with technique and providing administrative functions accounted for most of the implementing action. Many participants in programs of innovation in PRFs have expressed a sense of being "engineered" through the planning, design, start-up, and implementation phases. Michael (1973) has argued that most approaches to changing public organizations treat the various activities of change—planning, designing, training, administrating, evaluating, and so on—as social engineering problems requiring a social engineering technology. He describes social engineering as an elitist, top-down attitude toward planning characterized by impatience and resistance to feedback from the receiving environment. Goals tend to be set rigidly and the problem remains fixed; that is, its nature or defintion tends to go unexamined during the life of the project. Social engineering, in this view, seems to produce precisely aimed action programs pursuing predetermined outcomes and directed by self-assured individuals confident both of the outcome and the means selected to achieve it.

Care must be taken in characterizing either an individual project or a systemic program of innovation as powered by any one single attitude. Many factors influence the course of most reforms, and these often occur as a function of agency differences. Still, the social engineering attitude toward innovation and problem solving has a long and entrenched history in public organizations (Michael, 1973). In varying degrees, it is likely to be an explicit or implicit influence on the design and implementation of innovation. In many projects across several PRFs, I have observed it to be the controlling point of view.

Michael's (1973) extensive study of long-range planning for change in public organizations concludes, among other things, that social engineering attitudes and approaches to change misconstrue the requirements that will need to be satisfied if the turbulent conditions of organizational change are to be managed responsibly over the long term. Instead, his work suggests an alternative philosophy that views the planning and application processes of innovation as being: (a) flexible, not certain, about outcome; (b) experimental, not foreclosed, about means; (c) open, not closed, to continuous feedback from all environments associated with the intervention; and (d) alterable by such feedback. Under this thinking, innovation is a continuous act of revision for the organization and its people. Short-term outcomes are planned and revised in terms of conjectures about longer range futures that seem worth achieving. It is never assumed that all factors or events associated with conditions of change can be controlled.

If the process of implementing any of the ideas for future residential facilities discussed earlier is viewed through the lens of a philosophy of application such as Michael's (1973), two operational questions follow: (a) what will be the required competencies of people who might adopt this view; and (b) what would it take to make both the philosophy and the competencies acceptable as approaches to organizational change in facilities interested in designing new futures.

Suggested Competencies

The discussion thus far argues that a residential facility, having decided to conduct major reforms in its concept and function, will have to revise how it considers its process of applying those changes. It will have to make repeated checks on its goals and implementation procedures during the course of reform in order to maintain a valid sense of its progress and a clear view of its problems. Argyris (1982), reviewing several case studies of organizational change, suggests that an organization can acquire such a valid image of itself through a commitment and an ability to subject both the goals and the means selected for implementation to scrutiny by all those who will use them. He provides convincing evidence that most organizations cannot do this well. Many "consumers" (i.e., direct care staff, middle management personnel, professionals, support staff, clients, parents) of program reforms in PRFs probably would agree.

What Argyris (1982) is calling for presents a difficult challenge to those planners and administrators overcommitted to predetermined outcome states and biased toward a social engineering mentality about reaching them. The difficulty exists because the overcommitment and bias promote conditions that suppress or discard information revealing error about the outcome states or the implementing process. For residential concepts that venture into previously uncharted areas of role and function, this error rate should be higher. At nearly every stage, complex questions about the very values and assumptions of these roles and functions may arise. Previous ways of looking at the workplace and its personnel may have to be revised. This is to be expected in settings characterized by high levels of uncertainty and change. However, the capacity to detect errors validly and then to provide corrective response becomes more crucial in these circumstances. When this capacity is undeveloped, inhibited, or otherwise deficient, the organization is likely to evolve into what Argyris (1982) calls a "limited learning system." Such a system is apt to produce consequences (for this discussion, outcomes of reform) it does not intend. For similar reasons, those controlling or directing the implementation process are likely to be defensive and self-protective about their actions, thus "sealing in" conditions for uncorrectable error.

These considerations argue for the necessity to conduct valid inquiry into the process of reform *as it occurs*. To accomplish this, the organization must become an *active* learning system for which five initial competencies are necessary:

1. Competency to Design and Use Corrective Feedback Systems. This is the foundation requirement. All other competencies derive from the organization's ability to continuously evaluate its course and process of reform. To introduce and maintain a system that will perform this function, the organization's staff (from the chief administrator on down) must learn how to do three things. First, it will have to create throughout the work force conditions that encourage open and continuous questioning of both the goals and the actions to implement them. We are beginning to develop a data base suggesting that such conditions (e.g., supervisors and management willing to subject their ideas and beliefs to open review by their subordinates) do not exist in residential facilities, and further, that such questioning may be treated punitively (Thaw, Thibeault, & Johnston, 1985).

This is not a superficial notion of feedback. Rather, the conditions required must legitimize broad and deep inquiry into the organization's approach to reform by *any* member of staff regardless of rank. If, during the course of such inquiry, key values or assumptions behind policies or program choices are confronted, or even threatened, the inquiry must still be permitted to proceed without interference. If the inquiry is thwarted, the conditions of the competency are unsatisfied. As an illustration, recently the administration of a PRF directed its professional staff to cease using certain behavioral intervention procedures. The directive was in response to external pressures that had developed out of a litigation involving the facility. Members of the professional staff felt the directive was clinically unwise. However, they were unwilling to question the directive, because no feedback was requested and because they were reluctant to risk testing the authoritarian, nonnegotiable tone of the directive. They may also have been unskilled in ways to conduct such questioning were they willing to take the risk in the first place. In short, both staff levels, administrative and professional, were deficient in the competency being suggested. It is important to note that the competency does not require that the feedback always be used. Indeed, there are times when administrative directives are necessary. What must be legitimized, however, is acceptability of the inquiry without penalty.

The second thing to be learned is how to develop the capacity to gather reliably and analyze effectively information relevant to the questions asked. In many facilities, this capacity is underdeveloped. Many are unaware that this is so. Managers and professionals in many of these organizations do not see this evaluative capacity as a priority. For example, some years back, the administrator of a smaller facility refused to support the need to evaluate a major staff training program. "If we've decided to do the training," he reasoned, "let's assume it will have some benefit." Chapter 7 of this book addresses the design and utilization of evaluative systems at great length.

The third requisite is that individuals or groups be able to give evaluative information back to the organization in such a way that recipients find it acceptable and usable. *Acceptable* means nonthreatening; *usable* means recipients can act upon it in a manner that produces effects responsive to the question or problem. In the illustration about the directive to cease certain behavioral procedures, neither party seemed able to do this well. In consulting with numerous interdisciplinary groups in PRFs over the past 10 years, I did not encounter one group where these skills were sufficiently developed. More often, they chose feedback strategies that were polarizing, judgmental, or inflexible. What they encountered in return frequently were responses to their style rather than to the substance of their feedback.

If the three conditions of this initial competency are satisfied, the process of reform becomes a continuous act of inquiry and revision. This would replace the view (and the competencies associated with it) that reform proceeds by placing all bets on one plan, one form of application, and one view of outcome all fastened to a reluctance to reconsider any of it during the course of the project.

2. *Competency to Embrace Error.* Effective feedback systems detect error. Earlier it was argued that previous approaches to reform in residential facilities promoted conditions that suppress information revealing error. This contradiction is resolved by reconsidering the role of error in the reforming process. Thus, the second proposed competency is the ability of individuals, groups, and the organization itself to regard error (especially in uncharted areas of planning and implementation) as a learning experience rather than as a performance deficit. Michael (1973) had identified this kind of competency as essential for people working in organizations with major agendas of reform.

At present, in many residential facilities and especially those under strong external scrutiny by federal courts, state legislatures, or various monitoring agencies, error committed in the process of implementing change is too often viewed as performance weakness or even imcompetence. This happens because the organization perceives that the necessary abilities to conduct reform are certainty, control, and self-assurance. Stated differently, the organization places an excessive priority on its members' "being right." This priority calls for skills that emphasize "knowing" rather than "learning" as the active response in conducting change. The proposed competency rejects these assumptions and reflects instead Friedlander's (1980) view that it is necessary for the organization to "learn how to learn" from its own experience and actions.

In this alternative view, individuals and work groups within the organization become skilled at examining mistakes, errors, and incorrect or incomplete ideas for where these may lead, rather than in terms of their failure to be right. Many observers of individual, group, and organizational problem solving processes (e.g., Argyris, 1982; Burke, 1982; deBono, 1970; Ulschak, Nathanson, & Gillan, 1981) have pointed out that producing effective ideas, programs, and solutions does not require being right at every step in the process. The need to be right all the time may actually obstruct these processes. For example, in my work with interdisciplinary teams in residential facilities, I found large numbers of professionals, paraprofessionals, and middle level managers reluctant to contribute to program development or problem-solving discussions because the risk of having their ideas immediately judged as right or wrong was too high. Fisher and Ury (1981) have demonstrated the importance of separating the act of inventing and developing ideas from the act of judging them. When this skill was acquired by the interdisciplinary groups, the levels of members' participation increased, as did the range and depth of their ideas.

Similarly, the act of judgment itself must be reconsidered. Judgment typically is used as a rejection device. Instead, it should be employed as an evaluative tool that (a) searches for and extracts usable elements of ideas, concepts, and opinions; (b) identifies concerns about these contributions; (c) separates directly useful notions from those that represent areas for further exploration; and (d) permits reexamination of the nature of the problem (deBono, 1970; Ulschak, Nathanson, & Gillan, 1981).

Other skills also have been associated with the constructive use of error (see Argyris, 1982, and deBono, 1970, for discussions in organizational and individual contexts). It is not the purpose here to develop a detailed profile of such specific skills, but rather to illustrate the type of abilities that will have to become normative at all staff levels in residential facilities if error is to be treated as a learning opportunity rather than as a performance deficit.

3. Competency to Accept Uncertainty.   Harris (1980) has identified the ordeal with uncertainty as a major factor in organizational change. Nonetheless, organizations tend to see uncertainty as a liability and therefore avoid it, often by constructing what Harris calls ''the illusion of certainty.'' For example, they devise strategies that assume certainty of outcome rather than accept, at best, the probabilistic nature of outcome likelihoods. Michael's (1973) work reaches similar conclusions and advises that long-range social planning and reform will require that organizations openly acknowledge and live with great amounts of uncertainty.

The third competency develops from these considerations: the capacity to expect, acknowledge, and accept experiences of substantial uncertainty. For residential facilities faced with redesigning their futures, the periods of uncertainty may be protracted; the levels of uncertainty may, at times, exceed that which is tolerable; and some of the uncertainty may be irreducible. The competency on uncertainty requires that individuals and groups within the residential organization judge it an asset to own up to uncertainty when they experience it and live with it when it is irreducible. The prevailing wisdom seems to counsel avoiding this confrontation (LaPorte, 1971). In Chapter 4 of this book, we discuss in detail the dilemma uncertainty presents for the professional community in the larger residential facilities.

Michael (1973) suggests that acknowledging uncertainty would make at least three contributions to the conduct of reform. First, sharing the experience of uncertainty regarding such things as one's job role, the process of implementing various program interventions, or even the plans for the facility's overall mission could help ease the difficulty of carrying it alone. I have observed that although many individuals in residential facilities experience high levels of uncertainty, most seem unsure whether uncertainty is an appropriate reaction to the circumstances at hand. Second, acknowledging uncertainty would increase the chances for the exploratory mood necessary to view reform and change as learning processes rather than as engineering procedures. Third, openly acknowledging limitations to ''what there is to know'' would encourage a work climate of trust and a work attitude that permits continuous reexamination of the organization's goals and problems. Such conditions should also reduce the premium on ''being right," challenge the conventional view that being right is competence, and restrain the tendency to punish or phase out of the action those who are "not right."

4. Competency to Respond to Staff Needs Produced by Conditions of Reform. There is mounting evidence that staff members in human service organizations are experiencing major problems in job adaptation, morale, turnover, absenteeism, and stress (e.g., Cherniss, 1981; Reppucci & Saunders, 1983; Sarata & Jeppesen, 1977; Zaharia & Baumeister, 1978). Scholom and Perlman (1979) have directly raised the question of staff neglect in mental health facilities. Pines and Aronson (1981) report research findings indicating fully one third of staff in residential facilities for developmentally disabled clients meet criteria for physical, mental, and attitudinal exhaustion. Levinson (1980) points to failures at the organizational level: (a) the inability to recognize the devastating effects of change on employees; and (b) the absence of systematic efforts to support people through the process of change. Moore and Eddy (1980) find employees experiencing job stress paradoxically victimized by the organization. The employee is the recipient of stress from activity and effects produced by the organization but is held individually responsible both for coping with it and resolving the causes. These authors conclude that the problem requires system-level intervention.

These circumstances in the workplace recommend the fourth competency: the ability of the residential facility to scan for, identify, and proactively respond to the needs of staff affected by the conditions produced by reform. Working closely with staff at all levels of the service system for 15 years, I have observed these needs to be devalued as legitimate matters for attention. Often the devaluation is less a matter of organizational preference (the needs may be seen by administrators genuinely sensitive to their importance) than of the influence exerted on the facility by external forces such as state officials, court appointed monitors, advocacy groups, and the media. These groups tend to pressure residential facilities toward service outcomes, with limited regard and patience for the effects absorbed by staff along the way. These groups typically have enormous leverage and power, leaving facility leadership with few options.

The emphasis on proactive response is meant to distinguish anticipatory interventions from those that occur (if they occur at all) after difficulties have emerged and job-disabling conditions have begun to set in. For example, instruction of employees on the potential social and personal effects of accelerated rates of organizational change, coupled with supervisory attention to the earliest signs of such effects, would constitute a more proactive response than would the provision of counseling to employees who, having experienced extended periods of job stress, suffer a precipitous episode of anxiety.

To secure this competency, residential facilities will have to revise their obligations to their employees in at least four respects. First, they must recruit and hire specialists whose sole functions will be (a) to evaluate the system regularly for the presence of staff problems, and (b) to design and implement interventions in response to needs and problems identified. Most personnel departments in residential facilities do not or cannot perform these functions. Many supervisors are untrained even to scan for these types of employee problems as part of their normal supervision. In one facility, this supervisory deficiency prompted the chief administrator to direct higher level management to initiate corrective action if supervisors failed to react to their employees' concerns. This kind of decisive administrative action, however, is less helpful when the problem is a broad based skill deficiency in supervisory ranks.

Second, it will be necessary to persuade the high players external to the facility (e.g., state officials, federal inspectors, advocacy groups, etc.) that the needs of the staff evolving from the process of change are important factors, that they affect client service, and that they require recognition, resources, and priority. An adequate data base to support these arguments probably will be required, but the pivotal issue here may be the nature of the risk that facility leaders will perceive in taking this step. Some, perhaps many, may be unwilling to act if the personal risk seems too high.

Third, the beliefs and practices that place sole responsibility for coping with the demands of the reforming process on the shoulders of individuals must be disengaged. The residential facility will have to develop norms that view the staff fallout effects as legitimate variables rather than distractions to be overlooked. Further, the leadership will have to regard proactive and therapeutic response to these effects as a duty of the organization.

Fourth, it will probably become necessary to facilitate, rather than take for granted, the transition of staff from present conditions to future goal states. The organization will have to develop plans and design strategies to do this. Typical plans might provide for such things as: (a) identification of problem-solving and performance skills for employees at each stage of transition; (b) redesign of staff incentive systems to correspond with their needs for recognition, professional growth, and ownership of the programs of reform; and (c) development of assessment systems to anticipate employee needs in relationship to their assignments, task and support groups, supervision, and the total work flow of the organization. Carlson (1980) has described a model for this type of endeavor in considerable detail.

5. Competency to Use Historical Perspective. To utilize the first four competencies—indeed, to understand the problems that have characterized the residential facility's ordeal with reform over 2 decades—individuals will need a firm sense of their organization's history as well as the history of their own roles in the organization. This may actually prove to be the minimum requirement. An historical awareness of the broader social, political, and cultural developments that have influenced the course of events in the human services field also seems necessary. A working knowledge of the nature and effects of change, especially accelerated rates of change (see, for example, Toffler, 1970) probably should also be job required.

It is therefore troubling to observe that an indeterminant, but apparently large, number of persons working at every level in residential facilities and often in the systems that house them, are "ahistorical." In 15 years working with and consulting to professionals, administrators, supervisory personnel, and direct care staff, I have found surprisingly few with an interest in, much less an understanding of, events prior to their tenure. This shortcoming extends forward as well. Few of these people seemed to have a long-range vision of their facility. Even among those with 15 or 20 years' tenure, seldom was there an organized sense of their own job experiences over time that could be called on in present circumstances.

To illustrate, I have observed numerous interdisciplinary service teams to be literally transfixed to next week's agenda. The reports due on Monday, the meetings scheduled for Tuesday, the ICF/MR survey by inspectors on Wednesday—these types of events seem to control their use and concept of time. Developing both a predictive and postdictive vision about their work, their organization, sometimes even their clients, is difficult, often distracting for them. Many do not see its relevance anyway. On several occasions, I have asked members of these teams if they ever seriously discussed as a group the possible, probable, or potential circumstances of their clients 2 or 4 years ahead. The answer, which was always no, seems paradoxical in view of the requirement that they complete long-range plans for all their clients. The apparent contradiction is resolved, however, if preparing the long-range plans is conducted as an "ahistorical" exercise. Put differently, these professionals were satisfying present obligations ("We have to produce a long range plan today!"), and they did so by the act of selecting a single-point option (e.g., community placement in a group home, movement to a less restrictive environment, independent living, etc.) in the future. What they did not do was discuss a process, namely, the probable course of development for a client from which they could make a clinical prediction. There was no sense of a client's movement through time in their choice. Thus, despite files full of long-range plans, their answer to my question was perfectly truthful.

Recently, researchers have begun formally to study time perspectives—partitioning time into past, present, and future—and their influence on such things as work behavior, creativity, and problem solving (e.g., Gonzalez & Zimbardo, 1985; Levine & Wolff, 1985). Gonzalez and Zimbardo talk about an individual's "temporal bias," suggesting, for example, that some people never develop a meaningful sense of the future. Others may see the past as irrelevant to achieving future objectives. Reppucci and Saunders (1983) have emphasized the direct relevance of time perspective to understanding change in human service institutions. They point out that change agents infrequently attempt to gather the organizational equivalent of the standard clinical case history. Instead, participants in change are restricted in their focus to parameters of the immediate situation.

Reppucci and Saunders (1983) argue strongly that historical perspective should "be actively used as a conceptual stimulus to alter the field of problem definition and broaden the range of strategy formulations for bringing about change" (p. 518). Providing case evidence to illustrate the value of both general social history and historical knowledge of specific institutions, they conclude that such perspective sensitizes individuals implementing change to the important relationship between the internal practices of an organization and the external systems of society of which it is a part. In effect, these authors and others (e.g., Falck & Barnes, 1975) are calling for the skilled use of time perspective in the conduct of organizational change or reform.

Earlier, I described the inadequate preparation of persons providing and persons receiving reforms in residential facilities as a deficit in knowledge about and responses to the conditions of accelerated rates of change, the overemphasis on preset outcome states, and the social-interpersonal working environments these conditions produce. This deficit, at least in part, reflects the absence of temporal perspective. In Chapters 3 and 4 we describe the vulnerability and disorientation of individuals who become trapped in these circumstances and are unable to develop a bearing about it.

It is clear that those who plan, manage, and implement future valid residential facilities for mentally handicapped persons require such a bearing. They have to be practiced at developing broader views of the events in which they will be emersed, views continuous both with interpretations of past events and with informed conjectures about future conditions. Those individuals who cannot or will not develop this ability may be at some greater risk of not coping with the demands generated by future concepts and the transitions to them. Such individuals, if supervisors or managers, will likely be unable to assist their subordinates in dealing with the process of change.

These five proposed competencies are not intended to be exhaustive. Nor do they represent a complete operational strategy for organizational effectiveness in developing the potential futures of residential facilities. Instead these proposals represent a reorientation of focus for such facilities and those who will act upon their destiny. The effectiveness of organizations that adopt these particular competencies and other future-required capacities will have to be systematically evaluated. What has been suggested here is a starting point, a framework within which to consider alternative approaches to the process of applying innovative concepts and functions to the residential facility.

Making the Competencies Acceptable to the Organization

Establishing the view of reform and the notions of competency proposed in this discussion will require a significant value change for most residential facilities.

Specifically, reform will have to be regarded as learning procedures conducted in learning situations, not solely as technical procedures engineered in predictable and certain environments. Moreover, those involved with the conduct of reform will have to believe that embracing such a value will increase the likelihood of achieving valid, durable futures for their facilities.

There are important reasons why making all this acceptable will not be easy. First, adopting this value change and the concrete requirements it will have for many job incumbents in the organization will be burdened with the same dilemmas associated with any other change. For example, earlier we discussed the reluctance of residential facilities to recognize and respond to the preparation deficits of staff coping with high rates of change. Many of the same factors contributing to that reluctance will form a resistance not just to the acceptance of learning based competencies, but even to their very consideration. Foremost among these factors is the extent to which traits antagonistic to the competencies are already deeply embedded in the organizational and social culture of residential facilities. To repeat a previous emphasis, in times of rapid and continuous change at or beyond levels considered manageable, the preferred and rewarded abilities tend to be certainty and control. Leaders see themselves as turbulence reducers and clarifiers for their organizations. They assign to their principal managers the same functions. Collectively, the impression to be conveyed is "being in charge." Even if things are obviously confusing or turbulent, the leadership understands the confusion and turbulence and possesses the solutions leading to clarity and stability.

To accept the alternative standards of competency being recommended here would call for these people to rethink and perhaps significantly revise their beliefs about what their contribution to the organization should be. It seems unlikely that they could do this to the extent suggested without reexamining the professional images they have of themselves and their coworkers. Both tasks will require courage, especially in environments where even the effort may be viewed as an indication of weakness or incompetence. It is probably still the case in most facilities and in the bureaucratic systems that house them that those who would reject the necessity to adopt these standards or to reexamine their job roles still outnumber those who would be willing to try. At present, the former group also probably has enough power to keep the activities of the latter group well restricted.

Further resistance will develop from those who are overloaded by their job experiences and overwhelmed by the complexity of any longer term course of change. These people are fastened to short-term thinking as they search for quick relief for work situations they typically find unpleasant and unsatisfying. They possess little energy or desire to act otherwise. Over the past 15 years, I have observed several independent groups of staff at various levels disregard or actively repel opportunities to review and amend circumstances they were experiencing as personally unpleasant and professionally objectionable. One group, provided with the time and consultation to deal with a highly stressful set of new changes thrust on them, rebuffed the opportunity as an intrusion on time they could be committing to the very tasks they were rejecting as unacceptable. This response developed quickly and was protected by the membership. It was, in effect, a request to be left alone in their misery. In a not so curious way, they resemble some patients who develop a kind of investment in their psychopathology, which, for all its trouble, is safer and easier than the prospect of improvement. We are just beginning to develop a data base to support these observations (Thaw, Thibeault, & Johnston, 1985).

A third form of resistance will occur because social and organizational change technologies are underapplied in public human service settings. Many residential facilities will have to catch up with available technologies that deal with such things as organizational diagnosis, change facilitation, quality of work life, work redesign, and other issues (e.g., Argyris, 1982; Beckhard & Harris, 1977; Burke, 1982; French & Bell, 1978; Huse, 1980; Kilburg, 1984; Meltzer & Stagner, 1980; Schein, 1980). The problem is that such approaches are not widely viewed as legitimate ways out of current organizational change dilemmas by those owning the dilemmas. These approaches are also unattractive due to their costs and time requirements. Further, many of these technologies have been developed for use in industrial settings and thus are not human service system-specific interventions. Therefore, individuals who might be able to commit to major revisions in their approach to reform will not find an economical, efficient, and situation-specific portfolio of methods to assist them. This, too, will impede the process of acquiring new standards of competency.

In a sense, these and probably many other forms of resistance will emerge because most of the individuals and work groups involved are anchored more to previous ways of thinking and doing things than to the risk of experimenting with alternatives. They perceive the future in such a way as to permit their established beliefs, roles, and practices to be felt and experienced as remaining legitimate. As Michael (1973) puts it, these people either see the future as similar to the contexts in which they have succeeded or believe it to be different but requiring the same means of intervention.

The reluctance to adopt competencies that may be essential for responding to change and conducting valid innovation in PRFs makes it imperative that we introduce these notions about competence in ways that do not lead to their rejection. In selected contexts, parts of this book make a few initial recommendations toward this end. Generally, there appear to be four avenues through which acceptance could occur. First, the competencies and the values associated with them could be imposed upon the organization in response to ideological groundswells in the field. Such a circumstance would not be new to residential facilities. The concept of normalization (Nirje, 1969) compelled sweeping changes in policy as well as values, and it did so without the presence of a solid empirical base. In industry, there is much precedent for this type of transformation, such as the changes the American corporate sector had to make in response to the Japanese challenge (e.g., Peters & Waterman, 1982).

A second possibility involves research developments. To date, there have been very few formal empirical studies on issues relevant to the consideration and acceptance of alternative values and competencies in residential facilities. For example, there is limited data on administrative effectiveness (e.g., Sluyter, Schnittger, & Malmberg, 1985) and virtually none on supervisory personnel (e.g., Zaharia & Baumeister, 1978). Quality of work life factors are only beginning to be studied (e.g., MacEachron, Zober, & Fein, 1985), and little empirical research exists on the widely used interdisciplinary process (e.g., Bailey, Helsel-DeWert, Thiele, & Ware, 1983). Organization development programs have been limited in the human services field generally (e.g., Glaser & Backer, 1979), and few have been systematically evaluated (Jerrell & Kouzes, 1982). In short, our knowledge base concerning variables that would influence the effectiveness of residential facilities in conducting reform is weak. In Chapter 7, George Allen and his colleagues discuss why evaluative information has been so difficult to acquire and utilize in residential facilities.

Should this deficit in formal empirical knowledge be corrected such that a reliable data base on organizational effectiveness develops; should such data, for example, suggest the need to develop more effective approaches to change in residential facilities; and should such information be accessible to policy makers—should these and no doubt other conditions come to occur, it could facilitate the formal consideration and acceptance of alternative views of organizational competency.

These first two possibilities for acceptance largely involve the activity of forces external to the organization itself. The final two address internal factors, the first of which is leadership. It is conceivable that top leadership in individual facilities or at the systems level (e.g., state commissioners) may observe the unfavorable effects and disappointing results with previous approaches to instituting change and be prompted to consider alternatives. However, to do this, the leaders would probably be required to: a) examine feedback from the work environment some of which might reveal their own errors; b) tolerate this information and develop ideas from it; c) suspend some current practices in the organization (such as the pursuit of outcomes without reexamination of the problem along the way) despite the uncertainty this might produce; and d) subject ideas for new policies, procedures, and approaches to review by the consumers (e.g., staff at all levels). These activities, of course, involve using some of the very competencies proposed. Thus, the paradox develops whereby the act of introducing and adopting alternative values and competencies for conducting reform requires that leaders utilize the competencies themselves. This, in turn, requires high calibre leaders who are able to develop perspectives beyond the events of the moment and willing to take what could be considerable personal and administrative risks to apply such perspective.

The final possibility considered here focuses on lower rank staff and smaller work units within the organization. These individuals and work settings may be better suited to experimenting with the proposed alternatives than is top leadership. Theoretically, if smaller groups had successful trials with these approaches, they might be able to ''spread'' the effects laterally and then vertically up through the organization. For the past few years, I have been conducting training with such groups (e.g., individual professional departments, interdisciplinary teams, small supervisory groups) in skills and methods deriving directly from the competencies proposed in this discussion. Although this training is in its early stages, I am encouraged that it can lead to normative use of the proposed competencies by small units of staff and, further, that such staff groups can promote a more generalized consideration and acceptance by other individuals and work groups in the organization.

FINAL THOUGHTS

It may already be obvious to the reader that, in many instances, the issues raised in this chapter and the recommendations in response to those issues are at the earliest stages of conceptualization and practice. For example, in the current absence of systemic applications of the proposed competencies and formal evaluation of their effectiveness, refined conclusions calling for precise actions from practitioners of reform in residential facilities are not available. Indeed, the questions themselves are only beginning to be appreciated. This discussion, and many of those that follow, may therefore be best viewed as an early perception both for the questions raised and the actions suggested. What seems without question is the need to consider these issues.

REFERENCES

Argyris, C. (1982). *Reasoning, learning, and action.* San Francisco: Jossey-Bass.

Bailey, D. B., Jr., Helsel-DeWert, M., Thiele, J. E., & Ware, W. B. (1983). Measuring individual participation on the interdisciplinary team. *American Journal of Mental Deficiency, 88,* 247–254.

Balla, D. (1976). Relationship of institution size to quality of care: A review of the literature. *American Journal of Mental Deficiency, 81,* 117–124.

Baroff, G. S. (1980). On ''size'' and the quality of care: A second look. *Mental Retardation, 18,* 113–117.

Baumeister, A. A. (1981). The right to habilitation: What does it mean? *Analysis and Intervention in Developmental Disabilities, 1,* 61–74.

Beckhard, R. (1974). Organizational issues in the team delivery of comprehensive health care. In I. K. Zola & J. B. McKinlay (Eds.), *Organizational issues in the delivery of health services.* New York: Prodist.

Beckhard, R., & Harris, R. T. (1977). *Organizational transitions: Managing complex change.* Reading, MA: Addison-Wesley.

Begab, M. J. (1975). The mentally retarded and society: Trends and issues. In M. J. Begab & S. A. Richardson (Eds.), *The mentally retarded and society: A social science perspective* (pp. 3–32). Baltimore: University Park Press.

Bennis, W. G., & Slater, P. E. (1968). *The temporary society*. New York: Harper & Row.

Bensberg, G. J. (1974). Administration and staff development in residential facilities. *Mental Retardation, 12*, 29–32.

Bensberg, G. J., & Barnett, C. D. (1966) *Attendant training in a southern residential facility for the mentally retarded*. Report of the SREB attendant training project. Atlanta: Southern Regional Education Board.

Bevin, W. (1976). The sound of the wind that's blowing. *American Psychologist, 31*, 481–491.

Birenbaum, A., & Re, M. (1979). Resettling mentally retarded adults in the community—Almost four years later. *American Journal of Mental Deficiency, 83*, 323–329.

Bock, W. H., & Joiner, L. M. (1982). From institution to community residence: Behavioral competencies for admission and discharge. *Mental Retardation, 20*, 153–158.

Bogdan, R., Taylor, S., deGrandpre, B., & Haynes, S. (1974). Let them eat programs: Attendants' perspectives and programming on wards in state schools. *Journal of Health and Social Behavior, 15*, 142–151.

Boles, S. M., & Bible, G. H. (1978). The student service index: A method for managing service delivery in residential settings. In M. S. Berkler, G. H. Bible, S. M. Boles, D. E. D. Deitz, & A. C. Repp (Eds.), *Current trends for the developmentally disabled* (pp. 153–195). Baltimore: University Park Press.

Bruininks, R. H., Kudla, M. J., Wieck, C. A., & Hauber, F. A. (1980). Management problems in community residential facilities. *Mental Retardation, 18*, 125–130.

Bucher, R., & Stelling, J. (1977). *Becoming professional*. Beverly Hills, CA: Sage Publications.

Burke, W. W. (1982). *Organization development: Principles and practices*. Boston: Little, Brown.

Butler, E. W., & Bjaanes, A. T. (1977). A typology of community care facilities and differential normalization outcomes. In P. Mittler (Ed.), *Research to practice in mental retardation: Care and intervention* (Vol. 1) (pp. 337–347). Baltimore: University Park Press.

Carlson, H. C. (1980). A model of quality of work life as a developmental process. In W. W. Burke & L. D. Goodstein (Eds.), *Trends and issues in OD: Current theory and practice* (pp. 83–123). San Diego: University Associates.

Cherniss, C. (1981). *Staff burnout: Job stress in the human services*. Beverly Hills, CA: Sage Publications.

Cherniss, C., Egnatios, E. S., & Wacker, S. (1976). Job stress and career development in new public professionals. *Professional Psychology, 7*, 428–436.

Christian, W. P., Hannah, G. T., & Glahn, T. J. (Eds.). (1984). *Programming effective human services: Strategies for institutional change and client transition*. New York: Plenum Press.

Clements, J. D. (1970). Planning a residential facility for the mentally retarded. In A. A. Baumeister & E. C. Butterfield (Eds.), *Residential facilities for the mentally retarded* (pp. 59–116). Chicago: Aldine.

Cohen, H. J. (1975). Obstacles to developing community services for the mentally retarded. In M. J. Begab & S. A. Richardson (Eds.), *The mentally retarded and society: A social science perspective* (pp. 401–421), Baltimore: University Park Press.

Cook, T. (1983). The substantive due process rights of mentally disabled clients. *Mental Disability Law Reporter, 7*, 346–357.

Crawford, J. L., Aiello, J. R., & Thompson, D. E. (1979). Deinstitutionalization and community placement: Clinical and environmental factors. *Mental Retardation, 17*, 59–63.

Crissey, M. S. (1975). Mental retardation: Past, present, and future. *American Psychologist, 30*, 800–808.

Crissey, M. S. (in press). Program components of a therapeutic environment. In M. Rosen & M. S. Crissey (Eds.), *The comprehensive residential institution: A community resource*. Austin, TX: Pro-Ed.

Crosby, K. G. (1976). Essentials of active programming. *Mental Retardation, 14*, 3–9.

Cullari, S. (1984).   Everybody is talking about the new institution. *Mental Retardation, 22,* 28–29.

Davis, H. R. (1973).   Change and innovation. In S. Feldman (Ed.), *The administration of mental health services* (pp. 289–341), Springfield, IL: Charles C. Thomas.

deBono, E. (1970).   *Lateral thinking: Creativity step by step.* New York: Harper & Row.

Dyer, W. G. (1977).   *Team building: Issues and alternatives.* Reading, MA: Addison-Wesley.

Edgerton, R. B., & Bercovici, S. M. (1976).   The cloak of competence: Years later. *American Journal of Mental Deficiency, 30,* 485–497.

Edgerton, R. B., Bollinger, M., & Herr, B. (1984).   The cloak of competence: After two decades. *American Journal of Mental Deficiency, 88,* 345–351.

Ellis, N. R., Balla, D., Estes, O., Warren, S. A., Meyers, C. E., Hollis, J., Isaacson, R. L., Palk, B. E., & Siegel, P. S. (1981).   Common sense in the habilitation of mentally retarded persons: A reply to Menolascino and McGee. *Mental Retardation, 19,* 221–225.

Eyman, R. K., & Borthwick, S. A. (1980).   Patterns of care for mentally retarded persons. *Mental Retardation, 18,* 63–66.

Eyman, R. K., & Call, T. (1977).   Maladaptive behavior and community placement of mentally retarded persons. *American Journal of Mental Deficiency, 82,* 137–140.

Eyman, R. K., Demaine, G. C., & Lei, T. L. (1979).   Relationships between community environments and resident changes in adaptive behavior: A path model. *American Journal of Mental Deficiency, 83,* 330–338.

Falck, H. S., & Barnes, R. E. (1975).   The change agent in the organization. *Administration in Mental Health, 3,* 3–11.

Favell, J. E., Favell, J. E., Riddle, J. I., & Risley, T. R. (1984).   Promoting change in mental retardation facilities: Getting services from the paper to the people. In W. P. Christian, G. T. Hannah, & T. J. Glahn (Eds.), *Programming effective human services: Strategies for institutional change and client transition* (pp. 15–37). New York: Plenum Press.

Fisher, R., & Ury, W. (1981).   *Getting to yes: Negotiating agreement without giving in.* Boston: Houghton Mifflin.

French, W. L., & Bell, C. H., Jr. (1978).   *Organization development* (2nd ed). Englewood Cliffs, NJ: Prentice-Hall.

Freudenberger, H. J. (1975).   The staff burn-out syndrome in alternative institutions. *Psychotherapy: Theory, Research, and Practice, 12,* 73–82.

Friedlander, F. (1980).   The facilitation of change in organizations. *Professional Psychology, 11,* 520–530.

Gardner, J. (1963).   *Self-Renewal.* Evanston, IL: Harper.

George, M. J., & Baumeister, A. A. (1981).   Employee withdrawal and job satisfaction in community residential facilities for mentally retarded persons. *American Journal of Mental Deficiency, 85,* 639–647.

Glaser, E. M., & Backer, T. E. (1979).   Organization development in mental health services. *Administration in Mental Health, 6,* 195–215.

Gonzalez, A., & Zimbardo, P. G. (1985).   Time in perspective. *Psychology Today, 19*(3), 20–26.

Granger, B. P. (1972).   Dilemmas of reorganizing institutions for the mentally retarded. *Mental Retardation, 10,* 3–7.

Gray, J. L. (1974).   Matrix organization design as a vehicle for effective delivery of public health care and social services. *Management International Review, 14,* 73–82.

Greenberg, S. F., & Valletutti, P. J. (1980).   *Stress and the helping professions.* Baltimore: Paul H. Brooks.

Halderman v. Pennhurst State School and Hospital, No. 78–1490 (3d Cir. filed April 24, 1985).

Harris, R. T. (1980).   Toward a technology of macrosystem interventions. In W. W. Burke & L. D. Goodstein (Eds.), *Trends and issues in OD: Current theory and practice* (pp. 62–82). San Diego: University Associates.

Hauber, F. A., Bruininks, R. H., Hill, B. K., Lakin, C., Scheerenberger, R. C., & White, C. C. (1984). National census of residential facilities: A 1982 profile of facilities and residents. *American Journal of Mental Deficiency, 89,* 236–245.

Huse, E. F. (1980). *Organization development and change* (2nd ed.). St. Paul, MN: West.

Intagliata, J., & Willer, B. (1982). Reinstitutionalization of mentally retarded persons successfully placed into family-care and group homes. *American Journal of Mental Deficiency, 87,* 34–39.

Janicki, M. P., Mayeda, T., & Epple, W. A. (1983). Availability of group homes for persons with mental retardation in the United States. *Mental Retardation, 21,* 45–51.

Jerrell, J. M., & Kouzes, J. M. (1982). Organization development in mental health agencies. *Administration in Mental Health, 10,* 22–39.

Kanner, L. (1964). *A history of the care and study of the mentally retarded.* Springfield, IL: Charles C. Thomas.

Kaufman, H. (1971). *The limits of organizational change.* University, AL: University of Alabama Press.

Kilburg, R. R. (Ed.). (1984). Psychologists in management [Special issue]. *Professional Psychology: Research and practice, 15* (5).

Kleinberg, J., & Galligan, B. (1983). Effects of deinstitutionalization on adaptive behavior of mentally retarded adults. *American Journal of Mental Deficiency, 88,* 21–27.

Landesman-Dwyer, S. (1981). Living in the community. *American Journal of Mental Deficiency, 86,* 223–234.

Landesman-Dwyer, S., Sackett, G. P., & Kleinman, J. S. (1980). Relationship of size to resident and staff behavior in small community residences. *American Journal of Mental Deficiency, 85,* 6–17.

LaPorte, T. (1971). *Organizational response to complexity: Research and development as organized inquiry and action* - Part I (Working paper No. 141). Berkeley, CA: Center for Planning and Development Research, Institute of Urban and Regional Development, University of California.

Levine, R., & Wolff, E. (1985). Social time: The heartbeat of culture. *Psychology Today, 19*(3), 28–30, 32, 34–35.

Levinson, H. (1980). Power, leadership, and the management of stress. *Professional Psychology, 11,* 497–508.

Light, D., Jr. (1979). Uncertainty and control in professional training. *Journal of Health and Social Behavior, 20,* 310–322.

Likert, R. (1961). *New patterns of management.* New York: McGraw-Hill.

Lippitt, G. L. (1973). Hospital organization in the post-industrial society. *Hospital Progress, 54,* 55–65.

MacEachron, A. E., Zober, M. A., & Fein, J. (1985). Institutional reform, adaptive functioning of mentally retarded persons, and staff quality of life. *American Journal of Mental Deficiency, 89,* 379–388.

Maguire, L. M. (1970). *Observations and analysis of the literature on change.* Philadelphia: Research for Better Schools.

Mayhew, G. L., Enyart, P., & Anderson, J. (1978). Social reinforcement and the naturally occurring social responses of severely and profoundly retarded adolescents. *American Journal of Mental Deficiency, 83,* 164–170.

McClelland, D. C. (1978). Managing motivation to expand human freedom. *American Psychologist, 33,* 201–210.

Meltzer, H., & Stagner, R. (Eds.). (1980). Industrial/organizational psychology: 1980 overview [Special issue]. *Professional Psychology, 11*(3).

Menolascino, F. J., & McGee, J. J. (1981). The new institutions: Last ditch arguments. *Mental Retardation, 19,* 215–220.

Merges, R. C. (1982).   Checking the cycle: The decline of community-based residential programs in New York State 1925 to 1950. *Mental Retardation, 20,* 180–182.

Michael, D. N. (1973).   *On learning to plan—And planning to learn.* San Francisco: Jossey-Bass.

Mintzberg, H. (1981, January-February).   Organization design: Fashion or fit? *Harvard Business Review,* pp. 103–116.

Moore, L. L., & Eddy, W. B. (1980).   Employee as victim: Distress as an organization development issue. in W. W. Burke & L. D. Goodstein (Eds.), *Trends and issues in OD: Current theory and practice* (pp. 240–254). San Diego: University Associates.

Nirje, B. (1969).   The normalization principle and its human management implications. In R. B. Kugel and W. Wolfensberger (Eds.), *Changing patterns in residential services for the mentally retarded* (pp. 179–195). Washington: President's Committee on Mental Retardation.

Peck, R. F., & Cleland, C. C. (1966).   Intra-institutional problems: Organization and personality. *Mental Retardation, 4,* 7–11.

Perloff, H. S., & Sandberg, N. C. (Eds.). (1973).   *New towns: Why—And for whom?* New York: Praeger.

Peters, T. J., & Waterman, R. H. (1982).   *In search of excellence: Lessons from America's best run companies.* New York: Warner Books.

Pines, A. M., & Aronson, E. (1981).   *Burnout: From tedium to personal growth.* New York: Free Press.

Pollack, M. J. (1978, April).   *Comparison of state guidelines for regulating behavioral procedures.* Paper presented at the meeting of the Connecticut Chapter of the American Association on Mental Deficiency, Hartford, CT.

Rappaport, J., Chinsky, J. M., & Cowen, E. L. (1971).   *Innovations in helping chronic patients: College students in a mental institution.* New York: Academic Press.

Raynes, N., Bumstead, D. C., & Pratt, M. W. (1974).   Unitization: Its effects on residential care practices. *Mental Retardation, 12,* 12–14.

Reid, D. H., & Whitman, T. L. (1983).   Behavioral staff management in institutions: A critical review of effectiveness and acceptability. *Analysis and Intervention in Developmental Disabilities, 3,* 131–149.

Reiter, S., & Bryen, D. N. (in press).   The institution as an adult social and vocational habilitative community. In M. Rosen & M. S. Crissey (Eds.), *The comprehensive residential institution: A community resource.* Austin, TX: Pro-Ed.

Report of the National Task Force on Mental Health/Mental Retardation Administration. (1979).   *Administration in Mental Health, 6,* 269–323.

Repp, A. C., & Barton, L. E. (1980).   Naturalistic observations of institutionalized retarded persons: A comparison of licensure decisions and behavioral observations. *Journal of Applied Behavior Analysis, 13,* 333–341.

Reppucci, N. D., & Saunders, J. T. (1974).   Social psychology of behavior modification: Problems of implementation in natural settings. *American Psychologist, 29,* 649–660.

Reppucci, N. D., & Saunders, J. T. (1983).   Focal issues for institutional change. *Professional Psychology: Research and Practice, 14,* 514–528.

Rickard, H. C., & Clements, C. B. (1981).   Administrative training for psychologists in APA-approved clinical programs. *Professional Psychology, 12,* 349–355.

Roos, P. (1966).   Changing roles of the residential institution. *Mental Retardation, 4,* 4–6.

Roos, P. (1972).   Mentally retarded citizens: Challenge for the 1970's. *Syracuse Law Review, 12,* 1059–1074.

Roos, P. (1975).   *Trends in residential institutions for the mentally retarded.* Columbus, OH: University Council for Educational Administration.

Roos, P. (1979).   Custodial care for the "subtrainable" - Revisiting an old myth. *Law and Psychology Review, 5,* 1–14.

Rosen, M., & Crissey, M. S. (Eds.). (in press). *The comprehensive residential institution: A community resource*. Austin, TX: Pro-Ed.

Rotegard, L. L., Hill, B. K., & Bruininks, R. H. (1983). Environmental characteristics of residential facilities for mentally retarded persons in the United States. *American Journal of Mental Deficiency, 88,* 49–56.

Sajwaj, T. (1977). Issues and implications of establishing guidelines for the use of behavioral techniques. *Journal of Applied Behavior Analysis, 10,* 531–540.

Saper, B. (1975). Confessions of a former state hospital superintendent. *Professional Psychology, 6,* 367–380.

Sarason, S. B., & Doris, J. (1979). *Educational handicap, public policy, and social history*. New York: Free Press.

Sarata, B., & Jeppesen, J. (1977). Job design and staff satisfaction in human service settings. *American Journal of Community Psychology, 5,* 229–236.

Scheerenberger, R. C. (1977). Deinstitutionalization in perspective. In J. L. Paul, D. J. Stedman, & G. R. Neufeld (Eds.), *Deinstitutionalization: Program and policy development* (pp. 3–14). Syracuse, NY: Syracuse University Press.

Scheerenberger, R. C. (1982). *A history of mental retardation*. Baltimore: Paul H. Brookes.

Schein, E. H. (1969). *Process consultation: Its role in organization development*. Reading, MA: Addison-Wesley.

Schein, E. H. (1980). *Organizational psychology* (3rd ed.). Englewood Cliffs, NJ: Prentice-Hall.

Scholom, A., & Perlman, B. (1979). The forgotten staff: Who cares for the care givers? *Administration in Mental Health, 7,* 21–31.

Scott, S. B., & Crosby, J. V. (1981). Applying organizational development to productivity: A case history. *Administration in Mental Health, 9,* 123–136.

Scull, A. T. (1977). *Decarceration, community treatment, and the deviant: A radical view*. Englewood Cliffs, NJ: Prentice-Hall.

Slater, M. A., & Bunyard, P. D. (1983). Survey of residential staff roles, responsibilities, and perception of resident needs. *Mental Retardation, 21,* 52–58.

Sluyter, G. V., Schnittger, E. J., & Malmberg, P. A. (1985). Administration of residential facilities: A literature documentation (1970–1982). *Mental Retardation, 23,* 3–5.

Standards for Intermediate Care Facilities for the Mentally Retarded. (1978). Code of Federal Regulations, Title 42, Public Health Subpart G, Special Edition of the *Federal Register*. Washington: U.S. Government Printing Office.

Stolz, S. B. (1977). Why no guidelines for behavior modification? *Journal of Applied Behavior Analysis, 10,* 541–547.

Sundberg, N. D., Snowden, L. R., & Reynolds, W. M. (1978). Toward assessment of personal competence and incompetence in life situations. *Annual Review of Psychology, 29,* 179–221.

Sutter, P., Mayeda, T., Call, T., Yanagi, G., & Yee, S. (1980). Comparison of successful and unsuccessful community-placed mentally retarded persons. *American Journal of Mental Deficiency, 85,* 262–267.

Thaw, J., Palmer, M. E., & Sulzer-Azaroff, B. (1977, June). The middle managers and program development: A longitudinal approach to training institutional supervisory personnel. In J. Thaw (Chair), *Direct care, middle management, and professional staff: Characteristics, conflicts, and the issue of program innovation*. Symposium conducted at the meeting of the American Association on Mental Deficiency, New Orleans.

Thaw, J., Thibeault, A., & Johnston, D. (1985). [Analysis of an interdisciplinary service system in a residential facility for mentally handicapped clients]. Unpublished raw data.

Thompson, V. A. (1976). *Bureaucracy and the modern world*. Morristown, NJ: General Learning Press.

Thompson, T., & Carey, A. (1980). Structured normalization: Intellectual and adaptive behavior changes in a residential setting. *Mental Retardation, 18,* 193–197.

Thompson, T., & Grabowski, J. (Eds.). (1972).   *Behavior modification of the mentally retarded.*
New York: Oxford University Press.

Thompson, T., & Grabowski, J. (1977).   *Behavior modification of the mentally retarded* (2nd ed.).
New York: Oxford University Press.

Tjosvold, D., & Tjosvold, M. M. (1983).   Social psychological analysis of residences for mentally
retarded persons. *American Journal of Mental Deficiency, 88,* 28–40.

Toffler, A. (1970).   *Future Shock.* New York: Random House.

Ulschak, F. L., Nathanson, L., & Gillan, P. G. (1981).   *Small group problem solving: An aid to
organizational effectiveness.* Reading, MA: Addison-Wesley.

U. S. Department of Health, Education, and Welfare. (1971).   *Developmental Disabilities Act*
(PL91–517). Washington: U. S. Government Printing Office.

Vickers, G. (1963).   Ecology, planning, and the American dream. In L. J. Duhl (Ed.), *The urban
condition* (pp. 374–395). New York: Basic Books.

Walker, C. E. (1981).   Continuing professional development. In C. E. Walker (Ed.), *Clinical
practice of psychology* (pp. 33–49). Elmsford, NY: Pergamon Press.

Wedel, K. R. (1976).   Matrix design for human service organizations. *Administration in Mental
Health, 4,* 36–42.

Willems, E. P. (1974).   Behavioral technology and behavioral ecology. *Journal of Applied Behavior Analysis, 7,* 151–165.

Wolfensberger, W. (1969).   The origin and nature of our institutional models. In R. B. Kugel &
W. Wolfensberger (Eds.), *Changing patterns in residential services for the mentally retarded*
(pp. 59–172). Washington: President's Committee on Mental Retardation.

Zaharia, E. S., & Baumeister, A. A. (1978).   Technician turnover and absenteeism in public
residential facilities. *American Journal of Mental Deficiency, 82,* 580–593.

Ziarnik, J. P., & Bernstein, G. S. (1982).   A critical examination of the effect of inservice training
on staff performance. *Mental Retardation, 20,* 109–114.

Zigler, E., & Balla, D. (1977).   Impact of institutional experience on the behavior and development of retarded persons. *American Journal of Mental Deficiency, 82,* 1–11.

Zigler, E., Balla, D., & Hodapp, R. (1984).   On the definition and classification of mental retardation. *American Journal of Mental Deficiency, 89,* 215–230.

2 Forces in the Administration of Public Residential Facilities

Roger D. MacNamara, M.Ed.

INTRODUCTION

The Joint Commission on Accreditation of Hospitals (1971) defined a residential facility as ''an organizational entity that has physical identity and administrative integrity and conducts a program of services directed primarily to enhancing the health, welfare and development of individuals classified as mentally retarded. The primary purpose of a residential facility is to protect and nurture the dignity, health, and development of each individual requiring twenty-four hour programming services'' (p. xiii). To accomplish such a broad objective, the residential facility must be capable of providing comprehensive services and security to its entire clientele and coordinating programs of maximum benefit to each individual in an efficient, proper manner. This chapter is concerned with the administration of publicly supported or state-owned residential facilities with substantial populations of developmentally disabled people. There are 279 public residential facilities for the mentally retarded in the United States, with an average census of 347 residents (Scheerenberger, 1982).

Public residential facilities (PRFs) have been described as colonies, hospitals, training schools and more recently as developmental or regional centers. Their administrative officers have carried the titles of superintendent, director, and program manager (Directory of Public Residential Facilities for the Mentally Retarded, 1980). Whatever the designation, a public residential facility is a personally demanding, highly complex and risky position of public responsibility. The functions of management are subject to considerable misunderstanding and misinterpretation by staff, clients, parents, advocates, elected officials, governmental officials, journalists, and the public.

THE RESIDENTIAL FACILITY AND ITS FUNCTIONS

The public residential facility is a microcosm of clinical and administrative services created for individuals with serious disabilities requiring specialized programs of care, training, and treatment by a wide array of professional disciplines: psychology, special education, medicine and the allied health services, dentistry, recreation, speech and language therapy, audiology, psychiatry, social work, and vocational rehabilitation. Supporting services must complement the habilitative programs designed for the clientele. Transportation, dietary, personnel administration, data processing, utilities, protective services (fire and rescue), skilled crafts (carpentry, plumbing, painting, locksmithing, electrical engineering, and environmental protection), communications, housekeeping, beauty culture, laundry, and finance and purchasing must be coordinated efficiently. No less important are employee training and supervision, volunteers and advocacy, and legal assistance. The very comprehensiveness and specialization required of such facilities have contributed to the high level of difficulty of administering organizations attempting to deliver interlocking services 24 hours each day, 12 months a year.

The Physical Environment

The physical structures and setting of the public residential facility are the framework for the lifestyles and programs of the clientele and the working conditions for staff. Buildings may be categorized as residential, administrative, and physical plant and include residences for the clientele, workshops, schools, infirmaries, power plants, fire stations, diagnostic facilities and clinics, conference centers, personnel offices, storehouses, laundries, and recreational facilities. The architecture of residential facilities varies with their age, size and history. It is not uncommon for a facility to consist of structures that were constructed over several decades and therefore reflect the prevailing philosophy of care and treatment and economic considerations of each period. Problems in the maintenance of residential facilities with aging, renovated buildings and recent construction are constants in administration. Older buildings' heating and plumbing systems require weekly attention, and failures frequently occur in spite of efforts to prevent breakdowns. Depending on the type of construction materials in them, newer buildings often are more fragile and subject to irritating troubles such as windows and doors that will not close securely, walls that are easily damaged, carpeting that stains, light fixtures that will not function, roofs that leak, and basements that are periodically flooded. The department of plant and maintenance at a major residential facility must respond to hundreds of requests for work to be performed each week.

Older facilities often experience problems of inadequate design or construction that appear in time, usually after the original architectural drawings have been misplaced or rendered useless by the number of unrecorded changes in the buildings. A classic illustration of this problem is underground heating and water supply systems that have been gradually expanded to accommodate additional facilities but for which there may be no accurate blueprints. When a main ruptures, the water surges through the soil to the surface following the path of least resistance and possibly emerging from an oblique direction from the line.

Modern requirements for residential units (e.g., fire alarms, smoke and heat detectors, sprinkling systems, and water temperature controls and alarms) are delicate mechanisms requiring constant maintenance and testing and considerable technical and mechanical knowledge on the part of the staff in the physical plant department. The grounds of a residential facility must receive attention regularly for cosmetic reasons as well as for the health and safety of the clientele and staff. Snow removal and groundskeeping must be planned and scheduled; otherwise areas of the facility become inaccessible or dangerous, menial concerns perhaps—until someone is hurt or complains to a higher authority.

Other essential operations that must function efficiently at a residential facility may include but are not limited to the following: (a) a highly trained protective services unit equipped with modern fire suppression and rescue apparatus; (b) a waste water treatment plant that conforms to state and federal environmental protection laws and regulations; (c) a safe, efficient heating power plant, unless all of the buildings are equipped with individual heating units; (d) a transportation unit that assigns vehicles to staff and dispatches vans, buses, and cars to and from clinics, school, therapies, recreation, and special events; (e) a laundry with a capacity for processing a variety and large volume of clothing and linen; (f) a food services department that prepares meals and special diets three times daily, 365 days a year according to modern nutritional standards and the instructions of medical personnel; (g) a housekeeping staff that maintains thousands of square feet of building space and has expertise in the use of bactericides, disinfectants, and sanitary techniques; (h) an efficient communications department that provides 24-hour-a-day telephone service, emergency communications, and routine mail delivery; and (i) a comprehensive storehouse for preserving and dispensing supplies, food, and equipment for the entire residential facility.

The chief executive officer of a public residential facility must be vitally concerned with its entire operation, including the daily activities of staff not normally associated with the habilitation of the clientele. Understanding administrators' responses to organizational change and the delivery of habilitative services begins with an appreciation of the scope and complexity of their responsibilities.

The Primary Responsibility of Residential Administration

The client is the raison d'etre of the residential facility. The administration is responsible for the welfare of each individual: medically, psychologically, spiritually and socially—not for part of the day or week, but for all the hours that each client resides at the facility. Admission to a public residential facility is a legal event in the life of a handicapped person. The language and stringency of state statutes vary, but the transfer of responsibility for an individual's well being from himself or herself, parents, or guardian to the administrator of a public residential facility is an onerous undertaking (Johnson & Wood, 1976).

The authority to exercise control over or to retain custody of disabled persons is instantly accompanied by specific obligations for protecting them from harm and providing them services essential to their development (Friedman, 1976). The latter dictate, better known as the right to treatment, has been a contested issue in well-publicized litigations (e.g., O'Connor v. Donaldson, 1974; Wyatt v. Stickney, 1972; Halderman v. Pennhurst, 1977, and New York State Association for Retarded Children v. Rockefeller, 1973). There is, however, little argument that the protection from harm clause in the constitution applies to individuals voluntarily or involuntarily placed in residential facilities (Halpern, 1976).

The administrator is responsible, above all, for the health and safety of each individual in residence. This straightforward charge, budgetary constraints and untoward events notwithstanding, may cause conflicts between the administrator and staff, clients, parents, advocates, and governmental officials. For example, the question of risk versus benefit to clients in behavior therapy, placement, or medical treatment are never easily reconciled especially when the administrator is ultimately responsible for the consequences of each decision. Parents and staff, together or in opposition, may vigorously support or oppose a particular decision, but the administrator has the inescapable legal and personal responsibility for the outcome. The outcome, contested by all interested parties often having their own notions about what constitutes client welfare, becomes a conflict in judgment. Issues such as consent for treatment, training, and placement are fraught with dilemmas for the administrator. The tests for adequate consent are often impossible to determine outside of court because of the nature and extent of clients' disabilities and the absence of legally liable relatives or guardians (Horner, 1979). Nevertheless, consent must be obtained, and the administrator is responsible for the process as well as the outcome.

The administrator of a residential facility must also translate the legal obligations to protect the clientele from harm into staffing patterns, essential services, and a wholesome, safe environment. Public residential facilities are allocated fixed operating budgets, and historically resources have been insufficient to protect the clientele adequately from harm or to satisfy the expectations of staff and parents. Governmental officials, however, tend to consider large expenditures at residential facilities as excessive and possibly unnecessary. The administrator must protect the clientele from harm, attempt to satisfy staff and parents, and practice sound fiscal management for state government. "This condition is the conflict of interest—the dual loyalties. . . ." (Shestack, 1974, p. 1524). It is also the deepest and most confounding conflict for the public administrator.

Habilitative Programming

Habilitation is the process of enabling individuals to achieve maximum competence in all aspects of daily living (e.g., personal care and health, human relations, occupations, and recreation) and promoting emotional and behavioral stability. Mere custodial care (i.e., the basics of life such as food, clothing, shelter, and medical care) generally is considered by professionals to be insufficient residential programming. The Joint Commission on Accreditation of Hospitals and the Department of Health and Human Services are requiring that residential facilities offer comprehensive developmental and therapeutic services. "Both accreditation as a residential facility and certification as an intermediate care facility require the provision of more than adequate custodial or domiciliary care. Instead, the facility must provide each resident with a program that is designed to enhance his development" (Crosby, 1976, p. 9).

Therefore, an habilitative facility is one that offers complete diagnostic services, prescriptive programming, intensive therapy, and continuing education for its professionals and paraprofessionals. The relevant service disciplines (e.g., medicine, psychology, education, and the allied health services) must be integrated into the facility's residential services. Moreover, children in residence must be offered a full educational program in the least restrictive educational environment as required by Public Law 94-142. Increasingly, the term habilitation is being replaced by the phrase *active treatment* designed within an individual habilitation plan by qualified mental retardation professionals (Scheerenberger, 1976).

The organization of habilitative services has evolved from a medical model in which the physician was dominant in determining all treatment and therapy to an interdisciplinary format (Crosby, 1976). In interdisciplinary teams, professionals representing multiple disciplines write program plans, initiate specific habilitative activities, instruct staff in effective programming, and evaluate the client's progress. For the administrator, the interdisciplinary approach is an added organizational dimension. Team members also retain strong identification with their disciplines. In effect, professionals are released from their traditional departmental responsibilities to join interdisciplinary teams that are directed by a generalist in program management. Service delivery in this form is a blend of departmental disciplines and program management. This arrangement of departments and teams comprises a matrix organization (Heyel, 1973). The advantages of the matrix are increased and varied opportunities for the administrator to apply the particular talents, knowledge, and skills of individual employees to specific problems or projects. Its principal disadvantage is the tension arising from the dual loyalties of team members.

The public residential facility for developmentally disabled persons is a social microcosm with a clinical mission; it is also a political entity with legal and ethical accountabilities. The realities of public administration from a practitioner's view are the subjects of this chapter. Topics include the personal nature of human services management, chronic problems in residential facilities, the changes that are occurring in and around them, and observations on the future of these establishments.

ADMINISTRATIVE PROBLEMS IN RESIDENTIAL FACILITIES

The workings of public residential facilities are best understood from several vantages. The purpose of this text is to offer students and practitioners the opinions and insights of people with varying perspectives and experience with these organizations. There are preconceptions of residential facilities that can diminish the efforts of change agents. First, observers of residential programs mistakenly may conclude that the actions of staff and their performance in delivering services are predetermined and rigidly controlled by the administration. Second, reformers may believe that problems in implementing rational change can be easily prevented or quickly eliminated by obvious managerial decisions or initiatives. In realtiy, organizations of any significant size have informal as well as formal structures that frequently function independently of administrative influence. Naive observers often wonder at the difficulty the administration has in solving routine problems and conclude that the management is largely uninformed or tends to ignore obvious options. Unfortunately, administrative discretion in budgeting, staffing, and supervising and evaluating employees is rapidly disappearing in public services. Two other factors—the increasing complexity of residential organizations and the multiplicity of problems that are inundating the administration—can be paralyzing unless the chief administrator is able to isolate the essential issues and address them in priority. The administrator's responses to developing situations, however logical and necessary from a larger perspective, may frequently conflict with the immediate needs of staff, innovators, advocates, and critics.

Administrators of residential facilities frequently refer to a crisis orientation in describing their work. Although an established cliché these days, the phrase does reflect an overload of chronic and situational problems. Public administration is subject to countless impediments to effective services, and the vexing problems of managing public residential facilities cannot always be neatly divided according to their origins. For example, understaffing at a facility may be the result of the failure of the state legislature to allocate sufficient funds, or the administrator may have miscalculated the effects of a union contract, a reduced work week, or the needs of any one department of the facility. The modern dilemmas in public residential facilities include insufficient resources, bureaucratic overregulation, legal interference, and collective bargaining. Persistent tensions arise from these sources and may conflict with the quality of care and treatment of the clientele.

Insufficient Resources

The politics of public administration dictate that managers must compete for the funds needed to operate their programs. Congress and legislature expect administrators to justify their allocation of scarce resources by illustrating the unique needs or contributions of their constituencies. Consumers' sentiments must corroborate their claims (Wildavsky, 1964). Service providers usually are not allowed to engage in power politics; rather, in the search for adequate operating funds, they must assert the humanitarian or cost-effective qualities of their endeavor. This strategy has been effective with lawmakers in the past, but it has become a familiar scenario to them. Humanitarian arguments for increased funding seemingly have lost their appeal as legislators have found effective challenges to administrators' arguments. Politicians will, of course, rhetorically endorse the needs and demands of the elderly, the poor, the blind, deaf, mentally retarded and chronically ill, the illiterate, and the unemployed. The difference, more recently, is the effect of several consecutive years of general economic strain. The taxpayer is more resentful of public spending, and thus it is politically respectable to question humanitarian programs.

In state government, commissioners, who are appointed by the governor, submit budgets that must be approved by a fiscal authority also appointed by the governor. Subsequently, the commissioner must appear before the state legislature to testify on that budget and answer questions about its sufficiency from representatives who are variously sympathetic and antagonistic to the administration. The public administrator is immediately placed in a tenuous and conflicting circumstance. Questions from the opposition party member will be designed to discredit the budget and the governor. The loyalists will seek from the commissioner responses that endorse the incumbent's fiscal policies. What of the bona fide needs of the mentally handicapped clientele? If politics is the art of manipulating power by arranging advantageous compromises among multiple constituencies, as analysts suggest, then the needs of handicapped people may be secondary in the process of democratic government (Lyden & Miller, 1978). However, consumers and advocates of programs for the disabled long have recognized the limitations of state officials in securing public funds for their programs. Consequently, they have developed potent lobbying forces for influencing the outcomes of congressional and legislative sessions. The philosophies of these special interest groups are not always harmonious with one another or consonant with that of the service provider. This complicates the process of acquiring funding and adds yet another dimension to the administration of public facilities. External influences, including the interactions among governmental officials, professionals, parents, and advocates are discussed in the next section of this chapter.

The process for gaining financial support of public programs at best is an uncertain one, and therefore residential facilities are typically underfunded.

Scheerenberger (1979) determined in a national survey that 31% of clients in public facilities still had needs requiring additional resources. "Of particular note was the expressed effort to meet the challenge of the more difficult-to-manage or emotionally disturbed resident by the heightened interest in recruiting psychiatrists and psychologists" (p. 32). Insufficiency of resources for operating public residential facilities has had considerable fallout. It creates a serious gap in the continuum of services needed to insure an optimum quality of life and effective habilitation for the clientele. A serious shortage of operating funds inevitably has consequences for the entire pattern of service delivery within a state.

Altering priorities or reducing expenditures in discretionary areas will not isolate the effects of significant shortages. Nevertheless, such recommendations are frequently articulated by staff, parents, consultants, and politicians, who presume that if the limited resources were managed more adroitly, the necessary services could be provided. Other naive solutions proffered by critics and consultants include the reassignment of staff from one unit to another, the conversion of support or supervisory positions to direct-care staff or professionals, and the elimination of paperwork, research, and peripheral programs such as volunteer services or staff training. Obviously, minor budgetary deficiencies can be absorbed by controlling spending that does not threaten the quality of life at the facility, but significant shortages disrupt the complex patterns of care and habilitation for the clientele and result in multiple administrative, clinical, and personal problems for staff and clientele.

An effective program of habilitation ideally occurs in an environment where the clientele are protected from harm, receive individualized care, participate in programs that enhance their development, and obtain clinical treatment for specific psychological, social, or physical problems. Here staff are well supervised in all aspects of residential treatment and receive continuing training in the form of workshops, seminars, and coursework in nearby colleges or universities. Administrative and programmatic organizations are designed to facilitate communication, coordination, and full participation by all staff in program development and evaluation. The residential units are properly maintained, and the needed supplies and equipment are readily provided by support personnel. Parents and relatives of the clientele participate in program development and question any plan about which they have concern. The adminstration of the facility has published policies and guidelines for the care and treatment of the clientele and periodically assesses staff and the habilitative programs to be certain that the quality and quantity of services are appropriate to the needs of the clientele and that its policies are followed consistently.

This description may be somewhat unrealistic, but it does reflect the intent of the Developmentally Disabled Assistance and Bill of Rights Act of 1975 and the regulations promulgated by the Department of Health and Human Services governing the administration of Intermediate Care Facilities for the Mentally Retarded (ICF/MR). Active treatment for each client must be the highest goal for all residential facilities—attainable only with sufficient resources (Crosby, 1976). When a facility is underfunded, the quality and sufficiency of programs are adversely affected. The administrator will be confronted with the discomforting decision of providing less service to all clients or concentrating resources in certain living units for limited periods of time.

Understaffing

The most critical of the circumstances that obtain from insufficient operating funds is understaffing. Shortages interfere with the facility's primary responsibility of caring for and protecting the clientele from harm and diminishes the effectiveness of habilitative programming. The usual cause of understaffing is insufficient operating funds; however, it can also be the consequence of high rates of sick and workers' compensation leaves, uneven work schedules, employer-union contracts, and an excessive number of employee separations from the facility. To compensate the units for decreased staffing, the administration may resort to the use of overtime, requiring personnel to work additional hours and days. As employees tire from working excessive hours, the possibility of client abuse and negligence increases; labor-management relations become strained, and healthy communication in the facility declines. A cycle of frustration and bitterness and defensive maneuvering by the administration is created, and the interpersonal stability necessary for an effective, habilitative environment is jeopardized.

There are no absolutes in determining the optimum level of direct-care staff for clients with varying types and degrees of handicapping conditions. The Accreditation Council for Services for Mentally Retarded and Other Developmentally Disabled Persons published recommended ratios that administrators have used as guidelines (Accreditation Council, 1978), but these are subject to differences in the clientele, physical environment, and personnel policies of states. The sequence for certifying facilities as Intermediate Care Facilities for the Mentally Retarded allows for progressive adjustments in staffing based on the documented needs of the clientele. The federal surveyor may cite a facility for lack of staff when the level of care and interaction between employees and residents is insufficient. The administrator must respond with a plan of correction, an agreement to provide additional staff, for the state to endorse. If the state does not do so eventually, it will lose the federal government's share of the cost of care and treatment in the facility as a result of decertification. Of the 278 public residential facilities questioned by Scheerenberger (1979), only 169 responded that at least part of their programs qualified as ICF/MR's.

Insufficient staffing in direct care and supervision leads to inconsistent treatment and managerial expedience. Fairly common practices in residential facilities with insufficient direct-care staff are the use of fluid assignments and involuntary overtime. Staff may be reassigned temporarily to relieve acute shortages in particular residential units. Such reassignments may become commonplace, and staff quickly lose their identification with a specific work group and, worse, their personal attachments to individual clients. When staff members are constantly rotated through a number of units, true program continuity and accountability become impossible to maintain. Clients' individual program plans contain numerous instructional procedures and specific therapeutic contingencies with which staff must be proficient. When supervisors are constantly confronted with employees sent to them from other units who are unfamiliar with their clientele and the programs that have been designed for them, they may be forced to compromise their usual standards. Supervisors may be able to provide a cursory orientation for temporary employees, but the unit schedule may be unimplementable under such conditions. Knowing that these employees have been transferred to the unit for a short duration, the supervisor usually will assign them menial duties such as housekeeping or custodial responsibilities rather than attempt to integrate them into habilitative programs.

As a result, the continuity of supervision rapidly deteriorates. Employees receive insufficient direction and support, and their strengths and weaknesses are not observed. Employees may begin to feel that their work is not appreciated, that supervisors are concerned only with a mechanical adherence to rules and policies. A negative relationship between supervisors and staff usually creates resentment and suspicion, and trust disintegrates. This is a serious circumstance in an already stressful job context. Uncorrected, it can intensify and become the norm. The relationship between direct-care staff and their supervisors is extensively discussed in Chapter 3 of this volume.

Tired staff become susceptible to injuries and illnesses; this leads to increases in workers' compensation cases and rates of sick leave. Tired staff also become irritable; their self-control with clients, other employees, and supervisors predictably deteriorates, resulting in disciplinary actions and flurries of employee grievances. Indeed, all aspects of residential treatment (e.g., routine activities of daily living, programming, interactions with parents and visitors, and responses to policy) can suffer. More than an administrative inconvenience or minor irritation for the staff, in its chronic state understaffing is an insidious problem that adversely affects the very management of the facility and the welfare of employees and the clientele. Unchecked, it can develop into an organizational pathology that money alone will not cure.

Understaffing has equally unpleasant consequences for professional services. The majority of professionals approach their responsibilities earnestly and are gratified by the results of their efforts with clients and line staff. However, they cannot avoid the problems that accumulate within a facility that lacks the resources with which to accomplish its basic organizational goals and objectives. The morale, competence, and personal status of psychologists, social workers, nurses, and other service professionals are subjected to many pressures in residential facilities: pressure from direct-care staff (see Chapter 4) who may resist program ideologies, pressure from administrators to be loyal and effective, and pressure from their own expectations for recognition and achievement. Providing optimum services with inadequate staff creates yet another quandary for the chief administrator.

There are three primary administrative concerns in providng acceptable levels of service in a residential facility: coverage, supervision, and staff development. Each client, in accordance with the standards promulgated by the Accreditation Council, the Department of Health and Human Services, and numerous professional organizations, must have a complete diagnosis and evaluation that defines the individual's personal, social, physical, and psychological status and indicates areas for additional assessment. Diagnosis must be followed by treatment with well-defined goals and methods for promoting the individual's development and an optimal life adjustment. Each person who is significant to the client should be knowledgeable of the habilitative strategy. The regulations require professional staff representing the pertinent disciplines in sufficient ratios to clients to provide diagnostic and clinical services and to offer counseling and training for staff and relatives of the clientele. An acceptable ratio of professional staff to clients is determined by the needs and problems of the clientele and the complexity of the treatments recommended during diagnosis and evaluation. It is often difficult to predetermine minimally adequate levels of professional staffing for a given number of clients with precision, but there are clear signals when insufficiencies exist.

Professional staff should be comfortably occupied by their responsibilities. They should have active schedules with reasonably defined priorities for their time that emphasize interaction with clients and paraprofessionals. However, when these staff must routinely chose between equally important activities because they are overextended in their attempt to respond to the multiple needs and problems of their clientele, the quality of habilitation is seriously threatened. The sequence of diagnosis and evaluation, program development, staff preparation, and program implementation may be substantially impaired. Each element is indispensible and integral to the habilitative process. Chronic understaffing forces the administration to deploy its professionals according to the severity of the current crisis that may exist in any one of the residential units. It may be important to reevaluate clients periodically but a client with a serious behavioral or medical problem must receive attention at once, not when a schedule indicates the date for review. Acute shortages of professional staff almost certainly guarantee that existing staff will become specialists in crisis intervention, a role that soon becomes self-limiting and frustrating as problems that otherwise could be resolved through comprehensive client treatment and staff training constantly repeat themselves as crises. Under these difficult circumstances, good professionals often seek other employment. If they remain, they may attempt to isolate themselves from the clientele and direct-care staff by resorting to the subterfuge of meetings and paperwork.

Administrators have tried various means to alleviate the frustrations of professional staff. A common approach has been to encourage innovation with small groups of clients. Creative projects yield positive clinical results and general acknowledgement of the skills of the practitioners. However, concentrating the uneven resources of the facility on certain clientele also means that others receive little or no service. Thus understaffing has forced administrators into a delicate balance. Obligated to serve the clinical needs of all their clientele, they must do so through professionals whose needs are frustrated by conditions of overextension. It is at once, an administrative conflict between equally disagreeable courses. More recently, strong external pressures on facilities from advocates, lawyers, and others have forced the choice at the expense of the professionals' needs. In many facilities, this has caused significant tension between administrators and professional staff. This problem and other aspects of the professions in facilities for the mentally handicapped is discussed at length in Chapter 4.

The problem of inadequate resources can frustrate the facility's mission. When the shortages extend into middle management and support staff, the organization may become directionless and decline. These are serious matters, and chief administrators must devise strategies for obtaining increased support and create new designs for deploying staff, possibly making radical changes in organizational configurations for delivering services. Typical departmental structures and the recent interdisciplinary approach may have to be re-thought in favor of more efficient models.

Not all the problems confronting administrators are a consequence of insufficient operating resources. The budget provides the framework in which services must be provided within the facility, and it certainly does affect the quality of life of the clients and the working conditions for the employees, as discussed previously. Finance alone, however, does not determine the efficacy of the habilitative programs offered in the facility. In fact, during the most austere of times, a common lament of administrators is not insufficient funds, but the lack of freedom to expend their funds prudently to the greatest advantage of the clientele and with as little external and internal interference as possible. The erosion of the right to manage, to be accountable for one's responsibilities while retaining the authority to respond to them, is a serious administrative problem, one that produced this classic advice to future administrators: ''Never accept responsibility without authority.'' Two dominant forces that contravene the administrator's freedom to manage are unionism and bureaucratic control.

Unions

Unions and their activities create serious problems for administrators of public residential facilities. This statement is not a judgment of employee organizations; nor is it intended to suggest that existence of unions is always counterproductive. It is simply fact that for a significant number of administrators, unions are a daily reality. ''Thirty-one (64%) of the forty-eight continental states sanction labor organizations and nine (19%) permitted employee associations. Only twelve states (25%) indicated that neither unions nor associations existed'' (Scheerenberger & Jones, 1980, p. 16). For many managers, unions create obstacles to the timely delivery of effective services for their clientele. Conflicts typically arise when the union's objectives are in conflict with the administration's priorities. Unions strive to protect the interests of the employees and the union. Unions are organizations with highly political and financial foundations and goals. Their existence depends on a constituency that perceives a continuing need for protection and advocacy. Hence, union organizers, representatives, delegates, and stewards constantly strive to dramatize the membership's need for a defense from authority.

Higher salaries and increased staff, with the revenue their dues represent, stimulate vigorous competition among groups hoping to represent employees. Two imperatives emerge for union organizers: (a) employees must be concerned about the inadequacy of their wages, working conditions, and rights; and (b) employees must be convinced of the superiority of representation of one group over others. The incumbent union, if there is one, enjoys only temporary status and the financial rewards of its plurality. It will be tested periodically by rival groups attempting to discredit its effectiveness. The measures applied to the representing union to determine its successes or failures include wage advances, improved working conditions, staffing ratios, fringe benefits, working hours, and clear evidence of the protection of employees from administrative actions brought against them. In states that have legislatively endorsed employees' rights to bargain collectively, the contract not only represents a legally binding agreement between employers and employees; it also serves as a valuable public relations document for unions to announce their successes in confrontations with the state. The contract, once printed and distributed to the membership, also becomes a guideline for determining the validity of the instructions employees receive from their supervisors. It may specify under what conditions employees are required to perform their duties, how they are to be evaluated, where they can be assigned to work, and the process for appealing the decisions of management.

Unions have other means to communicate their successes with the administration: news letters, general membership meetings, angry demonstrations that attract the news media, conversations between stewards and employees, voluminous grievances against the administration, well-publicized defenses of employees involved in disciplinary actions, and public denouncements of administrative decisions. Administrators of public residential facilities reported to Scheerenberger and Jones (1980) that the two most severe problems created by unions "involved protection of the inadequate (and frequently abusive) employees and the loss of flexibility, which is actually reflected in several of the items, e.g., loss of flexibility, limited management's rights to use staff as needed, staff schedules and seniority" (p. 18).

Depending on the nature of the labor management climate prevailing at the facility, the administration may be characterized by union leaders in at least three contexts: (a) it is well intended but powerless to obtain adequate support for employees and clients, given the state bureaucracy and government; (b) it consists of inept, aloof managers who are unaware of, or unconcerned about, the problems and needs of the employees and clients; or (c) it is an oppressive dictatorship that readily resorts to coercion and punishment to control employees. Under all three perceptions, an intelligent, energetic union organizer is usually able to translate reasonable administrative policy, disciplinary action, and rational responses to financial or clinical problems into certain danger for the employees. The strength and credibility of the union is often dependent on such translations.

An individual for whom discipline is pending for a breach of policy has the right to representation by the organization that has been officially recognized as that employee's agent. A full analysis of the just cause for the disciplinary action will be argued at each level of the appeal sequence until the issue has reached arbitration, or, in the absence of a collective bargaining agreement, a hearing officer or panel. This process, however, does not prevent discussions of cases with other employees or presentations in the union's literature. Here the interpretation is subject to considerable bias and may be slanted for the purpose of demonstrating the insensitivity or severity of the administration.

The central problem in the adversarial nature of labor-management relations is the deterioration of that intangible quality known as trust. Administrators begin to suspect that unions and their representatives will exploit any situation to their advantage and will resist each initiative to improve or expand services for the clientele. Increasingly, employees come to view the administration negatively, constantly watchful for signs that it is about to encroach on their rights. Compounding the problem of distrust is the difficulty for the administration to discern accurately the actions of individual employees from organized efforts by the union to subvert administrative policy or to resist reasonable change. Trust between labor and management tends to fluctuate with the feelings of security or insecurity of the employees, the aggressiveness of the unions, and the temper of the administration.

The mission of unions is to counterbalance the authority of the administration in all aspects of personnel management, with particular emphasis on promotions, assignments, and employee evaluations. Generally speaking, unions would prefer that these issues be decided on the basis of seniority, whereas longevity is typically only one of several factors management would choose to consider in determining employee assignments and upward mobility. Under a strict seniority system, employees may bid on vacancies in the residential units. The most senior employee would be granted first choice for a transfer to a preferred unit. This provision automatically constrains rational decision-making by the administration with regard to both the needs and problems of the clientele and the physical and emotional characteristics of employees deemed most appropriate for successfully responding to the clientele.

Failing to negotiate seniority as a unilateral focus for all administrative decisions, unions have emphasized the rights of their employees to due process in evaluations, promotions, and disciplinary actions. The burden of proof and the documentation to support a judgment about the performance or conduct of employees must be thorough and compelling. Although it is difficult to reject this seemingly democratic and just concept, when it is applied in the extreme supervisors and managers must reduce all their observations to statistics and highly factual documentation, an effort that requires considerable time and effort. For example, simply to note in an evaluation that an employee has been unable to achieve meaningful rapport with the clientele is insufficient. Such an observation may be successfully challenged during an appeal. The party hearing this case will require dates, times, and criteria for determining acceptable employee-client relationships and behavioral indications of the failure of the employee to achieve such relationships.

Similarly, disciplinary actions must be accompanied by voluminous documentation of violations of policy, proof that the administration has disseminated adequate information to all staff. Administrators have lost disciplinary cases at arbitration by failing to prove that their policies and standards were well known by employees who were disciplined. Except in cases of gross negligence, client abuse, or rank insubordination, employees' rights to protection from judgments against them are assured by the principle of progressive discipline. Arbitrators consider suspensions or dismissals to be extreme measures warranted only after employees have been repeatedly counseled and warned of the consequences of their infractions or undesirable behavior. Naturally, these counselings and warnings must be finely documented in order to prove that the administration is carefully following the precepts of progressive discipline in spirit and in context.

Two additional consequences of unionism impair the management function. First, opportunities for redress offered employees provide alternatives to solving their problems with or resisting the instructions of their supervisors. Therefore, the delicate authority of supervisors, who are responsible for the daily care, training, and treatment of the clientele is subject to serious question. The very foundation of managerial authority is the right to assign, direct, and evaluate employees. When supervisors realize that employees may challenge their decisions by filing grievances that result in formal hearings, they may become intimidated and begin to avoid controversial decisions and supervisory confrontations with their employees. Rather than collect voluminous observational data on the performance of employees and to avoid the anxiety and pressures associated with the grievance procedure, supervisors may file satisfactory performance evaluations on employees they know are less than competent. The administrator of the facility suddenly discovers that the critical dimension of management by supervision has diminished significantly. Supervisors are not directing or correcting their employees, and they are failing to evaluate performance properly.

The second difficulty for administrators is the princple of past practices. If employees have been accustomed to certain procedures, schedules, assignments, or privileges, union representatives may insist that these are binding and may not be modified by management. Their argument is that once a practice has been established it becomes a condition of employment. Therefore, when the administration wishes to modify a program, the duties of employees, or their schedules, such initiatives may be regarded by the union as violation of past practices. Organizational change is always difficult to achieve; the doctrine of past practice is an additional and formidable barrier to progress.

Historically, labor organizations have played clear and necessary roles in the protection and advancement of public employees. This discussion does not question the importance of these functions. The purpose here is to observe unionism as another force that affects administration of a residential facility. From that view, it must be concluded that union activity, by definition an adversary process, absorbs incalculable amounts of time from the administrator and distracts managers and supervisors from their primary objective: the provision of habilitative services to the clientele. The skillful manager must learn and apply strategies that accommodate the union's goals yet do not compromise care and treatment of the clientele.

Bureaucratic Problems

This chapter has emphasized the complexity of managing a public residential facility. Services must be provided 24 hours a day, 365 days a year without interruption and usually without sufficient resources. In addition, managerial and clinical problems occur regularly: a client becomes acutely disturbed; the facility loses its electrical power; a highly communicable disease is detected in a residential unit; a client wanders away from the facility; staff threaten to strike; parents demand an immediate investigation of an injury; a building is damaged by fire; the union protests involuntary overtime. The administrator must have written contingency plans for responding to these eventualities. The plans must detail the actions of personnel during emergencies. Seldom will there be adequate resources with which to react to all possible difficulties; therefore, managers and supervisors must be willing to accept multiple responsibilities depending on the circumstances of the facility. The ultimate paradox in the administration of a public residential facility is the obvious need for optimal managerial flexibility in responding to multifarious problems and the limitations on the use of resources and the paucity of options readily available to management. For example, if a disease epidemic threatens the welfare of the clientele, the director of the facility knows that there are too few nurses to contain the problem. The director immediately requests an additional 15 registered nurses from the commissioner, who requests an emergency authorization to expend funds for this purpose from the state's finance department, who consults with the commissioner of the personnel department, who questions the number of positions requested by the facility. The director is asked to rejustify the request, which may or may not be approved. Because the positions have not been budgeted by the legislature, the authorization from the finance department permits assignment of only temporary nursing personnel. Unfortunately, the director of the residential facility is unable to recruit nurses who are willing to work only for the duration of the epidemic.

In the larger bureaucratic system of which the residential facility is but one element, the administrator's problems are not considered particularly significant—until they become a focused concern of the public and therefore a political issue for the governor, legislators, and commissioners. The public residential facility usually is an administrative unit within a state department of mental retardation, mental health, or mental hygiene. Or it may be a mere microscopic element in an even larger bureaucratic amalgam referred to as a "superagency," in which the formerly separate departments of mental retardation, mental health, and corrections may be combined. Parallel departments (e.g., the departments of transportation, personnel, and public works) that may also be subsumed by a higher authority (e.g. the departments of budget, finance, or general operations) complicate the administrator's task by further removing the ultimate decision-maker from the problems of the local administrator. In state bureaucracies, people responsible for controlling and monitoring the expenditure of public funds greatly influence general administrative policy. Budget directors receive instructions from the governor and their legal mandates from the legislature. The commissioners of the various state departments are appointed by the governor and are expected to respond to and favorably reflect the incumbent's philosophy and policies. When the governor practices austerity, the commissioners of service departments are expected to cooperate with directives on fiscal management.

Bureaucracy significantly affects the public residential facility's operations in several areas: the budgeting and management of funds, the administration of personnel, the expansion of programs, and the resolution of problems with political overtones. The facility's budget frequently is determined with no opportunity for the administrator personally to describe to the legislators the needs and problems of the clientele. Bureaucratic reasoning holds that if all administrators were free to advocate for their facilities, unfair and possibly destructive competitions might result. If the more persuasive administrators were successful in their budget presentations, clientele in other facilities would suffer. Therefore, the commissioner must argue for all the facilities in his or her purview, balancing their diverse needs and problems, and somehow organizing them into a reasonable budget. The confounding problem is that the budget process is more likely to be an occasion for the defense of the department's request than an opportunity to inform the governor and the legislature of the circumstances and needs of residential facilities. This important education, then, must be accomplished informally and with the assitance of third parties.

The initial fiscal problem for the administrator is the adequacy of the budget. The second problem is the lack of discretion in expending funds in response to the needs of the clientele and problems of the facility. Funds for personnel, supplies and sundry services, and equipment are appropriated by the legislature and signed into law by the governor. Actual expenditures, however, may be controlled through the use of a strict, line-item budget that details amounts for travel, food, clothing, utilities, overtime, and other expenses. A budget of this type dictates to the administrator. Most budgets provide for a degree of flexibility, but it is a clear violation of public accounting for the administrator to commingle funds in the three distinct categories of personnel, supplies and services, and equipment. Staff and parents frequently suggest to the administrator that certain problems (e.g., lack of staff, furniture, vehicles, or appropriate clothing) could be easily rectified by merely restructuring the budget. In state government, ingenious systems have been designed specifically to prevent such manipulations of funds.

Administrators of public residential facilities must contend with authorities on various levels of state bureaucracy with explicit areas of responsibility. The department of the budget may determine, through the allocation of funds, the maximum number of staff that may be employed at the facility at any one time. For example, 30 million dollars may have been budgeted for personnel. The fundable number of positions for the year, assuming there are zero vacancies, is 1200 employees. However, vacancies will occur throughout the year and funds will accumulate creating a significant surplus. If the sixth month accumulations could be reinvested in additional direct-care staff, basic services at the facility could be improved, albeit temporarily. However, this flexibility is seldom permitted; nor can the administrators, within the fundable number of positions, increase and decrease services by hiring more of one classification and fewer of another. The substitution of a physician for a nurse or a teacher for a social worker typically requires a written authorization from one or more departments and considerable time for approval—if it is granted. The state personnel department is responsible for ensuring that positions are used correctly. Personnel technicians, applying a mathematical formula, often determine how many positions are required for a certain number of clients or how many drivers are needed to transport clients to and from programs. Administrators of residential facilities must convince them, with documentation and pertinacity, of the logic of their organizational patterns. Lodged in state office buildings miles from the facility, these technicians frequently question the administrator about the appropriateness of requested staff positions, although they seldom argue about the clients' need for care and treatment. They bring mathematical precision to the ever-varying nature of administering programs of human service; in so doing, they represent another obstruction to responsive administration.

The budgetary process is highly influenced by the mood of the constituents and therefore the attitudes of the governor and the legislature. The administrator knows that the quality of life at the facility is determined by the balance of essential services. Direct care and medical supervision of the clientele are critical elements, but psychologists are no less important for units with individuals with extreme maladaptive behavior. The buildings and grounds should be maintained adequately, not only to protect the value of the property but to provide an environment that contributes to the happiness of the clientele and the morale and productivity of the staff. During periods of fiscal restraint, the administrator may be disallowed positions other than those that relate to the immediate care of the clientele, no matter how vigorously the administrator demands the right to determine needed personnel. Managerial and supervisory positions in particular are scrutinized carefully, and there is usually great reluctance to grant additional positions at higher salary levels. However, when the news media report the misconduct of an employee or an injury to a client, it is the administrator who must explain the circumstances of the facility without offending the commissioner, the governor, and the legislature.

The administrator of a public residential facility is constantly responding to conflicting priorities within state government. The legislature may have mandated that all clients must receive daily habilitative services, for example. In response, the administrator requests and receives positions to provide special education, occupational therapy, vocational education, and recreation. Such expanded services will automatically strain the facility's capacity to transport clients. The legislature simultaneously may have limited spending in several areas of state government, perhaps in the acquisition or maintenance of vehicles owned and operated by the state. The commissioner of transportation proclaims the intention to reduce the size of the fleet at the very time that the administrator of the public residential facility must request additional vehicles. The legislature has already concluded its session, and the parties are unable to obtain clarification of the issue. Neither the director nor the commissioner is willing to renounce or ignore the lawmakers' mandates.

A related illustration of the administrator's difficulty in gaining understanding from the state bureaucracy is the way the commissioner of transportation may typically approach the problem just described. The public and the legislature may suspect that state departments have acquired unnecessary vehicles. A study is ordered to identify facilities with underused vehicles as determined by monthly mileage reports. On the basis of mileage alone, the administrator of the residential facility would be required to release stand-by vehicles that are driven only during emergencies. Approximately one half of the facility's delivery vehicles would also have to be surrendered; because they are operated in reverse much of the time, that mileage is not recorded on the equipment's odometers. This scenario is hypothetical but far from uncommon. Across a vast public bureaucracy, one small agency facility may experience countless contradictions of this sort during the course of a year.

When administrators are not defending their existing resources, they may be found writing elaborate plans to justify needed improvement and expansion of client services. Program development can be accomplished by expanding the facility's budget or by converting existing positions into new classifications, both of which require approval by higher authorities. If timing is significant to organizational change, the administrator must either possess a high degree of prescience or develop considerable tolerance for delays in his or her initiatives. Innovation is applauded when it is successful, but governmental leaders also fear possible adverse consequences of experimental programs. This causes them to be cautious and to create bureaucratic mechanisms for limiting them. Commissioners of state departments must be able to justify the logic and prudence of their programs to the governor, legislators, and fiscal and personnel departments.

From the bureaucratic perspective, there are two fundamental indicators of stability in public programs: uniformity of operations and an unambiguous central authority that monitors and controls its administrative units. This is accomplished by the installation of an approved process by which the initiatives of local administrators must be reviewed and approved before their implementation. Fortunately, the bureaucrats' desire for uniformity seldom reaches the extreme they sometimes express; but for the administrator of the facility, it is a constant struggle to maintain a reasonable amount of discretion in the use of resources or the deployment of staff. The technicians who monitor the acquisition of equipment have been known to question why one facility requires more wheelchairs than a comparably sized unit. The monitors are remote from the problems, and it does not occur to them that the percentage of physically handicapped persons varies among residential units. These questions frequently are repeated in response to administrators' requests that reflect differences in the age, level of functioning, and clinical problems of the clientele and residential configuration.

To accommodate state government's need for clear accountability in program development, large central offices develop around the commissioners. Central offices become state governments in miniature, with bureaus specializing in finance, purchasing, staff development, housing, planning, evaluation, and other services. However, they are seldom mandated to provide direct services; rather, they become professional program reviewers. Originally designed to coordinate program development of facilities, the central office gradually begins to have needs and problems of its own. In time, it becomes an entity as important as the facility in which clients are living and receiving daily services. It becomes another layer of control not always comprised of personnel with the greatest expertise. In fact, the central office, like other state departments, tends to lack generalists. It is usually staffed by specialists who wonder why their particular interests are not appreciated by facility administrators beset with multiple problems. As state systems serving the mentally handicapped gravitate toward expanded central office operations of this nature, one may confidently predict that administrators responsible to that office will experience more complications in the management of their programs.

The budgetary requests and program proposals submitted by the administrator of a public residential facility must be reviewed at the central office, in parallel bureaucratic departments, in the governor's office, and by the legislature. Advocacy groups and parent organizations submit their own requests. The advocacy group may be seeking additional group homes and sheltered workshops. The facility's parent organization may be adamant about increases in direct-care staff and improvements to the residential units. The administrator may agree in part with both groups, except that his or her strategy includes improvements at the facility and expanded services in communities. Legislators become confused by equal and contradictory initiatives—unless, of course, the intensity of lobbying is one sided. This usually occurs only when one group misperceives the strength of the other or when one of the organizations has become lethargic. Simultaneously, the electorate may have expressed its mandate to the general assembly: decrease taxes by curtailing expenditures. Someone is going to lose in this contest, and the governor and legislators are certain to avoid blame. Parents, advocates, and unions will demand an explanation for the administrator's failure to obtain the necessary funds for their particular priorities. The result is a climate highly favorable to lawsuits in behalf of individuals, organizations, and the classes they claim to represent. More important for this discussion, in such firestorms of competition for limited resources, the facility's chief administrator is likely to be at the pivot, the most readily accessible target for all contestants. It is a losing game even for the most agile administrator.

The director of a public residential facility is responsible for solving administrative problems and preventing their re-occurrence. Administrative problems, however, are not necessarily limited by the boundaries of the facility. Controversies may be communicated to the governor or a legislator in an impassioned plea by a parent or advocate for relief from an administrative decision or for an investigation of an incident. Within a facility itself, there may be mechanisms and procedures to respond to such complaints or charges. For example, the administrator may have written, disseminated, and actively enforced specific policies protecting the clientele and employees (e.g., a process for appealing decisions that aggrieve parents and personnel and an administrative mechanism for investigating complaints against the facility). These procedural safeguards can be activated in response to the problems. Designated committees can be directed to review accidents, abuse, employee morale, and staff development. The events of the review will be recorded and the conclusion of administrators, supervisors, and committee members will be documented for the record.

However, once a problem is communicated to other branches of state government, the process for review changes. When a legislator or an aide to the governor calls the administrator and asks for an explanation of an incident, the administrator is expected to respond immediately with all of the pertinent facts and recommendations for reassuring the complainant. For that single instant, the administrator is assumed to be thoroughly knowledgeable of the incident, regardless of when it occurred or the people it involved. A report must be submitted within 24 hours, certainly no later than 2 days. The incident becomes priority number one, no matter what its importance compared to other issues or problems facing the administrator.

There are many such "instant priorities" for facility administrators. The transfer of a client from the residential facility to an alternative setting is a clinical decision until a parent or advocate questions the wisdom of the transfer and communicates his or her concerns to a political figure. Governors, their aides, and members of the legislature tend to respond to impassioned complaints from employees, parents, or advocates in a less than unbiased manner. Perhaps it is understandable that politically sensitive officials may be influenced by what appears to be a consummate lack of wisdom by one of their administrators. However, complainants infrequently include a full description of the context in which the decision was rendered or the incident occurred. The result is that the administrator is forced into a defensive position, required to prove that a decision was not arbitrary or capricious or that an incident was not the consequence of negligence. Complaints by parents and advocates about the care and treatment provided in public residential facilities have become highly frequent occurrences over the past several years. The director of any facility can be expected to devote considerable time and effort to explaining why events occur and defending staff actions.

Administrative Problems: One Illustration

Client abuse is perhaps the most unsettling problem administrators of public residential facilities must confront. It is a disturbing, highly charged, deceptively complex matter that interrelates with many of the issues discussed earlier. In many ways, it is *the* most difficult administrative problem and thus is presented in detail to conclude this section.

The word abuse evokes an emotional reaction from administrators, staff, parents, and the general public. Virtually every one concerned about the happiness and well being of handicapped people will agree that abuse is intolerable and must be eliminated wherever it exists. There is much less agreement, however, about the causes of abuse and methods for preventing it. Parents and advocates insist that abuse is the result of inadequate procedural safeguards for the clientele. Administrators argue that it is a consequence of inadequate supervision. Unions proclaim that it is a result of insufficient staffing, training, and professional support. Personnel specialists offer that it is a result of poor pre-employment screening.

To understand abuse, it is important to identify its basic types: (a) reactive abuse, (b) sanctioned abuse, and (c) pathological abuse. Reactive, or reflexive, abuse is an overreaction by a staff member to pain or frustration during an encounter with one or more clients. Under stress, tired and without conscious thought, an employee reacts to an assault by a client with unnecessary force or employs force to gain the compliance of a client. Sanctioned abuse is that level of force that is generally accepted by employees as necessary in order to maintain order in the residential units. Pathological abuse is utter cruelty perpetrated by employees with character disorders.

There are several dimensions to the prevention of abuse. The starting point seems to be an honest recognition of the stresses associated with continuous contact with severely disabled, multiply handicapped people. The degree of psychological stress on employees can be tremendous (see Chapter 3), and the attendant frustrations at times overwhelming for them. These stresses are often unacknowledged by supervisors and administrators in ways meaningful to those experiencing it. Thus, when an abusive incident does occur, the quick solution that often follows may be unrelated to the causes of the event. For example, administrators are told regularly that well-trained staff will not abuse handicapped people. Certainly training is important, but it does not guarantee the healthy emotional development of staff. The problem is an extremely complex one that resists simple solutions, but there are a few administrative provisions that can minimize mistreatment of clientele.

The administrator should publish a strict, clearly written policy on the subject of abuse. All employees, parents, advocates, and clients should be fully apprised of the policy and the certain consequences for its violation. All supervisors should be specifically trained in the detection of the symptoms and signs that predict possible abuse in employees and clients as well. Staff should be thoroughly trained and practiced in the use of specific techniques for responding to acutely disturbed clients, including the concept and practice of the least restrictive procedure for protecting clients.

These measures will help, but no matter how stringently the policies on abuse are applied or how thoroughly staff are trained in acceptable methods of behavior management, abuse can still occur. The single greatest protection for the clientele is an employee peer group that adamantly rejects abuse in any form. When employees are completely protective of the handicapped people for whom they are responsible, abuse will be eliminated. The emotional bonding of employees to clients is a protection far beyond any written policy, and it cannot be achieved through a single approach. It is prompted or discouraged cumulatively over time with virtually every message delivered to employees about their worth. Employees in regular contact with the clientele must know the importance of their work and feel appreciated for performing it in a human, effective manner. That recognition occurs when they share the facility's mission, indeed when they own it. The extensive discussion of this subject in Chapters 3 and 4 is highly relevant to the understanding and prevention of abuse.

It follows that the forces that fractionalize the work group tend to dissolve this identification with client and mission and thus increase the risk of abuse. Intrusive advocates, combative parents, rigid administrators, and aggressive unionists create distrust and insecurity among staff members. Initially, employees may have approached their responsibilities with genuine concern about the needs and problems of the clientele. In time, though, under the pressures that surround them and with the growing suspicion that they, and not the clients, are the true victims of bureaucracy, employees may begin to regard the clientele indifferently and, later, possibly resentfully.

Knowing the difficulty of achieving the emotional climate conducive to consistent care and protection of the clientele, administrators of public residential facilities must employ every possible safeguard for them. Human rights offices should be established to provide counselling to staff, clients, and parents. Human rights committees composed of clients, parents, and staff should be maintained as open and persistent forums for discussions of issues and proposals that will obviate conditions in which abuse can occur. Supervisors should be trained in detecting the signs and symptoms of chronic stress and in counselling techniques and interventions. Equally important, it must become an accepted norm of the facility's entire managerial system that employees be given regular opportunities to express their frustrations and feelings about clients and client behaviors. Such opportunities must be fully nonjudgmental, or they will not be trusted and hence will be ignored.

Mixing these requirements into a method that protects clients and yet responds to staff and is simultaneously trusted by external observers and critics is a monumental task for the administrator. It is also a necessary one upon which the credibility of that administration may rest.

Administrators of public residential facilities are acutely aware of their vulnerabilities in legal actions, that is, lawsuits initiated on behalf of individual clients and class actions on behalf of large groups of clients. The background and context of litigation against public institutions is discussed and analyzed in Chapter 5 of this volume. The purpose of this discussion is to observe litigation as it reflects the administrator and the staff of the facility.

There are likely to be several defendants in major litigation, including commissioners of various state departments and possibly the governor, but it is the local administrator who will be most affected by and most central to the case. Therefore, litigation is examined here for its effects on the director of the facility and its operations.

In addition to litigation, administrators are experiencing peripheral legal problems. Their mail increasingly contains letters by lawyers demanding the release of clients' records, investigations, changes in residence, the provision of immediate treatment or the immediate cessation of treatment. At conferences on legal issues in residential administration, administrators are being advised to hire staff attorneys to respond to emerging legal problems that only recently were considered to be administrative problems. The activities of attorneys, sometimes with reasonable cause and occasionally favorable results, represent an entirely new dimension in public administration. It is the fortunate director who receives legal advice from a knowledgeable, sympathetic attorney general familiar with developmental disabilities and the problems of administering a public residential facility. Clients' or parents' dissatisfactions that are translated into legal complaints are of great concern to administrators and require considerable time to formulate appropriate responses; but it is grand-scale litigation, the class action suit, that has completely changed administration of the public residential facility.

The formal process of class action litigation commences with the filing of a written complaint in federal court charging that the personal and constitutional rights of certain individuals, the named plaintiffs, were violated while those individuals resided in the facility, and further that the circumstances of the named plaintiffs represent those of all those in residence. A sequence of legal contests between the lawyers for plaintiffs and the lawyers for the defendants is activated. There are motions and countermotions, beginning with a debate before the judge on the validity of the complaint and its relevance to the federal court. Before the case can actually be tried, the judge must accept the complaint and rule against the defendant's usually automatic motion to dismiss it. The suit must be certified as a class action, and the lengthy period during which both sides collect facts, identify witnesses, and plan their legal strategies must be completed. Hoping that the issue will be limited to the experiences and circumstances of the named plaintiffs, lawyers argue vigorously against the certification of the class action. The difference between the status of a suit involving several plaintiffs and one that has been certified as a class action, and thereby encompasses the entire population of a facility, is monumental. A facility with several hundred people in residence will require years of legal research and investigation for the preparation of the adversaries' cases. This phase of litigation, commonly known as discovery (Allen & Miller, 1969), is highly disruptive.

There are two immediate and serious side effects of litigation regardless of the sincerity of the plaintiffs and their legal representatives or the reasonableness of the changes they seek in court. The complex and intensive nature of large-scale litigation (a) temporarily paralyzes the administrative function of the affected organization and (b) threatens the professional and personal security of the leadership of the facility. The administrator may, in fact, agree with the basic demands of the litigants for improved residential centers or expanded community services; however, the legal process is unavoidably adversarial in nature and the conduct of litigation is patently intrusive and extremely unsettling for clients, parents, and staff.

A proper legal defense requires the collection of factual exhibits for the judge; recruitment and coordination of expert witnesses; training of staff to be witnesses; and a complete clinical review of the clientele, the physical environment, and the programs of the facility. The administrator must also prepare personal testimony describing his or her tenure at the facility in fine detail. This recitation describes the organizational structure of the facility, staffing patterns, administrative and clinical policies, the manner in which services are provided to the clientele, and the clinical process governing admissions and discharges. The problems, progress, obstacles, and the administrator's plans of correction must be outlined carefully for the judge. In court, the administrator must illustrate his or her competence, perceptions of the facility's problems, and the determination and ability to correct them. An acute awareness of societal changes and their implications for the purposes and future of public residential facilities also must be demonstrated.

The administrator's testimony is designed to protect his or her right to manage the facility and the clients' and parents' rights to have several choices available to them for residential placement and habilitative services. The administrator must attempt to control the momentum of litigation to ensure that change is meaningful and manageable. This is best approached by providing the court with an honest perspective about the following matters: (a) the needs of the clientele; (b) the problems and potential of the facility; and (c) the financial, social, and governmental changes that must precede the development of new, applied models of service delivery for developmentally disabled people.

Quite often parents and state officials are greatly disturbed and confused by the sudden confrontation between former allies. Unfortunately, the pressures of litigation tend to intensify differences in advocacy, philosophy, and management style among the concerned parties. A destructive cycle can easily result in staff, administrators, and state officials blaming one another for the litigation instead of forming a coalition of people determined to preserve their rights and mission during and after the legal contest. In creating a coordinated legal defense, the administrator of the facility, who is the most immediately responsible party for the circumstances and habilitation of the clientele, must demonstrate his or her centrality in the case. Once this has been established, parents, clients, staff, state officials, and the attorneys can discuss their preferences and fears in a meaningful context that encompasses needed changes and reasonable protections for the clients and the interests of parents and administrators.

The relief sought by the plaintiffs can range from massive reforms at the facility to its closure in favor of small, family-scale living arrangements established throughout the state for the clients. The legal complaint, unfortunately, neither explains the motives of the plaintiffs nor describes their plan for successfully implementing the judicial order they seek. Dialogue between the parties is drastically constrained by the nature of the adversarial process. The bases for agreement between the contestants are concealed by the need for secrecy in preparing for the trial, and the possibilities of compromise are severely reduced by the transfer of authority from the parties to their legal representatives. Administrators, knowing the experiences of their peers in other states, generally will not entertain the possibility of consent decrees that legally bind them to a rigid course of change with small margin for discretionary judgment. Plaintiffs are generally unwilling to withdraw their suit in favor of a nonbinding agreement that subsequently could be abandoned by the administration or ignored by the state legislature.

With organized advocates demanding immediate and systemic change in states' programs for developmentally disabled people and with administrators' growing resentment of the intrusion of legal antagonists into their facilities and programs, collaborative strategies must become the preferred method of creating responsible agreements. The courts have been asked to interpret case law or to settle the disputes of individual parties, to judge history, and to implement by judicial rulings fundamental social changes that would be better addressed by legislative and administrative processes. Chapter 5 in this book examines the success of these rulings and their implementation.

State legislatures are beginning to rebel against decisions that force them to raise the tax base and the ire of their constituents (Mensh, 1980). The obligation of the states to provide treatment services to all disabled citizens has been limited by the Supreme Court, and the right of all handicapped people, in all circumstances, to live in community settings awaits unequivocal confirmation. Professionals, parents, researchers, and advocates may have to reconcile, outside the courts, their disagreement on fundamental questions pertaining to the quality of life of severely developmentally disabled people.

THE FUTURE OF PUBLIC RESIDENTIAL FACILITIES

The future of public residential facilities may be determined by cumulative litigations or by adverse decisions by the United States Supreme Court. Their destiny will also be influenced greatly by the attitudes and values of the public, the stability of the economy, the political climate, changing professional standards, and the findings of researchers. Roos (1978) questioned several nationally recognized experts in the field of mental retardation about the future of residential services. He found that "agreement was higher on degree of desirability of items than on the likelihood of their occurrence, suggesting that, in general, experts agree on what should take place, although they are less confident that it will take place" (p. 356). The prognosticators suggested that residential facilities will be smaller (150 or fewer beds) and that community living arrangements and support services would proliferate. "Large multi-purpose institutions of five hundred or more residents will no longer have a useful function and will have been phased out toward the end of the century" (p. 356). The experts unanimously predicted that living units will be designed for fewer than 20 residents and that the principles of normalization will be incorporated into the architecture, but that individuals with multiple and profound problems will continue to require specialized environments.

Members of the professional community currently differ widely on the future of public residential facilities. Dybwad (1978), Wolfensberger (1971), and Blatt (1977) have crusaded against institutions in and out of the court room, declaring them dysfunctional and harmful to handicapped people. Their remarks often contain sharp reprovals of professionals who support or are employed in residential centers. Conversely, Throne (1979), Schwartz (1977), and Rhodes and Browning (1977) express concern for the well being of disabled people who have been discharged to satisfy a single principle. These countervailing viewpoints are, to a degree, influenced by emotional attachments to causes or to experiences with residential centers. Wagner (1979) systemically examined the problems of providing effective services to mentally retarded people. He concluded that a unified system was necessary that would include institutions for the foreseeable future. Gettings and Mitchell (1980) analyzed residential services (i.e., community living arrangements versus institutions) by conducting a survey of the capital expenditures of forty states. "If there is a general lesson to be drawn from this analysis of state capital improvement budgets and plans, it is that extreme care must be taken in reaching any conclusions about the direction and pace of change at the state level—especially in such a volatile and emotionally charged area of policy as residential services for mentally retarded citizens" (p. 47). Although there has been a notable increase in community living arrangements in states across the country, the maintenance and renovation of public residential facilities continue to be important priorities for state officials and legislators.

The future of public residential facilities will be influenced by political, social, and economic developments, but from the administrator's perspective, the most serious challenge is the extent to which they can be managed properly and effectively. Historically, public institutions have been underfinanced and overpopulated. As admissions and censuses increased, buildings became overcrowded and personnel became overburdened. Administrators were confronted by the impossible task of serving large, diverse populations with insufficient resources, inadequate facilities, and a small, overworked complement of employees. Under these circumstances, the managerial imperative was to provide the basics of life to as many clients as possible in the most efficient way possible. Only the most expedient methods of feeding, bathing, dressing, and managing the clients were acceptable. Custodial care on a large scale was an absolute necessity merely to sustain the population. In the majority of states, the public residential facility was the only alternative for families and the disabled person; despite overcrowding and understaffing, the administrator was compelled to admit people whose situations had become desperate. The conditions in which handicapped people lived became intolerable, and reform was inevitable.

The quality of life and habilitative services in public residential facilities has improved remarkably but not completely. Today, administrators are striving to reduce their residential populations and provide specialized, comprehensive services to discrete groups of people with extraordinary developmental, behavioral, and medical needs. Administrators are attempting to achieve a reasonable balance between organizational resources and the clinical needs of their clientele. When a facility consistently protects its clients from harm, provides effective, specialized services, and helps clients to attain their highest developmental potential, it has achieved a state of manageability. The two greatest obstacles to proper management are (a) the tendency of public services to become ponderous, and (b) a sudden redirection of resources from residential centers to other systems of residential treatment and care.

The inherent difficulty in managing public residential facilities is the multiplicity of priorities and accountabilities that the administrator is required to satisfy. Each may be important, but in combination they have a consuming momentum all their own. Basic managerial functions are extremely difficult to maintain in organizations that are overregulated and in which union, advocacy groups, parent associations, and state and federal officials constrain the administrator's authority or limit discretion in planning, staffing, and evaluating services. The first symptom of organizational dysfunction is the disruption of basic communications because of the administration's inability to concentrate on the fundamental mission of the facility. When managers must be concerned equally about affirmative action, labor relations, state and federal regulations, litigation, inflation, public relations, and the habilitation of the clientele, their effectiveness is quickly diminished. Townsend (1970) emphasized that organizational success is directly related to the ability of managers to concentrate on specific, achievable objectives that are directly related to the central mission of the organization. When administrators' concentration is continuously interrupted by problems that are at best tangential to the facility's goals and objectives for the clientele, proper management is subverted.

Historically, public residential facilities have attempted to serve large, heterogeneous populations of handicapped people of all ages with emotional, social, physical, and intellectual handicaps ranging from moderate to profound. These diverse clientele have presented intense and chronic problems, overwhelming the administration and ultimately resulting in difficulties that have become the subject of numerous lawsuits.

Administrators of public residential facilities must gain the needed legislative, legal, and social support for their programs. The mission of their organizations should be clear and clinically defensible. Admissions should be restricted to those seriously handicapped individuals urgently in need of concentrated services in specifically designed, clinical environments. Clients should remain in any one program for only as long as it is beneficial for them. They should then move progressively to settings that enhance their habilitation and in which their personal needs can be met. Administrators must articulate ambitious goals for the future and pragmatic solutions for the daily problems of their clientele. Public residential facilities may eventually be replaced entirely by noninstitutional facilities and services, not necessarily because of internal dysfunction, but because of overreliance on them. Any system, no matter what its composition, will fail when it cannot be managed properly. Perhaps the problem today is that administrators and advocates speak too much of systems and too little of individuals' needs and problems. Blatt (1979) has warned his followers about the dangers of replacing one system with another without understanding the reasons for its problems and admitting that there are no quick and simple solutions to complex problems: "If we are not careful, there will someday be advocacy movements created to protect people who have been hurt by certain brands of our advocacy" (p. 10).

It is difficult to predict the future of public residential facilities with any degree of precision. Their size and scope of responsibilities for handicapped people are clearly diminishing. Their mission is becoming more definitive, their services more specialized. These trends may continue unabated; or social, political, or economic events could disrupt or reverse them. The atmosphere surrounding public residential facilities has been charged by the intensity of reformers' efforts to eliminate them and their defenders' growing resolve to protect them. Neither effort produces constructive dialogue or concepts for the future.

Recent Supreme Court decisions have been interpreted by experts to sound a caution to future litigants to consider their cases carefully in the light of other possible remedies, such as legislation (Bateman, 1982). The energy and money that has been expended on legal conflicts should be reinvested in implementing an enlightened social policy that recognizes the right and potential of persons with developmental disabilities. Clearly, institutions are in a period of decline in favor of supported community living. However, the fact remains that today public residential facilities are caring for the most delicate and complex individuals, and until the current trend becomes a unified practice, complete and comprehensive, they must be supported vigorously; otherwise there is the risk of default with the subsequent human damage that tends to accompany the deterioration of social structures.

There is also an urgent need for greatly expanded basic and applied research. The missing reference in too many discussions regarding the future of disabled persons and the structures that have served them is a rational base of information for making informed decisions. An intuitive approach, one that emphasizes presumptions on the universality of human nature and the commonality of needs of people irrespective of their outward differences may be a legitimate one for advocates. Managers, however, have to contend with restless governors, legislatures, and the public, whose first concern is the cost of care. The previous questions demand careful, scientific scrutiny. Without better information than currently available, private and public endeavors in behalf of the developmentally disabled may be directionless.

REFERENCES

Accreditation Council for Services for the Mentally Retarded and Other Developmentally Disabled Persons (1978). *Standards for services for developmentally disabled persons.* Chicago: Joint Commission on Accreditation of Hospitals.

Allen, C. & Miller, A. (Eds.). (1969). *Federal practice and procedures.* St. Paul: West Publishing.

Bateman, B. (1982). Youngberg v. Romeo. Analysis and commentary. *Analysis and Intervention in Developmental Disabilities, 2*(4), 375–382.

Blatt, B. (1977). The family album. *Mental Retardation, 15,* 3–4.

Blatt, B. (1979). Once upon a time I was a segregator. *The Exceptional Parent, 9,* 3–9.

Crosby, K. (1976). Essentials of active programming. *Mental Retardation, 14,* 3–9.

Directory of Public Residential Facilities for the Mentally Retarded. (1980). Madison, WI: National Association of Superintendents of Public Residential Facilities for the Mentally Retarded.

Dybwad, G. (1978, December). *A society without institutions.* Paper presented at the Residential Alternatives Symposium, Hartford, CT.

Friedman, P. (1976). *The rights of the mentally retarded,* New York: Avon Books.

Gettings, R. & Mitchell, D. (1980). *Trends in capital expenditures for mental retardation facilities: A state-by-state survey.* Arlington, VA: National Association of State Mental Retardation Program Directors.

Halderman v. Pennhurst, 446 F. Supp. 1295 (E.D.P.A. 1977).

Halpern, C. (1976). The right to habilitation. In M. Kindred, J. Cohen, D. Penrod, & T. Shaffer (Eds.), *The mentally retarded citizen and the law* (pp. 384–406). New York: Free Press.

Heyel, C. (1973). *The encyclopedia of management.* New York: Van Nostrand Reinhold.

Horner, R. (1979). Accountability in habilitation of the severely retarded: The issue of consent. *American Association of Educators of the Severely and Profoundly Handicapped, 4,* 24–35.

Johnson, R. & Wood, J. (1976). Legislative and administrative competence in setting institutional standards. In M. Kindred, J. Cohen, D. Penrod, & T. Shaffer (Eds.), *The mentally retarded citizen and the law* (pp. 528–562). New York: Free Press.

Lyden, F. J., & Miller, E. G. (1978). *Public budgeting: Program planning and evaluation.* Chicago: Rand McNally.

Mensh, S. (Ed.). (1980). *Capitol Capsule, 10.*

New York State ARC v. Rockefeller, 357 F. Supp. 752 (E.D. NY 1973).

O'Connor v. Donaldson, 493 F.2d 507 (5th Cir. 1974).

Rhoades, C. & Browning, P. (1977). Normalization at what price? *Mental Retardation, 15,* 24.

Roos, S. (1978). The future of residential services for the mentally retarded in the United States: A delphi study. *Mental Retardation, 16,* 355–356.

Scheerenberger, R. C. (1975a). *Administrative problems.* Madison, WI: National Association of Superintendents of Public Residential Facilities.

Scheerenberger, R. C. (1975b). *Managing residential facilities for the developmentally disabled.* Springfield, IL: Charles C. Thomas.

Scheerenberger, R. C. (1976). *Deinstitutionalization and institutional reform.* Springfield, IL: Charles C. Thomas.

Scheerenberger, R. C. (1979). *Public residential services for the mentally retarded.* Madison, WI: National Association of Superintendents of Public Residential Facilities for the Mentally Retarded.

Scheerenberger, R. C. (1982). *Public residential services for the mentally retarded.* Madison, WI: National Association of Superintendents of Public Residential Facilities for the Mentally Retarded.

Scheerenberger, R. C., & Jones, E. (1980). *Administrative problems.* Madison, WI: National Association of Superintendents of Public Residential Facilities for the Mentally Retarded.

Schwartz, C. (1977). Normalization and idealism. *Mental Retardation, 15,* 38–39.

Shestack, J. (1974). Psychiatry and the dilemmas of dual loyalties. *American Bar Association Journal, 60,* 1521–1524.

Standards for Residential Facilities for the Mentally Retarded. (1971). Joint Commission on Accreditation of Hospitals.

Throne, J. M. (1979). Deinstitutionalization: Too wide a swath. *Mental Retardation, 17,* 171–175.

Townsend, R. (1970). *Up the organization.* Greenwich, CT: Fawcett.

Wagner, B. (1979). *The future of institutions from a system analysis point of view.* Madison, WI: National Association of Superintendents of Public Residential Facilities for the Mentally Retarded.

Wildavsky, A. (1964). *The politics of the budgetary process.* New York: Little, Brown.

Wolfensberger, W. (1971). Will there always be an institution? II: The impact of new service models. *Mental Retardation, 9,* 31–38.

Wyatt v. Stickney, 325 F. Supp. 781 (M.D. Ala. 1971).

3 The Direct-Care Worker: A Socio-cultural Analysis

Jack Thaw, Ph.D.
Scott F. Wolfe, M.A.

INTRODUCTION: THE PRINCIPAL OTHERS

The drawing taped on the wall in the residential unit's living room is a client's self-portrait. The artist has his likeness speak these words: "I love the aides." There is a simple but uncommon grace to the drawing but a perspective as well. Through the prism of the mentally handicapped client's view, the direct-care worker, the aide, is the linkage with life. For many such clients, it will not be otherwise in the foreseeable future whether public residential facilities remain as they are, undergo revision, or are disassembled in favor of smaller facilities.

Direct-care staff, variously called attendants, aides, or client care workers, are the largest group of personnel that has ever served mentally handicapped individuals in public systems of care. They are the most important figures in the lives of clients in residential facilities. Even as many larger, total care facilities have been deinstitutionalized into smaller, community-based settings, some variation or derivative of the direct-care role has remained central to client services (e.g., Glahn & Chock, 1984; Slater & Bunyard, 1983). It seems likely that the men and women in these positions will continue to be "principal others" in the client's existence. This present and future significance advises the discussion in this chapter.

Client Habilitation and Direct-Care Workers

It is broadly understood that the direct-care role is critical to the treatment and habilitative services provided to mentally handicapped clients both in the larger public residential facilities (e.g., Bensberg & Barnett, 1966; Burgio, Whitman,

& Reid, 1983; Quilitch, 1975) and in community residential settings (e.g., Baker, Seltzer, & Seltzer, 1977; Landesman-Dwyer, Sackett, & Kleinman, 1980; Slater & Bunyard, 1983). Residential staff behavior, interaction patterns, and orientation to program services have been demonstrated to have a strong relationship to the behavioral growth of clients (e.g., Eyman & Call, 1977; Mayhew, Enyart, & Anderson, 1978). It is clear that future program initiatives in residential facilities will, in large part, depend on the performance of these personnel for success. Their history, attitudes, norms, practices, and working conditions will be active variables in this process.

Although the empirical evidence supporting these ideas is more recent, for years it has been recognized that direct-care staff cannot be taken lightly in the provision of services to clients. Earlier observers of institutions (e.g., Belknap, 1956; Cumming & Cumming, 1957; Goffman, 1961; Stanton & Schwartz, 1954) noted the relationship between staff attitudes and program effectiveness as well as the affects of programmatic "intrusions" on staff morale. Attendants historically have regarded program professionals with suspicion and disapproval (e.g., Klaber, 1970). Their capacity to oppose programmatic interventions and to control the outcomes of such efforts always has been considerable inasmuch as they own most of the clients' time and space (e.g., Bogdan, Taylor, deGrandpre, & Haynes, 1974; Cleland & Dingman 1970; Scheff, 1961). Later in the discussion we describe the practice of staff resistance and the choice to engage it.

In recent years, much attention has been devoted to improving the performance of residential staff as service providers (e.g., Prue, Frederiksen, & Bacon, 1978). This work has utilized the procedures of applied behavior analysis (Baer, Wolf, & Risley, 1968). Initial efforts sought to teach staff new job skills, but the training was not maintained by staff in their day-to-day work routine (Whitman, Scibak, & Reid, 1983). Recent studies have addressed skill acquisition and maintenance in the daily job situation. Reid and Whitman (1983) have provided a thorough review of this research. They report effectiveness in improving several specific areas of staff performance utilizing such approaches as feedback procedures (e.g., Greene, Willis, Levy, & Bailey, 1978); modeling (e.g., Gladstone & Spencer, 1977); lottery contingencies (e.g., Iwata, Bailey, Brown, Foshee, & Alpern, 1976); and multifaceted procedures combining several techniques (e.g., Korabek, Reid, & Ivancic, 1981).

In evaluating this body of research with direct-care staff, Reid & Whitman (1983) reached several conclusions that will help develop the focus of this discussion. Despite considerable progress in the development of technical procedures to improve staff performance, they do not believe behavior management practices can be considered scientifically validated or ready for general clinical use. Some of their reasons involve methodological concerns. Results have not been replicated across different settings, staff, and clients; long-term effectiveness of most procedures has been largely unanalyzed; there has been minimal examination of increased client benefits resulting from interventions with staff.

(Chapter 7 of this volume describes a project that provided both long-term follow-up and an evaluation of client improvement.)

Reid & Whitman (1983) raise three additional concerns that bear upon historical and socio-cultural factors of the direct care role. First, the acceptability of these procedures by staff and supervisors, even when the results are favorable, seems questionable. Some of the studies reviewed (e.g., Seys & Duker, 1978) reported staff resistance and strong negative staff reactions to the behavioral management interventions. Staff acceptability has not been well addressed as an empirical matter, and thus little is formally known about the apparent broad-based rejection (e.g., Mayhew, Enyart, & Cone, 1979) of behavioral management interventions at the primary care level in residential facilities.

A second question concerns supervisory personnel and whether the requirements to implement these management procedures are prohibitive, given their own job roles and responsibilities. What may be at issue here is whether the technology developed thus far is too cumbersome to install as a normative practice. If so, it would be useful to examine the competition of other demands and changes being imposed at the direct-care and supervisory levels, another matter we pursue later.

The third, and perhaps most important, conclusion of the Reid and Whitman (1983) review of the literature is that the ''natural'' contingencies that shape and maintain the daily work behavior of direct-care staff require systematic examination. They imply that these contingencies may control the performance of staff in providing program services. They suggest that some of the controlling variables may include the following: (a) the effects of peer models (e.g., more tenured staff); (b) the number of job responsibilities for which the direct care worker is held accountable; (c) management's use of civil service regulations such as service ratings, disciplinary actions, and merit benefits; and (d) the effects of supervisory, administrative, and professional interactions with direct-care staff.

To examine these three areas of concern is, in effect, to address the beliefs, values, norms, rules, and practices that govern the workplace of direct-care employees in residential facilities. These may be viewed as internal factors because they are restricted to the direct-care membership and are closely guarded there. Historically, access to such internal domains by outsiders has been difficult. One purpose of this chapter is to explore the operation and effects of these factors based upon long-term access to them.

The findings of the Reid and Whitman (1983) review disclaim any widespread adoption of behavioral management approaches to improve staff performance in client habilitation. What, then, are the prevailing approaches or orientations of direct-care workers to their jobs and their clients? Empirical evidence is beginning to emerge in response to this question, both for the traditional public residential facilities and community residential facilities. These recent studies are instructive because most of them report information obtained subsequent to the incorporation of judicial, legislative, and other regulatory requirements for provision of habilitative services (e.g., Crosby, 1976; Martin, 1979) by most systems of care in the last decade. These requirements mandate the provision of active treatment to clients as a matter of job definition for direct-care workers. Thus these studies provide some formal indications about the effect of the requirements on staff practices at the residential level. In one of the earlier studies of staff-client interaction patterns, Veit, Allen and Chinsky (1976) reported that of 7,790 interactions observed over a 7-week period, 68.3% of all staff-initiated activities with clients occurred in the context of custodial tasks. Formal training of clients was the least observed situation (8.9% of staff-initiated activities). In the great majority of interactions with clients, staff issued instructions or commands reflecting directive or supervisory aspects of the attendant's role. When clients took the initiative to interact with staff, they were ignored nearly one third of the time. The authors reported these patterns were observed with considerable stability over the 7 weeks.

Repp and Barton (1980) used a somewhat similar observational procedure to determine whether residential units (in a large state institution) that were licensed under ICF/MR guidelines differed from unlicensed units in terms of the active programming behaviors of staff and clients. The intent of the guidelines (Crosby, 1976) and the funding program that supports them is to provide both a system of active programming for clients and added resources to implement that system. Data yielding about 160,000 observations across 16 days revealed virtually no difference between licensed and unlicensed units—both were seriously deficient in providing habilitative programming. For licensed and unlicensed units alike, staff were found not interacting at all with the clients for the overwhelming percentage of the observations recorded. For the two licensed units, no programming was recorded 77% and 98% of the time; for the six unlicensed units, this figure ranged from 92% to 99%. The authors describe their results as extremely discouraging and conclude that facilities can be licensed under ICF/MR and better resourced as a result yet still not provide habilitation for their clients. Despite available teaching and training technologies, many developmentally disabled clients in residential facilities remain unaffected—the direct-care staff are not using these methods even at modest levels.

Other observers (e.g., Cullari, 1984; Favell, Favell, Riddle, & Risley, 1984; Realon, Lewallen, & Wheeler, 1983) suggest that these findings are representative of the general condition in large residential facilities. There is growing evidence that parallel conditions exist in community residential facilities as well. Landesman-Dwyer, Sackett and Kleinman (1980) observed the daily behavior of 240 mentally retarded clients and 75 staff members in 20 community group homes of varying sizes. Among several findings, they report less than 1% of staff members' behavior fell into categories typically associated with a training orientation (e.g., praising, rewarding, assisting). They point to a great need to encourage and train residential staff to perform more effectively with clients.

In a self-report survey of primary-care providers in community residential facilities, Slater and Bunyard (1983) found that the majority of respondents viewed their basic role as fulfilling maintenance responsibilities such as housekeeping, bookkeeping, and meeting clients' life-sustaining needs. Fewer than 25% viewed their primary responsibility as training, and fewer than 50% could correctly define or illustrate basic training concepts. No respondent was able to identify all eight components of an individual habilitation plan (IHP) as contained in Public Law 95–602 (1978). Slater and Bunyard suggest that providing a well-trained residential staff may prove to be a most difficult goal to meet in the development of a community-based service system for developmentally disabled clients. Importantly, they emphasize the need to begin identifying elements of effective client-direct care staff relationships occurring on a moment-to-moment, day-to-day basis, a conclusion similar to that reached by Reid and Whitman (1983). The development of sophisticated training curricula should follow, not precede, this attention to daily interaction patterns.

In a national survey of some 2,000 community residential facility administrators, Bruininks, Kudla, Wieck, and Hauber (1980) reported that recruitment of qualified staff, reduction of staff turnover, and staff training were the most pressing difficulties for respondents. George and Baumeister (1981) found a significant problem of controllable turnover of direct-care staff in a random sample of 21 small and large community residential facilities. Turnover problems have also been reported by others (e.g., Hung & Drash, 1984; Landesman-Dwyer et al., 1980; Slater & Bunyard, 1983). George and Baumeister also found generally low job satisfaction and major deficiencies in staff training and personnel management practices. They present additional information suggesting that employee morale and stability problems become more critical when staff are working with severely handicapped clients who present behavior problems as well. If this finding is supported by further research, it has implications for the general system of community residential services. If deinstitutionalization is to continue, more severely impaired and behaviorally disordered clients will be placed in community settings requiring, in each location, a stable corps of well-trained staff to meet their needs.

These community studies do not discredit the moral and ideological intentions of community-based residential settings or the clear gains made by many clients in these settings, especially where carefully designed programs exist (see Christian, Hannah, & Glahn, 1984, for examples). However, they do indicate the presence of distinct problems in establishing an habilitative role for direct-care staff in these facilities, both with respect to training staff and sustaining treatment-focused performance over time. Taken together with the direct-care studies in the larger, more traditional public residential facilities, these data prompt the conclusion that active habilitative treatment has been embraced by primary care providers neither as a belief nor as daily practice. Despite the presence of treatment methodologies usable by these staff, utilization apparently is not a normative job theme in many, perhaps most, residential facilities. The major questions to be addressed in this chapter may be developed from this state of affairs.

The Issues

There is a suggestion running through both the formal empirical studies and the earlier essays on direct-care staff that we simply do not understand these workers well, especially in the longitudinal sense of their job experience. It has been our personal experience that many of those people planning habilitative program interventions and many of those assigned to implement them are largely uninformed about direct care staff and the forces that surround their work lives. These planners and implementers thus are likely to misdiagnose staffs' actions in response both to their interventions and their intervention behavior. The failure to transform the traditional direct-care role into a broadly accepted habilitative role is due, at least in part, to these shortcomings.

To sharpen the focus, we argue that administrators, program managers, professionals, and any others who would reform client services at the residential level first will have to acquire a highly developed operational and historical understanding of direct-care workers in at least four respects: (a) as members of an autonomous social system within the organization; (b) as the lowest point in the facility bureaucracy; (c) as possible and worthy opponents of change; and (d) as potential allies in effecting durable program reform. Next, they will have to develop a diagnostic sensitivity to the attitudes, concerns, anxieties, and conflicts of these workers. Finally, they will have to use this understanding to build stable, meaningful work relationships with staff over longer units of time, not just for the run of a specific program intervention and not restricted only to the content of a specific program intervention.

All this insists that establishing habilitative treatment as normative activity at the residential level will require viewing direct care personnel as co-owners of these services rather than as reluctant technicians or implementers of procedures designed within the compound of the professional community. Their trust and support, both crucial to successful program interventions, will depend on this ownership. Although there has been philosophical and conceptual endorsement for this position (e.g., Crosby, 1976), there appears to be limited application in practice. These matters seem to have been bypassed or underemphasized in reported efforts to improve the work performance of direct-care staff in delivering habilitative services (e.g., Reid & Shoemaker, 1984; Reid & Whitman, 1983).

McCord's (1982) observations are instructive on these arguments and help frame the specific agenda of the discussion that follows. Writing about the acceptance in practice of the normalization principle (Nirje, 1969), McCord states that normalization radically redefines the traditional social functions of human service agencies. Thus, administrators and direct service personnel react to it as if their work paradigm (i.e., their construction of a human service reality) were under assault. It seems reasonable to raise the equivalent question about habilitative program interventions at the residential level: Despite the noble intentions of the interventionists and the rightfulness of the programs for the client's welfare, are these efforts experienced by staff as assaults on their "constructions" of human service realities?

McCord (1982) develops the issue further in reference to the difficulties of achieving maximal physical and social integration of disabled people into community life. He states, "The *acceptance* (italics added) of disabled persons into community life is far more a matter of people's perceptions of its meaningfulness and importance (to them) than of their ability to learn new ideas or their willingness to do the 'right thing' " (p. 252). It may be argued that the same would be true for direct-care workers' acceptance of the integration of habilitative program themes into their community. If so, it is understandable that the research reported to date, emphasizing as it has staff's learning of new ideas (i.e., program technologies) over the meaningfulness and importance of the programming to the staff, has encountered problems with acceptance.

McCord (1982) suggests that adoption of major new human service paradigms will be hampered by the history of any competing functions. Acceptance of the new paradigm, then, becomes less a problem of finding the correct technological solution than of guiding an evolutionary process rooted in the historical concepts, practices, and images of those affected. The performance of active habilitation treatment by direct-care workers is, for them, a major new paradigm that competes both with the history of their role in residential facilities and with their present construction of human service reality. Converting them to accepting the new paradigm would seem to require, at a minimum, understanding the competing history, the factors governing the evolutionary process, and the present construction of human service reality at the direct care level.

All these considerations can be organized into four areas of understanding and ability that may be viewed as required competencies for those individuals who seek to install enduring, stable program reforms at the residential level:

1. *The operation and effects of factors that govern the day-to-day patterns of activity in the direct-care work place.* These are the beliefs, values, norms, rules, and practices observed by members of the direct-care community and responsible for the evolution of their images of human service at the residential level.

2. *The effects of almost 2 decades of accelerated change in residential facilities.* This change has, at least in an official sense, revised most of the traditions and practices of the direct-care role. The focus here is the experience of the direct-care community during the transition from decades of historical motionlessness during the first half of this century to a period characterized by rapid

rates of change in areas such as client advocacy and human rights, technological advances, treatment methods, legislative reform, judicial intervention, and organizational management approaches.

3. *The errors associated with the introduction of program interventions in the residential unit.* The subject matter here is the process through which staff expectancies about performing formal habilitative treatment duties were developed and impressions about program specialists were formed.

4. *The interpersonal, social, and political strategies to be utilized in gaining staff acceptance of program interventions.* Attention is addressed to managing the interventionist's behavior in an effort to overcome staff resistance and to secure staff collaboration. The approach will emphasize constructing stable and meaningful work relationships over longer units of time.

We shall consider each of these areas in some detail and through the historical context from which their importance emerged. There is little hard data on these matters, as Reid and Whitman (1983) and Slater and Bunyard (1983) have noted. Our information is gathered from several sources. Both of us have worked closely with direct-care staff in residential facilities for almost 25 years collectively. One of us (S.F.W.) was employed as an attendant in a traditional setting for an extended period. Additionally, we have interviewed and informally discussed our subject matter with literally hundreds of direct-care workers over nearly a decade. Some of these men and women we knew for brief periods of time; a great many of our respondents became close working associates over long periods of time. For the latter, we had what amounts to intimate access to the internal work life of their residential units, access typically denied to most outsiders. For several years, we also conducted a practicum for college students that required, in part, that they work as direct-care staff for several months across first, second, and even third shift. They, too, earned their "rights of passage" with direct-care staff and this, incidentally, became another source of information. The principal purpose of their staff experience was to develop a higher level of acceptance by the regular staff when program interventions were subsequently introduced. This was achieved in virtually all cases.

In sum, although our information does not qualify as formal empirical data, it does provide a sense of the issues at question as seen from the perspective of direct-care workers themselves. In many ways, what follows is their viewpoint about the residential facility for mentally handicapped individuals and the people who endeavor to reform it.

It is necessary to mention at the outset that, in our personal experience, the overwhelming majority of direct-care workers in residential facilities are courageous and effective human service providers, sometimes miracle workers. They do, often with unnoticed skill and care, what generations of communities had decided were the useless tasks of servicing a handicapped population that those same generations had rejected as socially unworthy. As we argue firmly later in the discussion, the potential of direct-care staff as a corps of habilitators for even the most severely disabled clients is enormous. However, they all share a role history designed in large part by our nation's own social history and views about handicapped people. We intend to describe, not judge, the patterns of belief and practice that evolved from that history. We do so candidly, in the hope that the reader will know our admiration, respect, and confidence in these men and women.

SOME OUTCOMES OF THE HISTORICAL DEVELOPMENT OF THE DIRECT CARE ROLE

In their book, *Educational Handicap, Public Policy, and Social History,* Sarason and Doris (1979) argue that mental retardation is not comprehensible apart from American social history, culture, and values. The direct-care worker, in many ways, bears the imprint of our culture's views about the persons we have identified as mentally handicapped. Nearly 100 years of varying beliefs and practices regarding mentally handicapped persons are etched in the roles we have assigned to direct-care workers, the places we have provided for them to work, the assistance we have placed at their disposal, the wages we have offered them, and many other dimensions of their experience. This conclusion is inescapable as one reviews works of various social scientists who have examined public residential institutions (e.g., Allen, Chinsky, & Veit, 1974; Blatt, Ozolins, & McNally, 1978; Bogdan & Taylor, 1976; Braginsky & Braginsky, 1971; Goffman, 1961; Scheerenberger, 1982; Stanton & Schwartz, 1954; Ullmann, 1967; Vail, 1966; Veit, Allen & Chinsky, 1976; Wolfensberger, 1969). Perhaps more than anyone else, even the parent, the direct-care worker reflects the culture's choices about the mentally handicapped individual.

We do not present here a chronological account of either the care and treatment of mentally handicapped citizens or their caretakers. Competent reviews are available elsewhere (e.g., Scheerenberger, 1982; Vail, 1966; Wolfensberger, 1969). Instead, we describe the *outcomes* of that history that became resilient social and political norms in the direct-care community of virtually every public residential facility in the country and persisted there for decades. It seems safe to suggest that some elements of these norms continue to exert influence in "reformed" residential facilities of today. In some facilities, no doubt they exist nearly intact. There is also evidence to suggest their present influence in community residential settings (e.g., Bruininks et al., 1980; George & Baumeister, 1981; Slater & Bunyard, 1983). Thus, attempts to introduce program reform at any residential level can be expected to encounter these normative patterns of behavior and belief.

We have selected several aspects of work life in the direct-care community that representatively embrace these historical outcomes. For the most part, our descriptions are in the present tense to emphasize their active implications for competing interventions.

Pre-Service Training and the Direct-Care Routine

Despite the questions that have been raised about the usefulness and generalizability of pre-service training programs (e.g., Ziarnik & Bernstein, 1982), most new staff members begin their employment at this point. The pre-service experience usually provides an overview of the facility's mission, its organization, and its clients. The curriculum typically includes several areas of instruction: (a) a summary of the etiologies of developmental disabilities; (b) basic client care techniques such as feeding, taking a temperature, hygiene procedure, and so on; (c) upkeep of the residential environment; (d) procedures for handling emergency situations; (e) important policies and regulations; and (f) a basic overview (usually a film, lecture, or demonstration) of behavioral training methods.

One clear purpose of the pre-service program is to communicate to the new staff members a sense of optimism about working with mentally handicapped clients. This is done by emphasizing the developmental nature of the handicap and the potential of the clients to learn. Another purpose is to emphasize that the direct-care job is vital to the organization and requires training (Bensberg, Barnett, & Hurder, 1964). After completing the pre-service program, which can range from a few days to a few weeks, new staff are sent to their initial residential unit assignment, where a process of acculturation begins.

It is not uncommon for the first few weeks on the job to fall short of pre-service expectations. In many facilities, new staff will confront an established routine and a tightly knit social system that preserves that routine. It has been described as a lonely, frightening, and disillusioning experience (Cleland & Peck, 1967), made uncomfortable by strong pressure to conform to traditional, custodial-oriented routines (Allen, Chinsky, & Veit, 1974). These routines are at the core of the acculturation process and probably can be found in some parts of most facilities. The routines come to dominate the workers' day, tend to discourage their initiating new activities, and may serve to maintain the status quo against change through rigid task schedules, written rules for performance, and unwritten norms for behavior (Goffman, 1961; Rappaport, Chinsky, & Cowen, 1971). The routine also can reduce uncertainty about job performance through the standardization of a predictable set of basic tasks. In short, the routine facilitates order.

In many facilities, four characteristics of the residential unit routine account for most of the staff member's daily job behavior. The first is the predominance of custodial chores that must be done. Though it varies considerably from setting to setting, the majority of staff time is still today likely to be spent performing custodial jobs. This not only includes washing floors, scrubbing bathroom fixtures, and doing laundry, but may also spread to interactions with clients. A custodial emphasis applied to clients means performing tasks *for* them. For example, on a unit for severely mentally retarded clients, a new staff member may be taught and then required to dress clients, to brush their teeth, to toilet them, to wash their hands and face, and to feed them. It's quick, it's efficient. Teaching the clients to dress themselves, to brush their own teeth, and so on is less quick, less efficient, and often not encouraged by senior or tenured staff, except in some specialized or model program units.

A second characteristic of many routines is what has been called by many direct-care staff ''the rush to do nothing.'' New staff often are puzzled why veteran staff rush to get their chores done, only to find that when the chores are completed, there is little to do but stand around. For example, on a unit for profoundly retarded adult males where one of the authors worked, it was common practice to group 20 to 30 clients together and escort them to the dining hall for breakfast. Their meal would last about 20 minutes; then they would be taken back to the day hall. It was now time for showering. Two attendants would put about 15 clients through the shower, soap them up, rinse and dry them, and send them to the dormitory to be dressed. When dressed, they would be put back on the day hall—to do nothing! All of this took from about 7:30 to 8:45 in the morning. There was ''no time'' to systematically train independent eating, showering, or dressing skills. Instead, to the new staff member, there seemed to be one overriding concern for the staff: get to the first coffee break by 8:45!

A third aspect of unit routines is really the consequence of this rush to do nothing: an idleness of activity for both clients and attendants. In fact, several studies have documented that the most typical activity of many direct-care staff is idleness, or a lack of interaction between attendants and clients (e.g., Repp & Barton, 1980; Veit, Allen, & Chinsky, 1976). Sometimes for hours, clients move through nonhabilitative cycles of idle or stereotypic behaviors while the staff on duty stand or sit by.

A final characteristic often observed as part of the routine is the modeling effect of tenured and experienced staff. The new employee watches closely as the veteran attendant interacts with clients and runs the routines. Modeling by senior staff can be negative at times. To illustrate, the first day on the job for one new employee was filled with such modeling incidents. In the living area, he was told that no client was to sit on the staff's table. The penalty for doing so was a loud reprimand. Having watched other staff yell at clients for this trespass, the new employee understood that he had better start following ''the procedure.'' So when he saw a client sit on the table, instead of ignoring him (which is what he wanted to do), he reprimanded the client. Later, in the dining hall, he tried to get a client to feed himself. Across the table, another client stole food. The supervising attendant called to the employee, ''Feed him yourself, and if that guy steals food, remove him from the dining hall.'' After observing the supervising attendant removing clients from the dining hall, the new employee followed suit. It also seemed appropriate to stop teaching self-feeding, which wasn't winning any friendships with the senior staff. Similar modeling effects may hold for other activities as well.

Of course, there are also instances of constructive modeling. Our point here is that, in an indeterminate number of residential units, negative modeling has, over the years, come to set some norms for client care activities and interactions. These norms may be difficult to undo even when client care ideologies change. At the bottom line, the negative modeling seems related to job survival. Residential environments, especially those for severely disabled or behaviorally disordered clients, can be highly stressful places to work large blocks of time continuously. In such situations, getting the minimally acceptable amount of work done in the fastest time can be adaptive. If it is, the pressures to conform to these adaptive behaviors will be strong. When this happens, the incoming optimism for working with and teaching clients generated by the employees' pre-service training is compromised.

In addition to being acculturated by fellow employees, the new direct-care worker often is acculturated by the clients themselves (Cleland & Peck, 1967). Over time, a recurring pattern of interactions (or noninteractions) emerges in which behavioral expectations are created by both clients and staff. Certain client behaviors can be expected more than others to generate responses from direct-care workers. For example, in the past, when residential units typically had client-to-staff ratios on the order of 15:1, a client defecating on the floor was more likely to occasion the staff's attention than if that client independently and appropriately voided on the toilet. The client thus learned to defecate inappropriately because this behavior received attention. In a similar manner, new staff may come to rely on behaviors that elicit predictable responses from clients; for example, responses that contribute to an orderly, disciplined residential unit.

The comparative influence of the unit acculturation process over the formal pre-service training model can be substantial in many public residential facilities. There is little evidence to suggest that pre-service or in-service training results in improved staff behavior and more appropriate staff-client interactions (Ziarnik & Bernstein, 1982). Roos (1970) proposed that a possible reason is that a small group of attendants and supervisors undermine the pre-service training program by controlling staff behavior. We agree but argue further that the influence of the unit model over the pre-service program goes beyond a system of controls over staff behavior. Faced with a daily schedule that is at least tedious and sometimes quite stressful, new client care workers require structure and assistance to carry them through. They observe those who have established their routines, witness their apparently successful coping behaviors, and soon adopt the routine as their own. Gradually, sometimes even quickly, their actual job behavior drifts considerably from the job expectancies held at the conclusion of pre-service training. We have observed this discrepancy countless times. Energies readied for client habilitation and change may become invested in a long established regimen of noncreative care. What is happening here is more than a simple result of imposed control by a few veteran staff attendants. It is more systemic. The new direct-care employees are not merely yielding to a few constraints on their enthusiasm. They are actively developing a loyalty.

There are some important implications in this picture for program specialists and administrators. It may be risky to construct a set of optimistic expectations for new staff about their work with mentally handicapped people (as most formal pre-service training programs attempt to do), and then deliver the reality described. The risk is the precedent it establishes for these staff. The pre-service training assurances may be but the first in a line of unfulfilled expectations. Other expectations (including programming) will be thrust upon the units by administrators and professionals. Each of these new ideas, goals, or procedures inevitably will collide with the specific realities that exist on each unit. In each case, for the direct-care worker, skepticism and doubt may be what will be reinforced. The surviving and usable expectations may become limited to the order, sameness, and stability of the routine itself. Nothing may be able to compete effectively with it, not even larger amounts of resources such as those available under programs like ICF/MR.

Bureaucratic Organization and Direct-Care Staff

Residential facilities are bureaucratic organizations displaying most of the structural and operational characteristics associated with such places (Scheerenberger, 1975). With respect to formal power, mobility, status, and wages, direct-care staff sit at the base of the organization. This condition affects their perceptions about the rest of the organization and its mission. It also influences their response to planned change and program reform. For many of these men and women, their image of human service has been shaped by their experience with the human service organization. In this section we explore briefly the bureaucratic organization of the residential facility as experienced by direct care workers.

Experience with Administration.   The direct-care view of administrative function and of administrative personnel develops from a contradiction and the organization's response to it. Even with recent advances in treatment methodologies, human services to developmentally handicapped individuals still rely on uncertain technologies producing interventions of uncertain efficacy and durability (e.g., Baumeister, 1981). The application of these services by the organization is further complicated by changing, often impatient, demands for results coming from a diverse community of influences such as federal courts, advocacy groups, legislative regulations, parents, and so forth. This elevates the levels of uncertainty and confusion experienced by the service providers. The contradiction occurs because a principal administrative response to these legitimate conditions of uncertainty has been to act as if they were not uncertain. As Mechanic

(1973) suggests, administrators under scrutiny from external sources are unwilling to advertise their limitations. Instead, it is often essential to their political survival that they exaggerate their accomplishments and command over the facility's operation and direction, and they are thus encouraged to impose control and order.

There are many ways to achieve order and control. For example, policies, directives, and rules can be developed to prescribe clear, "certain" procedures in various domains of staff performance and client care. Professionals and middle-level managers can be assigned the task of reducing uncertainty by developing "solutions" or "programs" for difficult and confusing problems. (In Chapter 4, we describe the dilemma this role presents to the professionals, who may themselves be uncertain.) Mintzberg (1979) has observed that under conditions of uncertainty plus strong external pressure, top management may also suspend democratic administrative approaches and centralize the decision-making process.

In short, the administrative response is first to avoid acknowledging the real and legitimate uncertainties associated with human service in residential facilities; and second to deny that the response to those conditions is contradictory. Direct-care staff experience the contradictions daily. As Mechanic (1973) suggests, staff see diffuse agency goals, unclear performance standards, and less than effective treatment procedures but are expected to behave as if this were not so. They hear official agency philosophies of shared decision making and participatory management, typically under the conceptual character of the interdisciplinary system, but they experience a tightly controlled, rule-governed organization to which they have minimal input. The contradictions for them are real. Their own responses tend to become cynicism and distrust.

Rogers (1975) has argued that direct-care staff feel victimized by those who control the institution. Our interviews and experience with these staff confirm this. For example, direct-care staff report few rewards, such as promotions or recognition, contingent upon commendable job performance, yet they describe the organization's response to substandard performance as precise, often severe. They characterize themselves as recipients of arbitrary, conflicting, often unexplained decisions coming from multiple levels of supervisors, managers, and professionals. Historically, these and other staff perceptions are deeply rooted in actual events. For example, until recently it was not uncommon for an attendant to be penalized for some minor transgression by being sent to a "punishment unit," a back ward with aggressive clients.

Another historical outcome is that staff learn never to question openly the decisions handed down from the administrative and medical hierarchy. Although this has changed somewhat with the growth of labor unions in residential facilities, the learned response is now applied to confirm negative perceptions about administrators and supervisors, even where these views are unjustified. Direct-care workers often choose not to test their impressions of being victimized, even when they can. Where opportunities exist to request explanations for decisions or to clarify administrative intent, they reject the chance, infer a conclusion, and thus seal-in the perception.

Like many beliefs and practices backed by historical momentum, these perceptions about administration do not come unstuck easily. Even in more enlightened residential facilities today, inadequately trained supervisors and middle-level managers confirm these views on a daily basis. Where direct-care staff hold these beliefs strongly, we find they rely more heavily on the traditional routine described earlier. In the face of the uncertainties described and distrusting administrative intent and action, they retreat to what is safe, predictable, and certain. It is adaptive, if not logical, behavior.

Experience with Communication. Communication processes have long been of interest to organization specialists (e.g., Haas & Drabek, 1973; Schein, 1969). Mechanic (1973) advises that human service organizations should develop a theory or set of perspectives about what the agency is supposed to be doing. Such a model should include a clear sense of the limitations and constraints under which the agency must work. To these recommendations we would add that the organization should develop a coherent association between its mission, goals, and limitations on the one hand, and the priorities and performance requirements of staff on the other. This association should be reliably understood by staff so that they can identify their efforts with some larger notions of achievement.

Seen from the direct-care level of the facility's bureaucracy, these necessary communications do not occur. Staff awareness of the overall mission of the facility often is poor, making it difficult for them to identify with it. For example, in many facilities, concepts such as active programming and the interdisciplinary approach (see Crosby, 1976) were introduced very rapidly, often to capture federal reimbursement funds under the Title XIX, ICF/MR program (U.S. Department of Health, Education, & Welfare, 1974). The paper transitions occurred quickly, but the role and job adjustments for staff were more difficult. Some facilities literally sent teams of managers on a quick sweep of all units to explain the new goals and concepts. From that point on, the facilities acted as if the changes were both understood and embraced by the direct care staff, although neither was true. With goal changes and job requirements unclear, many staff members found a stricter adherence to the daily routine a graspable way to handle the situation.

This kind of communication experience is rooted in three problems. First, unlike industrial organizations, where most goals are specific, quantifiable, and product oriented, goals in human service organizations often are plural and less quantifiable (Maloof, 1975). "To normalize the lives of mentally handicapped clients"; "to provide active treatment"; "to prepare clients for community placement''—these are lofty goals but difficult to define operationally for staff and to measure against success criteria in their jobs. Behavior modification specialists, whose technologies require precisely operationalized objectives, often have been surprised to find that direct-care workers do not experience the same kind of clarity about behavioral goals. Similarly, major developments in the field of developmental disability typically are not well understood by many direct-care staff. For years, the important landmark case, *Wyatt v. Stickney* (1971), has been well known to most professionals and administrators, but most direct-care workers do not have a clear reference point for it in their daily experience. Where communications about these sorts of issues are not well developed, supervised, and evaluated for understanding by recipients, we have observed that direct-care staff tend to dismiss them as irrelevant to their working realities.

This suggests the second problem: managerial and supervisory competency in communication skills. Put candidly, too many managers and supervisors, especially at middle levels in the organization, do not communicate well, either in writing or orally, individually or in groups. The strongest deficits seem to be in asking questions, listening skills, and feedback abilities. For example, direct-care workers often report that their supervisors do not invite inquiry into important messages or new information. It is not difficult to understand why direct-care staff find their facility connected more reliably by rumor tracks than by official lines of information flow. Once again, these conditions tend to diminish the credibility of the bureaucratic organization for the primary care providers.

The third difficulty develops from the public human service organization's general reluctance to advertise its uncertainties and shortcomings. Rather than assist direct-care staff in coming to terms with the changing, often turbulent, nature of the contemporary residential facility and therefore the "non-permanence" of many new occurrences in their work setting, many of those responsible for communicating new information, procedures, policies, and so forth to staff mistakenly promote the expectation that the particular changes are permanent. Indeed, they may well believe it themselves. Over time, however, as the direct-care staff become repeatedly exposed to expectancies of permanent changes and experience that contradicts it, their belief in and use of the organization's formal communication system is undermined. (See Chapter 1 for an extended discussion of this and other effects.)

Experience with Rules.   Residential facilities have evolved over many decades into heavily rule-bound organizations. If one examines the archives of a particular facility, the various periods in its history often can be identified by layers of rules and procedures, each reflecting the thrust of its time. Typically, more rules are added than are discarded. In one facility, nearly 200 administrative and personnel procedures were introduced over a 4-year period, although only a handful were discontinued. In Connecticut, a state policy regulating the use of behavior modification methodologies contained 115 pages of procedural standards.

Bureaucratic organizations tend to establish rules to regulate and standardize the activities of their employees. Mechanic (1973) describes the function of rules as defining expected behavior under ordinary circumstances. As such, an organization's rule system guides proper behavior and deters improper behavior. For these functions to be effective, the rules must be seen as instrumental to job performance by those subject to their guidance. "When rules proliferate mindlessly and deal with every triviality, they tend to lose their power of guidance. . . . When persons are required to violate numerous rules to do their ordinary work, the rules themselves may become debased. . ." (Mechanic, 1973, p. 159).

This appears to have been the experience with organizational rules for many direct-care workers in residential facilities. Their daily activity is regulated by multiple sets of rules. For example, beyond the expected scheduling, work assignment, and personnel rules associated with most organizations, they face rules for enforcing residential fire and safety code standards; health code standards for storage and use of clients' clothes, towels, toothbrushes, etc.; rules governing therapeutic and safety restraint of assaultive clients; rules for repositioning bedridden and wheelchair clients; rules for infection control and preventive health procedures; rules for food handling; and rules to safeguard client rights. There are countless other rules, coming from many independent sources in the facility, that guide or control the direct-care worker's day. We have found it instructive to follow staff members through one day, observing their obligations to just one source of rules, for example, the documentation and procedural requirements under the ICF/MR program. The experience can disarm the most compulsive rule followers.

All these rules are intended to insure order and consistency in essential client care. Clearly, this is accomplished to varying degrees across individual facilities. Yet, many residential facilities seem less aware of the extent to which the growing system of rules is seen by direct-care staff as noninstrumental to the effective performance of their work. Even less attention is addressed to the gradual erosion of respect for rules as a general matter at the direct-care level. The responses that reflect this erosion are seldom public, often subtle, and always based in the direct-care staff's control over the residential unit's routine. We return to this matter in our discussion of staff resistance.

There are important lessons for program interventionists in this problem of rules being perceived as not facilitating job performance. To many direct-care workers, behavioral and other program procedures constitute more rules. If the particular staff have had the experience with rules described earlier, they are likely to judge additional rule sets unfavorably and to do so without a fair test. We know many program specialists who missed this point and were unable to manage the resistance that followed. In a similar way, the rule system imposed by the ICF/MR regulations has, in some facilities, forfeited its guidance function, with the result that required active treatment outcomes have been difficult to achieve.

Experience with Accountability.   Staff perception of formal accountability has evolved from the history of their role in the organization. Paul (1977) has suggested that accountability is the flow of responsibility in a particular organizational culture. It is a complex phenomenon that cannot be understood apart from that specific culture. Paul reasons that once assuming responsibility for the care of disabled persons, society, through its designated agencies (in this instance, residential facilities), institutionalized the means by which the responsibility was implemented. Thus it institutionalized the caregiving function into systematic, mechanistic routines that reflected a set of values and beliefs about the clientele and their needs. Over time, these routines were elaborated and stabilized into a sense of responsibility for the primary caregivers. This responsibility flowed from them, *through the routine,* to the clientele. We described the basic elements of this routine earlier. Its thrust is custodial, and it is decades long in momentum.

Despite the development of many conceptual and functional models of accountability to provide services reflecting *habilitative* values (e.g., Paul, 1977; Scheerenberger, 1975), the direct-care worker's sense of responsibility has remained fastened to the conventional routine. This is easily understood when one considers that the defining characteristics of their work structure and environment (i.e., long standing, stable, standardized, and repetitive routines occurring in relatively old and large settings) are not suited to adapting to new purposes (Mintzberg, 1981). Hence, many direct-care staff do not feel any conceptual accountability to habilitative purposes. Those who do attempt to conduct habilitative tasks often are simply reading the flow of power on their routine rather than embracing an habilitation-based sense of accountability.

It should be emphasized that the accountability anchored in the residential routine is unequivocal about responsibilities for clients' health, safety, and comfort. Indeed, the compassion and determination in exercising these obligations can be extraordinary.

The more equivocal response to responsibilities for clients' habilitation is also a function of the accountability arrangements that have come with the habilitative program systems. Historically, direct-care workers were responsible to one supervisor. It was a simple and predictable arrangement. With interdisciplinary systems as the principal organizational vehicle for habilitative services, staff have become accountable or partially accountable to many others as well: psychologists, occupational therapists, unit managers, human rights advocates, and even teams of specialists, monitors, or inspectors. It is not unusual for any one of those individuals or groups to impose requirements that conflict with or complicate those of another individual or group. The direct-care staff members are thus multiply subordinated, a condition not only confusing for them, but also threatening because they become potential explanations (or alibis) for the failure of subordinators to reach client habilitative goals in the residential unit. The call for a return to a single line of accountability for program systems in residential facilities (e.g., Favell et al., 1984) is well conceived.

An Autonomous Social System

The evolution of the residential facility created what amounts to a regional social group of primary-care providers. Over time, this group of employees developed characteristic patterns of behavior sufficient to distinguish itself from other groups in the organization. Embraced within this subculture (we use the term descriptively, not judgmentally) is a system of relationships, practices, and beliefs largely inaccessible to nonmembers. In this section we examine this autonomous social system through the direct-care workers' encounters with stress and morale difficulties and through their relationships with the principal members of the system: residential supervisors, fellow workers, and mentally handicapped clients.

Job behavior for direct-care staff is purposeful behavior. Among the purposes it promotes are daily social and occupational survival, protection from intrusion, and maintenance of stability. We have argued that the residential unit routine serves these purposes. The experiences with stress, morale, and social relationships are expressed through the routine often in an effort to control the job.

Stress and Morale.   The working world of a direct-care employee is alien to most people on a continuous basis. Even today, program personnel assigned directly to specific residential units spend significantly shorter blocks of time there than does the staff. Even with many units now normalized in appearance and with good programs of client activity, visitors to facilities for mentally handicapped people often are puzzled why anyone would want to work at a job that may tax the senses, press an individual against people with terrible handicaps and deformities, be at times physically dangerous, have little status, provide little recognition and much criticism, and promise meager opportunity for promotion. Some direct-care staff have confided to us that they are embarrassed to reveal their occupations to members of their communities. Male employees in particular, especially older ones, often are uneasy about and ashamed of their job, describing it as unmanly to clean up after incontinent clients and to perform domestic chores such as bedmaking, mopping floors, and scrubbing bathrooms. Some tasks of the direct-care staff can force them to extremes of activity and physical exhaustion, such as when a severely assaultive client is in a continuous rage for hours. At other times, the work experience can be one of profound boredom, also lasting for hours. The multiple demands described earlier overextend the staff emotionally. Most of the recently imposed changes arrived precipitously—without staff inclusion in decision making and with little notice or meaningful preparation for the new responsibilities attached to the change.

In this brief profile are the seeds of the stress and morale difficulties that, in the view of most direct-care workers, cannot be understood by those who have not shared the experience. It is our contention that the stress endured by direct-care staff in residential facilities has been significantly underestimated, perhaps because limited access to the direct-care subculture precludes direct observation of most of the symptoms. Of course, the stress felt by individual staff members will vary across facilities and perhaps also with factors such as the nature of client handicap, unit census, quality of supervision, staff turnover rates, and many other things. We do, however, see common threads of the stress experience.

There are several sources of stress. Michael (1973) suggests that role conflict or role ambiguity can produce serious personal stresses on the role incumbents in public agencies undergoing change. Role conflict occurs, according to Michael, when an individual tries to carry out directives that require what the individual believes to be behaviors incompatible with one another. Multiple subordination and the two-boss phenomenon would be examples. With the increasing shift to decentralized and interdisciplinary systems in public facilities, role conflict has become an increasing phenomenon affecting direct-care staff. The related experience of role ambiguity is, in Michael's view, the degree to which the required information for a given position is unclear or uncertain to the role incumbent. Our earlier discussion of communication and accountability suggests that the degree of role ambiguity is high. The disorienting role change many staff members experience when they move from their pre-service experience to the residential unit realities also promotes role ambiguity. Their fairly quick acculturation to the routine may be seen as a viable alternative to the stress of role ambiguity.

There are many other explicit aspects of day-to-day life on a residential unit that produce stress for the staff. For example, a severely retarded client may become disruptive in the dining hall, perhaps to attract attention or obtain more food. Although other clients are in no physical danger from the outburst, they may be agitated by it. Should the staff ignore the disruptive behavior as the unit psychologist advised? Should they attempt to restrain the client? Should they terminate his meal and send him back to the living area, perhaps courting a criticism by the unit physician or possibly the human rights advocate? Or should they simply give the client more dessert, an approach that will surely stop the annoying disruption, at least this time, but may incur the disapproval of the unit nurse who says the client is overweight and must reduce caloric intake? Dilemmas such as these occur daily. The staff are the single source of control but have multiple possibilities for response, each favored by different subordinators, who may not have met and problem-solved their differences together. Under these conditions, the event can be very stressful.

Certain medical conditions are distinct sources of stress for direct-care staff. A contagious disease on the unit can produce a sustained period of stress. With limited hospital facilities at many residential centers, clients must remain on the unit even when contagious disorders occur. Staff shortages and the physical geography of many residential units pose substantial obstacles to maintaining hygienic conditions at the criterion of a general hospital ward. The frequent incontinence of severely and profoundly retarded individuals intensifies the problem if the disease occurs in a unit with this type of client population. The possibility of contracting the disease is no small fear for staff members. Bearing the open cuts and scrapes that often mark their trade, direct-care workers are easy candidates for infection from many diseases.

Some years ago an outbreak of infectious hepatitis occurred at a large facility. Strict sanitary and disease control procedures were imposed and closely monitored by doctors and nurses. Some residential units were placed in isolation. Direct-care staff working through this period reported extreme emotional and physical exhaustion. Because the incubation period was several weeks, staff in constant direct contact with infected clients had to wait out long periods of time in anxious agony to learn whether or not they had been infected. One of the attendants on a quarantined unit was bitten by a client suspected of having the disease, which is communicated through direct body fluid contact. The employee's wife was in the early months of pregnancy. Not only did the employee wait apprehensively for days to learn whether the client was incubating the disease when he inflicted the bite, but he also had to anticipate the possibility of infecting his wife. Thus, he was faced with the distress of having to consider living away from home for a long period of time. He described the experience as emotionally debilitating.

Of course, hepatitis outbreaks on a large scale do not occur frequently. However, when it does occur, it is the direct-care worker who bears both the stress of caring for the client and the highest risk of infection among staff groups. The anticipatory stress of possible infection can occur with the presence of just one case of the disease. On a smaller scale, similar stress conditions occur with the presence of other, more common diseases on the residential unit. Streptococcus, staphylococcus, pinworms and diarrhea alter the unit routine and its stability. Unit-wide diarrhea can tax attendants' senses and nerves to the limit. Clients react behaviorally to a frustrating disease and the equally frustrating constraints imposed by treatment. In all cases, the direct-care staff—not the doctors, the social workers, the psychologists, or management—shoulder the consequences of the client reactions, and this, too, causes stress.

Perhaps the least recognized source of felt stress experienced by line staff is assignment to unfamiliar units. When a unit is below the minimally safe number of staff due to employees' calling in sick, employees on special duty, or other reasons, coverage is supplied by staff from other units. This sort of situation occurs regularly in many large facilities. For the covering worker, the new unit usually is a zone of many uncertainties—the clients, the procedures, the staff. For example, there may not be time to learn which clients suffer epileptic seizures or which are assaultive and what triggers their aggression. This uncertainty literally can be frightening and the covering employees must rely almost completely on regular staff members who are present. If, for some reason, covering staff are alone on the unfamiliar unit, the experience is even more difficult. We know one woman for whom it became unbearable. Sent out to cover another unit, she was left alone for a brief period when the charge attendant was called out of the unit on an emergency. The clients were severely retarded, aggressive, and aware of the absence of the regular staff. When the charge attendant returned, she found a terrified young woman, who despite her strong interest in working with mentally retarded clients, resigned soon after the incident and left the field.

Although this young woman's experience may be atypical, being "sent out" (to an unfamiliar unit) as the staff refer to it, is not. Seniority plays a role here, and usually the new employee is most likely to go if a call for coverage comes in. It probably is the case that many staff workers are sent out to several different units several times a month. The effects can be serious. Not only are there fresh doses of uncertainty for most of the work week, but also continuity and role legitimacy in one's assigned unit are reduced. The sense of filling what Toffler (1970) calls a fixed slot in their working environment decreases as they move back and forth, adjusting and readjusting to new places.

The worker's morale is bound up inextricably in these experiences. Webster's New Collegiate Dictionary defines morale as the mental and emotional attitudes of individuals to the function or tasks expected of them by their group. It is further described as a state of individual psychological well being based on such factors as a sense of purpose and confidence in the future. The discussion thus far raises concern about direct-care staff morale.

Some 30 years ago, Hill (1953) stated that direct-care staff morale suffered from too many duties and multiple roles. The situation is no less true today and is even more complex. These employees are surrogate parents, nurses, doctors, physical therapists, and psychologists, as well as general life care providers. But where these men and women become passive recipients of externally imposed changes in their work place; where they experience multiple, but uncoordinated subordination; where they are everyone's available excuse if something goes wrong; where they find the agency's goals and their daily work experience contradictory; where they cannot find guidance from the organization's rule system; where their experience of approval from other parts of the facility and especially their superiors is limited or absent; where their expertise and competence with clients go unacknowledged; where their stress reactions are not seen as legitimate matters for supportive intervention—where these circumstances exist, direct-care staff morale is unsteady. Symptoms such as high absenteeism, highly critical attitudes toward work, negative coping strategies like resistance, and related behaviors typically reflect these morale difficulties.

Recent research on the phenomenon of burnout (e.g., Pines & Aronson, 1981) confirms these observations about stress and morale. One study investigated the incidence of burnout in state-run institutions for developmentally disabled clients (Weinberg, Edwards, & Sternau, 1979). Their research specifically studied direct-care personnel, along with administrative and professional staff. Fourteen residential facilities in 11 states participated in the study. Subjects included 224 direct-care workers. Using physical, emotional, and attitudinal exhaustion as the index of burnout, these authors found an incidence of 16% for direct-care staff. Across facilities, direct-care burnout ranged from 0% to 33%, suggesting a situationally specific nature to the problem. However, the authors describe their figures as underestimating the problem, because their sampling procedure could not reach those staff who had already left work as a result of burnout or those who had not yet reached their measurable criteria of burnout at the time of the study. They suggest the possibility that as many as 50% of the staff at a residential facility may experience burnout at some point in their employment. Also of interest to our discussion was their finding that burnout was correlated with such job factors as work overload, conflicting demands, and the experience of administrative hassles.

Staff-Supervisor Relationships. Within the residential unit social system, a curious relationship exists between the direct-care worker and the unit supervisor. Having earned their positions by rising through the ranks, most supervisors can identify with the plight of their staff working in direct care of clients. Unfortunately, this rise to position typically occurs without needed training in management and supervisory skills. Leadership and independence are thus weak traits with many of these supervisors, and they come to overdepend on their subordinate staff for approval and acceptance (Thaw, Palmer, & Sulzer-Azaroff, 1977). The dependence is widespread in many facilities.

For many years it has been recognized that, of all the members of the institutional community, the actions of the unit or ward supervisor most directly concern the line staff (Hill, 1953). The supervisors occupy key positions on the unit. Their role as a communications filter, a gatekeeper of information, and a power implementer is crucial to an understanding of the staff's working realities. It is still the case in many facilities today that the supervisors are the spokespersons for the rest of the organization to the direct-care workers. The information they choose to communicate (or not to communicate) and the manner in which the message is transmitted affect what the staff believe, how they feel, and what they do. New treatment methods and programs, for example, often are introduced to staff by supervisors, especially on the second and third shifts. The supervisor is accountable to the program specialist for the program's progress. A supervisor who neglects to convey fully all procedures or who edits the information and its meaning for the unit's routines can influence the staff's acceptance and conduct of the program. The supervisor may also use this situation to frustrate the program specialist: "I told my staff about the program and its procedures, but they just won't do it.'' In our experience, this type of socio-political commerce is still fairly common in residential settings.

Control of communication is important to the unit or middle-level supervisor. Some use it constructively, while others rely on it for other purposes such as safeguarding their authority. The methods and patterns of communication control vary widely across and sometimes within residential units. This variability, coupled with its importance to unit affairs, makes it necessary for program specialists or other change agents to study the information flow and learn the patterns prior to attempting program interventions. Program results may depend upon success at this effort.

Supervisory control is practiced in other ways as well. Typical supervisory functions include scheduling staff work assignments, planning holiday and vacation time, introducing new policies and procedures to staff, training new staff members in the unit routine, evaluating staff, and recommending transfers and promotions. These tasks all have gatekeeping, filtering, and power functions. When a particular supervisor, armed with this leverage, deliberately or inadvertently rewards staff behaviors that may not support client programming—for example, when a supervisor approves cleanliness, order, and quiet to the exclusion of teaching self-help or social skills to clients—program professionals are unlikely to have incentives to compete.

Some years ago, Amble, Bellamy, Gideon, Parks, & Shafter (1971) investigated how supervisors rate their employees in residential facilities. Their data showed supervisory support for the custodial model. They found that supervisors did not view intelligence as an asset for being a direct-care worker and further that attendants with lower intelligence more often were rated higher by supervisors on job performance skills than were those with higher intelligence. Yet the study also revealed that the more intelligent workers had attitudes more favorable to helping and training clients. This takes on even greater significance when one looks at another finding: Supervisors focused on skills related to management of clients rather than skills involving training and habilitation of clients. It appeared to be the custodial activities staff performed, not the training, that held the highest job performance value for supervisors. Well over a decade later, these results seem surprisingly fresh and germane (e.g., Cullari, 1984; Reid & Whitman, 1983).

We conclude this brief profile of supervisory control with a consideration of the formal work evaluation or the *employee service rating* as it is called in many states. In many ways, it is pivotal to job survival for the direct-care worker. Here, too, the supervisor has much control. Although most evaluations genuinely attempt to assess an employee's work performance and provide motivation, the evaluation can, in some cases, serve other, more ''political'' purposes. For example, it can facilitate compliance and keep staff in line. Because salary increases, even routine annual increments, often are linked to service rating results, this is no small bit of leverage. We have known rating supervisors disinclined to have program development on their unit (formal facility goal plans notwithstanding) who utilized the service rating as a quiet instrument of persuasion. Because program personnel seldom complete service ratings for direct-care staff, even in the progressive, interdisciplinary systems of care, the concentration of power lodged with the rating supervisor must be reckoned with by all who would ask staff to conduct program or other interventions. The grievance procedure provided by most collective bargaining contracts has taken some of the sting out of the improper use of evaluations, but the grievance procedure is itself an adversary process, where private differences may have to be exposed and documented before an impartial hearing officer. Witnesses, frequently co-workers, often are involved, and the whole experience can have enough discomfort and unpleasant aftereffects to make it a less tolerable alternative than accepting the supervisor's standards. Also, some supervisors do not know how to conduct a meaningful service rating and have never received instruction on how to do so.

Thus far, we have presented a profile of a supervisor who is in control of the unit, a supervisor who can exert tremendous authority over the staff. However, in the complex relationship between supervisors and staff, just the opposite often is curiously the case. In many facilities for mentally handicapped clients, the staff, not the supervisors, are in control, setting the real unit policy while the paper policy yellows on the bulletin board. We can identify at least three reasons for this situation, each with strong historical roots.

First, direct-care staff usually have the edge on information—information on clients, information on events, and information flowing along the rumor tracks. The proximity of the staff to the clients provides information typically inaccessible to other people (Bogdan et al., 1974), and it is not uncommon to find attendants who feel that their supervisors misunderstand the needs of mentally handicapped clients, especially when the supervisors are "office" rather than "unit" bound. Thus, as Scheff (1961) pointed out, staff often can exact from supervisors compliance to their demands simply because they hold the trump card, information. To illustrate, when a parent request, program audit, or some other event calls attention to a particular client, a predictable response chain is engaged. The Superintendent or perhaps another official, will send inquiries to the unit concerning the client in question. Although professionals assigned to the unit can supply some information, as can the unit supervisor, only the direct-care staff have continuous, uninterrupted contact with the client. They are, in effect, the ultimate information source, and those supervisors who are to respond to the Superintendent's request must depend upon them. The packaging and presentation of that information by the direct-care staff can be surprisingly influential in the decision rendered. Often the recipients are unaware that they are being influenced.

Recently in our experience, a few direct-care employees were asked for input on a program for a highly aggressive client who had been assaulting other clients and staff. Their hidden agenda was to have the client transferred out of the unit, as his difficulties compounded the workload considerably. Armed with scores of reasons why a program solution would not work with this client in this unit at this time, the staff effectively countered every program suggestion "in the best interests of the client" (e.g., "We'll try any program, but these assaults don't have a pattern and we can't guarantee the safety of the other clients."). Indeed, the staff genuinely were concerned about the client, although whether a transfer was the best intervention was perhaps questionable. The inability of the supervisor and program personnel first to recognize the hidden agenda and then to deal with the informational leverage precluded any real chance for program intervention.

A second explanation for staff control over residential unit operations lies in the supervisor's roots in the direct-care staff subculture. As noted earlier, most supervisors have ascended from the ranks of line staff. Thus, they were trained and seasoned first as attendants. To a noticeable degree they identify with attendants. More importantly, if their skills as managers are weak, they will tend to depend more on attendants for approval and even success in their job. This makes their supervisory authority tenuous at times, such as when program changes are being attempted. If, for example, a group of staff view program intervention as intrusive or "more work with the same pay," their supervisor's authority may well be more secure in the safety and status quo of the staff's preference.

A final reason for supervisors' relinquishing control to their staff rests in the typically inadequate, often nonexistent, managerial training they receive. Supervisors are expected to perform many administrative tasks, usually without the benefit of instruction in management areas such as leadership, supervisory skills, goal planning, conflict resolution, team process, and problem-solving skills. Some facilities recognize this and are struggling to do something about it. Others assume that a supervisor's "acquired" experience and residential unit "savvy" are sufficient for tackling the job. Thaw, Palmer, and Sulzer-Azaroff (1977) have discussed the possible consequences of these matters for facilities serving mentally retarded clients:

> The precise effects of these multiple training deficits are difficult to determine. . . .
> It is not unreasonable, however, to suggest that these failures in training may well be associated with a number of traits characteristic of many middle-level supervisors in our institutions: a) the experience of threat or discomfort with change; b) a survival-like grasp on past practice; c) ignorance, disbelief in, and inability to cope with more recent ideologies and methods in mental retardation; and d) highly developed responses with which to resist intrusions. . . . (p. 3)

Thus, we have an alternative perspective on supervisors. They may be decidedly untrained in management and supervision, perhaps compromised as leaders by overdependence on their "followers," and on the short end of the information network. Their retreat to the certainty of the routine, their caution in risking challenge from below, and their diluted authority become understandable if not predictable.

In sum, the attendant-supervisor relationship is a delicate one that must be carefully and continuously negotiated in order to maintain harmony and efficiency in job performance. It is a relationship not easily accessible to observation and study, although it is essential to understand it in order to introduce meaningful change into the residential unit. One must learn to identify the pattern of relationships, the distribution of control and power, and the situation-specific conditions in which these arrangements function and vary. Change interventions without this assessment will be at some higher risk.

Staff-Staff Relationships.   A second component of the residential unit social system concerns relationships among direct-care workers themselves. Fellow staff often are the primary source of social and motivational incentive at work. Particularly in units with severely impaired residents with whom staff cannot converse, a fellow employee may be the only social relief from the boredom and stress of the job. The purpose of this section is to describe some aspects of worker-worker relationships, how these interactions protect attitudes, and why it is all so important to program development.

The process of residential unit acculturation, mentioned earlier, is a continuous action of conformance. Once the initial breaking-in phase is completed, it is relatively easy to maintain the attitudes, approaches, and adherence to the routine. Fellow employees do most of the maintenance work, and they do it in many ways. Though without official rank, experienced colleagues have seniority and unit savvy that often function to enforce compliance with the internal standards of the unit.

Their methods, some covert and harsh, still are used in some residential facilities. For example, some approaches may be broadly characterized as variations of ''blackballing.'' Any violation of the unit's established rules or norms is met by rejection of the offender. The blackball victim may find that his peers have seen to it that his midmorning coffee breaks ''inadvertently'' get delayed by last-minute, ''have to be done'' tasks. Or the victim finds that her coffee break is missed entirely. Lunches may become lonely times. Less desireable work assignments may become frequent. Temporary transfers to unfamiliar units (a typically unpleasant experience) may become common. Though far less frequently than in past years, fellow staff have been known to disappear mysteriously during emergencies, either medical or behavioral, and other staff may encourage client misbehavior to discourage program-oriented newcomers. In short, the price for nonconformance can be high. The routines and acculturation traditions are strongly lodged in place. Even something as commendable as interacting with clients in a play situation may become a focus of discouragement, resentment, and prohibition for other direct-care staff (Allen, Chinsky, & Veit, 1974). We are convinced that good working relationships with fellow staff are necessary for the direct-care worker's job survival.

It would be incorrect for the reader to infer and inaccurate for the authors to imply that residential units for mentally handicapped persons are staffed with insidious and calculating people manipulating their colleagues and uncaring of clients. We are describing patterns of staff behavior that evolved from several decades of neglect and inertia in our mental health institutions during the early and middle part of this century. It would also be incorrect to conclude from these descriptions that the direct-care workers displaying these patterns of response care less about mentally handicapped persons than do those who would reform the system. They may, in many instances, care more. We would also caution the reader that differences, sometimes large ones, exist among residential units, among facilities, among systems of facilities. In some units we know, the "rules" and status quo being enforced by senior staff are program priorities.

Compared to conformance demands, camaraderie is an elusive component to define in the unit's social system. Camaraderie among fellow workers, as in most settings, is largely an individual matter. Still, some features tend to characterize the direct-care system. First, as noted, fellow workers may be the only people to talk to most of every working day. Second, issues external to the unit, particularly those posing potential threats to the routine, such as programs or new administrative policies, tend to unify staff. Finally, the job setting itself tends to promote camaraderie. Direct-care staff share an experience few outsiders can understand or tolerate. The staff know this, and handling the experience promotes a curious bond among them.

Yet our anecdotal, observational, and interview evidence about the content of their interactions does not argue for a firm sense of interpersonal closeness among direct-care workers. As observed and reported by present and former attendants from several facilities, conversational content, for example, appears to concern a limited number of subjects: clients who give staff trouble, outsiders who threaten to intrude upon their routines, gossip, the "state," and news from other units. Over time, an observer begins to notice the sameness of the conversations and of the interactions among staff. Cleland and Peck (1967) have noted that it is as if the nonstimulating residential setting elicits stereotypic staff behaviors comparable to repetitive client behaviors.

Although camaraderie seems to exist around these topics of discussion, the loyalty seems to break down beyond these issues. On many units, conflict, rather than unity, predominates. The most striking example of this occurs between shifts. The rush to get things done, the failure to finish, and the reaction of those who must complete the duties on the next shift—all of these can merge to produce resentment, even hostility, across shifts. First shift complains that second shift has it easier (with the clients asleep for a large part of the staff's working hours) and thus should assume more task responsibilities. Second shift complains that first shift should do most of the chores anyway because typically there is more staff coverage on first. Third shift frequently feels left out al-together. These conflicts produce unreliable communication and task inconsis-tency across shifts. Service delivery to clients often reflects this deficit. "Gap-bridging" across shifts thus becomes a requirement for program interventions applied throughout the day.

In its many forms, the relationships among staff can be an imposing force with which outsiders to the unit must contend. Attitudes and behaviors that were formed during the first weeks of assignment to a unit are maintained through a series of subtle, but strong, peer processes and typically function to preserve the status quo of the environment. For the program specialist, for example, it may mean that direct-care staff mutually reinforce and protect the objective of the least possible intrusion. It may also mean that the potential to reject and resist training and new treatment methods is substantial. The long history of program failure in many institutional settings reflects, among other things, the nature of worker-to-worker relationships and its control over the operations of the residen-tial unit. We develop these considerations later, in the discussion of program resistance.

Staff-Client Relationships.   Perhaps the most significant relationship at facil-ities for mentally handicapped citizens is that between the direct-care worker and the client. It has long been clear that the lives of clients at facilities for mentally handicapped persons, their daily routines, and the rhythm of each day are all structured by the direct-care staff (Belknap, 1956; King & Raynes, 1968). The direct-care staff structure the lives of clients along dimensions of possessions, time, and space (Cleland & Dingman, 1970). Even in more progressive inter-disciplinary program systems, staff members decide such things as where a client's clothes are kept. They determine what recreational and other materials are permitted on the unit and what "ownership" clients may have over these. They decide whether and when a television may be used. They often determine whether activities such as off-grounds trips, recreation periods, and even training programs will be held, and when. This is possession control.

The direct-care staff also decide, in many cases, when clients wake up and when they go to sleep, when many of them are toileted, when they eat their meals, and how long a meal lasts. They often set the times for showering, dressing, shaving, and haircuts. They schedule access to snacks and refresh-ments between meals. A client who wishes to take a nap may be interrupted by a staff member who feels the nap will preclude a full night's sleep. These are illustrations of time control.

Direct-care personnel also exert control over clients' use of living space. Often some clients are restricted to the unit during certain hours. Doors may be locked, further limiting access. Some clients with severe assaultive or self-injurious behaviors often are restrained in their chairs for protection. Many clients are discouraged from interacting with one another for fear of an injury occurring. Staff shortages, preference, or possibly even agency policy may deny clients access to offices, kitchens, employee bathrooms, and other settings. Finally, despite major improvements in recent years, depersonalized physical plants still prevail in some facilities, further aggravating the space restriction. Beds resting one against another in large dormitories prohibit privacy, as do large bathrooms where open toilets and group showers facilitate staff supervision and work expediency, but limit a client's sense of personal space.

The extent of this system of restriction varies greatly from facility to facility, even from unit to unit. In some cases, the nature of client disability requires some restriction of time, space, and possession. This is a complex matter because often it is hard to determine the boundaries of necessary restriction. The absence of habilitative technologies in some areas of client disability (Bailey, 1981) sometimes leaves restriction as the only alternative to self-injury or assault. Limited staffing resources may lead to the same result even when the technology is available. There are also some situations when restriction is the staff preference because it is the easiest and least complicated intervention. The control of clients' routines and their access to possessions and space has influenced the development of staff relationships with and perception of clients. In this section we attempt to characterize the social relationships that exist between direct care staff and clients in many places. We discuss how traditional attitudes and beliefs held by staff about mentally handicapped citizens have persisted, often with support from the organization itself.

Relationships between client-care workers and clients are determined by a number of factors. One of the most significant is the traditional perception that staff, indeed the public in general, hold toward mentally handicapped people. Our conversations with direct-care personnel revealed the presence of attitudes not unlike many beliefs about this population held at different periods of history (Wolfensberger, 1969). Some staff members still see retarded people as ''acts of God,'' mistakes of nature not responsible for their actions, despite official philosophies to the contrary. For others, the clients in their charge are objects for pity or not capable of learning. We cannot place hard percentages on the prevalence of these beliefs (reliable data not confounded by social desirability response effects are difficult to acquire), but their existence is undeniable, possibly more widespread than generally acknowledged. More clear is the purpose the beliefs can serve (e.g., helping the direct-care workers to rationalize their performing basic self-care responsibilities for clients, rather than taking the time to teach them self-care independence).

Although it is difficult to accept, there are some direct-care workers who perceive mentally handicapped people as less than human. (Wolfensberger, 1976, has argued that some highly trained professionals seem to hold the same belief.) What staff see day after day may serve to confirm their belief. Some years ago, one client-care worker assigned to a unit for severely and profoundly retarded clients put it this way: ''What do you expect me to think? All day long I see people urinating and defecating on themselves and playing in it. I see people biting and kicking other people and hurting themselves. There are people eating things off the floor, eating grass and leaves outside. Other clients here yell and scream all day like wounded dogs.''

Still another perception of mentally handicapped people is reflected in the belief that they are "troublemakers." Indeed, many staff label various clients according to their predominant maladaptive behavior, often to reduce the uncertainty that exists regarding their handicap and its treatment (Caudill, 1958; Scheff, 1961). Labels such as the "head-banger," the "biter," the "spitter," the "window-breaker," or the "basket case" may exist. They make sense for the employee, and they further increase the resentment sometimes felt toward the clients (Bogdan et al., 1974).

Negative feelings toward clients, such as resentment, especially if the particular clients have severe behavioral disorders, are logical, as logical as the feelings of compassion that often exist concurrently. Anyone who has spent time at the direct-care level of a facility will readily understand this. The existence of the feeling does not necessarily imply its direct expression either—it is a highly individual matter. It is also the case that some of the beliefs mentioned, particularly the "act of God" and "object of pity" perceptions, often are held nonjudgmentally; the view is benign rather than biased. To indict direct-care staff for their feelings or their beliefs is to misunderstand them. Instead, the first step is to understand the circumstances that generate the perceptions.

Another factor that seems to affect a direct-care worker's perception is the degree of a client's physical abnormality. Here we find some empirical data. Dailey, Allen, Chinsky, and Veit (1974) found that clients who were rated more favorably on physical attractiveness and likeability received more positive affect, more social praise, and more interactions from attendants than clients rated considerably lower along these dimensions. A curious, but persistent, implication concerning physical abnormality seems to be that some staff may believe that behavior change and skill development are not possible without first altering the client's physical appearance.

Attendant-client interactions tend to gather about the client's maladaptive behavior (Warren & Mondy, 1971). Where staff have not been trained or do not accept program philosophies, or where staff shortages exist, the only time many clients receive attention from staff is when they misbehave. If they get "in trouble," for example, by annoying or assaulting another client, or if they do something disapproved by the staff, they receive quick notice. Over time, this pattern of attention intermittently reinforces undesirable behaviors, but staff often fail to see this. Instead, they tend to interact mostly in response to client maladaptive behavior. This is perceived by many as a job requirement; continuous positive interaction often is not. The reinforcing effects of even simple reprimands or corrective interventions in situations where any attention may be at a premium seems not well understood in many residential units. As the pattern recurs, it can generate *categories*. Clients may be regarded as either good or bad according to their degree of passivity or misbehavior in the face of staff demands for obedience and dependency.

We have suggested that a major concern of client-care workers is control over their work place. To maintain control, certain patterns of interacting with clients have evolved over time and, in some units, become encoded as unofficial policy. For example, staff often feel control can be secured by keeping clients quiet through reprimand or through discouraging interactions. In measuring attendant attitudes toward mentally retarded clients, Overbeck (1971) confirmed that control is a major concern for these staff. He stated that authoritarianism was positively correlated to the belief that mentally retarded persons should be separated from society. The residential institution is one of society's instruments for expressing that belief, though not the only one. This study seems to support the relationship between perception of clients and the control-dominated atmosphere of their care.

These traditional staff perceptions of clients and the behavior generated by them both evolved from the general culture's history of belief and care of mentally handicapped individuals. Not all direct-care workers share this set of perceptions to the same degree. Many do not share it at all—and many people who do hold these beliefs are not direct-care workers or even employees at residential facilities. Our severe description argues, perhaps, that these views of clients are intractable. This is not necessarily so, as we contend later. The attitudes can indeed change, as can the system of conditions that support them. However, these traditional beliefs and the patterns of interaction, where they exist, should not be taken lightly. Often they amount to a daily theme of life in a residential unit months, even years, deep in practice. Systematic investigations measuring staff-client interactions have confimred the predominance of these patterns even in units officially pursuing habilitative treatment themes (e.g., Gardner & Giampa, 1971; Repp & Barton, 1980; Veit, Allen, & Chinsky, 1976; Warren & Mondy, 1971).

It is paradoxical that the administration of the facility may confirm for the direct-care workers many of their beliefs about mentally handicapped persons. First, as stated earlier, custodial routines often are reinforced by supervisory and other authority figures much more regularly than efforts to develop habilitative programs. Second, the medical department may inadvertently confirm the staff's attitudes concerning control over the clients by prescribing the use of restraints and/or psychotropic drugs. "Why prescribe such large amounts of tranquilizers if they are not to control these people?" The power, prestige, and long tradition of the physician's status in public institutions makes this particular confirmation of belief persuasive and compelling. We should note, however, that in recent years many residential facilities have begun programs of drug and restraint reduction. Third, behavior reports, written up on the unit and routinely distributed to professional departments such as Psychology, Social Services, and

Medicine, often focus on maladaptive behaviors. Over time, a massive amount of material documenting a client's history of such behavior is collected. These behaviors and the clients who display them thus become the facility's attention getters. It is less often that one regularly reads reports detailing some constructive, positive activity of clients.

Finally, the formidable history of program failures on many units further confirms staff views of mentally handicapped clients as unchangeable, unable to learn. Clients who are returned to their units from training or educational sessions because they are disruptive; clients who are dropped after months of training because no progress has been made; failures to significantly reduce a client's maladaptive behavior after several procedures have been tried—all these program casualties reinforce the staff's belief that clients cannot be taught. It is curious that so often the program failures have less to do with client learning than with naive training personnel who themselves have not learned how to implement laboratory-developed procedures in residential unit ecologies (Reppucci & Saunders, 1974; Willems, 1974).

It is important to emphasize that direct-care staff often perceive mentally handicapped clients positively and interact with warmth and closeness. Observing these interactions, one gets an impression of defiance: staff rejecting the norms, beliefs, and practices that have shaped their job behavior over the years in favor of more instinctive reactions to clients. These interactions are most visible when a client becomes separated from the group, for example, during illness. Another time to observe it is on Sundays or holidays, when relatives and friends of clients come to visit. Typically, the visited client is showered and dressed in a nice outfit quite unlike the usual polo shirt and pull-on pants. The staff become involved in the client's appearance and experience as part of a family or social group outside the unit. Many staff report feeling proud as the client leaves the unit to spend the day with family or friends. Cumming and Cumming (1957), writing about the mentally ill, observed that when a patient is being considered for discharge, the staff forms the implicit hypothesis that this person is now able to carry on an acceptable social life in the outside world. They begin to interact with the patient as if he or she were "normal." It's almost as if the decision to discharge disengages the staff's belief system, and their behavior alters accordingly.

Clients also are given much attention when they are hurt or injured. Injured clients usually are taken aside to receive one-to-one attention for their wounds. These are often times when the compassion of the client care workers noted earlier is clear and intense.

This description of staff-client relationships, like other parts of our direct-care profile, will vary from facility to facility and often within facilities. The relationships must be viewed in a context. Staff are required to spend all their working hours with individuals who have complex, often severe, behavioral and developmental disabilities. The job has been described as exasperating (Realon,

Lewallen, & Wheeler, 1983). The handicaps themselves historically have been judged harshly by our society (e.g., Wolfensberger, 1969), and the afflicted individuals seldom have been favored members of our culture, even in more enlightened times. Staff-client relationships are best understood in this perspective.

To conclude this discussion, we have sought to describe some outcomes of the historical development of direct-care work in residential facilities. The beliefs, attitudes, norms, and patterns of behavior described have converged to yield a role that has decades of continuity. This role, or some parts of it, can be expected to persist even where it is held in official disfavor. We have argued that this role concept still directs or influences much of the day-to-day experience of client-care workers. In the next section we examine the effects of recent periods of rapid change and reform on the role incumbents.

TWO DECADES OF REFORM: THE DIRECT-CARE EXPERIENCE

By 1960, the normative patterns of work life that we have been describing, as well as the value and belief system that underbraced them, had become extremely stable. They had evolved slowly and settled into a kind of inertia that was essentially undisturbed for several decades. Beginning in the early to mid-1960s, a period of rapid change and upheaval across the entire field of developmental disabilities has prevailed that contrasts dramatically with the years preceding it. For direct-care workers in residential facilities, the nature of these changes and the rate at which they occurred have called into question the very foundations upon which the beliefs and practices of the previous period had been constructed.

The events that re-formed our society's consideration of developmentally disabled persons and the institutions responsible for their care are well documented elsewhere (e.g., Begab, 1975; Kugel & Wolfensberger, 1969; Roos, 1970; Sarason & Doris, 1979; Scheerenberger, 1983; Wolfensberger, 1971). In broad perspective, several major forces acted as propellants for these events: the personal interest of John F. Kennedy and his appointment of the President's Panel on Mental Retardation in 1961; congressional initiative resulting in specially funded programs on a large scale; the emergence of fresh conceptual approaches such as normalization and the developmental model; the growth and availability of treatment technologies such as applied behavior analysis; the intervention of the federal judiciary in behalf of mentally handicapped citizens; and the influence of advocacy groups such as the National Association of Retarded Children.

Many, if not all, of these forces and the reforms they generated would eventually titrate down to affect the daily direct-care experience in residential units. Scheerenberger (1983) has described one of these events as the *"tour de force* of institutional reform.'' This was the inclusion of residential facilities under the 1971 amendments to Title 19 (Medicaid) of the U.S. Social Security Act. This action brought new standards of treatment and service to the residential setting, along with financial support and an independent review system to ensure implementation. It also produced a showdown between the direct-care worker and accelerated social change because, in direct-care terms, it was a mandate for a massive intrusion of new service providers, new rules, new managers, and new obligations into the previously well-secured domain of residential life.

Bennis (1965) observed some time ago that theories of social change are rather silent on matters of directing and implementing change; that is, they tend to be more useful for observers of change than for practitioners. Our aim is to demonstrate why, from the perspective of the direct-care worker as recipient of change, these observations have merit. In the previous section, we described incidents of administrative and supervisory mishandling of new events at the direct-care level. Often even one such event produces multiple repercussions when entered into the socio-cultural system of the residential unit. However, when changes come in rapid succession, when they tend to be uncoordinated, when they come without clear images (for the recipients) of future direction, when they radically alter the balance between the familiar and the unfamiliar elements of the daily work experience in favor of the latter, when the recipients are inadequately prepared for the changes, when the internal configuration of the facility changes so frequently that it threatens one's relationship with the organization as a whole—when these and other circumstances associated with accelerated rates of reform occur, staff capacity to process the events, let alone adapt to them, may be exceeded.

This appears to be what has been happening to many direct-care workers over the past 15-20 years of accelerated reform in residential facilities. In Chapter One, we explored the effects of rapid rates of change on those forced to cope with it in residential facilities. The reader is referred there for extended consideration of the subject. For the present discussion, two observations need to be made. First, the increased turnover of change sustained over months, often years, has weakened the direct-care workers' reference point for their jobs, their facilities, even their clients. Their job images are no longer reliable for them, and the changes too frequently have not been anchored to goals and directions that are clear and meaningful to them. Stated differently, there have been too many revisions in too many important parts of their work lives, and they have become disoriented. Some seem fatigued with their job experience—not tired of working, but tired of repeatedly having to adapt to circumstances that are less and less predictable. As one worker put it, ''I don't know what to pay attention to anymore.''

The second observation is that these workers suffer the effects of their facilities' also being unable to manage the rate of change. Most residential facilities, philosophical postures notwithstanding, are traditional bureaucratic structures unsuited to managing rapid change. They cannot assist or support those employees confronting the effects of rapid change. Nor do they prepare them adequately for the experience of rapid change. Many facilities are not aware or choose not to acknowledge that the adaptation problems of their staff are legitimate matters requiring intervention at the organizational level. Some wrongly diagnose these problems as performance deficits requiring disciplinary action.

Davis (1973) has cautioned that the management of change calls for scrupulous and sincere regard for the rights and feelings of those involved with the change. In many residential facilities over the past several years there has been a careless disregard for the experiences of direct-care staff as recipients of high rates of reforming events. This has been costly because, for many reforms, it is these workers who must translate the new ideas, plans, even ideologies into experiences for clients. Thus, their response to organizational failure to understand and manage the effects of rapid change becomes a strong determinant in the eventual success of the reforms themselves. This response of the direct-care staff is the subject of the remainder of this section.

The initial response of direct-care staff to extended periods of unmanaged change has been confusion. Reforms such as the ICF/MR program, interdisciplinary systems of service, human rights procedures, behavior modification interventions, normalization philosophies, deinstitutionalization movements, and many other innovations all transform the responsibilities of direct-care workers in some way. Many of these changes alter the competencies required for their position and classify at least some of their traditional job practices (e.g., controlling, rather than teaching, behaviorally active clients) as officially extinct. The confusion occurs because the worker is expected to respond as a specialist in each area of responsibility, but probably was poorly prepared for the new tasks and the transitions to them. For example, in the process of introducing ICF-funded interdisciplinary systems, it was not uncommon to find groups of professionals, administrators, perhaps advocates, and others designing new procedures, routines, guidelines, or policies, and then "delivering" them to the direct-care staff for implementation. These planners often left the staff out of the planning process and underestimated the staff training requirements for achieving successful, durable implementation. For the staff, this precluded their buying into the new ideas comfortably, but it also produced role confusion—the new demands came suddenly, often were unclear, sometimes called for job behavior incompatible with what their supervisors endorsed, and generally conflicted with past norms on the residential unit.

This kind of confusion, over time, produces problems of identity, as we have noted. It also stimulates distrust. When reforms are introduced in the manner we have described and when demand for program outcomes from external sources (e.g., federal inspectors, courts, advocacy groups) preoccupies administrators and distracts them from the impact of reforms on staff, those confused will find it adaptive to distrust what they perceive to be the cause of their confusion, be it person, policy, or program.

Trust problems have underbraced many direct-care workers' perceptions and relationships with individuals and groups associated with programs of change. In our experience, those introducing reform at the residential level underestimated the trust factor and the effects it produces. We have also observed that the day-to-day ordeal with distrust is an unstable experience in the socio-cultural environment of the residential unit; that is, it tends to set off other reactions, notably fear, defense, and resistance.

A dramatic illustration of this shift in reaction occurred in one facility undergoing extremely high rates of change in areas of court-ordered deinstitutionalization. Within just a few days, a wildcat strike of direct-care employees was threatened, then barely averted at the last minute. Clearly, there were some grievances that needed to be resolved, but the rapid escalation to the tactic of an unlawful job action seemed puzzling to many observers. These workers were bypassing previously utilized approaches, such as negotiation, to risk dismissal, the consequence for an unlawful walkout. The risk appeared disproportionate to the stated grievances of the staff and its union. However, the strike threat and the frantic pace at which it developed was being powered by the work force's deepening distrust of deinstitutionalization and other changes. The facility was under judicial constraint to place hundreds of clients in community settings within strict time frames. For some of its residential units, ICF/MR decertification and subsequent loss of federal funding were becoming realities. At the same time, the facility was receiving continual media attention, most of it unfavorable. Finally, new roles and new expectations for the organization were being formulated, but largely without input from direct-care staff.

These changes all converged on the staff, who were confused about its meaning for them and untrusting of those they thought were in charge of the decisions. Eventually, many became frightened, because the real issues embedded in the changes were ones of job security: Will I be transferred to work in another part of the state because of deinstitutionalization? Will my job responsibilities be altered? Will my job be eliminated? Am I to blame for the well-publicized failures in the facility? Will I be punished? Will I be necessary? The threatened job action was a defensive, resistant response to these concerns.

One can find daily examples of this kind of reaction to accelerated change in a great many residential units. Less commonly are the responses as pronounced as in this case; more often they are subtle, almost understated, as we demonstrate in the next section. Taken together, these are patterns of adaptive behavior that evolved in response to years of stable, predictable paradigms of work life during the early and middle part of this century, followed by a quantum leap forward in change over a few short years. For many direct-care staff, accelerated rates of complex social change have brought discomfort and anxiety to the work environment. Many of these people are, in a sense, caught in time, working in places where the beliefs and practices of past ideologies became quickly and officially unacceptable. Yet, as often happens, acceptance of the newer ideologies considerably preceded the more complicated matter of implementing them. Thus the transition has been difficult for the direct-care worker, more so when the new approaches have been hurriedly imposed with inadequate preparation of those affected.

Although some staff have adapted smoothly and successfully to institutional reform, our own experience suggests most are still at some earlier stage of adjustment. A review of the literature about direct-care staff tends to support this conclusion (e.g., Allen, Chinsky, & Veit, 1974; Balla, 1976; Bogdan et al., 1974; Boles & Bible, 1978; Cullari & Ferguson, 1981; NARC, 1972; Panyon & Patterson, 1974; Quilitch, 1975; Repp & Barton, 1980; Repp & Dietz, 1979; Thompson & Grabowski, 1977; Ziarnik, 1980).

Nowhere has this adjustment been more difficult than in behavioral habilitation programs. In many respects, behavioral technologies and the interventionists that employ them represent the most penetrating and demanding form of change experienced by direct-care workers during the past two decades. It is not surprising that reviews of the research on behavioral interventions with direct-care workers (e.g., Reid & Whitman, 1983) report staff nonacceptance of such programs as a major problem. We turn our attention to this subject in the following section.

THE NONACCEPTANCE OF BEHAVIORAL PROGRAM INTERVENTION

Broadly viewed, the methodologies of behavior analysis have been applied to the residential unit in two ways: a) as specific treatment procedures for clients; and b) as training and management approaches to improve staff performance and/or work skills. Both interventions intrude upon the day-to-day routine in the unit. The intrusion also is more severe (particularly with regard to client treatment procedures) than that of other professional disciplines such as physical therapy, occupational therapy, or speech and language. This is because behavioral treatment strategies make more requirements of staff: more time, more accountability and documentation, more procedures to learn. Staff perceive all this as more rules injected into a system that, to them, is already overloaded with rules. They do not experience many of the organization's rules as guiding or supporting job performance, and their respect for certain sets of rules is limited.

The unwillingness of staff to accept behavioral habilitation and management interventions cannot be understood apart from staff's broader experience with accelerated change over the past several years. Behavioral methodologies were introduced and widely adopted by residential facilities during a period characterized by multiple reforms in many other areas of residential operations. The direct-care workers' experience with this entire period has influenced their reaction to any single unit of innovation such as behavioral interventions. This point seems to have been overlooked by many behavior management interventionists. In this section we examine the application of behavioral technologies to the residential unit from the perspective of the direct-care worker.

The Early Efforts

It is important to understand the direct-care staff's experience with the first efforts at behavioral programming, because it had strong implications for their response to broader scale interventions that came subsequently. The early program interventions were largely client treatment procedures conducted as demonstration projects. They faced two problems: (a) limited emphasis on maintenance or follow-up over time (Boles & Bible, 1978); and (b) concern with only a small part of the institution (Reppucci, 1973). In both cases, the longer term role of the direct-care worker in programming was reduced, or at least deemphasized. This was a misjudgment, because direct-care staff own most of the clients' time, and durable program success would inevitably be linked to their prolonged participation in the implementation. More importantly, these narrowly focused demonstration programs shaped attendants' perceptions of behavior method interventions.

To illustrate, several years ago the senior author, exploring the possibilities for a ward-wide token economy program, had several discussions with the lead charge attendant. The attendant's skepticism about behavior programming was instructive: "We had programming here a year ago. A few people came in every day to work with some of the residents. They were nice but didn't bother much with us. After several months they left, and the residents were back doing the same things they always did. Programming didn't help anything."

This man was describing a federal grant project in behavior modification. His views reveal much about the framing of the early attitude toward such programming. Several authors have presented information that seem to support his outlook. In their review of behavior modification programming in natural settings, Reppucci and Saunders (1974) underscored the pronounced difference between highly financed demonstration projects conducted in atypically special research settings and the formidable constraints encountered in natural ward environments. They recognized the indigenous-setting personnel (such as line attendants) as essential programming engineers over whom professional behavior programmers have little control and with whom they have limited contact. Thompson (1975) specifically addressed the problems in maintaining behavioral programs in institutional settings for retarded persons. Willems (1974) described behavioral program interventions as intrusions into an ecological system. The intruding programmer tended to focus on narrow outcomes and domains of data and was noticeably less sophisticated about the complicated system in which the intervention occurred. According to Willems, an inherent shortcoming in the early application of many program technologies was that the more narrow and specific the application, the greater the array of phenomena the practitioner tended to disregard. This may still be the case in many facilities today. We know literally hundreds of direct-care employees who would count themselves as part of the phenomena disregarded by programmers.

Available evidence on early projects suggests that behavioral programming was not a theme direct-care attendants embraced easily (e.g., Bensberg & Barnett, 1966; Boles & Bible, 1978). For many attendants, these programs were seen as ineffective and experienced as an intrusion. They viewed programmers as naive in believing that simple contingencies could be organized to compete with the realities of ward life. To the extent that the program professionals excluded staff from the programming process, they were courting the noncooperation of the group who controlled those realities. That extent appears to have been considerable in numerous instances. Thus, direct-care workers generally were treated as marginal participants in many early behavior programming interventions. The designers and implementers of these projects seemed neither appreciative of nor interested in the powerful significance of the attendant as the defining condition for durable program success.

Against this unfavorable history with early program interventions, direct-care workers, under conditions that followed (e.g., the ICF/MR regulations), were required to accept, believe in, and conduct behavioral programming as a matter of duty. For many of these staff, the tentative and unsettling experience with the early efforts, followed by what amounted to a nonnegotiated and compulsory role in behavior programming was too precipitous a transition. Whereas early demonstration projects were time-limited intrusions for the staff (when the demonstration or grant was over, the "intruders" typically withdrew), the mandated, more permanent interventions were more threatening. Reaction to the former ranged from confusion to a kind of antagonistic tolerance. Response to the latter developed into active resistance.

Resistance to Behavioral Interventions

The arrival of mandated client programs and broadscale adoption of behavior methodologies as the technological vehicle to manage the mandates presented three problems for direct care staff: (a) it accelerated the pace of their work life; (b) it made their jobs more complex; and (c) it increased stress. In short, these interventions penetrated more deeply into the stability of the traditional routines that had defined direct-care work for more than half a century.

The presence of resistance at the residential unit level is not a new discovery. Numerous observers of these settings have noted its occurrence in response to program change (e.g., Baumeister & Klosowski, 1965; Gardner, 1975; Thaw & Cuvo, 1974; Thompson & Grabowski, 1972; Watson, 1970). Many program innovators, however, seem to misunderstand staff resistance. For example, we have observed many behavior specialists misread it as a personal attack. Indeed, it easily can be experienced this way. But resistance is purposeful behavior, not personal. It is aimed at roles, positions, and events, not at individuals. In any residential unit where program resistance occurs, it will have distinct roots and it will involve specific methods. We shall examine both factors.

Resistance: Roots. Resistive behavior is a self-protective response to change. We can identify five principal roots to this response at the direct-care level. The first and perhaps the strongest source of resistance is the tradition and priority of the residential unit routine discussed earlier. This routine, with its rituals, rules, relationships, and perceptions, is a daily rhythm of life with a history that spans generations in many facilities. Even where morale is low and job dissatisfaction high, the fierce stability of the traditional routine is a curiously strong source of gratification for staff compared to the prospect of program change such as behavioral interventions. Staff will tend to resist the latter to insure the former. Under conditions of rapid change where individuals are inadequately prepared to manage the experience, clinging to past practice as a response to new and threatening demands becomes adaptive behavior. It is also effective, because seldom are the change agents present on the residential unit long enough to learn the meaning of the routine for staff and how to compete with it.

A second source of resistance evolves from certain messages and expectations that the habilitative orientation in general, and the behavioral approach specifically, bring to the residential unit. That the clients in your residential unit are not trained or need to be trained can be interpreted to mean that you have not done so and should have. That your work performance can be ''managed'' through techniques introduced by outsiders to the job domain can be experienced as surrender of control over one's job. Both interpretations suggest that the incumbent has failed in some way in his or her work. Not infrequently, direct-care staff make these interpretations when behavioral programming is introduced. Naive, overzealous, and sometimes less than tactful program personnel have aggravated the situation by making interpretation unnecessary. The result is the same in either case—failure-sensitive people resisting the efforts of those who have inadvertently or directly exposed what are felt to be their shortcomings.

Training clients requires knowing training methodologies. Learning those methodologies or the prospect of having to learn them is another message filled with anxiety for many direct-care employees. Most staff have been out of school for years. Many never finished high school; some barely made it through elementary school. The thought of training workshops or learning new skills can be scary to them. The authors have heard numerous direct-care staff voice serious concerns about looking stupid in front of their peers in a learning situation. If training personnel or program innovators cannot spot this anticipatory anxiety and help the staff members work through it comfortably, the only adaptive alternative may be to resist and block the whole notion of the intervention.

Some resistance is also rooted in the messages received by direct-care staff during the years when demonstration programs were conducted so widely. From where they observed it, what did work didn't maintain once the programmer withdrew. Understandably, many staff members saw these programs primarily serving the professional interests of the programmer. "He wants to put this project on his resume," one attendant remarked to us candidly. We heard this often where demonstration programs were in progress. Many well conceived programs simply didn't work out, and many laboratory-trained programmers clashed with the circumstances of the residential unit instead of addressing them as program variables. For the residential care staff, it all formed a kind of baseline experience with behavior-based programs, which seemed to generate an expectancy about any activity utilizing behavior management procedures. The experience and the expectancy thus prompted resistance to subsequent interventions.

A third source of resistance develops from the behavior of the interventionist or programmer, whose entrance to the residential environment often is seen as presumptuous, at least by the staff who work there. Trained to be a technical expert, the program specialist proceeds to act like one. We have noticed the disinclination of many young psychologists and other professionals to admit to direct-care staff that there are things they don't know. Failure-sensitive themselves, these professionals tend to cling to their knowledge and methods, which, for them, are able to explain almost anything. Not surprisingly, this attitude tends to discount the worth of the workers' own experience on the job and with the clients. Also, it provides a new, sure-fire way for the attendant to resist, as we shall see shortly. The presumptuous posture of some program specialists often masks their discomfort with residential units, direct-care workers, even clients. In more cases than program professionals would publicly acknowledge, they are simply uneasy on the client living units.

Related behavior exhibited by program personnel may compound the problem and strengthen the staff's inclination to resist. Exclusion is a case in point. Having secured a training grant, a small team of program specialists met with administrators and middle level supervisors to select a target residential unit for the project and to plan a tentative schedule of objectives. Among the first steps in the project was a series of meetings with first, second, and third shift direct-care staff in the designated area. Although the meetings were well intentioned, the program team found themselves describing *to* the staff a training program based on decisions *already made*. For this error, they paid a price in several months' resistance. Not all decision-making can be shared, and there are proper ways to share decisions already made. However, it generally can be expected that excluding direct-care staff from the program development process, starting with the very inception of the idea, will promote resistance. Meaningful programming will never work, in any systemic sense, without the direct-care workers, and they are acutely aware of this. To exclude them or to disconfirm their contribution, even if accidentally, is to court their opposition.

A fourth root of resistance concerns the change in norms that behavior programming usually requires. Implementing habilitative training for mentally handicapped clients requires team work and coordination across shifts for countless procedures. As Moos and Daniels (1967) observed some time ago, program operations also generally call for more confrontative and interactive modes of behavior as well as more open accountability, and this runs contrary to the informal code of norms rooted in the traditions of most residential units in facilities for mentally handicapped clients. The traditional code keeps accountability vague, less traceable, especially between shifts. It permits job functions so routine that staff can work parallel to one another without need for extensive interaction, never mind team work.

Finally, we see a source of resistance in the staff's beliefs about the clients themselves. Where they adhere to the belief, however private, that mentally handicapped clients are unable to learn, it is reasonable to assume that direct-care staff really will not see behavior programming as relevant to their job roles and their working lives. It is impossible to determine how widespread this belief is. First, it is now a matter of official orthodoxy in contemporary institutions to view with disdain any disbelief in the developmental learning potential of clients. Second, it is not a simple two-choice issue of belief versus disbelief. There are many views between a unilateral position that all clients can learn and the polar position that they all cannot. Nor is the dilemma of belief the exclusive province of the direct-care worker. Whether they would admit to it or not, all staff, including professionals and administrators, are probably distributed somewhere between the extremes. There is also the belief that some clients are so profoundly handicapped that meaningful learning through any known technology may be questioned. Bailey (1981) and Baumeister (1981) have discussed this matter at some length. Nevertheless, we feel that where the belief that clients cannot learn new skills and behaviors exists, it can prompt resistance to interventions that assume the contrary.

Resistance: Methods.   Resistance is defensive behavior. It is direct-care personnel protecting what is stable and predictable against what is confusing, intrusive, and alien. We have argued that this behavior is logical and justifiable when examined in context. It also is exceedingly effective. Staff are usually better at their defenses than behaviorists are at any of their therapies in the residential setting.

Virtually all methods of program resistance evolve from the direct-care worker's control of time, space, and information at the line level of the facility. Stated differently, the traditional routine is the principal instrument of resistance. This control can be harnessed in service of everything from simple noncompliance with a program initiative to active sabotage of whole programs. In workshop discussions on this subject with different groups of direct-care staff, one of the authors has heard this theme voiced repeatedly. Virtually all the participants felt they could "finesse" any behavior specialist because they held all the cards. If program procedures weren't carried out by the staff and the specialist inquired why, there were scores of "reasons" available: emergencies on the unit, covering staff sent in from other units, interferring priorities from other departments or supervisors, and so on. Details can be produced whose validity is nearly unchallengeable unless one lives on the unit. "Emergencies" that interfere with program procedures can be recited, chapter and verse. New staff sent to cover that unit (a frequent occurrence in many facilities) can be named, and the problems resulting from that situation can be set forth. The probability of communication failures across three shifts, across 24 hours a day, and across staff pass days is so high that the truth of these excuses or reasons is virtually trackless.

Direct-care staff who have not accepted a behavior management or habilitation ideology can also resist by dependency. Here the worker has "tried" the procedure, but it just isn't working. "We really can't do it right. If you could come in at 6:30 every morning when we do this program and help us with it, well, then there's a chance." Program specialists typically have a short fund of 6:30 a.m. appointments. A related method makes use of a residential unit universal: "There's not enough staff"; or "We need more staff to do all these things." These statements are accurate. There isn't enough staff on most units in most facilities in the country, though the situation is beginning to improve (Scheerenberger, 1979). However, the shortage is used here as a tactic to distance the staff member from responsibility for accepting the intervention.

Another form of resistance that develops from the staff's control of residential unit life is more aggressive. They can make programs fail. Owning practically all the client's time and acutely aware of the contingencies that affect a client's behavior, most direct-care staff can control program success even with the program specialist present. For example, we recall an instance where program personnel had set up certain skill training procedures for a group of profoundly retarded clients. The direct-care staff were to conduct these procedures daily. The staff, unsupportive of this program, inserted the training into the routine just prior to meal time, when the clients were more likely to be distractible and uncooperative. The program specialists, less aware of the specific changes in client responsiveness across the day, literally were watching while their training program was being subverted.

We have also seen program personnel victimized by their own rescue fantasies or enthusiasm. Many an attendant has suckered an overzealous new psychologist into tackling client behavior problems all by himself. The psychologist may observe the client religiously, prepare an intervention procedure, "teach" the staff how to implement the procedure whenever the target behavior occurs, and even monitor some of the interventions. He has learned an early lesson in the power of line level resistance when, even after weeks or months, there is no improvement.

Under certain conditions, this type of resistance can become systematically deliberate until it amounts to program sabotage. Data sheets can be fudged. Important anecdotal client information can be withheld. The most intractable clients can be recommended for inappropriate programs, and a new program professional may be totally at the mercy of this recommendation. Materials (e.g., keys to locked doors, towels and soap for hygiene programs, edibles used as reinforcers) can be "hard to locate" at program times. The program may be conducted only when someone is watching, as one staff member confided. The means are endless. They also can be more subtle, especially where the facility's programmatic mission has a wider base of acceptance. Program procedures can be passively endorsed, absorbed into the routine, and then watered down in implementation until they lose their clinical integrity. With behavior management contingencies to improve staff performance, direct-care workers can use their leverage with supervisors to make it too costly for supervisors to support the procedures. Moreover, program-stopping crises can always be manufactured or called upon for interference: (a) clinic runs for individual clients; (b) doctors coming to the unit; (c) a particular client "going on a bat" all day; (d) countless requests from other departments in the facility and from outsiders such as parents; (e) fire and life safety inspections; and (f) endless items of paper work demanded by official others in the organization.

Some resistance receives unsolicited help from the facility's bureaucracy. Delays are a good example (Roos, 1970). Program supplies can arrive weeks, sometime months, after a purchase requisition is submitted. Processing transportation requests for off-grounds trips earned by clients in a token economy program may be delayed so long that the contingency loses its programmatic meaning. Program meetings or training sessions can be postponed by supervisors faced with other priorities. Recognition for program achievement is frequently not forthcoming from a middle management accustomed to scanning their operations for errors rather than accomplishments. For direct-care staff, whose motivation for programming may be tentative already, these administrative delays, postponements, and disappointments tend to confirm their own reservations about the importance of program interventions.

Perhaps the most creative area for resistance is to work the communications system, which in so many places is already overstressed. As noted earlier, in any 24-hour residential setting, messages about client care, treatment, and anything else must flow horizontally across three shifts of staff as well as around the pass day arrangements used by the facility. Where that arrangement is rotating pass days (five days on duty followed by three days off duty set into eight separate cycles, or slots), the problem intensifies.

Some of these messages are written; many are in-person or telephone communications. The residential unit office in many a facility is a war zone of log books, scraps of paper with scribbled notes, and copies of directives, memos, and forms. It amazes us how much of this is processed as well as it is. At the same time, it is collectively a fine tool of ready confusion when messages about behavioral programming are introduced. As scores of staff have told us, it is easy to "lose," "forget," or "never receive" program information on the unit. In sum, the direct-care workers, if they wish, usually can deflect program innovation through the existing communications network. They understand that network better than anyone else and can manipulate it skillfully.

Direct-care resistance to behavior management and training interventions (and most other innovations as well) is predictable if staff feel defensive or if the changes are intrusive, seem permanent, or occur too precipitously. Nevertheless, staff resistance is a highly individual response to specific conditions. Its particular form and expression will vary across and even within facilities. Program specialists experiencing resistance thus will have to diagnose their own circumstances. In any unit, for example, they will need to know the history of those staff with previous programs of change. They will need to understand the day-to-day routines and practices which their presence and programs will disturb. In the following section, we propose some guidelines for managing these and related issues.

One final note on resistance seems warranted. It would be a misconstruction of the authors' view of direct-care workers to judge the practice of resisting program innovation as lack of concern for clients. This is seldom the case. It is also a mistake to regard staff resistance as unalterable behavior. We are encouraged that it can be modified, though through interventions of a different sort. We turn to those now.

MANAGING THE INTERVENTIONIST'S BEHAVIOR: INTERPERSONAL AND POLITICAL STRATEGIES

The central theme of this chapter perhaps has been that many of those planning reforms in residential facilities and many of those assigned to implement them do not adequately understand direct-care workers, especially in a longitudinal sense of their day-to-day job experience. We have suggested that many of the failures to transform the traditional direct-care role into a broadly accepted habilitative treatment role develop from this shortcoming. Applying McCord's (1982) reasoning, we argued that habilitative reforms and other types of change, as implemented, were being experienced by direct-care staff as assaults on their work paradigms. Acceptance of habilitative program paradigms into their construction of human service reality would depend less on finding correct technological solutions than it would on guiding a social-historical process to a point where such paradigms were perceived by staff as meaningful to them. In preceding sections, we examined some of the characteristics and events associated with that historical process. The remainder of the discussion concerns strategies for guiding the process.

In many residential facilities, especially those under strong external pressure to implement habilitative reforms or other changes, the preferred approaches to achieving direct-care staff acceptance of these themes are administrative, directive, and power-based strategies. Recently, the principal clinical officer in one residential facility, under pressure to provide active treatment to all clients, responded to the senior author's description of an effort to promote direct-care workers' acceptance of active treatment practices with this: ''We shouldn't have to spend a lot of time helping them accept active treatment. It's their job and they have to do it.'' This administrator is a skilled clinician, experienced with direct-care staff and better respected among their ranks than is typically the case with such officials. His comment reflects the strong attraction of directive, power-based strategies in places impatient for results, even with knowledgeable, staff-sensitive administrators. Despite their popularity, such strategies are rarely successful at achieving staff acceptance and usually are costly to employ because, without such acceptance, constant vigilance is required.

In contrast, what follows is biased by the belief that the principal means for changing the attitudes of direct-care staff and facilitating their acceptance of habilitative treatment interventions is to alter the behavior of the interventionists who cross their path, intrude into their work place, and otherwise propose to meddle with their working lives.

Changeworthy ideas cannot begin to be introduced until the complex issues of relationship with direct-care staff are adequately resolved. Where these issues are disregarded, the change specialists and the staff will be gathered around different sets of interests with the distribution of real power tipped in favor of direct-care norms and traditions. Building successful relationships with direct-care workers requires certain tasks and calls for some specific skills. What we propose is less a formula than a set of guidelines ordered in the sequence in which they tend to be required. Some of the guidelines are simple principles of interpersonal competence adapted to the roles and issues of the residential unit. Others are recommendations specific to the special conditions of the residential unit. Much of the content reflects several years of experience consulting and working with hundreds of direct-care workers in many different units across a number of facilities. Special workshops and interviews with direct-care staff on the subject also contributed significantly to this material.

Learning the Residential Unit

The first strategy, and a continuing requirement, is knowledge acquisition. Anyone with designs to change things at the residential level will first have to learn about the residential level. All of the components that make up the direct-care staff's working life—the routine, the unit acculturation process, the rules, the controls, the stress, the patterns of interaction with supervisors and clients—these must all be observed and understood. For example, who the key people are on a given unit seldom is apparent from the official organization charts. It could be a tenured charge attendant, a group of young energetic staff, or perhaps the supervisor. Knowing who holds the real influence is essential information for any planned intervention.

At the same time, the program specialist must have a current and accurate working knowledge of the capabilities, sensitivities, and vulnerabilities of the staff (Levinson & Klerman, 1967). The level of resistance and its preferred forms of expression by the staff are, as we emphasized earlier, significant variables in the profile of a particular residential unit. They must be understood precisely. The same requirement holds for every descriptive feature of the direct-care culture discussed in earlier parts of this chapter.

Realizing what must be understood is an easier task than acquiring the actual information. The reader will recall that the intimacy of the direct-care staff's working life typically is a carefully guarded matter. "Rights of passage" are earned only with time and through many tests of trust, commitment, and motive. For the new program specialist, the first step toward access to and learning the residential unit is presence in the residential unit. Several years ago, a young psychologist working for the senior author wished to introduce behavioral programming into a unit with emotionally disturbed clients. He sensed his own naivete about the unit and the people who worked there, and wisely resisted the urge to throw a paper program in at the top. Unsure of where to begin, he was advised to "live" on the unit for a month or so with no particular agenda. Though it was far from a comfortable experience, his logged time was surprisingly instructive and generated a revised program concept, a starting strategy, and a more sensible, if less ambitious, view of his own influence as an outsider.

We would advise all prospective change interventionists to log large blocks of nonagenda time on the unit before introducing their formal programs. This first presence is crucial, and it must present a low profile. Although who the program specialist is and what he or she does at the facility must be shared clearly, heavy doses of expertise, high expectation, and "Promised Land" ideas should be left in the office. The task at this point is to maintain a modest but sustained presence uncomplicated by any desire to make changes or to make a case for changes. A sustained presence means something beyond a visit. As professionals log more unplanned time in a residential unit disengaged from the practice of their formal role, their presence becomes less obtrusive, they lose much of their visitor's status, and they gain access to the naturally occurring norms and rhythms that will influence program implementation. In sum, a sustained, *nonprogram* presence on the unit breaks down initial barriers and permits both parties to learn about each other without having to deal with formal intervention procedures that might obstruct the learning.

Many professionals and administrators question this approach. They find it awkward to spend time on a residential unit pretending not to be the psychologist, social worker, speech clinician, or behavior specialist they are. We agree that the awkwardness or discomfort is indeed real. However, it is not caused by any contrived pretense but rather by the absence of one. We emphasized earlier that direct-care staff's reactions are most often to the formal roles of others that have a history of meaning for them. Thus the formal role of the program expert is, *for the staff,* the pretense. If it is all they see at the start, barriers will go up. The awkwardness of the outsiders is more likely a response to feeling vulnerable, uncertain, clumsy, even frightened in the presence of unaccepting direct-care workers on their turf, without being able to use the pretense of a formal role or expertise to reduce the discomfort. Managing these feelings is important, and we shall return to the problem shortly.

During this initial period at the residential unit, it is important for the program professionals to observe what happens to the staff and what happens to themselves. It is also important for them not to do anything about much of what is observed, at least then. For example, as one encounters the rules and norms that govern the staff's time and activity (e.g., schedules, chains of communication, seniority-based decisions, antagonism toward program personnel), it is best to refrain from judgments. As consultants, we have advised program interventionists at this early phase in developing relationships at the residential unit simply to "blend, not compete." The general mission here is to learn, not to alter.

It would be useful for the reader to review the discussion in previous sections because that discussion describes in detail what should be observed. Additionally, it is usually very helpful to study what it is like to be an outsider while feeling like one. Individuals should carefully register the things that happen to them on the unit. These experiences will be useful reference points later on. To illustrate, we have observed and experienced numerous occasions in which the outsiders, as they begin to break the ice with direct-care staff, feel that their presence is received with a kind of "antagonistic tolerance."[1] As one program specialist put it: "During the first month or so, no one minded my being around and no one said I was in their way, but somehow I felt they were putting up with my presence and that I was cramping their freedom." The feeling was very instructive and, it was discovered later, had a lot to do with the staff's reaction to getting program help they didn't think they needed.

In summary of this initial guideline, learning the residential unit amounts to working in it for prolonged periods of time with as little dependence as possible on the constraints and protections of one's official role of change agent, program specialist, professional psychologist, or whatever. In several years' experience with this approach, we have seen marked success despite the discomfort that goes with doing it. In a few instances, we have formalized the process into a requirement for new program staff. A brief review of one of these required procedures concludes this part of the discussion and raises the questions for the following section on relationship building with direct-care staff.

In the initial phase of an internship for college students training to be behavior program specialists with mentally retarded clients, all interns were required to

---

[1]The authors wish to thank Vivian Batterson for her helpful and insightful observations concerning the material in this section.

spend several weeks working on a residential unit. They had neither special status nor specific instructions. Over the 4 years this project was conducted, students were unanimous that it was an intense but necessary experience. Most had doubts they could complete the program after their first few days. Every participant, months later, judged the unit experience requirement essential to their overall training and confidence as programmers. We have selected below a sample of reactions and observations made by some of these interns just after their first few days on the unit:

> I felt great anxiety. I did not know my place in the flow of things. . . . Boredom was frequent.

> I experienced clients differently than if programming had been my first and only relationship with them. I felt strong affection for them and found myself responding to their emotion whereas I think a programming relationship to start with would have forced me to focus on them technically.

> I felt welcome as an observer but not as a member. The staff seemed to think of me as "theory informed" but "reality ignorant" about clients. . . . I started to initiate my own interactions with clients which led me to participate in the custodial duties of the ward routine. This helped lead to my being accepted.

> I felt a strong lack of confidence. When I tried to get into things it was uncomfortable and I was embarrassed at having to ask about every detail of doing a task. . . . I also felt pressure to be meaningful and act like a professional. . . . It was lonely.

> I had encounters with client behavior I would never had had if I came in as a program specialist. I experienced sudden assaultive, aggressive behavior; I was scratched, and got a feel for existing with the constant threat of sudden client behavioral disruption. I developed enormous respect for the aides. . . . My expectations about what could be done with program change were really lowered.

> I observed emotions in myself I don't usually experience so intensely and at the same time: fear, uncertainty, frustration, anger, happiness, concern. . . . The staff were cleverly unreceptive to my presence, and I think this is probably an unfamiliar experience for many professionals.

> I felt incredible respect for the aides. I could never do their job.

> A prolonged experience with nonverbal clients is extremely frustrating. I felt despair at the lack of communication. I wonder how the staff cope with it over long periods.

These descriptions reveal important personal perceptions, emotions, and interactions that would likely have been filtered out of notice, if not experience, had these people entered the residential setting under the protection of a special program role. The things they encountered and the feelings they could not escape are important factors affecting the introduction and acceptance of program interventions.

The interns' commentaries also suggest the somewhat unstable nature of an assignment that requires an outsider merely to spend unplanned time in a residential unit. All of our interns, often at different rates, moved from observer to participant. This movement was prompted very much by the awkwardness and vulnerability they felt. As noted before, managing these discomforts and such other feelings as fear, clumsiness, and uncertainty is important. It becomes the first problem in the phase of relationship building with direct-care staff.

Constructing Relationship in the Residential Unit

Earlier we discussed the direct-care workers' perception of being abused by the organization's bureaucracy. When people feel ignored, excluded, used, and misunderstood by a system, it probably doesn't matter that well-intentioned program interventionists are genuinely motivated to help them. What does matter is how these newcomers behave. Many innovation-minded professionals, administrators, and program specialists tend to engage client-care staff with what we call "role constrained" behavior; that is, they interact in terms of their intervention ideas, their professional positions, and their desire to make needed changes—they relate formally through their official roles, rather than informally as persons.

In addition to providing safety from the vulnerable feeling and fears the interns described, this professional behavior seems the logical approach with which to begin the process of change. Unfortunately, it is not a useful strategy this early in the process of developing program change. Invariably, it sends messages that presume the program specialists know what the direct-care worker's job is really like when, in fact, they do not. Even if they do, the staff won't believe it. Role-constrained behavior also presumes that the outside programmers are acceptable, trusted, service providers desired by the residential staff. This is rarely the case at the start. Finally, program personnel usually come with things to teach direct-care staff that *they,* the program personnel, have chosen. The not so subtle presumption here is that what the staff have been doing on their own is wrong, or not useful, a notion mentioned before as one of the roots of resistive behavior.

Some program specialists appear not to realize that the goodness of their concepts and products typically is a moot point at the outset. The overriding issue is the process of constructing a relationship with the men and women who staff the residential unit. The concepts and products will stand or fall with that relationship anyway.

The First Risk.   Relationship building with a staff group that feels abused by the system and has defensible reasons for distrusting outsiders does not begin with products or even promises. It begins with feelings, the outsiders' feelings. Rather than relate through their role or expertise, they must relate through the uncertainty, discomfort, awkwardness, and apprehension they predictably will experience. These reactions, when they occur, must be shared with the direct-care staff. There are surprising payoffs when, for example, the program specialist begins his or her relationship with staff with comments such as: "I've never worked in a unit like this before, and I'm a little unsure of myself"; "I'm quite naive about this place, and I'm not certain what I have to offer will be acceptable or if it would even succeed"; "I'm very uneasy around aggressive clients I don't know well. I'll need your help when I'm with them." These and other sentiments that truly reflect the outsider's first experience in the unit can be disarming. What they disarm are the initial expectations staff have about program interventionists, change agents, or other intruders.

The dynamics of this approach appear to involve reactions to people who are genuinely vulnerable and admit it. They tend not to get kicked if they are down but say so. It has been our consistent observation that direct-care staff do not take advantage of persons who own up to not knowing everything about the residential unit. To the contrary, the admission engages a responsive chord, probably because of its unmistakable honesty. It thus seems good advice for outside program specialists to have the courage to expose their vulnerable feelings rather than use their expertise to mask these feelings. This is, for many situations, the first step in constructing the relationship with direct-care staff, and the initiative rests with the interventionist. Program personnel confide that such candidness is not easy to display—perhaps this is why so many people conducting program reform in residential facilities choose not to be so open. Thus, the generally perceived performance requirements for bringing change to the residential unit do not include disclosure of weaknesses. In Chapters 1 and 4 of this volume we discuss at length why this is so.

The difficulty notwithstanding, disclosure is a workable strategy. Perhaps its greatest value is that it allows other aspects of relationship building to occur. This, in turn, should increase the probability that staff will support program change and be willing to alter their roles accordingly. These other components of relationship building include permission, trust, responsibility, ownership, and shared expertise.

Permission.   The idea of giving people permission to be who they are or feel exactly what they feel is a human relations concept found in Gestalt therapy (Levitsky & Perls, 1970) and utilized often in the recent wave of self-help literature (e.g., Dyer, 1976). Historically, direct-care workers rarely have felt a safe permission to express, for example, their experience of being excluded or feeling distrust. For many, doing so would have been risky because such expressions might show up as "bad attitude" ratings on a service evaluation. But when outsiders begin their encounters with direct-care staff by risking self-disclosure about their own vulnerabilities, they make it easier for the staff to take similar risks with them. This changes things.

One program specialist we know encountered strong resistance by a group of direct-care staff and particularly from one senior worker who felt she would have to fight too many people if she gave her support to the proposed program. In recalling the incident, the program specialist first thought the worker was making excuses. "It was tempting to challenge her on the excuse," he told us, "because the facts didn't support her." Rather than challenge the worker, he chose to acknowledge and accept her feelings and reconstructed his response to the worker this way: "I can see you really feel strong about this, and I think you have a right to feel like giving up. That's OK with me. I know people sometimes get tired of fighting. I'm glad you told me because I don't want you to feel you have to fight against me too." Months later, this staff member confided to the programmer that he was one of the few people who ever listened to her point of view without attacking it.

The messages of permission, though quite simple, are almost therapeutic. What gets communicated to the staff is that they don't have to suppress the feeling that their job situation hurts or that they are frustrated. Acceptance for where they stand right now, on any issue, also is communicated. It is permission to have and express feelings openly. It is permission to have problems. It is permission without penalty. It is permission few others are likely to give to direct-care personnel.

We have noticed a curious paradox about this kind of permission. For many direct-care staff we have known over the years, change was more likely to occur when their right not to want to change was accepted. For the program specialists who have sensed permission needs and responded effectively to them, the process of relationship building should reach an important stage here. Having disarmed some traditional staff expectations about outsiders by curbing their expertise and sharing their own vulnerabilities, the program interventionists have now prompted the staff to take a similar risk. If they have listened to the staff nonjudgmentally, the result should be the first sense of trust, the third component in our view of relationship building.

Trust.   Trust is treated as an important variable in many recent approaches to organization and group change (e.g., Bennis, 1969; Bradford, Gibb & Benne, 1964; Schein, 1969, 1980). Direct-care staff historically have worked in job environments characterized by many norms against trust. Many still do. Developing trust with these staff, if one is an outsider, will be a formidable task. Maintaining an already established trust may be as difficult.

The first fragile sense of trust that should follow from the successful exchange of permissions between outsider and direct-care worker must be strengthened and tested over many trials. One seasoned and successful residential program specialist described trust building as a continuous effort: "You'd think you could build a feeling of trust and then it's over. But it isn't. It never stops, and you have to be prepared to be pushed three steps back to gain one significant unit of trust forward."

Nothing will arrest the possibility of trust or dismantle a developing trust quicker than errors of *exclusion*. Exclusion is the failure to inform, involve, or consult any individual or group who might feel even a small event as touching what they consider to be their domain of work. Second and third shift staff are groups typically excluded from things. We know many program specialists who set up effective projects on bankers' hours and learned later what loss of the second shift's trust was like.

To avoid exclusion, one must be overly *inclusive* at the residential level. When something is planned that will affect staff, they must be informed in advance. Verbal messages delivered through other people or across shifts may not be reliable. Written notes are more reliable but get misplaced. In terms of its effect on trust, inadvertent exclusion is indistinguishable from deliberate exclusion. Prudent program personnel, especially in the early phases of relationship building, will spend a good deal of time on all three shifts talking to all staff.

Trust with direct-care staff is fashioned from other encounters as well. Being visible on the unit is important, especially when the program specialist is there for large blocks of time. The most trusted program specialist we have known in 15 years spent hundreds of hours in long blocks of time on the unit she worked, particularly during second shift. She developed points of attachment with the staff beyond her role as programmer. For instance, she became one of the few people they knew who listened, who helped with routine custodial chores when they were short staffed, and who saw their working knowledge of clients as valuable. This type of time investment may be beyond the reach or interest of most program personnel, but the returns in trust and, later, in more substantive and stable interventions may not come otherwise. This particular woman was singularly responsible for the emergence of a commitment to program change by a second shift staff long since written off by many others as intractable.

Trust also is earned when the outsiders assist in events or crises that may occur on the unit when they are present, especially if these events are difficult or even unpleasant. For example, on units with incontinent clients, toileting accidents may occur frequently. The staff would never expect a program specialist to pitch in and clean up urine or feces, and most program personnel may not see their role as including this sort of thing. However, when they roll up their sleeves and help out with chores like this, particularly when the staff are overworked, the relationship undergoes a change and another piece of trust gets formed.

Responsibility and Ownership. The exchange of permissions and development of some trust clearly will improve the relationship between program personnel and direct-care staff. But it will not be enough to support the introduction of program change. Giving people unrestricted permission to express how they feel, or to have the problems they have, but going no further with them, makes it safe for them to stay where they are. Many program professionals get stuck at this stage in their relationship with direct-care staff. After some progress has been generated in their association with staff members, the relationship seems to run into a certain inertia we call *dead-ending.*

Many of the perceptions and feelings of direct-care staff are dead-enders, reactions that describe unsatisfactory conditions or circumstances but project blame for these situations elsewhere. The staff's detailed and indeed valid reasons for why things at the residential unit are difficult and can't change are, in the dead-end view, the fault of others—another department, the administration, the state. "If we had more staff, we could begin to do behavior programs down here." The direct-care workers, of course, are not responsible for poor staffing ratios and other difficulties, and thus having honestly expressed their feelings about it, they often claim exemption from having to problem-solve any of it. When confronted with this kind of situation, program specialists often feel dead-ended. Sensitive to the newly developing relationship with a potentially oppositional group, they are likely to be very cautious at this point and not push the relationship.

Almost as often, the relationship moves from this sense of impasse in the wrong direction. Dead-ender statements seductively invite argument. We have seen many staff make a statement like this to a program specialist: "There's no way you're going to get programs to work in this unit." The programmer, directed by superiors to get client programming started, may feel his or her professional worth questioned by the staff member's remark and may slide into a "yes-no" argument about why and how programming can be done. The outcome of this type of argument, whether the worker's dead-ender was intentional or unintentional and regardless of who "wins" the discussion, is the same: Relationship building with direct-care workers is set back.

There are more productive options for negotiating this point in the relationship process, and they require focusing on the staff's responsibility for even the least part of the circumstances they find objectionable. Enduring program change will not occur in residential units unless the direct-care staff can see and feel the changes as their own. When program professionals elect to persuade the staff why programming can occur or to demonstrate how it would work, they bypass the question of the staff's responsibility. This is an error in timing. The staff must own the problems and have a desire to make changes before either the wisdom or demonstration of program innovation will make sense to them.

The responsibility option can be pursued in a number of ways. In one case we recall, a series of meetings was held with direct-care workers to discuss a forthcoming staff training project for them. At the outset, the staff did little else but complain about all the barriers that existed to doing program work (e.g., poor staffing ratios, too much paper work, weak supervisory support, etc.). This "negative scanning" continued until the training consultant offered them a choice: They could continue to use the meetings to complain about things out of their control (e.g., the staffing ratios), or they could identify problems they *could* do something about and proceed to develop solutions. The consultant further emphasized that the choice was theirs, not anyone else's. If they continued to use their meeting time to complain, they would have to accept responsibility for that course of action. A dramatic turnaround followed. Over the next few meetings, negative scanning declined and problem-solving emerged as a theme.

Taking responsibility seems to become a possibility when the staff are prompted to see that they have the choice to work on problems (no matter how limited the work) or to leave problems as they are. Some staff (at all levels in the hierarchy) do not realize they have this choice. They seem almost to have learned a powerlessness that disallows them to take risks with problems, while at the same time helping to confirm their pessimism. With the choice, individuals may begin to consider that they are in their circumstances at least in part because they choose to be there. This is a different perception from a total feeling of being abused or victimized by the system. It is a perception that permits change.

The transition from permission to responsibility in the relationship process requires tactfully challenging the powerlessness of the problem holders rather than the validity of the problem. It is our experience that when outsiders to the direct-care culture challenge what the direct-care staff are complaining about, they quickly become part of the complaint.

The concept of ownership in interpersonal relationships has been discussed in the empirical literature (e.g., Argyris, 1982) as well as in the popular literature (e.g., Gordon, 1975, 1977). It is an important consideration to the introduction of change in residential units because successful program interventions require establishing different ownerships by direct-care staff. First, they must own their problems. Subsequently, they must also own solutions, outcomes, and the process by which both are achieved.

Given the general history of the direct-care worker in public institutions and their specific experience with program change, feelings of ownership do not come easily. Outcome ownership is an expecially sensitive area. Many direct-care staff become involved with program change only to see credit taken by or assigned to others. The opportunity for ownership occurs when staff members realize that their problems give them choices in responsibility and when they believe their expertise is both needed and desired. These two conditions improve their stake in the intervention process. This, in turn, diminishes their experience of that process as intrusive and lowers the need to resist it.

Shared Expertise.   The goal state of relationship building with direct-care staff is a professional collaboration with them. This not only is desirable to enable change to occur more smoothly; it is preferable, because the changes will be better. The expertise direct-care staff possess about developmentally disabled clients and their residential environments is extraordinary. It can be used to resist program change, as we have seen. It can also complement and improve a program specialist's portfolio of ideas and methods for change at the residential level.

Shared expertise is a logical outcome of outsiders' success in risking their vulnerabilities, building trust, utilizing permission, and promoting staff ownership. At its core, it communicates this clear message to the client-care worker: ''I respect what you have to offer and what you know about your clients. There's no way program work can be done without you. You have perspectives I could never have and skills I don't possess. Let's pool our resources and work together.''

If constructive relationships have formed, there are many possible ways to collaborate with direct-care workers in implementing program change. Interventionists who have done their homework in learning the residential unit will be much better prepared to recognize and seize these opportunities. Over the past 15 years we have conducted several staff training projects at the direct-care level. Our experiences with shared expertise in this context have been instructive. Presumably our training staff were the ''teachers'' and direct-care workers the ''learners.'' However, as these roles became reversed, blurred, disappeared, or simply became less important, the programs were more successful and decidedly more enduring. Some anecdotes from these programs illustrate the practice of shared expertise.

In one case, a staff trainer was showing a direct-care trainee how to task analyze the skill of handwashing into a series of smaller steps to teach to a blind, severely retarded client. The trainer's expertise was extremely useful, but the training procedure worked only after the trainee, thoroughly versed in the client's patterns of movement, sound preferences, and time rhythms, recommended which particular sink to use in training, what times of day had a higher chance of on-task success, and that softer tones of voice were more likely to elicit the client's cooperation.

In a different context, we recall one project where the direct-care staff taught us how to use to our advantage the unit's elusive communication system. By working messages in certain forms both horizontally (across shifts) and vertically (up the chain of command), we learned to transfer program information to all interested and disinterested parties in ways they were more likely to accept. Previously we had been victimized by that system and accused of excluding people.

Staff expertise was crucial in winning the support of resistive higher level supervisors in one program several years ago. The staff knew the specific incentives of authority and credit that would engage the supervisors' interest and support. They also knew what approaches to avoid when seeking cooperation from these supervisors. Here the expertise was an astute working knowledge of some key personnel in the facility.

Finally, a comprehensive maintenance system (Creamer, 1979) to sustain the program change accomplished in one unit was developed and implemented under the direction of the direct-care staff who initially had been trainees. Their sophisticated understanding of the staff, supervisors, clients, and operation of the unit provided the expertise to establish the system and keep it running successfully.

It is through this sense of shared expertise that program specialists can comfortably utilize their own professional skills in the residential unit. When the interventionist's role is no longer intrusive, expertise sharing can begin. If this phase in the relationship is achieved, staff resistance is much less likely to occur. What the interventionist has to offer now fits more acceptably into the staff's construction of human service realities.

Shared expertise between the direct-care worker and the program interventionist is an interdependence of process and product—the process of relationship building enables the application of products (in the way of concepts and methods) for effecting program change. When expertise sharing starts to occur, the collaboration gradually can begin to enlarge its domain of activity. More and different problems will be seen as workable. For example, in a longer term staff training grant, shared expertise between trainers and direct-care staff had been successfully achieved. With the grant ending and the trainers about to leave, the direct-care workers petitioned the administration to provide them with a new position designated to supervise maintenance of the program work established under the grant. They were successful and ventured into even more "forbidden" domains by asking to participate in the interviewing of prospective candidates for the position, a procedure usually reserved for hiring supervisors. This request was also granted. There are important changes to observe here. For these direct-care workers, the passive powerlessness we described earlier had been overcome. This was *their* program, and they were not about to surrender it for lack of resources. In making this choice, they had enlarged the range of problems they saw as their responsibility.

The collaboration or partnership between program personnel and direct-care staff can reach into other areas associated with the implementation of change itself. These include such administrative and clinical processes as decision-making, complex problem-solving, planning, and interpersonal processes like feedback and positive scanning. Briefly, let us examine illustrations of some of these effects.

Sharing candid feedback is a necessary norm in any atmosphere of change (Argyris, 1982). Yet, as indicated before, it can be an area of high risk where outside interventionists and client-care staff interact. However, we have observed repeatedly that relationships developed to the shared expertise stage are more likely to interpret frank feedback constructively rather than defensively. Positive scanning, or focusing on constructive perspectives, outcomes, and interactions, as a choice over negative scanning, also seems to emerge as a more normative practice at or near the point where shared expertise occurs. One program specialist we know had the "strange" experience of sending someone in the unit a thank you memo only to have him send a return memo thanking her for the thanks! It underscored the importance of sending messages of appreciation in a bureaucratic system well drilled in finding negatives.

Another illustration of collaboration outcomes involves response to more complex problems and planning. One group of direct-care staff were the recipients of classic bureaucratic abuse. They had developed an habilitative program for their unit and had managed to adapt their thin staffing ratio to its implementation. One morning, the Chief Medical Officer arbitrarily transferred one of the facility's most difficult clients to their unit, bypassing the facility's formal client referral system. The client's behavioral disturbance was significant, requiring extensive staff time. The staff were given no role in the transfer decision; indeed, they were given less than one hour's notice to prepare for the client's arrival. Their resentment at being treated so inconsiderately was aggravated by their conviction that the new client's requirements would make their new habilitative program unworkable and thus force a retreat from their program initiatives. That the transferred client was seen as more appropriate for any of several other units only intensified the matter. Fortunately, this staff had worked through the phases of relationship with their program consultants over the preceding year and a half and were able to enlist that experience in responding to the Chief Medical Officer's action.

What followed was a curious, telescoped view of that relationship process. Their first reaction was to give up; they had been bruised by the system once too often. Some members of the group wanted to fight fire with fire and take on the medical director. They spent the time needed giving each other permission to be openly outraged and unproductive. This led gradually to a frank confrontation not with the medical director, but with their own responsibilities to the transferred client. With the negatives burned off, they began to examine the new problems and their whole unit more closely. They generated a number of choices but reached agreement on a strategy that, in effect, changed their whole operation. They would intensively program the new client, though he was reputed to be nearly unmanageable, and they would reorganize their work routines to accommodate the other programs.

These direct-care staff achieved both goals. Their success with the transferred client became well known throughout the facility, as did their decision to accept his programmatic challenge with no additional resources. The facility learned some valuable lessons as well. These staff members had worked the process of change in its most productive sense. They were true change agents and became a model for their colleagues as well as other facility professionals and administrators.

The confusion and threat that direct-care workers so frequently have felt in response to the turnovers of change in the past two decades are, in our view, inextricably bound to the absence of productive working relationships between them and the various planners, administrators, and implementers of that change. Constructing relationships at the residential level is, not surprisingly, similar to developing most other human relationships. The few differences, however, concern rather compelling historical circumstances that characterize the workers themselves, the evolution of their job, and their powerful learning experiences with outsiders. These circumstances, which we detailed earlier, sharply alter the nature and course of building relationships that will assist the direct-care staff to accept and support program change. These circumstances also charge the intruding change agents with the responsibility of developing the relationships. The process is tedious, but to believe that definitive and durable program change can occur in client residential environments without effective relationships with direct-care staff is naive. To fail to apprehend the habilitative possibilities of these settings with that relationship established is to be without vision.

REPRISE AND REFLECTION

In closing, we return to the client's self-portrait taped to the wall in the residential unit's living room. "I love the aides," were the words the artist had his image speak.

This voice instructs the singular significance of the client-care worker for any vision, mandate, mission, or program that would revise the residential facility. Yet too many of those with the visions, mandates, missions, and programs do not know the men and women to whom the client's drawing refers. They do not know the direct-care worker's history, but they plan his future. They disconfirm the direct-care worker's traditional role functions at the flash of a new concept, but then become impatient when she responds with resistance to the disorientation she feels. They overestimate what the direct-care worker can achieve with their programs given the manner in which these are introduced, but underestimate the clinical expertise he could contribute as partner in a collaborative relationship. Thus, these "change agents" bring interventions to direct-care workers but rarely offer them shares in the intervention process. They reflex at the staff member's resistance, but may not spend the time in a residential unit to appreciate the extent of the worker's potential. They throw change after change at the facility and assume its direct-care staff can digest it all in an instant, when they themselves took decades to embrace merely the humanity behind the change.

They do not know the direct-care worker as well as the client artist does. This must all be corrected. We have offered a few suggestions.

REFERENCES

Allen, G. J., Chinsky, J. M., & Veit, S. W. (1974). Pressures toward institutionalization within the aide culture: A behavior analytic case study. *Journal of Community Psychology, 2,* 67–70.

Amble, B. R., Bellamy, E., Gideon, C., Parks, W. G., & Shafter, A. (1971). Child care aides: Intellectual, personality, and preference patterns in relation to job performance. *Mental Retardation, 9,* 6–10.

Argyris, C. (1982). *Reasoning, learning, and action.* San Francisco: Jossey-Bass.

Baer, D. M., Wolf, M. M., & Risley, T. R. (1968). Some current dimensions of applied behavior analysis. *Journal of Applied Behavior Analysis, 1,* 91–97.

Bailey, J. S. (1981). Wanted: A rational search for the limiting conditions of habilitation in the retarded. *Analysis and Intervention in Developmental Disabilities, 1,* 45–52.

Baker, B. L., Seltzer, G. B., & Seltzer, M. M. (1977). *As close as possible: Community residences for retarded adults.* Boston: Little, Brown.

Balla, D. (1976). Relationship of institution size to quality of care: A review of the literature. *American Journal of Mental Deficiency, 81,* 117–124.

Baumeister, A. A. (1981). The right to habilitation: What does it mean. *Analysis and Intervention in Developmental Disabilities, 1,* 61–74.

Baumeister, A. A., & Klosowski, R. (1965). An attempt to group toilet train severely retarded patients. *Mental Retardation, 3,* 24–26.

Begab, M. J. (1975). The mentally retarded and society: Trends and issues. In M. J. Begab and S. A. Richardson (Eds.), *The mentally retarded and society: A social science perspective* (pp. 3–32). Baltimore: University Park Press.

Belknap, I. (1956). *Human problems in a state mental hospital.* New York: McGraw Hill.

Bennis, W. G. (1965). Theory and method in applying behavioral science to planned organizational change. *Journal of Applied Behavioral Science, 1,* 337–360.

Bennis, W. G. (1969). *Organization development: Its nature, origins and prospects.* Reading, MA: Addison-Wesley.

Bensberg, G. J., & Barnett, C. D. (1966). *Attendant training in southern residential facilities for the mentally retarded.* Atlanta: Southern Regional Education Board.

Bensberg, G. J., Barnett, C. D., & Hurder, W. P. (1964). Training of attendant personnel in residential facilities for the mentally retarded. *Mental Retardation, 2,* 144–151.

Blatt, B., Ozolins, A., & McNally, J. (1978). *The family papers: Documentation from the hidden world of mental retardation.* Glen Ridge, NJ: Exceptional Press.

Bogdan, R., & Taylor, S. (1976). The judged, not the judges: An insider's view of mental retardation. *American Psychologist, 31,* 47–52.

Bogdan, R., Taylor, S., deGrandpre, B., & Haynes, S. (1974). Let them eat programs: Attendants' perspectives and programming on wards in state schools. *Journal of Health and Social Behavior, 15,* 142–151.

Boles, S. M., & Bible, G. H. (1978). The student service index: A method for managing service delivery in residential settings. In M. S. Berkler, G. H. Bible, S. M. Boles, D. E. D. Deitz, & A. C. Repp (Eds.), *Current trends for the developmentally disabled* (pp. 153–195). Baltimore: University Park Press.

Bradford, L. P., Gibb, J. R., & Benne, K. D. (Eds.). (1964). *T-Group theory and the laboratory method.* New York: Wiley.

Braginsky, D., & Braginsky, B. (1971). *Hansels and gretels.* New York: Holt, Rinehart, & Winston.

Bruininks, R. H., Kudla, M. J., Wieck, C. A., & Hauber, F. A. (1980). Management problems in community residential facilities. *Mental Retardation, 18,* 125–130.

Burgio, L. D., Whitman, T. L., & Reid, D. H. (1983). A participative management approach for improving direct-care staff performance in an institutional setting. *Journal of Applied Behavior Analysis, 16,* 37–53.

Caudill, W. (1958). *The psychiatric hospital as a small society.* Cambridge, MA: Harvard University Press.

Christian, W. P., Hannah, G. T., & Glahn, T. J. (Eds.). (1984). *Programming effective human services: Strategies for institutional change and client transition.* New York: Plenum Press.

Cleland, C. C., & Dingman, H. F. (1970). Dimensions of institutional life, social organization, possessions, time, and space. In A. A. Baumeister and E. C. Butterfield (Eds.), *Residential facilities for the mentally retarded* (pp. 138–162). Chicago: Aldine.

Cleland, C. C., & Peck, R. F. (1967). Intra-institutional administrative problems: A paradigm for employee stimulation. *Mental Retardation, 5,* 2–8.

Creamer, J. (1979). *The clinical management system.* Unpublished manuscript, The University of Connecticut, Storrs.

Crosby, K. G. (1976).   Essentials of active programming. *Mental Retardation, 14,* 3–9.

Cullari, S. (1984).   Everybody is talking about the new institution. *Mental Retardation, 22,* 28–29.

Cullari, S., & Ferguson, D. G. (1981).   Individual behavior change: Problems with programming in institutions for mentally retarded persons. *Mental Retardation, 19,* 267–270.

Cumming, J., & Cumming, E. (1957).   Social equilibrium and social change in the large mental hospital. In M. Greenblatt, D. J. Levinson, & R. H. Williams (Eds.), *The patient and the mental hospital* (pp. 49–72). Glencoe, IL: Free Press.

Dailey, W. F., Allen, G. J., Chinsky, J. M., & Veit, S. W. (1974).   Attendant behavior and attitudes toward institutionalized retarded children. *American Journal of Mental Deficiency, 78,* 586–591.

Davis, H. R. (1973).   Change and innovation. In S. Feldman (Ed.), *The administration of mental health services* (pp. 289–341). Springfield, IL: Charles C. Thomas.

Dyer, W. W. (1976)   *Your erroneous zones.* New York: Avon.

Eyman, R., & Call, T. (1977).   Maladaptive behavior and community placement of mentally retarded persons. *American Journal of Mental Deficiency, 82,* 137–140.

Favell, J. E., Favell, J. E., Riddle, J. I., & Risley, T. R. (1984).   Promoting change in mental retardation facilities: Getting services from the paper to the people. In W. P. Christian, G. T. Hannah, & T. J. Glahn (Eds.), *Programming effective human services: Strategies for institutional change and client transition* (pp. 15–37). New York: Plenum Press.

Gardner, J. M. (1975).   Training non-professionals in behavior modification. In T. Thompson & W. S. Dockens (Eds.), *Applications in behavior modification.* New York: Academic Press.

Gardner, J. M., & Giampa, F. (1971).   The attendant-behavior checklist: Measuring on the ward behavior of institutional attendants. *American Journal of Mental Deficiency, 75,* 617–622.

George, M. J., & Baumeister, A. A. (1981).   Employee withdrawal and job satisfaction in community residential facilities for mentally retarded persons. *American Journal of Mental Deficiency, 85,* 639–647.

Gladstone, B. W., & Spencer, C. J. (1977).   The effects of modeling on the contingent praise of mental retardation counsellors. *Journal of Applied Behavior Analysis, 10,* 75–84.

Glahn, T. J., & Chock, P. N. (1984).   Transitional teaching homes for developmentally disabled clients. In W. P. Christian, G. T. Hannah, & T. J. Glahn (Eds.), *Programming effective human services: Strategies for institutional change and client transition* (pp. 407–432). New York: Plenum Press.

Goffman, E. (1961).   *Asylums.* New York: Doubleday.

Gordon, T. (1975).   *P.E.T.: Parent effectiveness training.* New York: New American Library.

Gordon, T. (1977).   *Leader effectiveness training: L.E.T.* New York: Wyden Books.

Greene, B. F., Willis, B. S., Levy, R., & Bailey, J. S. (1978).   Measuring client gains from staff implemented programs. *Journal of Applied Behavior Analysis, 11,* 395–412.

Haas, J. E., & Drabek, T. E. (1973).   *Complex organizations: A sociological perspective.* New York: Macmillan.

Hill, I. B. (1953, May).   *Factors influencing employee morale.* Paper presented at the meeting of the American Association on Mental Deficiency, Los Angeles.

Hung, D. W., & Drash, P. W. (1984).   Community-based residential treatment for autistic, developmentally disabled, and predelinquent children: The CIRT model. In W. P. Christian, G. T. Hannah, & T. J. Glahn (Eds.), *Programming effective human services: Strategies for institutional change and client transition* (pp. 457–489). New York: Plenum Press.

Iwata, B. A., Bailey, J. S., Brown, K. M., Foshee, T. J., & Alpern, M. (1976).   A performance-based lottery to improve residential care and training by institutional staff. *Journal of Applied Behavior Analysis, 9,* 417–431.

King, R. D., & Raynes, N. V. (1968).   Patterns of institutional care for the severely subnormal. *American Journal of Mental Deficiency, 72,* 700–709.

Klaber, M. (1970).   Institutional programming and research: A vital partnership in action. In A. A.

Baumeister & E. C. Butterfield (Eds.), *Residential facilities for the mentally retarded* (pp. 163–200). Chicago: Aldine.

Korabek, C. A., Reid, D. H., & Ivancic, M. T. (1981). Improving needed food intake of profoundly handicapped children through effective supervision of institutional staff performance. *Applied Research in Mental Retardation, 2,* 69–88.

Kugel, R. B., & Wolfensberger, W. (Eds.). (1969). *Changing patterns in residential services for the mentally retarded.* Washington: President's Committee on Mental Retardation.

Landesman-Dwyer, S., Sackett, G. P., & Kleinman, J. S. (1980). Relationship of size to resident and staff behavior in small community residences. *American Journal of Mental Deficiency, 85,* 6–17.

Levinson, D., & Klerman, G. L. (1967). The clinician-executive: Some problematic issues for the psychiatrist in mental health organizations. *Psychiatry, 30,* 3–15.

Levitsky, A., & Perls, F. S. (1970). The rules and games of Gestalt therapy. In I. Shepherd and J. Fagen (Eds.), *Gestalt therapy now.* Palo Alto: Science and Behavior Books.

Maloof, B. A. (1975). Peculiarities of human service bureaucracies. *Administration in Mental Health, 3,* 21–26.

Martin, R. (1979). *Workshop materials: Legal challenges in regulating behavior change.* Champaign, IL: Research Press.

Mayhew, G. L., Enyart, P., & Anderson, J. (1978). Social reinforcement and the naturally occurring social responses of severely and profoundly retarded adolescents. *American Journal of Mental Deficiency, 83,* 164–170.

Mayhew, G. L., Enyart, P., & Cone, J. D. (1979). Approaches to employee management: Policies and preferences. *Journal of Organizational Behavior Management, 2,* 103–111.

McCord, W. T. (1982). From theory to reality: Obstacles to the implementation of the normalization principle in human services. *Mental Retardation, 20,* 247–253.

Mechanic, D. (1973). The sociology of organizations. In S. Feldman (Ed.), *The administration of mental health services* (pp. 138–166). Springfield, IL: Charles C. Thomas.

Michael, D. N. (1973). *On learning to plan—and on planning to learn.* San Francisco: Jossey-Bass.

Mintzberg, H. (1979). *The structuring of organizations.* Englewood Cliffs, NJ: Prentice-Hall.

Mintzberg, H. (1981, January-February). Organization design: Fashion or fit? *Harvard Business Review,* pp. 103–116.

Moos, R. H., & Daniels, D. N. (1967). Differential effects of ward settings on psychiatric staff. *Archives of General Psychiatry, 17,* 75–82.

National Association for Retarded Children. (1972). *Residential programming for mentally retarded persons.* Arlington, TX: National Association for Retarded Children.

Nirje, B. (1969). The normalization principle and its human management implications. In R. B. Kugel & W. Wolfensberger (Eds.), *Changing patterns in residential services for the mentally retarded.* (pp. 179–195). Washington: President's Committee on Mental Retardation.

Overbeck, D. (1971). Attitudes sampling of institutional charge attendant personnel: Cues for intervention. *Mental Retardation, 9,* 8–10.

Panyan, M. C., & Patterson, E. T. (1974). Teaching attendants the applied aspects of behavior modification. *Mental Retardation, 12,* 30–32.

Paul, J. L. (1977). Accountability. In J. L. Paul, D. J. Stedman, & G. R. Neufeld (Eds.), *Deinstitutionalization: Program and policy development* (pp. 97–123). Syracuse, NY: Syracuse University Press.

Pines, A. M., & Aronson, E. (1981). *Burnout: From tedium to personal growth.* New York: The Free Press.

Prue, D. M., Frederiksen, L. W., & Bacon, A. (1978). Organizational behavior management: An annotated bibliography. *Journal of Organizational Behavior Management, 1,* 216–257.

Public Law 95–602. (1978). *The rehabilitation, comprehensive services, and developmental disabilities amendments of 1978.*

Quilitch, H. R. (1975). A comparison of three staff-management procedures. *Journal of Applied Behavior Analysis, 8,* 59–66.

Rappaport, J., Chinsky, J. M., & Cowen, E. L. (1971). *Innovations in helping chronic patients.* New York: Academic Press.

Realon, R. E., Lewallen, J. D., & Wheeler, A. J. (1983). Verbal feedback vs. verbal feedback plus praise: The effects on direct care staff's training behaviors. *Mental Retardation, 21,* 209–212.

Reid, D. H., & Shoemaker, J. (1984). Behavioral supervision: Methods of improving institutional staff performance. In W. P. Christian, G. T. Hannah, & T. J. Glahn (Eds.), *Programming effective human services: Strategies for institutional change and client transition* (pp. 39–61). New York: Plenum Press.

Reid, D. H., & Whitman, T. L. (1983). Behavioral staff management in institutions: A critical review of effectiveness and acceptability. *Analysis and Intervention in Developmental Disabilities, 3,* 131–149.

Repp, A. C., & Barton, L. E. (1980). Naturalistic observations of institutionalized retarded persons: A comparison of licensure decisions and behavioral observations. *Journal of Applied Behavior Analysis, 13,* 333–341.

Repp, A. C., & Deitz, D. E. (1979). Reinforcement-based reductive procedures: Training and monitoring performance of institutional staff. *Mental Retardation, 17,* 221–226.

Reppucci, N. D. (1973). Social psychology of institutional change: General principles for intervention. *American Journal of Community Psychology, 1,* 330–341.

Reppucci, N. D., & Saunders, J. T. (1974). Social psychology of behavior modification: Problems of implementation in natural settings. *American Psychologist, 29,* 649–660.

Rogers, K. (1975). State mental hospitals: An organizational analysis. *Administration in Mental Health, 3,* 3–11.

Roos, P. (1970). Evolutionary changes of the residential facility. In A. A. Baumeister & E. C. Butterfield, (Eds.), *Residential facilities for the mentally retarded* (pp. 29–58). Chicago: Aldine.

Sarason, S. B., & Doris, J. (1979). *Educational handicap, public policy, and social history.* New York: Free Press.

Scheerenberger, R. C. (1975). *Managing residential facilities for the developmentally disabled.* Springfield, IL: Charles C. Thomas.

Scheerenberger, R. C. (1979). *Public residential services for the mentally retarded, 1979.* Madison, WI: National Association of Superintendents of Public Residential Facilities for the Mentally Retarded.

Scheerenberger, R. C. (1983). *A history of mental retardation.* Baltimore: Paul H. Brookes.

Scheff, T. J. (1961). Control over policy by attendants in a mental hospital. *Journal of Health and Human Behavior, 2,* 93–105.

Schein, E. H. (1969). *Process consultation: Its role in organization development.* Reading, MA: Addison-Wesley.

Schein, E. H. (1980). *Organizational psychology* (3rd ed.). Englewood Cliffs, NJ: Prentice-Hall.

Seys, D. M., & Duker, P. C. (1978). Improving residential care for the retarded by differential reinforcement of high rates of ward-staff behavior. *Behavioral Analysis and Modification, 2,* 203–210.

Slater, M. A., & Bunyard, P. D. (1983). Survey of residential staff roles, responsibilities, and perception of resident needs. *Mental Retardation, 21,* 52–58.

Stanton, A. H., & Schwartz, M. S. (1954). *The mental hospital: A study of institutional participation in psychiatric illness and treatment.* New York: Basic Books.

Thaw, J., & Cuvo, A. J. (1974, June). Implementing progressive mental health ideas in traditional institutions: Some issues and rules of operation. In A. J. Cuvo (Chair), *Implementing and maintaining innovative programming in a residential setting.* Symposium conducted at the meeting of the American Association on Mental Deficiency, Toronto.

Thaw, J., Palmer, M. E., & Sulzer-Azaroff, B. (1977, June). The middle managers and program development: A longitudinal approach to training institutional supervisory personnel. In J. Thaw (Chair), *Direct care, middle management, and professional staff: Characteristics, conflicts, and the issue of program innovation.* Symposium conducted at the meeting of the American Association on Mental Deficiency, New Orleans.

Thompson, T. (1975, May). *I'm O.K. and you are O.K. too but the state hospital system stinks.* Paper presented at the meeting of the Midwestern Association of Behavior Analysis, Chicago.

Thompson, T., & Grabowski, J. (Eds.). (1972). *Behavior modification of the mentally retarded.* New York: Oxford University Press.

Thompson, T., & Grabowski, J. (1977). *Behavior modification of the mentally retarded* (2nd ed.). New York: Oxford University Press.

Toffler, A. (1970). *Future shock.* New York: Random House.

Ullman, L. P. (1967). *Institution and outcome: A comparative study of psychiatric hospitals.* London: Pergamon Press.

U.S. Department of Health, Education & Welfare. (1974). Regulations for intermediate care facility services. *Federal Register, 39,* 2220–2235.

Vail, D. J. (1966). *Dehumanization and the institutional career.* Springfield, IL: Charles C. Thomas.

Veit, S. W., Allen, G. J., & Chinsky, J. M. (1976). Interpersonal interactions between institutionalized retarded children and their attendants. *American Journal of Mental Deficiency, 80,* 535–542.

Warren, S. A., & Mondy, L. W. (1971). To what behaviors do attending adults respond? *American Journal of Mental Deficiency, 75,* 449–455.

Watson, L. S., Jr. (1970). Behavior modification of residents and personnel in institutions for the mentally retarded. In A. A. Baumeister & E. C. Butterfield (Eds.), *Residential facilities for the mentally retarded* (pp. 201–245). Chicago: Aldine.

Weinberg, S., Edwards, G., & Sternau, R. (1979, May). *Burn-out among employees of state residential facilities serving the developmentally disabled.* Paper presented at the annual meeting of the American Association on Mental Deficiency, Miami Beach.

Whitman, T. L., Scibak, J. W., & Reid, D. H. (1983). *Behavior modification with the severely and profoundly retarded: Research and application.* New York: Academic Press.

Willems, E. P. (1974). Behavioral technology and behavioral ecology. *Journal of Applied Behavior Analysis, 7,* 151–165.

Wolfensberger, W. (1969). The origin and nature of our institutional models. In R. B. Kugel & W. Wolfensberger (Eds.), *Changing patterns in residential services for the mentally retarded* (pp. 59–172). Washington: President's Committee on Mental Retardation.

Wolfensberger, W. (1971). Will there always be an institution? I: The impact of epidemiological trends. *Mental Retardation, 9,* 14–20.

Wolfensberger, W. (1976, June). *A look at the future directions of human services in the light of historical developments.* Plenary address to the annual meeting of the American Association on Mental Deficiency, Chicago.

Wyatt v. Stickney, 325 F. Supp. 781, 784 (M. D. Ala. 1971).

Ziarnik, J. P. (1980). Developing proactive direct care staff. *Mental Retardation, 18,* 289–292.

Ziarnik, J. P., & Bernstein, G. S. (1982). A critical examination of the effect of inservice training on staff performance. *Mental Retardation, 20,* 109–114.

4 The Professionals: Difficulties and Directions

Jack Thaw, Ph.D.
Edward Benjamin, M.S.
Anthony J. Cuvo, Ph.D.

INTRODUCTION

Agendas for changing public residential facilities (PRFs) for mentally handicapped persons that developed in the late 1960s and early 1970s (e.g., Kugel & Wolfensberger, 1969; Roos, 1970) called for active participation by professionally trained service providers. During the same period, reviews of services in fields such as psychology (e.g., Baumeister, 1967), speech pathology and audiology (e.g., Blue & Sumner, 1970), education (e.g., Younie, 1966), and social work (e.g., Krishef & Levine, 1968) described significant needs and problems for these and other professions serving mentally handicapped clients. Many professional departments, where they existed in PRFs 2 decades ago, were functioning on the margin. They provided limited services and perhaps were nearly uninvolved with the daily course of client activity. Clearly, the professions themselves were faced with ample agendas for change if they were to operate successfully within new philosophies and trends of institutional reform.

In the 1980s we find the professional service provider (we shall define this individual shortly) suffering the effects of responding to all these changes. Unlike their counterparts in the less active residential facilities of the 1960s, and perhaps ultimately for better reasons, today's professional is working in an increasingly unstable environment beset by multiple reforms and pressures for even more. Many of these changes came quickly and were forced into overly short time frames. Many were implemented with minimal planning; many persist without adequate evaluation; and, thus, many changes are in need of revision.

This text generally takes the position that the nature and rate of change in many PRFs have come to excede the system's capacity for administrative, technological, and personal responses to the demand. For most service professionals this situation is decidedly unlike the ones in which and for which they were trained. Though data are limited, there are recent signals that professionals are not coping well either with their work setting or the upheaval it is experiencing. The important relationship between effective internal functioning of a mental health organization and employee satisfaction have been explicated (Scholom & Perlman, 1979). Data from mental retardation facilities also support this notion and prompted Sarata (1975) to conclude that satisfaction with agency-related matters is a much more significant determinant of overall job satisfaction than satisfaction with the field of mental retardation itself. The authors cited suggest that the quality of service delivery is limited by a lack of the system's responsiveness to service providers. Not surprisingly, the needs of service staff (including professionals) often are neglected (Scholom & Perlman, 1979).

Recent attention to stress and the phenomenon of burnout among mental health workers (e.g., Maslach, 1976; Pines & Maslach, 1978) seem to confirm this belief. Although systematic data are limited, one large-scale study (Weinberg, Edwards, & Sternau, 1979) examined burnout across three staff levels in 14 PRFs in 11 states. Professionals (e.g., psychologists, social workers, teachers, nurses, physical therapists, speech clinicians) were one of three groups studied. Applying the Kafry and Pines (1977) definition of burnout (i.e., the experience of physical, attitudinal, and emotional exhaustion that results from the presence of stresses and absence of satisfiers in the work situation), Weinberg and colleagues reported incidences of burnout among professionals that ranged from 5% to 31% across facilities. More than 15% of the professional staffs in half the facilities described themselves as burned out; these people tended to be valued and dedicated workers.

One must be extremely cautious with methodologies and data at such an early stage of research on a subject. Nevertheless, these findings are consistent with our own personal observations of professionals in similar facilities. When situated in conditions of high demand and pressure for change, and when experiencing a rushed, uncoordinated, and unevaluated turnover of significant workplace events, these employees are vulnerable. In a sense, they are trapped in complex organizations structured in many ways to minimize the effectiveness of their new and often imperfect technologies. They are also trapped in these settings by virtue of being untrained to understand and manage them. Finally, they are trapped in chains of innovation and uncertainty that stress and overprocess them. This chapter discusses these circumstances as well as the vulnerabilities of the mental disability professional working in PRFs. Recommendations for revising aspects of professionals' preparation and function are offered.

DEFINING THE MENTAL DISABILITY PROFESSIONALS

The professional working in organizations has not gone unnoticed as a subject of social science (e.g., Abrahamson, 1967; Bucher & Stelling, 1969; Moore, 1970;

Ryan, 1974; Scott, 1969). Our focus is those service providers accorded the status of *professional* in PRFs. Formal research on this group is meager; therefore, it is important to develop some clarity about who these people are, what characterizes them, and what distinguishes them from other staff groups in the facility. Doing this requires not only definition but also examination of the relationship between professional training schools and the professionals' work environment. We shall treat both questions in turn.

Numerous definitions have been offered to describe profession and professional. Some time ago Cogan (1953) characterized a profession generically as a vocation founded on expertise in some area of learning or science applied to the practical affairs of man. Referring to the mental health field, Tucker and Tucker (1976) saw professional staff as a varied group of people linked only by their possession of one or more academic degrees. Michael (1973) provided a vernacular meaning—a specialist with credentials. Dolgoff (1970) characterized the mental health professional as an academically trained specialist with a code of ethics and a service commitment.

Beyond these and other formal descriptions, a local definition exists at every individual facility. There professions and their members are identified and sorted according to pragmatic and political considerations. as well as formal credentials. Status, power, and interpersonal reputation influence the perception of the individual professional or profession and in so doing alter the operational definition. Particularly important in this process is a judgment of the effectiveness of certain professions made by other staff groups, using their own criteria. For example, the sophisticated and well-trained psychologist who cannot translate his or her abilities into service usable and acceptable to direct care staff may come to be seen, and thus defined, by these staff as ineffective or unnecessary to the service operation. Repeated experience may likely generalize such attributions to the profession itself and all its members.

These local definitions are important for understanding the dynamics of professionals in PRFs. So, too, is the history of the definition in a specific facility. Newly arrived professionals too often neglect to review the record and tradition of their predecessors. Local viewpoints thus organize individual professionals and professions in context with other professions, employees, and the facility itself. Any formal definition must be filtered through these local considerations.

We suggest that the following formal features characterize professionals in PRFs: (a) standards of operation; (b) special language; (c) regulation and ethics; (d) specialized knowledge and technology; (e) presence of a power structure; and (f) overt symbolism.

Standards of Operation

A profession typically has formal mechanisms for defining its span of endeavor. It establishes credentials for admission to the field as well as standards for remaining credible in the occupation. Most professions develop formal competency standards that identify the nature and sophistication of practitioner responses. Additionally, the profession defines acceptable ways of developing knowledge in its field, provides vehicles for disseminating that knowledge, and rewards for those who contribute to these efforts.

Special Language

Another characteristic of a profession is its language. Technical concepts and methods often require a special vocabulary that becomes a kind of language code, a functional shorthand for members that is often identified by outsiders as a jargon associated with the discipline. This language code tends to produce an additional distinction, even an exclusiveness or touch of mystery, to the profession. The mystique often serves to separate professionals from nonprofessionals in terms of identity, prestige, and autonomy.

Regulations and Ethics

Most organized professions impose regulations to enforce their standards of operation. Regulatory procedures often exist to define both the domain and the quality of services and to monitor the conduct of members. These regulations may be issued from the profession itself or from agencies of the state or federal government. The formal professional organization usually prepares a written set of ethical standards that binds its members and provides sanction for violation (e.g., exclusion from the organization).

Specialized Knowledge and Technology

Another distinguishing feature of a profession is its claim to a body of specialized knowledge. One of the functions of the profession is the generation of that specialized knowledge through research. The knowledge is disseminated through institutions of higher learning to students of and apprentices to the profession. Similarly, an array of vehicles (e.g., professional journals, conferences, workshops, continuing education programs, etc.) distribute developed knowledge to the practicing membership of the profession. Many professions are currently experiencing a knowledge dissemination overload with increased specialization as well as volume. This has led to the creation of subdivisions of special knowledge within a profession. One distinguished observer in psychology (Koch, 1981) described his profession as a collection of fields rather than a single coherent discipline.

The methods, procedures, tools, and other devices that facilitate the application of knowledge to needs in human service may be described as the technology of a profession. Such technologies are developed through applied research. In PRFs, identified professions utilize technologies at various stages of development. The observed effectiveness of a profession's technology often affects the influence of the profession itself. The difference between the expectancy and performance of human service technologies is an important issue for professionals and will be discussed below.

Power Structure

The growth and survival of a profession depends on its internal power structure and its ability to use that power for its own interest. Training programs have the power of gatekeeping—they determine who is admitted to study for the profession and ultimately to its membership. Additionally, universities control the training curricula and standards of achievement for professional aspirants. The prestige of institutions of higher education derives from the reputation of their faculty, prominence of their graduates, and quality of their research. These, in turn, endow the individual professions at large with an elitism and image of expertise and strength, not unimportant elements in power.

Professional organizations have the power to admit, deny admission, and expel from their ranks professionals credentialed by the training programs. Although some of these organizations function entirely to disseminate scholarly knowledge, others are more socially and politically active, and may engage the legislative and executive political processes. More recently, many have played roles in litigation through *amicus curiae* briefs and by providing expert testimony. A great deal of this activity is targeted at increasing the influence of the profession in matters relevant to its protection, strength, and growth.

In the mental disability field, professional power is legally sanctioned in several instances. Medical testimony and, more recently, psychologists' testimony, typically are important factors in mental status and competency legal proceedings. The opinions of other mental disability professionals have a favored position of authority in still other formal proceedings such as civil commitment, workman's compensation claims, guardianship, and adoption. Professional power can be quite extensive in many of these areas. One of the authors recalls observing numerous civil commitment hearings in which judges had functionally abdicated their role to psychiatrists who had conducted one or two brief interviews with clients.

Finally, some professions enjoy another facet of power—privileged communication. Physicians, for example, may claim the privilege in certain aspects of their service relationship with consumers. The law has sanctioned nondisclosure of information obtained under the terms of that privilege by attorneys. The importance of this power is underscored by recent attempts to secure it on the part of certain human service professionals historically denied the privilege (e.g., psychologists, social workers, counselors).

Overt Symbolism

Unique markings and special environments often serve as identifying criteria of a profession. These visible symbols are generally recognized by the public and often anchor the perceptions of the profession by other groups in the human service system. The stethoscope and white coat, intelligence tests, and other symbols mark the professions that use them and help construct images or expectancies about those professions. These expectancies may inspire confidence in the professional service or they may invoke reactions not desired by the professional. For example, the images of manipulation and control that became attached to behavior modification in the early 1970s evoked in many consumers and administrators distrust and fear of those practitioners identified as behavior modifiers.

SERVICE AND TRAINING ENVIRONMENTS

Taken together, these defining parameters of professionalism imply certain priorities in allegiances for the practicing professional: to autonomy rather than supervised control, to service tasks rather than administrative policy, to standards of science and professional ethics rather than bureaucratic politics. Human service settings, especially large PRFs, can be expected to challenge these allegiances in many ways. For example, many contemporary PRFs are in litigation or under close external scrutiny by special interest groups, the media, and others. Administrators and managers in these PRFs, not surprisingly, are defensive because their careers hang in the balance. Administrators must depend heavily on their professional staffs to justify the organization's service integrity and competence. This dependence on professionals can easily blur into questions regarding their loyalty. What may be honest and healthy dissent between administrators and staff professionals may be parlayed to political advantage by the organization's critics. Administrators are acutely aware of this possibility. A professional service provider in such a facility is likely to experience steady tension, often quite subtle, between autonomy concessions and loyalty requirements.

Bureaucratic regulation provides another illustration of the challenge to professional allegiances. PRFs are today governed by extensive sets of standardized rules. Labor relations policies, federal regulations concerning client programs, and affirmative action standards represent just a few domains that are strongly rule bound. As Mechanic (1973) pointed out, rules define expected behavior under ordinary circumstances and deter behavior that would exploit the organization, its personnel, or clients. Though many rules do not interfere with professionals' applying their services, many rules present obstacles to professional values (e.g., flexibility of decision making). Thus, in many programs operating under the Title XIX ICF/MR guidelines, rules requiring individual habilitation programs (IHPs) for all clients have forced psychologists to produce scores of "paper" programs that meet compliance standards, but which may require questionable adjustments in actual implementation. For example, corners may be cut in training line staff to implement a client program so that the psychologist can "cover" all clients with a written IHP in the record.

Most bureaucracies, when sufficiently threatened or stressed, will suspend normal procedures and power will revert to the chief administrator (Mintzberg, 1981). In human service settings this will occur with varying frequency depending on how stressful or threatening administrators perceive certain internal and external events. Professionals are likely to experience pressure under conditions of centralized authority. In one facility under considerable stress, the superintendent issued a directive ordering that no client treatment program involving a restrictive procedure be implemented without his explicit authority, despite the existence of professional and human rights review mechanisms. For professionals developing these programs, some measure of their own standards of responsibility and independence was perceived to have been compromised by the directive.

This chapter examines the interaction of professional service providers and the organizational bureaucracies where they work. The illustrations just mentioned suggest the service system is capable of qualifying the very norms that traditionally define the professional. What may be more significant is that most professionals entering the field neither anticipate that this will occur nor have been prepared to manage it. This reflects a problem in the training setting.

The professional training school, whether a medical school, graduate school, or undergraduate college, is the site where aspirants to a profession follow a plan of study under the direction of experts of the discipline to become sanctioned members of the field. Subsequently, they enter one of several settings to practice the profession. Instructional research suggests that if generalized learning is to advance from a training setting to a different environment, the two settings should share as many elements in common as possible (Stokes & Baer, 1977). One would think, then, that the goals of university training programs would be compatible, though not identical, with those of the professional work place. One would expect academic professionals to be qualified to teach their students both to understand the ecology of work settings such as PRFs and how to apply their professional skills in that ecology. One would believe that the tasks and skills learned at the university would be valued by those in the work setting. One would hope that professionals' training practica and laboratory experience would predict the parameters of the work place. One would think, too, that the professional role promoted and developed in the training setting would be appropriate for the work setting. Unfortunately, for too many professions servicing mentally handicapped clients in PRFs, these expectations are mistaken. Not only may the training and work environments be separate worlds, but also in some instances they may be antagonistic entities.

This seemingly paradoxical situation is disappointing and accounts for some of the vulnerability of new professionals to the operating realities of organized human service systems. Despite the vast differences among professional training programs, as well as across various professional work settings, comparisons between these two environments seem to explain some of the difficulty in their relationship.

First, there is the issue of the goals for the two establishments. Broadly conceived, the goals of most major professional training programs include teaching and training of students, research, and professional service. Of these, research is the principal measuring stick for most universities seeking a reputation in the professions. Thus, university resources are likely to be directed toward research and publication support. Clinical Psychology at the doctoral level of training, for example, is principally a research focused curriculum despite the fact that most new Ph.D.'s from these programs take applied positions (Howe & Neimeyer, 1980).

In contrast, the goals of the mental disability workplace are overwhelmingly clinical service for all professions. In most public human service facilities, teaching, research, and service to one's profession are not primary goals. Facilities rarely make available either the resources or staff time for such activities. Under legal mandates such as ICF/MR or many current court orders, these PRFs could not engage in those activities even if they wished.

These differences in fundamental goals are significant. In training programs that provide a strong service emphasis (e.g., many programs in medicine, nursing, education, speech, and occupational therapy), the differences are more subtle but still significant. Although these programs accent clinical instruction, they typically teach little to their students about how human service organizations function. Courses or practica on organizational dynamics or interdisciplinary concepts of service delivery are virtually nonexistent. Graduates of these programs thus tend to be relatively well prepared to practice their techniques but ill prepared to do so in the settings where they take employment. As but one illustration, the powerful fact that most clinical services will in some way be handled or assisted by or be dependent on direct care staff in PRFs is virtually ignored by professional training programs. Although these gaps in training have been acknowledged (e.g., Cherniss, Egnatios, & Wacker, 1976), they still persist in too many programs.

The result of these goal incompatibilities is to lessen the contribution of new professionals. Over the past 15–20 years, we have found it necessary to provide in our facilities extensive and time-consuming instruction to new professionals who were unprepared to function effectively in a complex service system. The question whether the needed training is best conducted at the university or by the service establishment itself is a hard empirical matter further complicated by the typically poor communication at planning levels between the two settings.

Treatment related issues present a second contrast between the professional training schools and service environments. Light (1979) has noted that even masterly professions such as medicine are full of uncertainties in diagnosis, treatment, and client response. He suggests that trainees, in order to cope with these uncertainties, learn methods for control. For example, control of uncertainty in the treatment of disabilities can be achieved for the clinician by emphasis on technique. Given the tenuous nature of much professional knowledge, trainees come to emphasize the actual procedures of their craft more than the outcome (Bucher & Stelling, 1977). Thus, the certainty of clinical procedures predominates over the uncertainties of treatment outcome. Millman (1976) suggested that this also redefines professional competency in terms of technique—if you're applying the procedure correctly, you're competent.

Control is further enhanced by posturing "clinical experience" and "professional judgment." As trainees in all the human service professions acquire a collection of "success" cases, they de facto possess a body of wisdom over which they have complete control and which is relatively immune from criticism (Light, 1979). This becomes the source of powerful respect granted to practitioners and a means by which they can exert dominance over the work setting.

Professionals viewing either the process of treatment or their own roles through the prism of such trained control will likely experience some distress in many contemporary PRFs. The physician and the behavior modification practitioner illustrate this point. Physicians typically are trained with an orientation to the disability and the workplace that assumes medical dominance. Doctors "give orders." Other service providers "make recommendations." Direct-care staff and nonprofessionals "follow orders." Mental disability, for most physicians, is a medical condition; those afflicted are "patients" who receive care. In one facility, a physician reduced a client's dosage of psychotropic medication and "ordered" a behavior modification program as if it were a lab test for a white blood cell count. All elements of the physicians' trained orientation were expressed in that order.

Most of these medical assumptions no longer fit in the prevailing philosophy of habilitation governing PRFs, though of course they once did. Now the conceptual emphasis of mental handicap is developmental, not medical. Mentally disabled people are called consumers or clients rather than patients; their principal need is training rather than care. Clinical decisions usually are made by interdisciplinary or transdisiplinary teams rather than unilaterally by the physician. It is not unusual today for the facility's chief administrator to be an educator, psychologist, or some other nonmedical professional.

The design and application of treatments under these more recent conditions is unsettling for physicians trained to control their work settings. Although some have adapted quite well to reformed ideologies, many cannot reconcile the difference and retreat from interdisciplinary teams either to accept a more limited role or leave the facility. Other physicians are in frequent conflict with nonmedical personnel. These physicians seem so unaccustomed to sharing control and direction of the treatment process with other disciplines that they misunderstand how alternative approaches work. We know of several cases where physicians refused to accept that certain acute maladaptive behaviors could be due to anything extrinsic to the client's intrapsychic make-up or medication side-effects. These were not simply instances of belief in the intrapsychic origin of behavior; they were more fundamentally instances of serious misunderstanding about how other servic methods worked.

Behavior modification practitioners have also experienced problems as they made the transition from graduate school to PRFs. Behavior modification (or, more properly, behavior analysis), with its emphasis on visible, precise methods of measurement, is more clearly a body of observable techniques than most other therapies that have been developed through the social sciences. Its accent on observable response units characterizes both the diagnostic and treatment phases in behavior therapy. In behavior analysis, controlling operations are very visible and nonmysterious and have been demonstrated over 2 decades of fairly organized research. It is no wonder that many new professionals with credentials in behavior analysis enter the work setting with a confidence rooted in the demonstrated control and effectiveness of their treatment methods.

But evidence that behavioral treatments produce durable effects that generalize across the environments of residential settings is minimal (Baumeister, 1981; Foxx & Livesay, 1984). New practitioners become disaffected as they fail to replicate even basic procedural outcomes long established in the literature. Many cannot manage the issues presented to them by direct care staff who will handle or mishandle their procedures. This and other essential matters of the service ecology were probably unaddressed in their training. Thus, technique-based control does not always work well for them, and like many physicians but for different reasons, behavior analysts become disillusioned by expectancies acquired during their schooling.

A final concern in the relationship between service and training settings involves how rapidly the latter can modify its curriculum to be responsive to changes in PRFs, the philosophy guiding clinical practice, law and policy, as well as habilitative technology. For example, in recent years the steady increase in the proportion of more severely impaired and adult clients in PRFs has not always been matched by an instructional emphasis for this population in professional training schools. In many instances there is no attention to this client group at all. Until recently this problem was acute in special education, where university teacher training had been geared to high functioning students. Graduating teachers today are confronted with students with severe deficits in language, basic self-care, and other adaptive behavior whose education is mandated under PL 94-142. Since the passage of that law corrections are underway in special educational training, but uneveness remains.

Perhaps even worse is the virtual absence of course work and training experience with mental disability, especially severe disability, in the curricula of most medical schools, nursing programs, psychology graduate schools, and schools of social work. Many practitioners in these professions encounter their first mentally handicapped clients when they are hired by agencies that, for reasons developed later, presume their professionals' expertise with this population. PL 94-142 also mandates that psychologists assess students with severe handicaps. Deficiencies in assessment skills by psychologists who serve this student population have been revealed (Irons, Irons, & Maddux, 1984). During the past decade, for example, psychologists have had to acquire new skills in assessing adaptive behavior as well as intelligence. In addition to a new emphasis in the field of evaluation, there has been a shift in the professional activities that characterize the duties of psychologists in PRFs. In an analysis of the roles and fuctions of psychologists in PRFs in 1982, as well as changes in those activities since 1967, shifts in the major responsibilities of these professionals have been reported (Baumeister & Hillsinger, 1984). Psychologists in the 1980s have program development and behavior modification as their primary activities. Evaluation, ranked most important in the 1967 survey of PRF superintendents, ranked third in importance in 1982. These shifts in the roles and functions of psychologists serving mentally retarded clients have been influenced by basic research on intelligence, societal concerns regarding intelligence testing, the growth of effective behavioral procedures in the habilitation of developmentally disabled persons, changes in the AAMD definition of intelligence, the development of new assessment procedures, legal mandates, among others. Graduate schools must be aware of new developments such as these and translate them into curriculum modifications if they are to produce professionals who are at the cutting edge of their field. The failure of graduate schools to do so compounds the transition of novice professionals into service settings, and increases the burden of PRFs to provide inservice training to these underprepared new employees.

We have presented the notion that the nature and circumstances of human service settings, especially the larger PRFs, exert a force against some of the priorities, allegiances, and norms that tend to define the professional. We have also described several discontinuities and contradictions between the professional training settings and the service environments. These conditions apply a kind of disabling bearing for new professionals as they encounter the operating realities of service systems. The following section addresses these realities.

PROFESSIONALS AND SERVICE SYSTEM REALITIES

We endeavor to develop a representative sense of the experiences professional service providers have had in tangling with the public human service system, particularly when they are employed in PRFs. This section describes some of the structures, events, people, and conditions that exert an influence on professionals as they attempt to apply the service methods acquired through formal training.

The objective is diagnosis—a graspable way to view the experience so that its problems can be better anticipated and managed.

Uncertainty

It once was, but no longer is, amazing to us that so many new professionals enter the public human service field expecting certainty: certainty that techniques can be applied as they have been demonstrated in laboratory situations; certainty that the facility itself is responsive in structure and in operations to professional requirements; certainty that the system is stable and in control of its mission; and certainty that innovation is logically conceived, broadly accepted, and implemented in a linear fashion. Of course, few of these certainties exist normatively in most facilities, and most professionals see this before too long. Curiously, some do not. The authors know of a number of service professionals who, even after years of service, still performed as if their facility were a laboratory.

But most adjust to the reality that many kinds of uncertainty confront public human service organizations. The more difficult matter is whether the conditions of uncertainty are bearable. LaPorte (1971) has suggested that while uncertainty at low levels is adaptive in relatively stable situations, most contemporary organizations experience considerably destabilizing pressures and many unexpected conditions. When high enough levels of uncertainty exist in such a turbulent environment, LaPorte argued, it raises important questions of adaptability. It is clear that this view has validity for service professionals in PRFs. Less clear is how to identify the critical level of uncertainty which, if passed, generates discomfort or more serious problems of coping. Most facility managers are too absorbed with making and managing changes to consider properly the level of uncertainty as a confounding variable of administration.

It is apparent, however, that professionals are having problems with unhealthy levels of uncertainty. In one facility, a psychologist on an interdisciplinary team reported continual discomfort when his team was confronted with severely disturbed clients whose behavior seemed beyond the reach of available interventions and resources. There was often administrative and advocate pressure on the team to "do something" for these clients, and the team often responded with a knee-jerk reflex to the psychologist that amounted to the same message each time: "You're the behavior specialist. Can you take it?" The psychologist knew that he didn't know what to do with most of these referrals. He also knew that his credibility, especially with direct-care staff, would be called to question if he came up empty on these clients. Finally, he understood the team's strong desire not to have to face the administration (itself under external pressure about providing treatment for these clients) without resolution. Thus, this psychologist found accepting referrals, and the uncertainty that went with them, the preferred option. The psychologist was compelled to respond to uncertain relationships between administration and his interdisciplinary team as well as uncertain relationships and norms within his team. This only compounded the uncertainty he already felt concerning the referrals themselves.

In another example, a group of service professionals was called together to meet with the legal representative of a client. The legal representative was also a participant in a law suit against the facility. The meeting was chaired by the representative and indeed controlled by her. Otherwise competent service providers were cautious, tentative, and seemingly unsure of themselves as the discussion developed. Toward the end of the session the legal representative was calling for specific assessments and program procedures, some of which made no clinical sense. Nevertheless, she was relatively unchallenged. She was directing the clinical traffic in a group of service professionals, not because they were incompetent but because they were uncertain—uncertain about the risks for them and uncertain about the legal role in the clinical process. Clinicians had, as a response to uncertainty, in effect surrendered the clinical process itself to a nonclinician.

There are countless other situations that collectively present professionals in PRFs with uncertainty. Michael (1973), in a thoughtful consideration of uncertainty in modern organizations, suggested that professionals are looked upon to bring understanding and control where little existed before, and to resolve problems that otherwise would contribute to uncertainty. This is true in PRFs, but it complicates the situation. When given the role of uncertainty reducer, professionals are constrained in dealing with their own uncertainty. They must bring things into some rational order for many others, a task not compatible with acknowledging ambiguity or confusion.

Michael's (1973) work is instructive on this point. He presented evidence that disclosing high levels of uncertainty to self or others is especially difficult for those members of an organization who contribute to maintaining its rational order. Thus, unless the disorder or uncertainty can actually be reduced, these members will tend to repress awareness that "they know they do not know." According to Michael, they will avoid situations that confront them with uncertainty or will treat such situations as if they were not uncertain.

Although Michael (1973) did not address PRFs, we believe his reasoning is also valid for professionals who work in these facilities. We know of no empirical data, but our observations and experience in several facilities over a number of years is consistent with his information. For example, senior professionals have shared with us the extreme unpleasantness of owning up to their own confusion about various service system realities when supervising newer or lower rank professionals. Much like the team psychologist in the earlier anecdote, senior professionals feel pressure to have answers and understand all things. And so they generate reasons and solutions that may or may not correspond to the realities that exist. There is no better illustration of this than many professionals' understanding about direct-care staff. The reader is referred to Chapter 3 of this volume, where this issue is discussed extensively.

There are other ways to observe this response to uncertainty. If one samples meetings of professional departments in PRFs, even when staff are openly confused about events or circumstances, members act as if they know what is really involved. Michael (1973) called this translating uncertainty into risk. It allows the person doing it some emotional relief. Even if they cannot change the circumstances, professionals can at least assign probabilities to possible outcomes and thus present a posture of understanding what is going on. In this way, many professionals can explain the complex effects of reorganizing a centralized service system into an interdisciplinary one. They also can affix blame for conceptually sound programs that fail in the clients' residential unit. They can describe the weaknesses of middle management personnel and conceptualize a staff development curriculum to correct them. They can interpret bureaucratic decision making and "predict" the consequences of such choices. They can be seen to understand rapid change and turbulence in the service system.

These responses frequently are oversimplified and sometimes are just wrong. But they are self-protective responses, and herein lies their importance. In the turbulent environments that characterize many PRFs, professionals who yield to uncertainty are in danger of being phased out. They may not necessarily be phased out of the facility itself (union contracts may preclude that), but they easily can be phased out of the action by administrators.

This is especially so in institutions experiencing external threat, such as federal litigation aimed at closing them or transferring administrative control of their operations to outside agents. In such situations, the facility may be questioned, if not attacked, on every element of its program. In many class action suits against institutional services, scores of outsiders have visited the facility and gathered information used critically in court. A common approach in such proceedings is for plaintiffs to bring in outside professionals, often from academic settings, and have them review the facility's professional services. These individuals may visit for one day and conceivably testify in court for several. For the facility's own professionals, this experience is often a defensive one because, in the context of adversarial legal contests, the plaintiff's outside experts are looking to find fault. While a good defense team may successfully educate the judge about the uncertainties inherent in the available knowledge about the client disabilities and service methods, the facility's administration and its professionals may be formally asked to respond to the outside professionals' findings. The defendant professionals may experience a distinct expectancy that they be very certain: certain about the effectiveness of their services; certain about the reasons for program failures when these occur; certain about how to service clients through the organizational structures that exist; certain even about the problems and uncertainties confronting the service system.

Under these circumstances, professionals cannot afford to acknowledge that they are confused or uncertain. Even if their program is beset with shortcomings, they must act as if they understand clearly the exact nature of the difficulties and what is needed to correct them. Any impression short of this risks communicating to the court that they are not in control of their service program.

Turbulence and external threat have the dual impact of increasing the real level of uncertainty as well as the demand that professionals be in control of it. At stake are the self-image of the professionals and their superiors. In today's externally scrutinized institutions, both levels of staff may well be evaluated on the professionals' response to uncertainty. As we have indicated, professionals adjust to this situation by perceiving and communicating order where others might see enormous complexity and uncertainty. Although self-protective, this adjustment is, in truth, a serious maladjustment because it steers the organization incorrectly. For PRFs, the fact is, as Michael (1973) generally has cautioned, that deep and continuing uncertainty is likely to characterize contemporary and future efforts as social planning. Organizations embracing future responsive missions will have to confront such uncertainty, not avoid it. According to Thompson (1967), another fact is that many organizations will face consequences of simply being unable to reduce uncertainty to comfortable levels.

Acknowledging real uncertainty, confronting it, and managing the discomfort it will generate are, then, the only valid issues. What we are calling the maladjusted responses of professionals distract the organization from properly attending to these issues. In accepting the role of uncertainty reducers, and thereby neglecting to come to appropriate terms with their own uncertainties in the system, professionals ironically help escort the organization off course. What is needed is professional leadership that will guide the organization through the difficulties of limited technologies, turbulent change, and other real uncertainties while at the same time not yielding to the misattribution of those difficulties as weaknesses by internal or external forces. Whether selected professionals in any facility can assume some of this leadership is an empirical question that can be determined only after the valid matters of uncertainty are acknowledged.

Organizational Structure

Most professional service providers prefer a work situation where a client's needs can be identified and where any one of a set of available procedures can then be applied cleanly to the need. Where established or standardized procedures are not adequate, the majority of professionals prefer the freedom and support to develop and test alternative solutions (i.e., to innovate). With a limited store of validated treatment procedures in the mental disability field, the need for development and innovation is strong and some professionals would no doubt select work situations that allowed them to do this alone.

These are preferences of structure. We have never known professionals in public human service who desired an arrangement of the work setting that interfered with this ideal notion of human service. However, as Cherniss, Egnatios, and Wacker (1976) have observed, there is a basic incompatibility between the service tasks to be performed and the typical organizational structure in which to perform them. The tasks require the patient, longitudinal application of methods to clients; the structure imposes people, hierarchies, rules, procedures, policies, and many different views of the organization's mission between the application of service methods and the clients. This contradiction between the service ideal and the very nature of bureaucratic organization is a source of stress and confusion to professionals. One effective clinician we know expressed the problem with near outrage; "I am a competent professional and I know how to service my clients. This place just won't let me do it. Something or someone is always in the way."

This young man and many like him feel nullified by what they see as "the system." When examined more closely, much of what they are objecting to is the presence of several different structural arrangements in the same organization, each with its own set of expectations about the nature of the work and each with its own clusters of staff at ease with those expectations. In most facilities, professionals daily encounter other staff preferring work structures different and often contradictory to their own choice. The problem occurs because, while the work structure is different, the work site is the same. In the interaction at the work site, the professionals feel obstructed.

The simultaneous presence of incompatible structures in the same organization is hardly a startling observation. Thompson (1976), discussing organizations more generally, pointed out that bureaucratically organized production units often will not cooperate with innovation units. Lippitt (1973) noted that in hospitals some segments of the organization may be operating on the basis of one organizational model and other segments on another. One might expect this reality to be acknowledged and accepted over time by those experiencing it; however, we have observed that professionals in PRFs have considerable difficulty in doing so. For most of them, servicing clients should only be done ideally (i.e., through the pure service model they prefer). This view is strongly held. We find that, even after years of working in PRFs, most professionals cannot understand why the organization will not adopt or impose structures that support what is for them a valid approach to service. Why can't direct-care routines be made more flexible and thus more responsive to program interventions? Why can't middle level supervisors support habilitative innovations more vigorously? Why does the information flow across many staff groups servicing the same unit of clients seem so unhelpful to client programming efforts? Why does it seem that so many people working within a training and habilitation mission misunderstand the ingredients of a developmental program of habilitation?

Professionals who recurrently ask these questions probably have not come to terms with the coexistence of contradicting structures, but this may be only part of the problem. We also believe that many professionals, despite their strong beliefs about applying services, have come to function in a manner more consistent with the models of organization they reject.

To illustrate what we are suggesting, it is first necessary to be more precise about structure. Mintzberg's (1979, 1981) work on organization design is useful in this regard. He identified five major configurations of structure in which most organizations fall. The elements of structure include such things as: (a) the specialization of tasks; (b) the formalization of procedures; (c) the grouping of positions into units; (d) the performance control system in place; (e) the delegation of decision making; and (f) the formal training required of staff to perform tasks to a standard. Various situational factors, according to Mintzberg, influence the elements of structure. These factors include the age and size of the organization, the technical system or knowledge base that underpins the tasks performed, and various characteristics of the organization's environment (e.g., how stable or complex it is).

Mintzberg (1981) maintained that, in an organization, "... the central purpose of structure is to coordinate the work divided in a variety of ways" (p. 104). How that coordination is achieved dictates what the organization will look like in configuration. When the configurations of structure are mismatched to the tasks or missions (i.e., the wrong ones are put to work together), the organization does not function effectively.

The five configurations of structure identified by Mintzberg can be summarized briefly as follows:

1. Simple Structure: Coordination is achieved at the apex of the organization usually by direct supervision. There is a relative absence of standardization and little need for a middle line. Control is very centralized typically with a chief executive.

2. Machine Bureaucracy: Coordination depends on the standardization of work, and hence a large hierarchy becomes necessary in the middle line to oversee that standardized output. This production system requires a stable environment to function effectively; change tends to disrupt the standardized output. Thus, these structures tend to stabilize environments in which they find themselves. Machine bureaucracies become larger rather than smaller. Mintzberg (1981) described some of the associated problems of these structures as inadaptability, dull and repetitive work, and the kind of employee alienation that often goes with routine, circumscribed jobs.

3. Professional Bureaucracy: Coordination depends on the standardization of skills rather than tasks. Thus, the organization needs highly trained professionals who must be given considerable autonomy over their own work. This structure is, therefore, more decentralized. Mintzberg (1981) noted that the emphasis on standardization of skills (such as in general hospitals) also requires a fairly stable environment. This is not a good structure in which to innovate or impose change. It does better at perfecting what is known.

4. Divisionalized Form: Coordination is achieved through parallel operating units, each with fairly autonomous managers. However, to retain control over a

span of semiautonomous units, top administration usually designs and imposes performance control systems, leaving the operating details to the units. But because the unit managers are responsible for division performance according to those standards, in practice, this system gets driven toward bureaucratization. Goals get translated down the line into specific work standards supervised in a centralized fashion. Mintzberg (1981) pointed out that by emphasizing the measurement of performance as the means of administrative control, a bias develops in the units in favor of those goals that can be operationalized. Curiously, we have seen the same bias develop in some human service programs governed by performance control systems such as ICF/MR.

5. Adhocracy: Coordination occurs through project teams. The work here is innovation, and the environment tends strongly to be complex and nonstandardized. This is a fluid structure, with projects developed around specific missions providing the organizing factor. These projects fuse needed experts into task forces with integrating managers whose spans of control are usually confined to the project. When the project is over, the team disbands, with members going on to new projects. With adhocracy, standardized output, centralized administration, and performance control are all diminished. As Mintzberg (1981) described it: "Ambiguity abounds. . . . Adhocracies can do no ordinary thing well. But it is extraordinary at innovations" (p. 113).

It would be a mistake to view any human service organization in terms of its correspondence with any of these five structures. Mintzberg (1981) argued that these configurations are useful diagnostically only if we see them as "pulls" that may exist in one or more parts of an organization (e.g., the pull to centralize, the pull to formalize). Applying this approach to PRFs, we find much experiential validity, though we know of no hard data.

For example, the routines and tasks that exist with 24-hour residential care pull the organization of these units toward characteristics of Mintzberg's (1981) machine bureaucracy. The abundance of middle management personnel in large residential systems, the emphasis on standards of basic care, the sometimes uncanny ability of direct-care workers to neutralize or resist program change, and many other characteristics described in Chapter 3 of this volume tend strongly to favor this pull. As another example, the directors or coordinators in many ICF/MR units resemble Mintzberg's division manager in several important respects. They are responsible to administration for the operation of highly performance regulated programs. At stake in compliance with these regulations is ongoing federal financial support. Thus, it is not surprising to see many ICF unit directors maintaining fairly tight, centralized control over their programs. This control often is at the expense of innovation and to the dismay of professional staff.

To return to the issue raised, we suspect that professionals frequently function within organizational structures they reject as useful for applying their services.

They are strongly affected by other structural pulls that exist in the workplace. Our observations further suggest that many professionals yield to these other pulls for various reasons, with the consequence of having to settle for diminished if not compromised effectiveness. We are currently examining this question empirically, but a small preliminary survey completed by the first author is instructive. In this survey, 15 staff psychologists in a PRF first indicated their preferred work structure and then the one they were experiencing. All 15 described a disharmony between preference and experience. Twelve of the 15 described their predominant work structure as machine bureaucracy, the configuration perhaps most discrepant from their unanimous preference for a professionally autonomous adhocracy structure.

These respondents were also asked to identify two key position titles in the facility whose members most misunderstood the nature of the psychologists' professional services and contributions to the facility. They were also asked to indicate the structural configuration in which their "misunderstanders" worked and whether they believed these people were comfortable or uncomfortable in that structure. Although the 15 respondents nominated many different groups as misunderstanders and distributed them across all five major configurations, the overwhelming majority of these misunderstanders were seen as comfortable in their experienced structure. Of course we did not ascertain whether the misunderstanders, if given the same rating task, would judge themselves as comfortable.

If these findings can be confirmed empirically across representative samples of professionals and facilities, the implications are serious. A pronounced and continuous pattern of contradiction between the preferred organization of the service setting and the one experienced should be unsettling for professionals. People working in this kind of contradiction can be expected, at a minimum, to be unhappy. They may well be stressed by the circumstances. A separate and more formal survey of over 80 professionals from several disciplines in the same facility as the one above supports these suggestions. Respondents reported significantly more stress in work situations outside the structure of their professional department itself (Thaw, McLaughlin, & Ciarcia, 1982). They also reported experiencing limited control or influence in making the services they wanted to occur actually take place in the proper manner. Those professionals more extensively involved in work situations discrepant from their department structure felt this absence of control more strongly. Not surprisingly, respondents generally felt actual service efforts tended to be compromised in favor of paper compliance with performance control regulations. Of further interest to the present discussion, respondents strongly indicated that their training and supervision in professional school and through in-service programs at the facility were inadequate in teaching them how to function in the service structure to which they were assigned.

In the Weinberg, Edwards, and Sternau (1979) study mentioned earlier, data from 14 facilities in 11 different states revealed high rates of burnout for professional staff. These authors also found factors of bureaucracy, administrative hassle, reduced autonomy, and decision making difficulty among the major correlates of both job dissatisfaction and burnout for professional staff and other employee groups. These variables correspond quite well with some of Mintzberg's (1981) elements of structure. It suggests that a lack of fit between the professionals' tasks and the structures in which they must do them is associated with outcomes of job dissatisfaction and prolonged stress.

Taken together and with due caution, these findings prompt the conclusion that where professionals are working within nonpreferred or incompatible organizational structures, the possible effects warrant concern. In the authors' experience, contradiction between preferred and experienced structure is widespread, and only a few professionals acquire a working interest in the contradiction. Most find the incompatibility a source of irritating if not agonizing interference. Some are disabled by it.

The Unit System

". . . Organizations will continue to change slowly, and the difference between their rate of change and the speed of changes in human aspirations and expectations will generate familiar tensions for many generations to come. . . ." (Kaufman, 1971, p. 112).

In discussing uncertainty earlier in this chapter, we made the observation that many new professionals enter the public human service system believing that innovation proceeds in an organized, linear manner. In truth, experience runs counter to that belief most of the time. It is useful to consider Davis' (1973) distinction between organizational change and innovation. Change is taken to mean the adoption of a different response to ensure attaining the mission of the organization; innovation is a subset of change referring to the process of implementing new practices. The problem in contemporary PRFs is unmanageable change and unmanaged innovation. Many facility administrations are attempting to control and stabilize change demands thrust on them by various others whose impatient "aspirations and expectations" tend to misunderstand how change-worthy notions are best converted to changed realities. The task is frustrating if not time consuming. The more units of change to manage, the harder it is to develop innovations prudently in a logical manner consistent with the innovative concept. This issue is discussed in greater detail in Chapter 1 of this book.

There is perhaps no better example of an unmanaged innovation than the implementation of the so-called "unit system" in PRFs. It has become the general concensus (Crosby, 1976; Meyer, 1979) that the unit management system of service delivery is the one best suited to meet the developmental goals of a residential facility. But, as Granger (1972) and Sluyter (1976) suggested, the manner in which a facility adopts the unit system may result in only a partial application of the concept. We believe that in facilities overburdened with unmanageable change, professionals may be trapped in unit systems that are not faithful to unit concepts such as decentralized authority, interdisciplinary process, and collaborative programming with direct care staff. Their administrators may be too distracted managing multiple changes either to be aware of the problem or to respond to it if they are aware. The result often is that the unit system plods on almost as if the contradiction were not there. With the heavy paper and time frame accountabilities that attend most unit systems, they appear too busy ''performing their tasks'' to correct the errors.

We shall examine two aspects of the professionals' encounter with unit management systems: transition to it and operation in it.

Transition. Philip was hired through the state merit system as a staff psychologist in a moderately sized PRF. Like many who hold this position, he had a master's degree in psychology with only limited training and experience with mentally retarded populations. The day after he started working, he was assigned to an interdisciplinary team. The team was newly formed and charged with quickly bringing the assigned client population up to certification standards so that Title XIX funding could begin. This meant conducting a great many evaluations, organizing a service contract for each client, writing at least one program (IPP) for each client, and developing a record-keeping system responsive to the heavy paper requirements of the ICF/MR regulations. Philip was appointed team chairperson and given the responsibility of organizing these tasks. Administrative desire and subsequent pressure to certify this unit precluded any meaningful time by him to obtain needed professional supervision from his department despite his weakness in mental retardation and newness to the system. Like Philip, other professionals on the team were new and ill prepared with respect to the interdisciplinary concept and this particular unit system. Together they were setting in motion significant changes for the supervisory and direct-care staff who hardly knew this new mode of service delivery and were equally unprepared for the transition to unitization. Predictably, these veteran employees skillfully resisted the changes, which created frustration and considerable stress for the professionals. Philip shouldered most of this burden because his team had developed few norms as a cohesive group of professionals. Rather than operating as a team, they were a collection of individuals, each struggling to stay even with their caseload assignments in the stressful drive toward certification. Philip had the most extensive clinical caseload because the principal client needs were for psychological services. He found himself having to write programs for clients who really required more observation and assessment. There was little time to get to know, let alone train, the direct-care staff who were to conduct these program procedures. Additionally, he was the only team professional eligible to be a QMRP (Qualified Mental Retardation Professional), the designated accountability person in the unit. Thus, he had to sign-off on client contracts and programs that had been far too hastily thrown together. He felt ill at ease, if not somewhat compromised with this responsibility.

These and similar conditions persisted through certification. But very little changed after the unit was certified. Crisis norms of performing tasks had taken hold, and the problems left in the wake of crashing the program together became the daily agenda. There was no time to develop the interdisciplinary group process or to receive sufficient training and supervision. Philip continued to pour energy and dedication into the job, but in the best interests of his career resigned and left the field just a year after he began. Physically and emotionally, he was spent as a professional.

The unit concept has been introduced despite poor preparation in many facilities. Decentralized and interdisciplinary themes run counter to the machine bureaucracy characteristics discussed in the previous section, yet many unit programs are set into place through this structure. When the concept and the structure collide, there is much job discomfort for professional staff. Where these individuals receive minimal supervision in working through the transition, the discomfort can affect performance and morale.

Paper transition to a unit system usually occurs long before the functional or clinical transition. Thus, the paperwork often becomes the objective itself. We know of one professional department operating in the 2nd year of the facility's unit program that prepared a position statement documenting an average of well over 100% of a typical work week to meet paper work compliance alone. Such essential professional activities as training staff to conduct client programs, receiving supervision, and evaluating program outcomes occurred only after the paper tasks were completed. This often meant they were not done at all. The administration's response to the position paper was limited to sympathy.

It was perhaps inevitable that decades of unaccountable services would yield to some measure of excess in the accountability-based programs of recent years. Many facilities overlaid with regulations and guidelines for everything from the use of client restraint devices to the temperature of the food have responded with elaborate, often redundant, record systems. In one facility, a unit leader reported finding one item of client information documented in 14 places. We have found that excessive, cumbersome paper systems accompanying the transition to unit programming delay the development of sound interdisciplinary program norms.

Sluyter (1976) described the identity loss that professionals experience when changing to a unit system as disturbing. Unit managers, by the very nature of their responsibilities, become far more concerned with certification deadlines, client and staff schedules across three shifts, personnel matters, and numerous other administrative tasks than they do with the development of their professionals. The unit manager is charged with keeping the unit on course. The professionals' needs for autonomy, supervision, and growth often are seen to interfere with this responsibility. In facilities where the professional departments provide technical supervision to the unit professionals, a two-boss system may develop. If the transition has been accelerated and if the unit leaders and department heads have not developed a workable relationship themselves, the two bosses will probably conflict, especially over issues of how unit professionals utilize their time. We know of many battles between unit managers and discipline chiefs concerning who controls the professionals' time card, job service rating, and supervision. In establishing a comprehensive program of professional supervision for unit psychologists, the first author encountered the most resistance from unit managers, who saw supervision and the supervising psychologists as intrusions upon their authority and control of time.

Sluyter's (1976) review of the unit system also noted that unit leaders often are poorly trained for their extensive administrative, program, and personnel responsibilities. Frequently, they are appointed from within institutional ranks, provided little supervision, and given inequitable salaries. The requirement that unit leaders master a unit philosophy, create and maintain a decentralized authority structure, alter the job roles of numerous employees, put a program system on a tightly regulated schedule of accountability, and keep it there is beyond their preparation, if not their abilities. In the authors' experience, the compromises unit leaders will surely make under this pressure include minimal attention to the needs of their professionals.

Some years ago, Hersch (1968) described an "explosion of discontent" among mental health professionals in response to an unorganized transition from traditional to innovative service approaches. We sense the same response among professionals thrust into unit systems too fast to adjust effectively. Intuitively, it seems important that a professional entering a unit system facility know where in the transition the facility is. The facility, however, may not be able to provide this information, because it may not have examined the question. We believe that organizations without a good grasp of their own history will be at great risk when they attempt innovations such as unit management.

Operation.   The pressures that force a facility to introduce a unit system rapidly tend to continue once the system is in place. For example, after a service unit initially qualifies for Title XIX funding under the ICF/MR program, the continual cycles of maintaining certification largely define the unit's operation. Depending on the staff-to-client formulas adopted by the facilities, there may continue to be little room for developing an operation faithful to the unit concept. For the service professional, perhaps the most critical element of that concept is the interdisciplinary process. Under unit programs, the interdisciplinary team should replace the department as the primary point of identification for the professional. We have found the interdisciplinary team to be the governing factor of a professional's successful long-term adjustment to the unit system.

The interdisciplinary approach is the core of the unit concept and the ICF/MR program (Crosby, 1976). Its premise is a shared, fully integrated collaboration among professionals and direct-care staff in the evaluation, planning, and treatment of client habilitation needs. The boundaries traditionally assigned to specific professional disciplines blur under the interdisciplinary approach as physician, psychologist, social worker, physical therapist, speech clinician, direct-care attendant, and other participants each assume an equivalent primary role identification as team member.

To accomplish this integration of diverse professionals and paraprofessionals, each team member must surrender the single-profession view of servicing clients (the view usually acquired during formal academic training) and acquire a functionally different set of group-profession norms. Without these norms, the interdisciplinary process misfires and the unit system is strained. Among interdisciplinary process norms, the following are most essential: (a) interpersonal trust and safety; (b) active, nonjudgmental listening; (c) group ownership of successes, failures, and problems; (d) participatory, consensus decision making; and, (e) mutual support and willingness to take risks on behalf of the group.

These norms should bind a group of service providers to their mission and permit them to collaborate programmatically. Teams weak in these areas, however, tend to work as though their individual functions were independent. Members perform tasks, attend meetings, and produce products, all of which have the appearance of interdisciplinary activity. Observing such groups closely and over time, we have noticed members disinclined to invest energy either in the team's business or in its development. There is a low level of initiative, and members seem content to allow the "most relevant" professional to handle a particular problem. In short, the single-profession approach prevails under the guise of interdisciplinary process.

In an extensive analysis of one interdisciplinary staff unit, the first author found an uncoordinated and discontent group of professionals unable to admit its difficulties to itself. Members reported a high level of felt pressure to perform successfully for the facility but were unable to admit to each other that they were often stuck and without solutions. Thus, they tended to force solutions in response to the pressure instead of problem solving the real difficulty. Their decision-making seldom involved everyone's input and often occurred with only minimal evaluation of potential outcomes. Many members felt that opinions and solutions were "ramrodded" down the team's throat by a few members but that it was unsafe to comment on this openly. Most members felt little acknowledgment for their contributions, and no member rated the team as a responsive, sensitive group. Much dissatisfaction and anger were expressed privately in small subgroups but were unexpressed at team meetings. Members reported high levels of boredom, low levels of creativity, and limited identification with the team. They felt their professional work, for the most part, was not well respected or understood by the team. Once aware of the first author's findings, team members were genuinely motivated to improve. But they found little time to work on the problem, and their motivation fell victim to the weekly agenda of tasks. The unit system had acquired an inertia all its own, one that assumed the presence of an interdisciplinary structure was equivalent to the operation of an interdisciplinary process.

It is not surprising that interdisciplinary teams come to suffer this processless group process. Most professionals were trained in a single discipline. The character, time, and expense of professional training is such that new graduates tend to possess an overly strong belief in their profession's approach to human service. Few were instructed by members of other professions, let alone in an interdisciplinary program. In the service setting, the interdisciplinary method is, therefore, uncomfortable for them, if not undesired. This situation is aggravated by the relatively poor inservice training many facilities provide to their interdisciplinary teams in the process areas noted earlier. This, too, is not surprising inasmuch as certification- and funding-minded administrators are more concerned about their interdisciplinary teams' "performing" tasks than "norming" their process. Once in motion, as we have suggested, this conduct of the unit system is difficult to correct.

Mechanic (1973) has suggested that under conditions of innovation and uncertainty, "there is no force more important than a deep commitment to the job and a sense that one's agency has the capacity to do it" (p. 164). The unit concept enjoys widespread support despite little empirical data to confirm its incremental value to client services. Formal evaluation of facilities applying the unit plan (e.g., Granger, 1972; Raynes, Bumstead, & Pratt, 1974) reveals serious difficulties in operationalizing the concept and minimal improvement in quality of care for clients. The professional functioning in a unit system may well be committed by circumstance to an unmanaged, unevaluated, but officially embraced innovation. The extent of this contradiction will vary across facilities. We believe, however, that its eventual effect on professionals is to diminish confidence that their facility has the capacity to perform its mission.

Other Realities

The conditions we are describing have two characteristics in common. First, each exerts considerable influence on professionals' total job experience; second, it is unlikely these issues were covered either in the professionals' formal instruction or inservice training. Several other important conditions meet these criteria in many contemporary PRFs. We give brief mention to some of them.

Legal Forces.   Historically, the notion of external scrutiny has been foreign to human service programs (Gurel, 1975). For decades, the public impression (where one existed) was that PRFs were doing the Lord's work and that was sufficient. Professionals enjoyed this freedom with their motives, methods, and outcomes all largely beyond review. Obviously, all this has changed, and today legislatures, citizen advocates, federal surveyors, the media, and countless others critically monitor the activities of PRFs. This topic has been examined in considerable depth by Cuvo and Thaw in this book.

All these external observers in some measure affect the work experience of professionals. For example, these observers have influenced methods of human service including accountability requirements and policy restrictions on certain clinical procedures. However, none of these external groups has had nearly the impact on professionals that can be attributed to the legal community. As of this writing numerous PRFs are involved in legal proceedings, many of these major class action litigations before federal judges. The quality and quantity of professional services are often the subject of plaintiff grievances. Members of professions regularly give depositions and testimony concerning everything from the training of professionals to the number of hours per week they spend in direct contact with specific clients. As one superintendent put it in preparing his professional staff for their testimony: "If you think that you know more about the fine details of our operation than they (the plaintiff attorneys) do, you are in for a major surprise when you take the stand."

Because we have devoted an entire chapter of this volume to legal activity in the mental disability field, we confine comments here to some of the effects this activity has produced for PRF professionals. In the simplest sense, the effect has been to alter the professionals' choices in using time. At more serious levels, the legal intrusion of the 1970s and early 1980s precipitated anxiety, fear, and unwarranted decisions by professionals to exit the service arena. This culminated in the U.S. Court of Appeals decision in *Romeo v. Youngberg,* (1980), which established guidelines for assessing personal liability of PRF administrators for client abuse and mistreatment.

Although this decision was modified by the U.S. Supreme Court (see later discussion) many professionals still scan their methods and practice with legal sensing devices. Procedures that are clinically sound may be perceived as legally risky and thus be discarded from consideration, possibly to the clients' misfortune. Especially in litigated facilities, professionals have become extremely conservative and cautious in their decisions. While concern for legal rights of clients is essential, some of these choices by professionals amount to a surrender of the clinical process. This has occurred, in part, because legal scrutiny of clinical procedures begins with different assumptions from those of the clinical process, employs different methods, addresses different purposes, and uses different criteria for decisions. As Baumeister (1981) has suggested, the law and science operate at different levels of discourse. Clinicians are sharply aware that these differences exist, though they may not fully understand the legal process. The point is clinicians tend not to trust their ability to understand their own clinical and scientific process. It thus becomes necessary to adjust their choices to what they may see as the least questionable approach from a legal perspective.

Such caution is not without justification. We know of one facility where a court not only ordered evaluation and treatment plans, but also specified the procedures to be used by each professional. The team of professionals applied their skills to the task, presented its product, and were charged with contempt of court by the plaintiffs for not meeting the procedural stipulations of the order. Subsequently, the court stipulated what was to be done in a physical examination, what specific areas of development would be evaluated by the psychologist, and so on. It may well be that an independent peer review committee would have reached similar determinations, though we doubt this. The point, once again, is the extended reach of the legal process—in this case the judiciary—into professional clinical domains. Whether that reach is justified is an empirical question. That it is occurring is not in question.

There are numerous other consequences to professionals from increased legal activity in their service environments. Sajwaj (1977), for example, noted that due process interpretations can result in multiple steps of review for any innovative program or procedure. Any one of the reviewing bodies could require significant change in the procedure, causing the professional to retrace his steps through the chain. Disapproval by any reviewing body could amount to a veto of the procedure entirely. The draw on time and effort under this long line of checkpoints, merit notwithstanding, conceivably could reduce the inclination to innovate.

The clinical conservatism and anxiety shown by PRF professionals, as suggested earlier, has been a legal side effect of the avalanche of litigation that we have witnessed. That litigation has, in many ways, denigrated the opinions of professionals who work in PRFs. More recently, the status of professionals has been reinforced by the Supreme Court opinion in *Youngberg v. Romeo* (1982). The high court ruled that on issues of training PRF clients

> . . . courts must show deference to the judgment exercised by a qualified professional . . . interference by the federal judiciary with the internal operations of these institutions should be minimized. Moreover, there certainly is no reason to think judges or juries are better qualified than appropriate professionals in making such decisions . . . the decision, if made by a professional, is presumptively valid; liability may be imposed only when the decision by the professional is such a substantial departure from accepted professional judgment, practice, or standards. . . . In an action for damages against a professional in his individual capacity, however, the professional will not be liable if he was unable to satisfy his normal professional standards because of budgetary constraints; in such a situation, good-faith immunity would bar liability.

The *Youngberg* decision provides welcome relief to professionals whose opinions have been subject to scrutiny and criticism in recent years. Professionals have been particularly uncertain and fearful of their personal liability in situations where lack of resources precluded their delivering the quality of service they were capable of and wished to provide. Although the Supreme Court said in 1982 that the decisions of professionals were ''presumptively valid,'' the recent history of litigation has made professionals keenly sensitive in our litigious society. The *Youngberg* decision notwithstanding, substantial residuals remain of the clinical conservatism engendered by earlier opinions. The concerns of professionals described above have been abated to some degree but, by no means, eliminated.

In sum, our message is only that legal activity in PRFs has broad and deep implications for professionals. We are witnessing the very early and stormy phases of this activity, and the more prudent solutions may be some time ahead. Professionals will be able to negotiate the legal implications of their clinical work only if they are trained and supervised to do so. For now, significant deficiencies exist in both respects.

Labor Unions.   We have argued that professionals generally have not been able to secure identities commensurate with expectations established in graduate school. We have described the effects of uncertainty, the frequent lack of meaningful reference groups, the reduction in autonomy, and relatively high levels of stress and frustration often experienced by professionals. These factors plus any weaknesses in comparative pay, benefits, and work schedules together provide fertile opportunities for organized labor activity in professional ranks. When options to redress various discontents become less reliable, as they do in facilities experiencing large turnovers of change and external pressure, union affiliation becomes even more attractive.

Scheerenberger (1975) has described the rapid growth of labor unions in mental disability systems and the particular reasons for the expansion of organized activity among professional groups. Smartly prepared public employee unions have appealed to these conditions and in so doing have altered the very nature of professionalism in public service organizations.

Unquestionably, unions have provided several essential protections and benefits for professional employees that state government, by its very nature, could not or would not provide alone. In many instances, these have improved the respectability of professional positions in competitive job markets. But, much like factors discussed earlier, unionism can be a powerful variable in the work experience, affecting professionals, their supervisors, and their departments. Few of these people were ever instructed in formal labor relations before they encountered it, again a situation much like the issues we discussed before.

The impact of labor unions on professionals varies with the statutory authority of labor unions, the nature of particular labor contracts, and many local characteristics. Generally, we have observed several effects and believe they represent potential outcomes in most facilities. Perhaps most important is that for a growing number of professionals union activity has become more reinforcing than their jobs. It often has less uncertainty, more reachable rewards, and an easier road to identification. Union leaders acutely understand this. We know a number of professionals for whom the union has become the principal reference group of their work experience.

At another level, union activity and duties diminish service time, which is already at a premium. Union stewards, often staff professionals, must attend meetings, trouble shoot problems, participate in contract talks, and represent employees in grievances. These activities can be time consuming and under most labor contracts, be performed during normal work hours. Some grievance procedures, for example, have extended over weeks and months, consuming hundreds of hours of professionals' time. For chiefs of disciplines and professional supervisors, these labor procedures often can force clinical responsibilities to lower priorities. A few disgruntled employees can parlay the natural adversarial relationship between union and management into excessive and costly proceedings even over modest grievances (although this is relatively uncommon).

In some professional departments, the presence of organized unions, especially when more aggressive, can transform relationships based on clinical and collegial affiliations into impersonal labor management relationships. One labor incident, such as a challenge to work rules or selection for promotion, can make a department head extremely cautious with the staff in the future. Problems previously resolved informally now involve outsiders, personnel officers, union representatives, and sometimes arbitrators. A maverick employee skillfully using the union contract has a good chance of affecting his or her department even if unsupported by colleagues. Especially in the first years of union activity, nonsupport of a fellow union member's particular struggle often is reflected in silence rather than opposition.

What can result if these circumstances persist is not only cautious relationships between professional staff and supervisors, but distant ones. Distance can occur easily among union members as well. In one state, for example, failure to negotiate a labor contract as the established deadline approached raised the possibility of a job action or strike. Union pressure to support the action was deliberate and strong. Many professionals, however, had serious reservations about leaving clients unserviced and possibly unprotected. Having to choose to support a strike or cross a picket line created tension and conflict previously unknown in their professional ranks.

These outcomes, although all possible, are not necessarily probable. The key determinant is the professional leadership of the discipline chiefs or department heads. Despite some appearances, the preferred identity for most professionals continues to be their profession and their services, however bruised these may be. The novelty and appeal of union identification may tend to diminish over time partly because a mentality of adverse relationships is ultimately uncomfortable for many service professionals. It is too much unlike the scholarly, scientific, and clinical discourse in which they were trained and motivated. It is for the chief of discipline to rescue that motivation and at the same time to utilize the union process in a sensible manner that promotes support, defuses extreme responses, and reduces labor-management distance. For example, programs of inservice training responsive to the needs of alienated professionals may well renew professional motivation. Intensive, high quality supervision can have the same effect. At the bottom line, the chiefs of professional disciplines should understand the needs, discontents, and incentives of their staff better than others who do not share the same history of training, technology, standards of performance, and symbols. To develop these givens into a governing identification in unionized facilities will require that discipline chiefs be more assertive with administrators and unit leaders about their profession. If the discipline programs are well conceived, the administrators and units will see useful payoffs in morale and service. Ideally, strong professional identification should permit a labor union to provide its essential functions without holding the profession itself in its grip.

Technology: Promise and Performance.   In the early 1970s, a distinguished behavioral researcher spoke before a few hundred staff members at a large institution for the mentally retarded. He described a few studies of highly successful training procedures with severely and profoundly retarded clients and declared to his audience that nothing was impossible. Many employees did not believe him. They did not believe that in their residential units the maladaptive behavior he described could be so effectively reduced or that adaptive responses could be so easily acquired.

Both the speaker and the audience were accurate. The speaker's truth was the sterilized applications of a new technology under highly controlled conditions, a point that was never really clarified for the audience. Their own truth was the ecological reality of the residential unit, which would interfere with or nullify his applications. Each party, however, argued the relative worth of the technology, and it is in this miscommunication that one finds the source of a grand technological expectation and its equally grand misuse.

The technology of behavior modification or applied behavior analysis is learning based, whereas the foundation deficit in the facilities under discussion is developmental. It is thus not difficult to understand the status ranking that behavior modification has achieved in PRFs (Baumeister & Hillsinger, 1984; Ellis, 1979). In many respects, the condition of behavior modification in these organizations is much the condition of the habilitation program itself.

The numerous early demonstrations of behavioral technology under controlled conditions (e.g., Azrin & Foxx, 1971; Bensberg, Colwell, & Cassell, 1965; Gardner, 1971; Lent, 1968) generated an enthusiasm that led to its widespread application in PRFs. Working in these facilities in the late 1960s or early 1970s, one discovered that nearly everyone was doing "behavior mod." But, as Ellis (1979) pointed out, the quality of the effort was often poor. Worse, the use of the technology in uncontrolled environments occurred and expanded despite the fact that the empirical research on establishing, maintaining, and generalizing behavior in these settings had not been done (Bates & Wehman, 1977; Turkat & Forehand, 1980). As Baumeister (1981) observed, we have little systematic evidence showing that operant training consistently produces durable effects.

Today, those errors in applying behavioral technology are well known (e.g., Cullari & Ferguson, 1981; Ellis, 1979). The problem is, however, that at the level of the service facility and in the eyes of many policy makers, lawyers, judges, and advocacy groups, a belief about the long reach of technology has been set in motion and now has nearly 2 decades of momentum behind it. This expectancy dangerously exceeds the actual performance record of behavioral technology in applied settings. Indeed, there is growing opinion (e.g., Bailey, 1981) that the popular notion that all clients can benefit from training is unsupportable for many of the most profoundly handicapped persons. That is to say, the technology still is rudimentary, and demonstrations that meaningful behavioral responses can be taught to these clients are minimal (Bailey, 1981; Ellis, 1981).

This brings us to the reality faced by the service professionals working in the facility. These people must daily manage the divide between the technology's expectation and its performance. It is a monumental task in some instances. For example, in one facility, the medical staff began to reduce the level of client psychotropic medication in response to the general concern and sensitivity about overuse of these drugs. In many cases, as the maladaptive behavior increased with the medication reduction, the physicians "prescribed" behavior modification as a remedy. The behavior modification professionals were faced with the "ecological truth" mentioned earlier but found the various parties involved (physicians, some administrators, other professionals) not very sympathetic. They wanted the prescription filled.

The professional's difficulty with working his or her technology to useful service outcomes is serious. Here we have described some misunderstandings about the technology. In addition, applying technology often meets with broad and sophisticated resistance (see Chapter 3) at the residential level. Even where it is desired by direct-care staff, they may not know how to use it. Where they know how, there may be inadequate resources to make use of their abilities. These problems do not exist in every facility or in every unit in a facility. Our point is, simply, that the problem does exist and that the professional attempting to manage it was probably untrained for the assignment.

SOME REVISIONS AND NEW DIRECTIONS FOR THE PROFESSIONS

The profile of service professionals developed in this discussion contends that these men and women arrive at the PRF without reasonably accurate images either of the setting or of their role in it. Although expert in technical specialties, they are nonspecialists about the circumstances that will likely exert the most force against their career priorities, allegiances, even their definitions of themselves. This makes them vulnerable. We have suggested further that most contemporary facilities operate under conditions and norms that make it seem adaptive to conceal the vulnerability. The professionals are likely to comply, thus enabling the organization to be unresponsive to their needs.

It is tempting to conclude this chapter with an itemized prescription detailing specific actions both professionals and organizations should take to correct these matters. Although such actions are intuitively apparent to us after some 50 years' collective experience with PRFs, we know few successful changes that occurred simply by being declared. Instead, it seems more useful and fair to the reader to reexamine the assumptions and perhaps rethink the goals that underpin professional service in PRFs.

Preparation

Our profile of the professional, as is, is largely an attempt to construct an understanding of the dynamics of PRFs as they are experienced by those who work in them. If such an understanding can be reliably developed, then the first necessity is to convert it to instruction. This means revising the notion of training for service professions in university settings and introducing instruction in many service facilities. It also means developing a teaching continuity between the two settings that predicts to the real parameters of the jobs.

At first glance, such objectives seem to be monumentally improbable, especially in view of the goal contradictions across the two settings discussed earlier. But a closer look reveals that some basics are present already. For example, many programs currently have their students intern in PRFs where they conduct training with clients. University faculty often have special project units in these facilities as well. But the practicum training tends to be oriented toward clinical procedures, data collection, and first shift hours. Too often the student trainees practice in quasi-laboratory set ups or special conditions arranged to accommodate them or their professors. The students often train or work with clients before they acquire a working knowledge of the environment and the staff. Some are not required to develop that knowledge at all; it is viewed as a peripheral matter.

Training practica that predict real job parameters would use time and space differently. We believe no formal clinical training should be undertaken with clients until students have spent a large block of unstructured time observing the residential unit on all three shifts. Preferably they should roll up their sleeves and work alongside direct care staff with no special status. Some of the useful outcomes of doing this are described in Chapter 3. Especially important is the improved ability students develop in working the environment into program interventions, that is, designing and implementing procedures that the natural ecology of the residential unit can support and sustain.

But there is much more to be done with training practica. If the subject of instruction becomes the entire service setting, then we have to formulate a new agenda of training. To illustrate, one element of the curriculum might develop skills to identify the relative tolerance for change that exists in a given environment of staff and clients. In such practicum training, students might intern the service unit learning to assess the readiness of direct-care, supervisory, and administrative personnel for specific staff development and program interventions. They might examine these questions:

1. At a bare minimum, what has to be in place before an intervention can begin?
2. What is the precise nature and level of administrative support necessary to sustain an intervention at planning, implementation, and maintenance stages?
3. What is the history of similar efforts with these employees? How have they reacted in the past?
4. Is there awareness of the needs to which the program intervention is a response? What are the likely reactions of those who are aware and of those unaware or unwilling to become aware?

We believe that students who are career bound in the service professions can and should be taught these skills. From 1974 to 1979, the first author conducted a series of 1-year practica that focused heavily on this type of training. The student trainees, mostly from the disciplines of psychology and special education, provided evaluative information indicating that the practicum was significant in preparing them to understand, anticipate, and respond to many of the service setting realities discussed earlier in this chapter. Some students were informally followed for several years into their careers. These people continued to confirm the relevance and anticipatory value of the training.

These are hardly convincing data, but the necessity for conducting this kind of instruction in the service setting is clear enough. Thus, it is not at all farfetched for us to consider a curriculum of practicum or internship training that develops skill in the following areas:

1. Understanding and working with the social, political, and administrative norms that tend to control events at various levels of the PRF.
2. Reading the language, symbols, and secret codes of various staff groups that often signal important choice points for the professional.
3. Pre-assessing the impact of professional roles and service interventions on the staff, clients, parents, and external groups that have large stakes in the natural setting.
4. Assessing an environment for activities and routines that could compete with program interventions.
   a. Identifying likely points of resistance.
   b. Determining sources of interference that can and cannot be controlled.
   c. Pre-assessing the environment's capacity to maintain interventions.

5. Managing the delicately balanced relationships between professional and administrator and between professional and direct-care staff.

6. Using the natural incentive and power systems in the facility.

7. Diagnosing the goodness of fit between organizational structures and tasks.

8. Developing credibility and trust as an "outsider" in residential units.

9. Understanding and managing the differences in history, function, and expectancy that distinguish first, second, and third shift operations.

10. Promoting the growth of the interdisciplinary process.

11. Negotiating labor contract conflicts with program requirements.

This approach to practicum training for service professionals amounts to a systemic reality testing of the ecology. Taken together with technical practica, it should develop professionals who are sophisticated in managing the application of technical services in the complex environments of PRFs. The Report of the National Task Force on Mental Health/Mental Retardation Administration (1979) described a similar model of practicum training as essential for administrative trainees if they are to appreciate the field situations they will supervise.

The Task Force Report also indicated the need for planning and implementation continuity between training (i.e., university) and field staff. This is not less important in the training of mental disability professionals. Currently, however, there are weaknesses in this collaboration. Service professionals, even if knowledgeable in the areas listed earlier, often have not developed this information into useful instructional vehicles. Training universities or agencies, on the other hand, have neither solicited this expertise at the field site nor incorporated it into their field requirements.

University classroom curricula also have not reflected the importance of the relationship between clinical technologies and the ecological characteristics of the service system as the fundamental knowledge base on which contemporary professions must function. If they did, their catalogue listings would offer more courses in organizational systems and behavior, mental disability law, program administration, labor relations in the professions, public financial management, governmental process and policy formulation, history and sociology of PRFs, and supervision and leadership. Once again, the Report of the National Task Force (1979) suggests a curriculum of similar content as for administrative trainees. We would extend the requirement to the service professionals—it is inevitable that they will need the knowledge.

Servicing the Professional in the Work Setting

Any revision in the thinking and conduct of training professionals for public human service positions must be supported by revised methods of caring for them in the work setting itself. Cherniss, Egnatios, and Wacker (1976) have argued that because there is no longer a strong, unquestioned conception of what the new professional should become, the process of becoming a professional is more stressful. The contradictions, uncertainties, and other realities we have described as characteristic of the professionals' transaction with the work setting contribute to serious levels of stress and impaired morale. A growing literature on this subject supports this conclusion (e.g., Cherniss, Egnatios, & Wacker, 1976; Greenberg & Valletutti, 1980; Scholom & Perlman, 1979; Weinberg, Edwards, & Sternau, 1979). In the past decade or so, we have observed unhealthy and habitual cynicism, gallows humor, and other similar signs of distress among professionals in PRFs. Many of these people rage at the system, and their complicity in maintaining it as Rogers (1975) has observed. We have also noticed that some develop a curious investment in their resentment.

The work setting tends to be unresponsive to these difficulties even if it is aware of them. A major correction in the relationship of the facility to its professional service providers is, therefore, required. Their needs must be prudently assessed, acknowledged with priority and without stigma, and supported through competent supervision.

That there is considerable risk for individual professionals in sharing their job distress openly is an important issue. With their roles often fashioned in a way that precludes such disclosure, it becomes necessary first to identify the distress through more formal and anonymous assessment. Following such a premise, Thaw, McLaughlin, and Ciarcia (1982) surveyed virtually all members of the professions in one facility to determine their needs and reactions along a broad span of job factors. Some of the information gathered included the following:

1. Professionals' perception of the respect various other staff groups have for their work and the importance of that respect.
2. Relative discomfort in various work situations.
3. Professionals' judgment of the adequacy of their preparation for their current job responsibilities.
4. Rating of job enjoyment.
5. Level of stress experienced in each major job situation.
6. Perceived control in making services occur properly.
7. Major obstacles to implementing services.
8. Extent of compromise for purpose of compliance with paper requirements.
9. Difficulties in relationships with department heads and unit managers.
10. Quality rating of supervision received.
11. Attitudes toward various aspects of the job.
12. Degree of role confusion or ambiguity.

An anonymous but formal audit of the condition of a facility's professions can provide its administration with valuable information it would otherwise be unable to acquire in an organized way. More important, the decision to inquire systematically about the needs and problems of professionals legitimates the existence of the needs. It thus becomes more acceptable for individual professionals to have these needs. Properly conducted, such assessments can be powerful in compelling administrators and supervisors to respond to those needs with a sense of priority.

Evaluative data of the sort we are describing can be organized by profession, unit, interdisciplinary team, or other functional group. In our survey (Thaw, McLaughlin, & Ciarcia, 1982), we found considerable variability across groups for different items, suggesting that some areas of need are discipline or team specific. Once the auditing of this information becomes a normative activity, the facility can develop approaches to respond. These must be equally acceptable and nonstigmatizing.

Scholom and Perlman (1979) suggest several options in response to the kinds of problems professionals experience in PRFs. For example, they advise designated "mental health breaks," outside staff development seminars, and increased opportunities for staff input into agency policy development. They also recommend the use of outside consultants to meet periodically with staff on internal matters. These proposals should be helpful, and some agencies have adopted approaches of this sort; however, it is our belief that the principal intervention must be a program of continual and intense supervision. Staff development seminars, outside workshops, even breaks tend to be one-time propositions with limited follow-up.

There is an apparently widespread belief in PRFs that professional service providers do not need supervision or that they require only technical supervision. This belief is misguided. It is also common practice to qualify people as supervisors by reason of their degrees, status, or tenure in the system. This is an equally misguided practice although a very difficult one to question. Discontent, frustrated, uncertain, and overstressed professionals working in environments and under assignments with which they cannot come to terms need more than technical supervision. They also need supervisors competent to handle these difficulties.

A program of competency-based supervision for professionals is both possible and likely to succeed. Professionals can be stewarded through role confusion, uncertainty, mismatched tasks and structures, poorly applied unit concepts, legal activity, labor relations problems, and overly accelerated organizational changes with their sanity and professionalism intact. They can be redirected to view obstacles and resistance to their projects as important variables to problem solve rather than just as annoying distractions. To take a related example, many professionals are ahistorical about their work setting—it began when they arrived and it will discontinue when they exit. Such individuals tend to be constrained by a narrow view of change and innovation. They are likely to see barriers to progress and flaws in the system itself as insurmountable. They may be right in certain instances but probably not as a general rule. Quality supervision can help them to develop an historical sense of their organization, one that allows them to see that even a small unit moves through levels of maturity, each level with a different tolerance for program interventions and other events.

One pilot project responsive to the concerns under discussion deserves mention (Thaw, 1981). Based on results of a needs assessment of all psychologists in one PRF, a program of technical and process supervision was developed. The technical component had been in place informally for several years. It was formalized and updated. The process component was new and addressed coping with many of the factors of the professionals' job experience discussed in this chapter (e.g., ecological, legal, role, interdisciplinary process, organization dynamics, and stress). Four senior psychologists with previous supervisory experience were organized as a supervisory team. They received specialized training in supervisory and leadership skills germane to the problems their supervisees were experiencing. The team also met monthly to present and problem solve difficult individual situations. Finally, each supervisor met regularly with the Chief Psychologist to review his or her supervision. Ten psychologists received supervision in weekly or biweekly sessions lasting from 1 to 3 hours. Supervisee problems and needs were committed to formal goal plans and, in some cases, to contractual arrangements with supervisors.

Two evaluative instruments were designed to assess the effectiveness of the supervisory program (Thaw, 1981). One required supervisees to rate specific supervisory and relationship abilities of their supervisors as well as the general relevance and value of the program to their work experience. The second asked respondents to rate technical progress and judge the degree to which supervision had assisted them in problem solving several specific process issues (e.g., managing interdisciplinary conflict in their units, defining their roles as psychologists, handling job stress, relating to direct care staff).

The evaluation was conducted after one year of the program's operation using a retrospective pretest (Then/Post) analysis (Howard, 1980). The results were instructive. The data confirmed a unanimous positive response to the supervision. It was judged significantly more valuable than previous approaches to supervision these professionals had experienced. Supervisees reported increased perspective about their jobs and attributed that development to supervision. On the second instrument, a pre–post means comparison revealed a statistically significant improvement on 22 of 23 total items. Supervisees believed they were coping better with several parameters of their job and perceived the supervision as responsible for the improvement.

With only 10 subjects from one PRF, these results are merely suggestive and cannot be generalized. They are bound by the conditions of the specific facility, the nature of the profession studied, and the individual experiences of the personnel involved. We are encouraged, however, that intensive programs of supervision responsive to nontechnical dimensions of the professional job experience can be implemented effectively in the work setting. Whether administrators will see fit to elevate the priority of such efforts and invest the necessary time and resources in them is another matter.

A FINAL THOUGHT

In closing, some historical perspective of our own may be in order. We have described some troubling conditions confronting the professions in PRFs for mentally handicapped clients. Most of these circumstances have developed over the past 15 years. However, if we remember that prior to this period, most professions functioned marginally in these organizations and some not at all, then the current problems may be seen, at least in part, as a response to the acceleration of events that has affected the service system generally. These events have been of significant proportion. It is unreasonable, even naive, to believe that their effects and implications can be fully understood, let alone translated into stable, normative functions in such a relatively short span of time. If the required perspective is patience and the program of change and revision is sensibly farsighted, there is reason to be encouraged that the professions can contribute to needed systematic adjustments while coming to more constructive terms with the system itself.

REFERENCES

Abrahamson, M. A. (Ed.). (1967).   *The professional in the organization.* Chicago: Rand-McNally.
Azrin, N. H., & Foxx, R. M. (1971).   A rapid method of toilet training the institutionalized retarded. *Journal of Applied Behavior Analysis, 4,* 89–99.
Bailey, J.S. (1981).   Wanted: A rational search for the limiting conditions of habilitation in the retarded. *Analysis and Intervention in Developmental Disabilities, 1,* 45–52.
Bates, P., & Wehman, P. (1977).   Behavior management with the mentally retarded: An empirical analysis of the research. *Mental Retardation, 15,* 9–12.
Baumeister, A. A. (1967).   A survey of the role of psychologists in public institutions for the mentally retarded. *Mental Retardation, 5,* 2–5.
Baumeister, A. A. (1981).   The right to habilitation: What does it mean? *Analysis and Intervention in Developmental Disabilities, 1,* 61–74.
Baumeister, A. A., & Hillsinger, L. B. (1984).   Role of psychologists in public institutions for the mentally retarded revisited. *Professional Psychology: Research and Practice, 15,* 134–141.
Bensberg, G. J., Colwell, C. N., & Cassel, R. H. (1965).   Teaching the profoundly retarded self-help activities by behavior shaping techniques. *American Journal of Mental Deficiency, 69,* 674–679.
Blue, C. M., & Sumner, F. G. (1970).   Residential speech and hearing services. In A. A. Baumeister & E. C. Butterfield (Eds.), *Residential facilities for the mentally retarded* (pp. 272–314). Chicago: Aldine.
Bucher, R. & Stelling, J. (1969).   Characteristics of professional organizations. *Journal of Health and Social Behavior, 10,* 3–15.
Bucher, R., & Stelling, J. (1977).   *Becoming professional.* Beverly Hills, CA: Sage.

Cherniss, C., Egnatios, E. S., & Wacker, S. (1976). Job stress and career development in new public professionals. *Professional Psychology, 7,* 429–436.

Cogan, M. L. (1953). Toward a definition of profession. *Harvard Educational Review, 23,* 35–54.

Crosby, K. G. (1976). Essentials of active programming. *Mental Retardation, 14,* 3–9.

Cullari, S., & Ferguson, D. G. (1981). Individual behavior change: Problems with programming in institutions for mentally retarded persons. *Mental Retardation, 19,* 267–270.

Davis, H. R. (1973). Change and innovation. In S. Feldman (Ed.), *The administration of mental health services* (pp. 289–341). Springfield, IL: Charles C. Thomas.

Dolgoff, T. (1970). The organization, the administrator, and the mental health professional. *Hospital and Community Psychiatry, 21,* 25–32.

Ellis, N. R. (1979). The Partlow Case: A reply to Dr. Roos. *Law and Psychology Review, 5,* 15–30.

Ellis, N. R. (1981). On training the mentally retarded. *Analysis and Intervention in Developmental Disabilities, 1,* 99–108.

Foxx, R. M., & Livesay, J. (1984). Maintenance of response suppression following overcorrection: A 10-year retrospective examination of eight cases. *Analysis and Intervention in Developmental Disabilities, 4,* 65–79.

Gardner, W. I. (1971). *Behavior modification in mental retardation.* Chicago: Aldine.

Granger, B. P. (1972). Dilemmas of reorganizing institutions for the mentally retarded. *Mental Retardation, 10,* 3–7.

Greenberg, S. F., & Valletutti, P. J. (1980). *Stress and the helping professions.* Baltimore: Paul H. Brookes Publishing Co.

Gurel, L. (1975). The human side of evaluating human services programs. In M. Guttentag & E. L. Struening (Eds.), *Handbook of evaluation research* (Vol. 2) (pp. 11–28). Beverly Hills, CA: Sage.

Hersch, C. (1968). The discontent explosion in mental health. *American Psychologist, 23,* 497–506.

Howard, G. S. (1980). Response-shift bias: A problem in evaluating interventions with pre/post self-reports. *Evaluation Review, 4,* 93–106.

Howe, H. E., Jr., & Neimeyer, R. A. (1980). Job relevance in clinical training: Is that all there is? *Professional Psychology, 11,* 305–313.

Irons, D., Irons, T., & Maddux, C. D. (1984). A survey of perceived competence among psychologists who evaluate students with severe handicaps. *Journal of the Association for Persons with Severe Handicaps, 9,* 55–60.

Kafry, D., & Pines, A. (1977). The experience of tedium in life and work. Unpublished manuscript, University of California at Berkeley.

Kaufman, H. (1971). *The limits of organizational change.* University, AL: University of Alabama Press.

Koch, S. (1981). The nature and limits of psychological knowledge: Lessons of a century qua "Science." *American Psychologist, 36,* 257–269.

Krishef, C., & Levine, D. L. (1968). Preparing the social worker for effective services to the retarded. *Mental Retardation, 6,* 3–7.

Kugel, R. B., & Wolfensberger, W. (Eds.). (1969). *Changing patterns in residential services for the mentally retarded.* Washington: President's Committee on Mental Retardation.

LaPorte, T. (1971). *Organizational response to complexity: Research and development as organized inquiry and action - Part I* (Working paper No. 141). Berkeley, CA: Center for Planning and Development Research, Institute of Urban and Regional Development, University of California.

Lent, J. R. (1968). Mimosa cottage: Experiment in hope. *Psychology Today, 2*(1), 51–58.

Light, D., Jr. (1979). Uncertainty and control in professional training. *Journal of Health and Social Behavior, 20,* 310–322.

Lippitt, G. L. (1973). Hospital organization in the post-industrial society. *Hospital Progress, 54,* 55–65.

Maslach, C. (1976, September). Burned-out. *Human Behavior,* 17–21.

Mechanic, D. (1973). The sociology of organizations. In S. Feldman (Ed.), *The administration of mental health services* (pp. 138–166). Springfield, IL: Charles C. Thomas.

Meyer, R. J. (1979). A college-level course on mental retardation for professional and paraprofessional nursing staff of a residential MR facility. *Mental Retardation, 17,* 29–31.

Michael, D. N. (1973). *On learning to plan - and planning to learn.* San Francisco: Jossey-Bass.

Millman, M. (1976). *The unkindest cut: Life in the backrooms of medicine.* New York: Morrow.

Mintzberg, H. (1979). *The structuring of organizations.* Englewood Cliffs, NJ: Prentice-Hall.

Mintzberg, H. (1981, January–February). Organization design: Fashion or fit? *Harvard Business Review,* 103–116.

Moore, W. E. (1970). *The professions: Roles and rules.* New York: Russell Sage Foundation.

Pines, A., & Maslach, C. (1978). Characteristics of staff burnout in mental health settings. *Hospital and Community Psychiatry,* 233–237.

Raynes, N., Bumstead, D. C., & Pratt, M. W. (1974). Unitization: Its effects on residential care practices. *Mental Retardation, 12,* 12–14.

Report of the National Task Force on Mental Health/Mental Retardation Administration. (1979). *Administration in Mental Health, 6,* 269–323.

Rogers, K. (1975). State mental hospitals: An organizational analysis *Administration in Mental Health, 3,* 12–20.

Romeo v. Youngberg, 644 F. 2d 147 (3d Cir. 1980).

Roos, P. (1970). Evolutionary changes of the residential facility. In A. A. Baumeister & E. C. Butterfield (Eds.), *Residential facilities for the mentally retarded* (pp. 29–58). Chicago: Aldine.

Ryan, R. M. (1974, Summer). Managing mental health professionals: An alternative future. *Administration in Mental Health,* 68–73.

Sajwaj, T. (1977). Issues and implications of establishing guidelines for the use of behavioral techniques. *Journal of Applied Behavior Analysis, 10,* 531–540.

Sarata, B. P. V. (1975). Employee satisfactions in agencies serving retarded persons. *American Journal of Mental Deficiency, 79,* 434–442.

Scheerenberger, R. C. (1975). *Managing residential facilities for the developmentally disabled.* Springfield, IL: Charles C. Thomas.

Scholom, A., & Perlman, B. (1979). The forgotten staff: Who cares for the care givers? *Administration in Mental Health, 7,* 21–31.

Scott, W. R. (1969). Professional employees in a bureaucratic structure: Social work. In A. Etzioni (Ed.), *The semi-professions and their organization* (pp. 82–140). New York: Free Press.

Sluyter, G. V. (1976). The unit management system: Anatomy of structural change. *Mental Retardation, 14,* 14–16.

Stokes, T. F., & Baer, D. M. (1977). An implicit technology of generalization. *Journal of Applied Behavior Analysis, 10,* 349–367.

Thaw, J. (1981, June). *Department of psychology supervisory program* (Year End Report). Mansfield Depot, CT: Mansfield Training School.

Thaw, J., McLaughlin, D., & Ciarcia, J. (1982, June). *A survey of the professions in a facility for the developmentally disabled* (Draft report). Mansfield Depot, CT: Mansfield Training School.

Thompson, J. (1967). *Organizations in action: Social science bases of administrative theory.* New York: McGraw-Hill.

Thompson, V. A. (1976). *Bureaucracy and the modern world.* Morristown, NJ: General Learning Press.

Tucker, R. C., & Tucker, L. M. (1976). The role of paraprofessionals: An administrative dilemma. *Administration in Mental Health, 3,* 114–124.

Turkat, I. D., & Forehand, R. (1980). The future of behavior therapy. In M. Hersen, R. M. Eisler,

& P. M. Miller (Eds.), *Progress in Behavior Modification* (Vol. 9) (pp. 1–47). New York: Academic Press.

Weinberg, S., Edwards, G., & Sternau, R. (1979, May). *Burnout among employees of state residential facilities serving the developmentally disabled.* Paper presented at the meeting of the American Association of Mental Deficiency, Miami Beach.

Younie, W. J. (1966). Approaches to educational therapy in state supported institutions for the mentally retarded. In J. Hellmuth (Ed.), *Educational Therapy* (Vol. 1) (pp. 371–388). Seattle: Special Child Publications.

Youngberg v. Romeo, 50 U.S. Law Week 4681 (1982).

5 Mental Disability Law—The Politics of Human Rights

Anthony J. Cuvo, Ph.D.
Jack Thaw, Ph.D.

On July 4, 1776, the Congress of the United States unanimously approved the Declaration of Independence. One of the most widely recognized portions of that proclamation is: "We hold these truths to be self-evident, that all men are created equal, that they are endowed by their Creator with certain unalienable Rights, that among these are Life, Liberty and the pursuit of Happiness. That to secure these rights, Governments are instituted among Men, deriving their just powers from the consent of the governed" (Syrett, 1970, p. 81, 82).

Our wise founding fathers recognized an unfortunate irony that plagues us now, more than 200 years later. We have natural law rights that cannot be surrendered, but governments must be created to obtain those rights for us. Citizens can take little comfort in the fact that rights they may not have in reality cannot be denied in principle.

The Constitution of the United States defines the three branches of government and their role in securing our rights. A popular perception of some naive citizens is that the executive, judicial, and legislative branches of government operate fairly and, after carefully and objectively weighing factual evidence, reach decisions that are in the best interest of all people. Some may believe that executive orders, judicial decisions, and legislative statutes that define citizens' rights emanate in this manner. Such a perception misses the mark in many instances.

Instead, rights are generated by a political process characterized by negotiation of competing interests in an adversarial fashion. Legislators, for example, represent state constituencies that sometimes have multiple and conflicting interests; a legislator's vote on any issue may please some people and alienate others. The judicial process is characterized by resolving differences between parties using adversarial procedures. Both the executive branch of government and the legislative, are subject to the influence and even coercion of individuals, groups, and societal forces that are positioned nationally and indeed internationally. Most people are well aware of the competing interests that interact publicly in the political process to advocate or oppose, for example, the comparable worth of different jobs traditionally held by men and women, racial goals for employment, prayer in public schools, federal government payment for abortions, benefits for welfare recipients, and other similar issues.

The Declaration of Independence proclaimed that "all men are created equal . . . with unalienable Rights." Mentally disabled people were not excluded from these blessings. Unfortunately, they also were not exempt from securing those rights through the political process. The negotiation of rights for mentally disabled persons in the political arena has been labeled "psychopolitics," a term that describes the "general relationship between politicians and political systems, on the one hand, and mental health workers and mental health systems, on the other hand" (Greenblatt, 1978, p. 4). As suggested, the word political can be defined broadly to denote not only the three branches of government, but also a variety of other societal forces and institutions that attempt to exert control on governmental processes. These forces may operate in either an advocacy or an adversarial role with respect to mentally disabled persons, attempting to obtain or deny rights for them or otherwise influence the service delivery system. Examples of these nongovernmental forces include special interest groups, the media, and private citizens.

The political process scrutinizes the mental disability service delivery system and holds it accountable. It regulates the service system through policy powered by legislation and litigation if necessary (see Chapter 6). Politics also intrudes into the day-to-day operation of individual public residential facilities such as psychiatric hospitals and developmental centers. Sophisticated professional policies are influenced by elected and appointed politicians who have no expertise in mental disability. Additionally, institutions and community facilities often are political footballs that are exploited by politicians to further their own careers (Talbot, 1978).

Greenblatt (1978) perceptively observed that "a great deal of money and power is 'brokered' through interchanges between mental health system leaders on the one hand and watchdogs of government on the other" (p. 6). He noted that remarkably few mental health or governmental professionals have either studied systematically or at least described the psychopolitical processes in which they have participated. Greenblatt was Commissioner of Mental Health in Massachusetts between 1967 and 1973 and thus portrayed psychopolitics in mental health from the experiential perspective afforded him from his high executive position. The purpose of this chapter is to accept Greenblatt's challenge and portray from an internal perspective politics in the field of mental disability. This chapter focuses on political influence encountered at the national and state levels as well as the lower tiers of the mental disability bureaucracy (e.g., public residential facilities [PRFs] and their subunits). The first thesis of this chapter is a logical deduction from one of Greenblatt's observations. Specifically, the number and nature of individual rights garnered by mentally disabled persons and the manner in which they are implemented substantially depend on political struggles and involve money and power. The politics of human rights refers to the negotiating and sometimes adversarial processes by which mentally disabled persons gain and lose rights. Mental disability professionals, administrators, advocates, and others who participate in that political process have been termed psychopoliticians (Greenblatt, 1978). The process by which these rights are manipulated by psychopoliticians and their adversaries both in the formulation of law as well as its implementation is the concern of this chapter.

The second major thesis of this chapter draws an analogy to some of Alvin Toffler's observations of contemporary society. Toffler (1971) cited evidence that events in society are progressing at such a rapid pace that people have difficulty integrating change into their lives. It is as though the present were rushing into the future with time telescoped because of the rapidity of change. The perceived compression of time has caused citizens to become concerned about their role in the future. Long-range goal planning becomes difficult, and there is a reversion to a series of short-term goals. As a result, Toffler claimed, people in society are in a state of "future shock." More recently, Toffler (1975) turned his analysis to the world's economic condition. He noted that the economies of many countries on our globe are in an upheaval and on the brink of disaster. The futurist claimed that nations are suffering from "eco spasm" (i.e., traumatized economies).

Toffler's concepts of future shock and eco spasm are conceptually analogous to events that have occurred within public residential facilities for mentally retarded and mentally ill persons. The pace of legal events affecting the mental disability system has progressed so rapidly during the past decade that it has created a condition analogous to future shock—legal shock. Similarly, the impact of legal shock on PRFs has been so forceful that it has created, figuratively, "institutional spasm." Legally mandated reform has been thrust upon a formerly placid and impoverished mental disability service system in many cases too fast for it to respond adequately to the demands imposed. The avalanche of litigation, with concomitant legislation and administrative policies, has shaken many aspects of the mental disability service delivery system to its very foundation.

For example, the right to treatment class action suits of the 1970s brought to national attention the abhorrent conditions of PRFs for mentally disabled clients. This litigation, originating with *Wyatt v. Stickney* (1971) and followed by all its early progeny, was argued successfully on morally invincible principles. The use of the judiciary as an instrument of institutional reform in the early 1970s, however, put into motion a legal chain reaction that may have created unforseen consequences in the 1980s. Class action suits aspiring to secure various rights for disabled citizens have been undertaken in most states. At present, we are witnessing one PRF convulse after another as they try to comply with judicial decrees that may have poor formulas for implementation.

The third thesis of this chapter is that rights of disabled persons are established in *principle* by the official branches of government at the highest echelons and in *reality* at lower levels of the governmental structure (e.g., those persons that have the most contact with clients). Legislation may be passed by federal, state, or municipal governments; court orders may emanate from the supreme courts, courts of appeal, or trial courts in either the federal or state systems; and administrative policies may be issued by federal departments, state departments, and individual PRFs. Despite the sanctioned authority of the governmental source and the propriety of the rights proclaimed, legal documents may represent nothing more than shallow "paper victories" for clients unless there is an enforcement mechanism at the service system level that ensures the implementation of these rights (Lottman, 1976).

The rights that clients possess on paper and the ones they exercise in reality may b, quite disparate, and few of us may realize the magnitude of that discrepancy. The breakdown in the process of implementing legislation and litigation may be at any link in the chain, including professional and paraprofessional direct service providers. Ascribing the problems in securing client rights and delivering appropriate services to failures at the line level is, however, a miscalculation of the nature of the difficulties. Systemic problems in the mental disability bureaucracy, our communities, society at large, and in the legal process itself frequently contribute to, if not bear the major responsibilities for, the breakdown of rights implementation.

These three themes are interrelated and part of the politics of mental disability. Each is presented and illustrated with selected contemporary circumstances in the mental disability field. The picture that should emerge is that human rights, in this instance those of mentally disabled persons, may be bartered for money, power, or privileges. Rights create enormous problems of implementation for the service delivery network and can be denied or at least infringed by any one of the many components of our social system. That rights for mentally disabled people are a recent historical concern and legal action has come at such a rapid pace seem to have compressed significantly and thereby complicated and stressed this entire process of reform.

THE BROKERING OF HUMAN RIGHTS

Serious students of the development of law frequently consult Justice Oliver Wendell Holmes, a scholar of common law. He stated: "The life of the law has not been logic: it has been experience. The felt necessities of the time, the prevalent moral and political theories, institutions of public policy, avowed or unconscious, even the prejudices which judges share with their fellow-men, have had a good deal more to do than the syllogism in determining the rules by which men should be governed. . . . The substance of the law at any given time pretty nearly corresponds, so far as it goes, with what is then understood to be convenient'' (Holmes, 1881/1963).

Holmes' analysis of the development of law, written more than a century ago, is timely today and is perhaps a conceptual precursor of the term psychopolitics. The process of law is influenced by societal ''necessities,'' human ''prejudices,'' and ''what is convenient.'' People in our society, however, differ with respect to their perceptions of what is necessary. We all do not share the same prejudices. What is convenient for some is an insurmountable obstacle for others. Establishing a community facility for mentally handicapped persons may seem like an uncomplicated exercise of those individuals' rights until local property owners contend that a group home abridges their rights under ''protection of the general welfare'' clauses of land use control laws. As a result of these human differences, law is not a simple matter of benevolent governmental authorities dispensing human rights because it is the universally accepted and unquestionably just thing to do for citizens. Mental disability law, like perhaps all law, often is a matter of negotiated settlements reflecting prevailing conveniences. Thus, it is not immune to the brokerage process.

Adversarial contests have pitted various special interest groups against each other with each side arguing that its position is in the best interest of mentally disabled clients. Groups have formed coalitions with one another to increase their political strength on a particular issue. At times, the alliances have shifted, so that groups cooperating with each other on one issue may be adversaries on another. As Arthur Bentley said almost 70 years ago, groups are the ''raw material of politics'' (cited in Ornstein & Elder, 1978).

Special interest groups monitor governmental activity and attempt to promote their interests by lobbying for or against governmental actions. ''Regardless of the type of group, access to political decision makers is the key to group activity, and the nature of that access—the number of points of access, the ability to reach the 'right' people, the type of reception from the decisionmakers—is directly related to the resources of the group and its ability to utilize them'' (Ornstein & Elder, 1978, p. 54).

In recent years there has been increasing activity by mental disability service providers, especially unionized state employees, in the political arena. In still other actions, the rights of mentally disabled clients have been challenged by groups of citizens in their community or by politicians on their behalf. Professional organizations (e.g., medical societies) also have labored for or against proposed legislation purportedly benefiting disabled persons for what may be an ulterior motive of protecting organization members' welfare. Although the political process frequently involves organized groups, governmental branches, and large sums of money, the brokerage and advocacy action of individuals also is noteworthy.

Unfortunately, these political machinations generally are not reported in the professional literature. Political activity tends to occur privately as much as it does in public forums or in print. Systematic documentation is sketchy and less concrete than it is for most other professional practices. Evidence tends to come from the verbal reports of participants in or observers of the political process. The motivation of informants and the validity of their comments may be suspect. Consequently, conscientious reporting of the politics of human rights is difficult. In light of these caveats, some of the situations portrayed later are stated in general terms in order to protect individuals and facilities for unintended misrepresentation. The examples cited have been organized to reflect political activities involving special interest groups, individual service providers, and elected officials.

Mental Disability Politics Involving Special Interest Groups

The political dimension of human rights acquisition can be illustrated by some of the background facts in the landmark right to treatment and habilitation case, *Wyatt v. Stickney* (1971). In October 1970 the employment of 99 workers at Bryce Hospital in Alabama was terminated because of a budget cut at the facility. The reduction was necessitated because of a decrease in the cigarette tax revenues available to the Alabama State Department of Mental Health, as well as a legislated adjustment in the pay period for state personnel that would increase expenditures. Of the 99 staff laid off, 58 were members of various professions involved in direct client care.

The newly terminated state employees were unsuccessful in winning reinstatement to their positions through civil service appeals. Subsequently, the Wyatt law suit was initiated in federal court by the former hospital employees. The Commissioner of Mental Health in Alabama at the time claimed that, "the patients were added to the suit, almost as an afterthought, to bolster the employee plaintiffs' contention that if they were laid off, adequate treatment could no longer be offered at Bryce Hospital" (Stickney, 1976, p. 32). The federal court was sympathetic to the patients' portion of the suit on Constitutional grounds but rejected the employees' petition for an injunction against their termination. Subsequently, however, the plaintiff employees were successful in obtaining a restraining order against the Mental Health Department in a state district court in Tuscaloosa. "Some observers concluded this was a local political decision," said Dr. Stonewall Stickney, the named defendant (Stickney, 1976, p. 32).

These events seem to portray mentally disabled people as collateral in a larger political struggle of state employees to retain their jobs; the human rights issue merely was convenient in the contest over reinstatement and lost wages. The "accidental" nature of the *Wyatt* (1971) case prompts questions regarding the litigative register of the 1970's in mental disability law. When would reform in Alabama have been initiated had 99 people not been laid off? If those people had not lost their jobs in Alabama, would we have had the Willowbrook case (*New York State ARC v. Rockefeller,* 1973) in New York, the Pennhurst case (*Halderman v. Pennhurst,* 1977) in Pennsylvania, or dozens of other right to habilitation cases from coast to coast? Would anyone have had the rights of disabled persons as their primary concern? Although the former Bryce employees in Alabama were thwarted by the federal court in their initial efforts to win reinstatement, the eventual judicial orders required hiring large numbers of additional staff. Perhaps we should accept the good accidents of legal history along with the bad and be done with it; however, the unchartered early developments in *Wyatt* may remind us of the wisdom of Mr. Justice Holmes' reflection about the law's reliance on history for its expression.

It seems that approval for deinstitutionalization and PRF census reductions should be universal. Instead, it has created controversy that can be illustrated in proposed state and federal legislation. The argument has been made by some proponents of community living that as the populations of PRFs are reduced and clients are placed in community alternatives, the budgets of PRFs should be decreased proportionally and those funds diverted to community programs—the money should follow the clients. Community service providers have argued that they must absorb an increasing number of clients that are being funneled, if not dumped, into the community without the necessary budget to do so. PRF administrators and staff, not surprisingly, claim that their budgets should be maintained and preferably increased in order to provide newly mandated services to the more severely handicapped clients that remain in their facilities. Recent legislation, litigation, and policies, coupled with the greater proportion of institutional clients with special needs, require all the existing staff and resources, if not more, to provide necessary services. The struggle over funds for staff positions is fierce, and state employees and their labor organizations are among the most vociferous protagonists fighting for their jobs.

Unfortunately, in most states there are not enough staff positions to provide all the mandated services to clients in PRFs and in the community. Consequently, there is a tug-of-war between PRF and community special interests to retain or acquire positions, generally from the former to the latter. In this struggle, PRF employee labor organizations frequently have taken a proinstitution position and obstructed efforts toward community placement, the closing of PRF Living units, and the consolidation of old PRFs. As PRFs are effective in exerting political pressure to retain their staff, the rights of clients in the community may be jeopardized. On the other hand, as community facilities are successful in drawing resources from PRFs, the rights of institutional clients may be endangered. In this situation we have mental disability service providers as adversaries of other service providers in a competition for finite resources.

This point can be illustrated by a controversy that took place in Pennsylvania in 1980 centering on amendments to Senate Bill 581 that was before the State General Assembly. Essentially, the principal amendment required that at least 30 days prior to closing any mental retardation center or materially reducing (i.e., 5%) its bed complement, services, or staff, the Department of Public Welfare would hold a public hearing in the affected area and not take action without presenting its proposal to the general assembly. If either legislative body disapproved of the proposed action, it would not take effect. The bill, therefore, would require legislative authorization for closing institutions or reducing their staff or services.

This amendment to Senate Bill 581 was introduced in the House of Representatives after the Pennsylvania Public Welfare Department had proposed to close Retreat State Hospital in Luzerne County and considered eliminating chaplain, farming, and other institution positions. The House and Senate passed the amended bill; the governor subsequently vetoed it. The bill then went back before the state senate, where eight additional votes for an override were needed. At that point, the political battle lines were drawn sharply between special interest groups.

The proposed statute became known as the "Stop Retreat" bill. The jobs of a large number of Pennsylvanians as well as one of the economic bases of Luzerne County were in jeopardy. Political activity to introduce the amendments was spearheaded by the major state employee labor union, the American Federation of State, County, and Municipal Employees (AFSCME). Opposition to the amendments was led by The Pennsylvania Association for Retarded Citizens (PARC), which considered the proposed legislation to thwart the deinstitutionalization process and the right of clients to live in less restrictive environments.

The struggle was documented by PARC in several of its publications in the spring of 1980. AFSCME reportedly retained the services of the J. Walter Thompson advertising agency to develop a public relations strategy to influence key senators to change their vote from no to yes on the override vote. According to PARC's *Legislative Action* (May 9, 1980), nine senators were the principal targets for full-page ads that appeared in Pennsylvania newspapers and radio spot announcements within the districts of these public officials. Typical of those ads is one that appeared in *The Meadville Tribune* (May 8, 1980, p. 9). The full page ad stated in large print: "Senators Kusse and Dwyer: Don't be responsible for more unemployment in our community. . . . You have a voice when a hospital opens. Why surrender that voice when a hospital in your community—like Polk and Warren—may be threatened with closings?. . . Now, as a Senator concerned about all your constituents, it's up to you to *override* the veto, and make Senate Bill 581 a law." The ad was signed by the Coalition of Concerned Citizens, Pennhurst Parents - Staff Association, Pennsylvania Social Services Union, Pennsylvania AFL-CIO, and Pennsylvania Nurses Association, among others.

In response to these political efforts to gain support for the override vote, PARC, the Mental Health Association in Pennsylvania, the State Health Coordinating Council, and other groups influenced the Senate and public to continue opposition to Senate Bill 581. These organized and sophisticated special interest groups obtained endorsement for their position from church, disability, advocacy, and civic groups. Tactics recommended by PARC for obtaining support included writing letters to the editor and news releases, making appearances on TV and radio talk shows, and inviting the local State Senator to an annual ARC dinner meeting (*The PARC Hot Sheet,* May 23, 1980).

During this battle, each side claimed that its position was in the best interest of clients, that the other side was motivated by self-interests. The closing of institutions, it was argued by proponents of Senate Bill 581, would result in a disservice to clients by dumping them on an unwanting community. Opponents of Senate Bill 581 countered that the proposed legislation abridged clients' right to habilitation in the least restrictive environment. Eventually, amended Senate Bill 581 was defeated; however, a county ARC official in Pennsylvania said there is reason to believe that its proponents will try to attach the amendments to a future bill.

The principal point of the present discussion is not the outcome of the law but its political process. The Pennsylvania example illustrates how human service professionals, direct-care workers, parents of institutionalized clients, and others created an alliance to defend their self-interests. Deinstitutionalization represents a possible loss of jobs for workers and uncertainty for parents regarding where their children may be placed in the future. By their banding together, the financial and political power of these disparate groups could be enhanced. Does the right to habilitation in the least restrictive setting outweigh employees' interests in preserving their jobs and parents' concerns for maintaining the placement of their children? Rights won in federal courts by litigation may be thwarted by state legislators if sufficient political pressure can be brought to bear by their constituents. Such conflicts, therefore, are not always resolved by what is legally or morally correct, but by what can be ushered through the political process.

The politics of institution versus community habilitation also is being played out at the national level, specifically in the drama of the proposed Community and Family Living Amendments of 1983 (U.S. Senate Bill 2053). The bill, introduced by Senator John Chafee in the 98th Congress, would restructure Medicaid and phase out support for PRFs in favor of smaller, community-based programs. ARC-US has been a primary architect of this bill and one of its most visible proponents. The most detailed criticism of the bill has come from the National Association of State Mental Retardation Program Directors (NASMRPD). Parents and parent groups have taken positions on both sides of the issue, as have mental retardation program and facility administrators and state ARCs. Only two other senators have cosponsored this bill, and the majority of letters to the U.S. Senate Finance Committee as well as to Senator Chafee (1984) have been opposed to the proposed legislation. This debate takes place in a context where approximately only 4% of the mentally retarded population is institutionalized, yet institutions receive the vast majority of federal and state funding. Hearings on the bill were held before the Subcommittee on Health of the U.S. Senate Finance Committee in Washington on February 27, 1984, and in Minnesota in August of 1984.

As a result of the opposition to the bill, particularly by NASMRPD, ARC-US has compromised and recommended modifications. NASMRPD agrees with the basic premise that many institutionalized mentally retarded persons could benefit from less restrictive community alternatives, but it objects to S.2053 as a vehicle for accomplishing that goal (Gettings & Howse, 1984). Instead NASMRPD favors modifying the already existing Medicaid home and community care provisions. Interestingly, ARC-Illinois has come out in opposition to S.2053, and has taken a position in conflict with its parent organization (ARC/Illinois News, 1984). ARC/Illinois, a service provider as well as an advocacy organization, opposes the bill because it claims the proposed legislation does not support a full spectrum of residential services. Critics of the State ARC position have argued that S.2053 in its present form would jeopardize the organization's residential services, as well as the alliance it has built over the years with parents and institution service providers who have a personal investment in maintaining PRFs. ARC-Illinois has prepared an alternative draft bill to S.2053.

ARC-US acquiesced on a number of points in contention that might make the bill more palatable to its opponents (Everitt, 1984). For example, ARC-US has recommended a partial (i.e., 85%) withdrawal rather than a total withdrawal of federal Medicaid funds from institutions, and the withdrawal would take place over a longer time frame than originally proposed. Also at issue are defining the eligible population, grandfathering existing ICF-MR facilities for funding, reimbursing staff training, and a number of other matters. Although S.2053 died at the end of the 98th Congress in December of 1984, Senator Chafee introduced a revised bill, S.873 on April 3, 1985 (Chafee, 1984). The revised bill narrows the definition of entitled severely disabled persons, "grandfathers" certain existing facilities for funding, allows states to use 15% of Medicaid dollars for non-community-based services, adds individual and family support services, and reduces federal matching for individuals being served in nonqualifying facilities. We witness at the national level what took place in the Pennsylvania example cited above, the politics of mental disability involving billions of dollars, thousands of jobs, special interest groups, and a number of elected officials. It will be interesting to learn how full a measure of rights eventually will be delivered to disabled clients, and the degree to which those rights will be sacrificed in the political process to appease competing interests.

The evolution of the definition of developmental disabilities in federal legislation is another illustration of the political efforts of a special interest group operating nationally. The first developmental disabilities law was enacted in 1970 (Developmental Disabilities Services and Facilities Construction Act, PL 91-517). Developmental disabilities was defined categorically in that legislation and included mental retardation, cerebral palsy, epilepsy, and other neurological conditions deemed by the Secretary of the Department of Health, Education, and Welfare (HEW) to be related to mental retardation. Three essential components of the definition were that developmental disabilities have an onset during the developmental period, be chronic, and constitute a substantial handicap.

In 1970 empirical data were available to support the specific identification of the three named disability categories (Breen & Richman, 1979). Mental retardation, cerebral palsy, and epilepsy were the leading causes of disability in adults whose handicaps originated in childhood. Also, many people have diagnoses involving two of these disabilities; therefore, there is a clinical overlap among these conditions. It should be understood that the term developmental disabilities, unlike the three named categorical disabilities, is not a clinical entity, but a legislative term that defines categories of disabled persons eligible for services funded by the Act. Not surprisingly, by creating categories of haves and have nots, advocates of excluded disability groups (e.g., autism, dyslexia, learning disabilities) attempted to exert political influence to have their group included in a revised definition in future amendments to the Developmental Disabilities legislation.

The National Society for Autistic Children (NSAC) played a major political role in securing the inclusion of autism in the 1975 legislation known as the Developmentally Disabled Assistance and Bill of Rights Act, PL 94-103 (Akerley, 1979). The 1970 legislation was paradoxical in the sense that the congressional intent was that the term developmental disabilities should refer to a functional, *noncategorical,* severe, chronic disability that is developmental in origin; nevertheless, three specific categories were named (Breen & Richman, 1979). Blame for this lexigraphical imprecision has been placed on the coalition of national advocacy organizations representing the three included disability groups (not Congress) who drafted the proposed legislation in 1970 (Akerley, 1979). According to Akerley, NSAC's initial attempt to broaden the scope of the definition involved seeking to become a consumer representative for the fourth category of ''other neurological conditions'' on the newly created State Planning and Advisory Councils. NSAC's attempts to secure a place on the Councils were rejected because the Secretary of HEW had not ruled that autism was included in the other neurological category.

Thus rebuffed, autism advocates intensified the political process by petitioning the Secretary of HEW, lobbying Congress, and writing comments on proposed federal regulations that defined developmental disabilities. These efforts reportedly were fruitless. Akerley (1979) also described NSAC's political efforts to gain acceptance by the other ''in'' developmental disability organizations. Eventually, an effective coalition was developed—the Consortium Concerned with the Developmentally Disabled. When the 1970 Act was close to expiration and the topic of definition was under discussion in HEW and Congress, NSAC obtained an ally, the large, sophisticated Mental Health Association. In a *quid pro quo* arrangement, the Association reportedly assisted NSAC to lobby key Senate staff people and use the Association's 2,000,000 members to claim widespread support for a noncategorical definition of developmental disabilities (Akerley, 1979). Because the various special interest groups could not agree on a definition of developmental disabilities, Congress granted a 1-year extension of the Act and admonished the advocates to come to a consensus or lose the whole program.

NSAC developed two congressional allies in 1974, Ernest Hollings in the Senate and Yvonne Burke in the House of Representatives. Hollings successfully negotiated earmarking funds for autism in the National Institute of Neurological and Communicative Disorders and Stroke allocation, as well as the inclusion of autism in the definition in the Developmental Disabilities Act (Akerley, 1979). For these consessions in favor of autism, according to Akerley, Senator Hollings agreed not to push for passage of his own bill seeking funding for research and residential services for autism. Representative Burke was the only member of Congress who testified at the House hearings on the Developmental Disabilities Act, and she did so in behalf of making autism one of the disability categories included in the definition. As a result of this political action by NSAC, autism was unambiguously included in the definition of developmental disabilities in the 1975 amendments.

As a postscript and further illustration of the politics of mental disability, dyslexia also was included in the definition but only in a qualified manner (i.e., only if persons with dyslexia also had one of the four named categorical disabilities). Why? Allegedly because the ranking minority member of the House Subcommittee on Health had become a spokesman for the Association for Children with Learning Disabilities (Akerley, 1979). In the more recent 1978 amendments, the definition of developmental disabilities became entirely functional, with categorical disabilities per se not named.

The politics affecting the definition of developmental disabilities has obvious implications for funding qualified clients. The relationship between funding and subsequently implementing the right to habilitation (staffing, programming, physical environment), presumably is positive if not perfect. Ironically, with the battle to include additional categorical groups under the scope of the Act, it should not be overlooked that the definition of developmental disabilities excludes mildly handicapped persons. Are there special interest groups who will rise to their cause and attempt to have severity and chronicity removed from the definition of developmental disabilities?

The State of Illinois provides another illustration that the rights of retarded children sometimes are brokered by the political process with special interest groups playing a prominent role. Illinois has a statute requiring the screening of new born babies for PKU and hypothyroidism. The issue of concern in 1980 was a proposed state statute that would require all hospitals to send babies' blood samples to a state lab in Chicago for analysis. Private laboratories or hospitals had performed about 20% of the tests, with the other 80% conducted by the state lab. The state representative who sponsored the bill argued that the requirement would prevent cases from "slipping through the cracks." The bill was supported by ARC-Illinois, which lobbied for the statute and distributed a fact sheet espousing the merits of the legislation. Opposition came from the Illinois Medical Society and physicians who believed that the bill would place new controls on hospitals and laboratories. They feared "unwarranted government interference in the field of medicine and increased competition with private enterprise" (Briggs 1980, p. 8).

Dr. James R. Thompson, the governor's father and a pathologist, voiced his opposition to the bill, claiming that it would be an "invasion of private medicine" (Briggs, 1980). The battle lines were drawn between a coalition of politicians and special interest groups espousing rights to life and health for PKU children, and physicians contending the right to be free from governmental interference in their profession (arguably the right to money and privilege). A medical society lobbyist said, "This isn't easy taking on retarded kids but you've got to get beyond the emotionalism" (Briggs, 1980, p. 8).

In a related issue, ARC-Illinois lobbied for passage of a full, statewide newborn screening program but had to compromise by agreeing to a sunset provision (Staff, 1982a). The ARC, well versed in state politics, presented Governor Thompson an award at the Illinois State Fair in appreciation for signing the bill into law. The ARC included in its newsletter a picture of the Governor signing the bill while holding in his lap a child "saved from retardation by metabolic testing" (Staff, 1982b). This appears to illustrate the reciprocally reinforcing role of special interest groups and politicians.

Mental Disability Politics Involving Individuals

The theme under consideration has been illustrated to this point with situations involving primarily such organized special interest groups as state employees, parents, and advocacy associations. The politics of mental disability, however, operates analogously at the level of individual service providers and citizens. The bartering of favors between individuals in direct service positions also has implications for rights implementation. An example relevant to special education can be cited. In a PRF for developmentally disabled children in the Midwest, special educators were asked to write goals and objectives for each of their students in order to comply with the Individual Education Plan (IEP) requirements of the Education for All Handicapped Children Act, PL 94-142. In a situation known to one of the authors, a teacher agreed to change the oil and tune up the car of a graduate student friend if the student would write several short-term objectives subsumed under the long-term goals for his 12 students. The bartering continued, and the teacher promised to take his friend to a metropolitan zoo in exchange for her writing the long-term goals for the next school year.

There are several points to be made by this seemingly trivial example. One is that service providers are not always prepared to implement the mandates of new legislation or litigation. Professional and paraprofessional service providers may have skill deficits and not be able to perform as expected. Habilitative technology may be inadequate to meet client needs, and there may be obstacles to providing appropriate inservice training of staff. Whether either of these factors or sloth were operative in the foregoing illustration, the suggestion is that teachers may resort to negotiating an exchange of services to meet their professional obligations.

The implications of this brokerage process concern no less important issues than the quality of students' educational goals and the subsequent instruction they receive. This example also supports one of the themes of this chapter. The rights of mentally disabled people are established pragmatically at the service delivery level despite the mandate of federal law. The right of children to an appropriate education was dependent, in that case, on a teacher's having a friend presumably more competent than he at the mandated task and being able to negotiate an acceptable deal with her. If the graduate student did not need her car tuned up or if she did not want to visit the zoo, would the retarded students' right to an appropriate education have been jeopardized? In this case the students' right to education probably was enhanced by the brokerage between the teacher and his friend. Unfortunately, this illustration may not be atypical.

It would be misrepresentative to cite only examples of political action by PRF employees that are perceived as resistant to change, self-serving, and counter to the interests of mentally disabled clients. There are countless PRF administrators, professional and direct-care staff, and auxillary personnel who are politically active in support of legislation and policies beneficial to mentally disabled persons. The Willowbrook case illustrates not only the dedication, but also the political activity waged by some staff members on behalf of retarded persons. Taylor and Biklen (1980) write:

> "Staff members at Willowbrook, after months of trying to secure changes from within, blew the whistle on Willowbrook's abuses; they were reprimanded and two of them were fired. Dr. Mike Wilkins and social worker Elizabeth Lee had already been fired from Willowbrook when they appeared on the ABC-TV Dick Cavitt Show to reveal the horrors of their workplace. . . . Dr. William Bronston was not fired. But he was the first tenured doctor in the history of the institution to be given negative reviews by his supervisors." (p. 55)

In Illinois, whistleblowing by a PRF employee initially resulted in a reprimand and ultimately led to state regulations protecting workers from retribution. A speech therapist at the Lincoln Developmental Center challenged the planned transfer of some Lincoln residents to an unlicensed nursing home in Chicago. The speech therapist was cited by supervisors with "conduct unbecoming an employee" (Sevener, 1982). That supervisory response was a catalyst for

AFSME to lobby for legislation to protect state employees from whistleblowing. The law was necessary, argued the speech therapist, because "a bureaucracy exists to perpetuate itself and is willing to break the law to do that" (Sevener, 1982). In addition to protection by state regulations, a Pennsylvania court awarded unemployment compensation benefits to former employees of a group home who engaged in whistleblowing (*Kelly v. Pennsylvania,* 1983). The court ruled that the plaintiffs, relief weekend supervisors at a residential facility, had performed in good faith and in a reasonable manner in publicizing the conditions in that facility.

Whistleblowing is only one strategy to reform PRFs from within. In extreme cases, superintendents of PRFs may invite litigation and, in fact, instruct client advocacy groups, parents, and other parties with legal standing in bringing suit against a facility. Administrators may provide facts suggesting a cause of action. They do so, understandably, with mixed feelings, knowing that their careers may be jeopardized and they are inviting health threatening stress and countless hours of work for themselves and their staff. This ultimate step, of course, reflects administrators' profound sense of frustration in attempting to bring about institutional reform by operating within the constraints of the existing state bureaucracy. One of the underlying causes of this frustration is the constitutionally sanctioned separation of powers between the executive and legislative branches of government. PRF reform frequently is thwarted because the executive branch (e.g., a state Department of Mental Retardation or Mental Health) claims that the legislative branch does not allocate sufficient funds for PRFs to provide a humane psychological and physical environment, hire qualified staff in sufficient numbers, establish community service alternatives, and implement other mandated measures of reform.

In addition to individuals operating politically within the mental disability service delivery system, citizens positioned externally also may initiate actions whose effects are intended to influence the rights of disabled persons. A wealthy California businessman launched a one-man advertising campaign to unseat Senator Charles Percy in the 1984 Illinois election. Michael Goland purchased anti-Percy television and billboard advertising that characterized the Senator as a chameleon who changes colors, that is, political positions (Dold, 1984). Goland, disabled from polio contracted as a child, claimed his motivation to defeat Percy was based on the Senator's insensitivity to the disabled and his voting to kill funding bills for education and hiring the handicapped. In discussing his defeat on a television interview, Senator Percy claimed that Goland's more than one million dollar advertising campaign had played a role in the legislator's loss. Senator Percy's attorneys reportedly could not identify any other individual who had spent so much money to defeat a single candidate. Taking Goland's reported motivation to defeat Senator Percy at face value, which is doubted by his critics, this illustration shows the efforts of individual citizens to influence political outcomes to benefit causes of interest to them.

Mental Disability Politics Involving Elected Officials

Wolfensberger (1969) discussed how perceptions of retarded persons have affected the nature of institutional models that have been created. Perceptions of retarded people, for example, as being "dangerous," "a menace to society," and "subhuman organisms" have stigmatized them. Consequently, we have extruded mentally retarded people from society by placing them in large residental facilities in remote areas of our states. Although the role played by the perception of retarded persons in the selection of PRF sites has been well documented (Wolfensberger, 1969), the influence of money, power, and privilege in the creation of PRF models has been presented less articulately in the professional literature. The location of PRFs, their architectural design, characteristics of the staff hired, and institutions' admission policies all may be influenced by political processes. These factors have definite implications for the quality of services delivered to mentally disabled persons (i.e., rights implementation).

In the mid 1960s a commission was formed in a midwestern state to study the needs and services available to mentally retarded persons. The commission recommended that two new PRFs be built for children in the primarily rural region of the state where such institutions did not exist. A commission member recommended that one of the PRFs be located within 15 miles of the most populous city in the region. That town has a state university that was the largest employer in the area. The commission member claimed that the Republican governor had given his oral agreement to place the PRF near the city recommended.

Subsequently, the commission member reported, an influential Democratic state legislator from the region persuaded the governor to locate the PRF in the House member's district some 40 miles east of the original site. The legislator allegedly argued that the larger city had the state university as a source of employment, and the small town in the distant county had no substantial state employment. With the exception of farming and coal mining, there were few employment alternatives there, especially for women. The governor's motivation in changing the site of the facility, it was reported, was to gain the votes and influence of the powerful legislator of the opposition party.

To the degree that the commission member's report about these circumstances is valid, it suggests that political factors were responsible for the selection of the PRF site. The implications of this arrangement for the rights of the mentally disabled clients of the PRF may or may not have been a consideration. It seems reasonable that if clients were located near the larger community, potentially they would have had greater access to the facilities in that town: shopping, movie theaters, medical and dental services, recreation, and a larger variety of goods and services. Undoubtedly, there would have been greater university involvement had the PRF been located more convenient to the faculty and students.

The political trade between the governor and legislator (i.e., jobs for votes) was successful in its intended purpose, but at the possible expense of the PRF's clients. As it happens, in 1982 that institution was closed and turned over to the

Department of Corrections to be renovated into a medium security prison. Conversion of the facility to serve a new client population not only was less expensive than building a new facility, but also it maintained the employment in the community, both very desirable political outcomes.

Politicians at the local, state, and national level work for their constituents in a number of ways that can affect the administration and delivery of service to mentally disabled persons. Politicians, for example, may be employment brokers in a patronage system that produces government jobs for constituents who are politically loyal. Patronage may create jobs that previously did not exist, determine who fills available positions, and dictate who is terminated from employment. Political factors may influence selection of employees at highest level cabinet positions down to the lowest paid hourly workers at any level of government. The public mental disability service system, as part of the executive branch of government, is not exempt from patronage appointments. Illinois state politics is used here for illustrative purposes once again.

Patronage within a state legislative district may be under the ultimate control of a state senator or representative who may or may not consult his county political party committee. The day-to-day job of handling patronage may be delegated to a political ally who is put on the state payroll. It has been reported that a downstate Illinois Republican representative was involved in securing jobs for constituents 650 times between 1974 and 1980 (Koplowitz, 1980c). In this representative's district, the man charged with day-to-day patronage duties is in a $20,000 state position, with his employment line covered in turn by different state departments. The Department of Mental Health and Developmental Disabilities Regional Director allegedly was "asked" by the person in the state central office who handles patronage for the Department to put the man on the region payroll because it was "mental health's turn to pay [his] salary" (Koplowitz, 1980a). This person is responsible for making "job referrals" for the departments of mental health, corrections, and transportation in his district. As a "recruitment officer," he recommends people endorsed by area Republicans active in politics, especially the state representative.

Formerly, when a vacancy in Illinois PRFs was to be filled, the names of people who scored the highest on the Civil Service examination would be sent to the Region with a notation indicating whether they were referred on the basis of political patronage. A change in administrative procedures resulted in a process in which only one qualified person at a time is referred by the department to the region. That person likely has been referred by the patronage official. Commenting on the role of patronage in selecting employees for his Region's mental health and mental retardation facilities, the Region administrator was quoted as saying, "I would probably pick one by the way they dressed or a first impression anyway" (Koplowitz, 1980a).

The selection of Illinois Department of Mental Health and Mental Retardation Region administrators and even PRF superintendents may be political decisions made by the Governor's office. An Illinois regional administrator and a superintendent of a PRF in that region were both chosen after political pressure was exerted in their behalf (Koplowitz, 1980a). Although the then director of the department and a search committee each had another candidate, someone else was given the position of regional administrator. The director claimed that it had come down to who would be best liked by the legislative leadership (Koplowitz, 1980c).

In an analogous political action, the reportedly fourth-ranked candidate on the search committee's list was named superintendent of a PRF. A search committee member was quoted as saying that the department director had told him 2 days prior to the announcement of the new superintendent's appointment that the committee's first choice would be named (Koplowitz, 1980c). In explaining the appointment of the fourth-ranked applicant, the department director reportedly said that the district state representative did his lobbying for the fourth-ranked candidate at the governor's office. Interestingly, the local newspaper reported that the region director and the superintendent each had made monetary contributions either to the influential state representative or to the senator from the district.

In addition to wielding influence in the hiring process, legislators also may play a role in firing PRF employees. Once again, an Illinois state representative was cited in the local news. He and four other state officials were named defendants in a law suit brought by a PRF stationary engineer who was fired after 16 years' employment (Landis, 1984a). The suit claimed that the representative initiated efforts to have the employee fired when he supported the politician's opponent in the 1982 election. The former PRF employee alleged that the five state officials had violated the engineer's civil rights by conspiring to have him fired and keeping him from regaining his job (Landis, 1984b). Further, the state representative wa the subject of a probe by state and federal officials into buying and selling of state jobs. After more than a year the politician was cleared of the charges; however, in the interim he lost his bid to become a state senator (Landis, 1985). Now in a high position with the state Department of Conservation, the former legislator charged that the probe resulted from efforts of his political enemies to sabotage his race for state senator.

These illustrations of Illinois politics affecting mental disability should be understood in a larger context with nationwide implications. It has been said that, "the business of modern society is service. Social Service in modern society is business" (McKnight, 1978, p. 69). This observation is even more germane in areas where there is little industry. In deep southern Illinois, for example, one out of every six nonagricultural workers in the seven-county region works for the state (Davis, 1981). Prosperity there is dependent on state jobs, and most of those positions are in education and human service. A veteran state legislator commented, "There's not a thing wrong with patronage. The only thing that is wrong is that there is not enough of it". . . . [I] long for the pre-Civil Service days when state employees could be fired for belonging to the wrong political party" (Koplowitz, 1980b, p. 3). It would be surprising if this legislator were unique in his aspirations.

Wolfensberger (1969) has argued that PRFs often have been located away from major population centers because of the negative perception that society has held for mentally retarded persons. In rural areas, communities actively compete with each other to attract prisons and PRFs. Residents of a rural county helped convince the state legislature that "a setting such as we had here in Southern Illinois was much more conducive to rehabilitation" (Davis, 1981, p. 3). In Illinois the legislative trade off frequently is between Chicago and downstate. Human Service gains in Southern Illinois often are accomplished in exchange for downstate legislators' acquiescence in rapid transit, public school, and tourism funding in Chicago.

Other state legislatures also have political arrangements where parochial interests may be negotiated with concern for the self-interests of politicians. California State Senate Minority Whip H. L. Richardson (1979) revealed that "it's a rare legislative bird who even reads most of the bills. . . . Legislators consistently vote on legislation without understanding what is in it, especially when the final vote is taken" (p. 37). The state senator explained that legislators use a variety of techniques to decide how to vote on a bill including following the recommendation of special interest groups, adopting the administration position, revenging a colleague, repaying a favor, and yielding to pressure. Reason and logic were ruled out as bases for making voting decisions. The legislature is ". . . a body of men reacting to what they deem the most successful way to be reelected" (Richardson, 1978, p. 46).

In some of the examples of mental disability politics cited, there may have been, in part, an economic consequence for the political behavior of citizens (e.g., jobs, professional fees for service). The relationship between personal economic gain and the position that one takes, *pro* or *con,* on a human rights issue cannot be dismissed lightly. For example, state legislatures are under political pressure from various special interest groups to allocate funds in support of their concerns. The rights of mentally disabled persons are in competition with state road and bridge repair, transportation, public schools, universities, corrections, parks, law enforcement, employment security, national guard, fisheries and forestry, and so forth. Deinstitutionalization, for example, competes for funds with stocking state streams with trout and building rest rooms in state parks. Psychopoliticians are in a contest with "recreopoliticians," "educapoliticians," and others for the state coffers. Conscientious mental disability advocates, therefore, must learn how to play the game of politics and compete with proponents of other agencies to help secure client rights and quality service. Although these mental disability politicians can invoke more than a decade of litigation and legislation supporting their claim for more state resources, the political voices of other citizens can be quite persuasive with their state legislators and governor. In recent years all these interests for governmental services have had to contend with the taxpayers' revolt originating with Proposition 13 in California and continuing into the 1980s with the supply side tax cuts championed by the Reagan administration.

LEGAL SHOCK AND INSTITUTION SPASM

Since the *Wyatt* (1971) case, mental disability special interest groups have been successful in using the judiciary as a legal mechanism to seek large-scale reform of PRFs. Consequently, the rate of legal activity, litigation in particular, escalated in the 1970s so that by its very presence the activity itself has become a variable affecting PRFs in an unanticipated fashion. The rapid sequence of legal events during the past decade, the requirements they have imposed on PRFs, and the consequential effect on that bureaucracy have created analogs to future shock and ecospasm—"legal shock" and " institution spasm." The application of Toffler's concepts to mental disability can be understood best with a brief historical consultation. As Justice Holmes said, "The history of what the law has been is necessary to the knowledge of what the law is" (Holmes 1881/1963).

The perceptions that society has had of mentally handicapped people and, consequently, the nature of the service delivery systems that have been created are part of the relevant history (Wolfensberger, 1969). For more than a century and a half, with few exceptions these perceptions have been negative and the service systems meager. Not surprisingly, mental disability law prior to 1970 also was minimal, and existing statutes and policies primarily mandated what society could do *to* disabled persons rather than what it could do *for* them. State statutes passed under either the police power or *parens patriae* doctrines delineated how mentally disabled persons could be involuntarily committed to PRFs, sterilized, excluded from single-family living zones in municipalities, paid wages below the minimum standard for the rest of society, and denied education, their own children, and voting rights among others (Burgdorf, 1980). Also, they were subjected to inhumane physical and psychological environments and other privations, degradations, and abuses. The statutes and policies in effect from the mid-19th to the mid-20th century reflected Holmes' first requirement of a sound body of law: "that it should correspond with the actual feelings and demands of the community whether right or wrong" (Holmes, 1881/1963).

The explosion of legal events in the 1970s, class action litigation in particular, has created a special type of future shock, "legal shock," which has stressed many PRFs beyond their coping limits. A review of the impact of legal activity on PRFs now is becoming possible. Although no systematic data are yet available, a representative sense of the situation experienced by many facilities can be described. The discussion that follows addresses the effects of court orders and legislative mandates as they have been imposed on clinical systems. Emphasis has been placed on the systems' response to the intrusion rather than the merit of the legal doctrines involved. Legal activity has tended to grieve three areas of concern in PRFs—staffing, physical and psychological environment, and habilitative programming. We shall examine the effects of changes propelled by legal events in each of these domains.

Staffing Aspects of Public Residential Facilities

The annual budget of state mental disability programs is negotiated between the executive and the legislative branches of government through the political process. PRFs traditionally have received less money than they need to provide adequate staff, facilities, and programming. The budget for staff has been compromised in favor of funds for renovation and expansion of the physical plant, purchase of new equipment, habilitative programming requirements, and other facility needs. In many cases, PRFs' budgets for staff have been so inadequate that their high staff-to-client ratio precluded effective habilitation. Until only recently salaries were low, and PRFs were not viewed as productive career paths by professionals; however, these too are changing.

Litigation and legislation have improved the impoverished staff situation in many PRFs. For example, most right-to-habilitation lawsuit remedies have provided that the defendant facilities must have adequate staff to offer habilitation to their clients. In Alabama, New York, Maine, Minnesota, and other states, large numbers of direct-care, professional, and support staff had to be hired and pressed into service rapidly as a result of litigation. Certification of a PRF or part of it as an Intermediate Care Facility under the provisions of Title XIX (Medicaid) of the Social Security Act (PL 92-233) has resulted in a similar influx of large numbers of new staff in most states.

No one would dispute either the importance or the urgency of redressing staff shortages in PRFs. No one should. Yet, it is possible for a human service system to choke on its remedy, and this can happen with the acquisition of vitally needed staff. In one PRF, a superintendent received 40 new direct-care positions for use across three shifts in just one unit of 60 clients. With the new help came pressure to expedite the process of putting them "on line" to work. After these new employees had been on the job awhile, the superintendent visited the unit only to find the new staff standing around and disorganized. The unit was ill prepared to optimize its increased resources. Supervisory instruction, adequate inservice training, and reasoned planning had been nullified by expediency.

Similarly, in the March, 1972 Interim Emergency Order in the *Wyatt* (1971) case, Judge Frank Johnson ordered the hiring of 300 new employees within 30 days for Partlow State School (Fremouw, 1976). What is being described as "legal shock" and "institution spasm" occurs when just such remedies are imposed on a PRF with impatient regard for required planning and miscalculation of how much change the receiving units can process. When the remedy derives from the adversary forum of litigation, the impatience may be more pronounced and the miscalculation more severe.

These judicially sanctioned requirements can be traumatizing. First, there is the chronic problem of recruiting qualified staff in adequate numbers. Not everyone is attracted to work with severely and profoundly handicapped persons. Even among those who are so inclined, many will be unable to manage the stressful burdens of the job (see Chapter 2). More troubling in this regard is the relatively undeveloped personnel science that should provide a screening procedure with predictive validity to the employment situation. This problem may be related to the larger failure to recognize direct care as a highly specialized service that should be given as much attention in recruitment as in the acquisition of professionals. Under external pressure to implement improved staff ratios, the necessary filtering during the screening phase breaks down and too many unqualified applicants are hired.

It also is difficult to determine who will be a good client care worker during the hiring process. Information from most applicant forms and personal interviews does not seem to predict adequately who will be able to conduct client programming competently, administer medication as prescribed, do housekeeping, negotiate disputes between clients, prevent clients from harming themselves or each other, relate effectively with parents, and perform the many other duties. It is difficult to determine during the employee selection process who will have patience with clients, co-workers, and the PRF bureaucracy; who will risk bodily harm to protect clients; and who will function effectively under stress. As quoted earlier, one of Illinois' Department of Mental Health and Developmental Disabilities Region Directors, also a superintendent of a PRF, said regarding the selection of employees: "I would probably pick one by the way they dressed or a first impression anyway" (Koplowitz, 1980a). In too many instances, hiring occurs too quickly and with too much uncertainty.

A subsequent problem may develop when active and sophisticated labor unions act to protect the employment of marginal workers. Although unquestionably inadequate employees may be dismissed during probation without union protest, minimally adequate workers may be protected vigorously. The union, by doing its job, is protracting previous errors in employee screening. The recruitment and selection of professional staff also present difficulties as discussed in Chapter 4 of this book.

Recruitment is only the first phase in implementing staffing judicial remedies. As noted earlier, the importance of staff training has been recognized by NASMRPD in its efforts to include reimbursement for such training in the community living alternatives that would be created by S.2053 and its legislative successor S.873. Nevertheless, large contingents of new staff, especially at direct-care levels, are only as good as their preparation. All too often, staff development and inservice programs in PRFs are not geared to teach requisite skills to criterion in compressed time frames. Some may not be equipped to do it properly under any time frame; nevertheless, the same court order or legislative mandate that provided the additional staff is not likely to have the required resources for staff development efforts. Typically, staffing remedies pay less attention to these problems, and critical functions of supervision are left unimproved. The consequences of poor supervisory and management training filter downward. The operational questions that emerge from this situation are these: (a) How does a PRF orient and train large numbers of new staff? (b) How are these groups integrated with minimal systematic upheaval to the continuity of client care and treatment? and (c) Will the administrative and supervisory staff be able to cope with and direct meaningfully increasing numbers of employees?

Some court orders have addressed the question of staff development. Willowbrook (*New York State ARC*, 1973) and Pineland (*Wuori v. Zitnay*, 1978), for example, mandated that the PRFs develop a plan for staff orientation and training. Pineland must provide a minimum of 20 hours of orientation training programs during the first 3 months of employment. Orientation or preservice training has been part of many PRFs' programs; however, there is considerable qualitative variability in staff orientation and training programs throughout the United States. The requirement for appropriate staff orientation and training is laudatory, although it has created problems for PRFs. Having a staff training program presupposes that there is an adequate curriculum of instruction. Although we have come a long way in developing an effective technology of habilitation, our knowledge is markedly inadequate in many areas of mental disability and even weaker in the application of that knowledge in the natural ecologies of many human service settings (Reppucci & Saunders, 1974; Willems, 1974).

Further, court mandates often have underestimated the extent of staff development needs in most PRFs. Basic skill instruction as indicated in a staff member's job specification (e.g., how to bathe, dress, and feed multiply handicapped clients) sometimes is seen as the requisite for inservice training. In truth, it is barely the starting point. A host of skill functions and problems that exist for almost every staff group in almost every PRF are proper and necessary subjects for inservice programs. For example, communication difficulties plague most facilities. The flow of enormous amounts of information across three shifts and different sets of pass-days suffers frequent discontinuity and breakdown. Multiply that across many units, layers of supervisors, and professionals, and the system malfunctions. Closer inspection often reveals these problems to be deficits in communication skills at many staff levels. Staff training interventions in this domain also are required.

Similarly, problems in decision making, conflict resolution, supervision, morale, team building, interdisciplinary processes, coping with continuous change, as well as monotony; the development of trust across interacting staff groups; and the recognition and management of the damaging effects of job stress—all represent staff development needs in a modern PRF. The planning and preparation required to design and then implement such training systems require months, perhaps much longer, if they are to be done properly. The few days or weeks of staff training provided or implied by many judicial orders misunderstands the need and seriously compromises the function of staff training.

Additional and equally important aspects of staff development are the matters of staff evaluation and skill maintenance. At many staff levels, especially line levels, newly acquired skills often erode or slip in sharpness over time. This failure in skill maintenance is not a poor reflection on employees, but rather another item on the staff training and supervisory agenda, namely, provision for refresher or renewal instruction and reinforcement of staff behavior by supervisors. Staff evaluation and skill maintenance programs are costly and time consuming, but necessary. Where court orders have acknowledged their necessity (and this is atypical), they have provided facilities with little room and resources to evaluate and maintain staff development programs adequately.

In summary, many of the court-ordered staffing requirements are justified and long overdue. Many requirements and resources in developing that staff are still overdue and have been missed by legal decision makers. Problems in recruiting, screening, training, and supervising new staff remain and are serious in some systems. Tremendous financial and administrative resources have been expended in this process over an extremely brief period of time from an historical perspective. Expectations to fix these difficulties at the stroke of a judge's pen may be misguided. Efforts to implement these expectations in the "most restrictive time frame" contribute significantly to what we have called institution spasm. Creating new positions and putting large numbers of bodies in them is a highly disrupting process. The transformation of new recruits into seasoned and effective service providers is a time- and resource-devouring activity that is stressful to PRFs already made fragile by other litigative impositions. The goodness or justification of most of these legal requirements is not being questioned here. The process provided to fulfill the requirements, however, is in need of re-examination. Court orders have tragically miscalculated the range and depth of bringing to criterion the staff system that services highly disabled human beings. It must be assumed that despite the natural antagonism in litigative proceedings, neither the plaintiffs nor the courts desired these consequences.

Humane Physical and Psychological Environment

A second major element of right to habilitation case remedies is the requirement that defendant facilities provide humane physical and psychological environments. This mandate was created, in part, to rectify the dehumanizing manner in which staff perceived and related to clients, as well as to eliminate hazardous physical conditions. Like staffing orders, this requirement has created enormous stress on PRFs.

The requirement essentially has two facets—the bricks and mortar physical plant component and the human attitudinal/behavioral one. The living units in older PRFs may have been constructed more than 60 years ago at a time when our perception of mentally disabled people was more devalued than it is today. The then prevailing PRF model emphasized the warehousing of deviant people, who were seen as a menace to society (Wolfensberger, 1969). In other periods, the design of PRFs reflected the perception that mentally disabled persons were sick patients who should be housed in a medical facility and administered care by medical and nursing personnel (Wolfensberger, 1969). The developmental and humanitarian perspective in the mental disability field in recent years has obligated state governments to invest millions of dollars to demolish or renovate old PRFs and construct new residences that are humane, dignified, and normalized.

In some PRFs virtually every living unit would have to be modified to comply with an order such as that in Wyatt (1971), but compliance is a complex matter. Architects and interior designers have to collaborate with developmentalists to produce environments that permit habilitation and protect the individual dignities of a living space. The challenge is even more difficult because environments also must be responsive and thus adapted to individual needs and problems of clients. For example, some interior designs, though normalized, cannot withstand the behavior of severely disruptive and aggressive clients, who may punch holes in wall board construction, rip out electrical fixtures, or destroy furniture. Those who believed that the mere existence of a homelike environment would banish maladaptive behavior have been disappointed, and there is recent longitudinal research to support their disappointment (e.g., MacEachron, 1981). Maladaptive behavior seems to survive the change to more normalized living units; uniform construction across all new living units may be unresponsive to the real needs and differences that derive from the disabilities many clients possess.

Individualizing environments is a costly endeavor. It may be prohibitive when viewed in concert with client turnover rates in a given PRF. Resolving this problem varies from PRF to PRF. Nevertheless, the price for a normalized living unit for clients with highly specialized needs and disfunctions may be exacted from demands that staff manage the adjustment of clients to environments. No one argues the absolute necessity to pay this price; it is legally required. The point here is to underscore the intense demand this requirement generates for the facility. When underprepared to work these new environments with proper resources and planning, the PRFs jeopardize the intent of the environment itself.

Another major source of stress for PRFs is the disruption that occurs when a living unit undergoing renovation must be vacated by its clients and staff for 6 months or more. The stress on the PRF occurs when the displaced clients and staff are temporarily transferred to another overcrowded residential unit. Clients must adapt to new peers, staff, physical environment, and rhythm of day. The displaced employees must fit into an existing staff hierarchy with pre-existing working relationships, and deal with the uncertainties that the move produces. A great deal of ''newness'' and uncertainty turn over in the lives of staff and clients alike at a sometimes alarming rate. The disorientation and strain that result is yet another, perhaps unavoidable, sacrifice that this generation of mentally disabled persons and their service providers must make to secure client rights for decades to come.

The creation of a humane psychological environment presents an even greater difficulty for PRFs. It stresses them for a longer period of time and more pervasively than upgrading the physical environment because the problems of correction are more subtle and have years of humane inertia attached to them. As opposed to bricks and mortar, a humane psychological environment protects rights to dignity, privacy, and humane care. Once again it would be helpful to contrast the way PRFs are and the way courts have said they should be. Congregate living in the tradition of PRFs acceptable in earlier periods of this century precluded privacy and an individual sense of dignity. Because these traditions have persisted beyond the beliefs that gave birth to them, certain practices exist to the present time. Groups of men or women may be marched naked back and forth from a second floor dormitory to the basement group shower area of an old residential unit. The open dormitory and bathroom preclude privacy in dressing or performing personal hygiene. Patterns of interaction between staff and clients, both obvious and more subtle, often disconfirm a client's sense of worth. As Thaw and Wolfe point out in Chapter 3, the archaic physical environments conspire to support this pattern—how else should one relate to people judged by the general society to merit these living environments?

Additional violations in the physical and psychological environment in some PRFs have been noted. Inappropriate client behavior often has been treated with medication without concomitant programming; physical restraint and seclusion have been used for unregulated and extended periods of time; and aversive techniques have been employed without professional supervision. Clients frequently have had to wear stigmatizing institutional clothing, perform institution-maintaining labor for minimal or no pay, and been recruited as research subjects without the safeguard of informed consent.

All these conditions and far more subtle ones foreclose the possibility of a humane psychological environment. Such conditions are unacceptable and must be corrected. Court orders to that effect are as compelling as they are overdue. But what is to be corrected derives from a societal point of view about mentally handicapped persons that rooted and developed for nearly a century in some instances. The attitudes and practices derived from that point of view have enormous historical inertia. They too cannot be dislodged by the signature of a judge. Yet, once the attitudes and practices are legally affirmed as injustices, the expectation—indeed the demand—is that they be reformed at once. Between the demand and the reform exists monumental stress for the facility. PRFs cannot absorb massive requirements for change in such compressed time periods even if they wish to do so. Apart from more natural resistances to change in general, the reforms in planning, management, training, budget, and staffing alone call for longer range time frames.

Some types of improvement can be effected with dispatch. A facility's supply of institutional clothing can be burned in a day, and the acquisition of normalized garments may be but a purchase order and delivery away. Reshaping values and perceptions and committing them to instruction and norms take more time in any organization or community, as the past quarter century's pursuit of racial equality has demonstrated. Despite the ineffable nobility of the mission, forcing the process of correction at a rate that exceeds the system's capacity to cope, let alone reform meaningfully, compromises the outcome for the clientele. This may be why a number of judges, months and years after their order, have observed the inadequate resolution of problems cited in their initial interventions.

Let us examine one illustration of implementing mandates for humane psychological environments. PRFs have had to establish a variety of client rights committees. Similar groups have been formed in many states to develop guidelines on the use of medication, behavior management procedures, behavior modification techniques, physical restraints, and other methods of controlling client behavior. Additionally, interdisciplinary committees develop and review clients' individual habilitation programs as a due process procedure. Still other committees evaluate the propriety of research proposals and protect clients from participating in hazardous or intrusive experiments without procedural safeguards.

In the process of establishing and operating these committees, PRFs have had to invest tens of thousands of hours of personnel time. It is not uncommon for staff to be shuffled and reshuffled in and out of new roles, meeting mandate after mandate. Effort spent developing policies and guidelines can severely reduce time available for delivering service itself. Clients receiving only minimum services may have to receive even fewer if the expansive committee system is to operate.

In underresourced facilities, these kinds of demands can produce a cumulative stress that disables the program system. Most PRFs and their mental disability workers will be the first to admit their deficits in humane client physical and psychological environments. Many have good, even superior, expertise to correct the circumstances; however, when court orders arrive unaccompanied by resources for all corners of the system affected by the correction and without provision for workable time frames, the PRF can be expected to convulse in its effort to comply. This is what we have designated as legal shock—a disturbing fallout that presumably never was the intent of the judiciaries or legislatures. Where PRFs remain viable parts of the continuum of care, future formulas for their improvement will have to anticipate and regulate changes more reliably with respect to their tolerances in time, resources, and planning.

Habilitative Programming

A third requirement of right to habilitation judicial remedies, ICF/MR standards, and related legislation is the provision of habilitative programming. The demand to train clients tends to be all inclusive regardless of their age, number of disabilities, type of disabilities, severity of disabilities, past history of success in programming, prognosis of success in future programming, and availability of staff, time, resources and technology for training. A full panopoly of institutional and community-based services must be made available as needed on an individually determined basis. With requirements for habilitative programming come overwhelming requirements for recordkeeping.

A pattern of demands similar to those in staffing and environmental mandates occurs with habilitative programming requirements: sweeping reforms thrust upon PRFs ill prepared to manage them. Merit notwithstanding, the habilitative orders can contribute further to the spasm and breakdown of the PRF because their formulas have, in many instances, been misconceived or misapplied. This may have occurred because courts made several questionable assumptions in formulating their habilitative remedies.

One assumption was that there existed an adequate technology of habilitation. It was assumed that the medical, behavioral, educational, and social sciences had provided their practitioners with the tools to habilitate all clients within the constraints established by the law. That assumption is questionable on two counts. First, despite the monumental strides that our human service technology has made during the past 2 decades, it is not yet responsive to all clients' needs; even where it is responsive it still is in a state of development. This issue has been discussed in *Wyatt* (1971) as well as more recently in a published symposium addressing the question of whether or not all children really are educable (Kauffman, 1981). Our technology may be reasonably adequate for programming for clients who are mildly and moderately impaired by a single disability. Our technology is grossly deficient, however, in programming for people with multiple disabilities that render them severely or profoundly handicapped. We find it difficult to treat the blind-deaf, severely retarded child who engages in life threatening, self-injurious behavior. Our habilitative tools are limited when we attempt to train the nonambulatory, profoundly retarded person.

Another area of concern is the considerable divide between the controlled research demonstration of a technological procedure and its application in less sterile natural ecologies with numerous sources of interference (Cullari & Ferguson, 1981; Willems, 1974). Successful demonstrations abound. The more complex issue of demonstrating that the technology can be applied successfully in natural settings is far less conclusive. The same can be said about the maintenance of successful outcomes and their generalizability to other relevant settings. For example, a review of 56 studies on behavior management procedures with mentally retarded clients found information on the maintenance of the behavior change in only 29% of the reports; only three studies had follow-up information beyond 3 months (Bates & Wehman, 1977). Problems in direct-care staff implementing behavioral programs correctly and consistently have been attributed to staff's inadequate training (Cullari & Ferguson, 1981). Too often there is a great discrepancy between the resources typically available in most PRFs and the personnel and material resources brought to bear to produce client behavior change reported in published research articles. Facilities also have been faulted for their lack of maintaining programming efforts by direct-care staff because their supervisors lack a committment to programming (Cullari & Ferguson, 1981).

A second assumption of legal sources is that PRFs are prepared to implement habilitative programming for all clients immediately and at the level of competence mandated. The social history of our culture's decisions about mentally handicapped people fuses with the organizational configurations for their care to render this assumption unfair. For the most part, PRFs have not been prepared or resourced to be effective and efficient organizational systems of service delivery. There have been exceptions: a few scattered PRFs around the country provide large-scale habilitative programming by an effective and efficient staff, and in a number of places, resources have permitted adequate programming in two or three of the 20–30 residential units on a large PRF's grounds.

Although court orders and legislative enactments have mandated what PRFs must do, their history of organization has left them unready to respond to the demands. As described in other parts of this book, the tenacity of this historical inertia has been miscalculated and misunderstood by many reformers, the courts included. If PRFs are to become functional elements in the continuum of human service to mentally handicapped clients, then substantial preliminary work is required to develop the administrative, supervisory, professional, and direct-care networks to support extensive 24-hour habilitative programs. In some cases, new adminstrative and service models may be necessary. In all cases, those participating in the judicial process as an instrument of reform should recognize the fundamental importance of bringing PRFs to readiness either before or as part of the order to deliver full habilitation.

A third assumption of the legal interventionists has been that the required due process of habilitation would be a rather simple matter to accomplish. What was naively unforeseen by the attorneys, judges, and legislators, however, was how time devouring their accountability procedures could become. In many PRFs the paperwork generated by accountability requirements has run out of control (Cullari, 1984). In one PRF known to the authors, a unit director described having to document the same piece of information in 14 different places to comply with all accountability requirements. In another case, a PRF Psychology Department determined that the routine duties of the Title XIX ICF/MR, including paperwork requirements, consumed almost 4 of the 5-day work week for each ICF psychologist under the formula for that state. The "real" units of habilitation (i.e., direct treatment of clients and training direct care staff to implement programs) had to be distributed over the 7 hours that remained each week.

What develops in these circumstances for many service providers is a curious competition between the twin goals of implementing and documenting the habilitation mandates. The concessions usually are made on the implementation side because the documentation draws more attention from external reviewers. A classic example of this occurs with many ICF/MR inspectors, who pour over records and generate lists of citations that threaten continued accreditation and funding is not corrected. Rarely is actual service observed over meaningful time intervals (Cullari, 1984). The assumption is that the documentation will reflect service, and to varying degrees it does. What is disconcerting, however, is that service providers, mindful of the preeminence of the record, develop a rhythm of work that has the paper wagging the client. Greater priority is given to ''paper compliance'' rather than actual compliance to standards. This certainly is not the case in all PRFs, but it tends to exist with increasing frequency in facilities that have experienced poorly planned legal interventions.

In extreme cases, judicial or legislative mandates have been implemented so poorly by PRFs that still more legal initiatives have been required. The landmark Wyatt v. Ireland (1979) case, for example, has had a long and troublesome history of noncompliance with the original 1972 court orders. Willowbrook also has been plagued by incessant problems with compliance that have resulted in a series of court actions since the original decision in 1975.

Implementation of complex legal remedies has been underestimated. Further aggravating the matter, the principal players of the intervention (e.g., attorneys, judges, advocates, appointed masters, administrators, special interest groups, service professionals) had very little interaction prior to Wyatt. For the most part, they have neither a history nor a rhythm of collaboration, especially on intensive innovative projects. Worse yet, they think and operate through different systems of experience, training, and language; thus, the risk of misunderstanding in high stress circumstances is elevated. It is no wonder that a critical observer has been lead to characterize judicial decrees as paper victories (Lottman, 1976). Similar problems exist with implementing state and federal legislation.

These examples are not uncommon and perhaps suggest a general condition of protracted skirmishes between plaintiffs and defendants to secure or resist compliance, respectively. It is worth noting that within PRFs experiencing judicial intervention, one often senses an excruciating feeling of impasse between antagonists. Their points of view are heavily invested, and this seems to promote a strident pursuit of victory. After a little more than one decade in the litigative process, this all may be a passing developmental phase to be followed by revised forms of innovation. It may be the inevitable outcome when relatively sudden reverses in legal doctrine confront decades of historical inertia and too many untested applications of newer technologies. It also may represent a signal that judicial intervention is limited as the directing strategy of human service reform.

In sum, it was inevitable that legal activism would be extended to mentally disabled citizens in PRFs in response to social and human injustice. It also was of monumental human significance because even the most conservative reading of the constitution reveals that violations of clients' rights had been tolerated if not supported by public law for decades. Yet, it well may be the staggering depth of that contradiction that motivated a literal explosion of litigative and legislative activity during the 1970s following decades of relative silence from representatives of the law. It may seem to future historians that the legal interventionists of the 1970s attempted to undo or correct over a century of unjust beliefs and circumstances by sweeping orders from the bench. Indeed, this approach, as noted earlier, has been employed with other disenfranchised groups in recent years. The present discussion has no quarrel with these intentions. Instead, it has sought to grasp some sense of the interventions of relief and their consequences.

OUTLOOK FOR THE FUTURE

Although the relationship between politics and mentally disabled persons has been illustrated with contemporary examples, the linkage between law and the handicapped dates back to antiquity. Aristotle more than 2000 years ago opined, "As to the exposure and rearing of children, let there be a law that no *deformed* child shall live" (cited in Scheerenberger, 1983). In the United States, Dorothea Dix urged the Massachusetts legislature in 1843 to pass a law to provide assistance to insane persons who led an horrific existence in prisons, almshouses, and asylums (Rosen, Clark, & Kivitz, 1976). Several years later, Massachusetts created a commission to study the condition of idiots in that state, but a bill to do the same in New York failed.

Since the middle of the 19th century all state legislatures have accepted a duty to support services to mentally disabled persons. The decade of the 1970s witnessed the formation of a critical mass of societal, legal, and political events to unleash the judiciaries, legislatures, and executive branches at all governmental levels as vehicles for change on behalf of mentally disabled persons. It seems reasonable that the special interest groups, impassioned individuals, elected officials, service providers, and others who have been successful participants in the political process in the 1970s have been rewarded for their efforts, and their political activity will intensify in the future. The strategies of these astute players also should serve as a model for heretofore nonparticipants and unsuccessful players in the political process.

An even more active political future for mental disabilities can be envisioned as the competition for resources becomes ever keener. A number of advocacy and professional organizations have encouraged their memberships to voice opposition to human service budget reductions. One of their principal concerns has been that the rights to rehabilitation, education, and habilitation won through legislation in the 1970s would be denied in the 1980s by sharply curtailing or eliminating federal funding supporting these rights.

Another major concern has been that fiscal austerity would pit developmentally disabled persons against other disabled, poor, elderly, and children's groups. Will each group's measure of rights be determined at the expense of other groups? A third problem concerns the economic jeopardy to the wide range of human service workers who may face layoffs as a result of funding cutbacks. How many teachers, direct-care workers, and other PRF employees will have to be released from their jobs? Will workers have reduced hours? At this time the reduction in the growth of federal spending for human services is a *fait accompli* and threatens to be more severe.

It will take new strategies and vigorous political action to keep the rights of mentally disabled clients from vanishing. Advocates for mentally disabled persons should join in a coalition with those representing other disabilities. For some political battles, alliances with supporters of the elderly, children, the poor, and other disadvantaged people might be profitable. Rather than compete with each other over the fiscal pie allocated, these groups might attempt to increase the size of the pie by coalescing their political strengths. Many human service providers and advocates for disabled people believe that their share of the fiscal pie can be increased only by slicing it from the military portion. Human service special interest groups have fantasies about how many services for disabled persons could be purchased for the price of just one B-1 bomber or MX missile.

These fantasies notwithstanding, special interest groups operating in behalf of mentally disabled persons will have to sharpen their political tools. If Illinois is typical of other states, the most influential lobbying groups at the state level fall into three basic categories: business groups, labor unions, and professional organizations (Dowling & Strong, 1984). At the national level these same special interest groups have been joined by those championing the causes of the elderly, veterans, farmers, federal workers, and others who oppose budget slashing at their expense (Sheldon, Johnson, & Walsh, 1984). On the other hand, special interest groups in support of business, taxpayers, and conservatives lobby for budget cuts over tax increases. Special interests for mentally disabled persons will have to compete with these influential lobbying groups, which wield substantial political clout. The size of their membership, financial power, and impact on the economy make them formidable competitors for legislators' attention.

One of the most fascinating groups of players in the political arena are the parents of mentally disabled persons. Almost uniformly on the side of the plaintiffs in the early right to habilitation litigation, parents no longer are a monolithic political force. In recent years, they have divided their allegiance and united with pro- as well as anti-PRF forces. The major concerns underlying parental opposition to deinstitutionalization in Nebraska, for example, are quite illuminating (Frohboese & Sales, 1980). Parents questioned the adequacy of community-based services compared with those available in the PRF. Parents had concerns about the instability, lack of quality and comprehensiveness, and administrative shortcomings in the community based system. These parents also questioned the ideology underpinning community services including normalization, the dignity of risk, and habilitation in the least restrictive environment. They objected to loss of their parental rights in the community placement process and expressed concern about their offspring coping in the community. These findings might have generality across other states and could suggest that parents, too, may be suffering from legal shock. The pace of legal events may have moved too rapidly for them, and they cannot evaluate or adapt to the change. They have lost some control over their families. These parents have become a force with which the legislatures, courts, and special interest groups must deal in coming years.

A view toward the future should not exclude the possibility that mentally disabled persons themselves could become active politically. A 34-year-old mentally retarded man, an alumnus of an orphan's home, foster home, PRF, group home, and supervised apartment, ran unsuccessfully for the Boulder Colorado City Council (Randall, 1984). Charles Dieterle, who earned 1,333 votes, is president of a lobbying group, contributes to two newsletters, and sits on the ARC-US advisory board. Physically handicapped people have become politically active in recent years by forming a variety of self-advocacy groups. Whether mentally disabled people will become a genuine political force remains to be seen. Nevertheless, teaching self-advocacy skills to mentally disabled people should become another component of their training curriculum.

The conflict between client interests and those of their service providers will continue to be a thorny issue. The problem exists, in large part, because advances for the former (e.g., community placement) have been at the expense of the latter (e.g., job layoffs). As we look toward the future, it appears that this conflict will intensify. It is our opinion that the class action law suits starting with Wyatt have been a necessary vehicle for initiating PRF reform in the absence of more responsive legislatures and executive branches of government. It is hoped that all large institutions with hundreds or thousands of residents, with as many or more staff, on multi-acre campuses will fade from the scene in the very near future. It also is hoped that the momentum to deinstitutionalize, spurred by some of the lower court decisions of the 1970s, (e.g., *Wyatt*, (1971) *Halderman* (1977) will not be thwarted by the more recent U.S. Supreme Court decisions in *Pennhurst* (1981) and *Youngberg* (1982). These more conservative rulings limit states' obligation to provide training in the least restrictive environment.

What should be the future role of residential facilities for mentally disabled people? We believe that the large PRFs have suffered legal shock and institution spasm in large part because of their very size. The examples illustrated in the previous section of this chapter occurred, to a large degree, because the enormity of litigated PRFs had an exponential effect on the legal intrusions. Even if enormous sums of money were poured into large PRFs and they could be made to provide adequate habilitation, this favorable outcome still would meet with philosophical objections by many critics of institutions. Large institutions are in a no-win situation as perceived by a number of people.

It appears that the most judicious course of action would be for large PRFs to continue to engage in a reasoned process of deinstitutionalization. At least two critical elements are essential to make large-scale deinstitutionalization viable. First, there must be funding for community living alternatives to PRFs. The Community and Family Living Amendments bill proposed by Senator Chafee is one mechanism to accomplish this goal. Although there has been opposition to this bill during the 98th Congress, it is hoped that its rewritten form, S.873, will be politically more viable in the 99th Congress. An essential political compromise of that bill will have to be a provision to maintain PRFs in some form in the future. Although a number of philosophical, economic, and programmatic arguments have been made for closing all PRFs, it is our belief that the congressional votes would not be available to support such a radical approach to services. Too many special interests would be threatened (e.g., NASMRPD, AFSME, parents).

A related funding issue is to reduce federal incentives such as Title XIX (Medicaid) that help maintain old institutions at the possible expense of creating community alternatives. A solution should be found that eliminates this problem. Different state programs have developed various formulas for compliance within the bounds of these federal regulations. Some have been more clinically workable than others; some have become paper compliance operations. Currently, PRFs are elegible for Medicaid funding to help them fix and maintain their physical plant. Not surprisingly, there is tremendous financial incentive for them to do so. Pennhurst, for example, received one third of its budget from Medicaid (Laski, 1980). "Medicaid, by virtue of its open-ended funding with an average contribution of 56.8% . . . leads to maintenance of institutions for state fiscal reasons alone" (p. 175). These incentives to maintain PRFs seem counter to litigative powered deinstitutionalization objectives. Switching the incentive to community-based programming, as S.873 would provide in larger measure, appears to be a necessary step.

A second requisite for large scale deinstitutionalization is that there be community residential facilities and services prepared to habilitate and render medical treatment to the predominately severely and profoundly handicapped persons who still inhabit PRFs. This issue, in part—but only in part—is tied to the availability of funding as described earlier. Successful deinstitutionalization also is dependent on integrating clients into an accepting community, hiring qualified staff, and applying appropriate medical and habilitation technology. Deinstitutionalization to date has involved community placement of primarily mildly and moderately retarded clients. Although a number of follow-up studies have been published on the effects of deinstitutionalization, their outcomes have not been consistent and definitive conclusions cannot be drawn at this time.

The real test of large-scale deinstitutionalization and the future role, if any, of PRFs will come when efforts are made to place the most severely handicapped residents into community settings. Will there be appropriate community living facilities for profoundly retarded, nonambulatory persons with life-threatening medical conditions? Will there be a group home that will accept profoundly retarded, deaf-blind, persons who engage in life-threatening, self-injurious behavior? Will the community accept clients whose violent behavior is a threat to neighbors or their property?

It will take careful planning and preparation to place clients such as these in the community and insure their health and safety as well as satisfactory habilitative programming. It well may be that in the decade of the 1980s not all corners of this country will be prepared to accept that responsibility. Despite the social desirability of placing all clients from all PRFs into community settings, workers in the field are well aware of dentists and physicians who will not treat retarded persons, communities where there has been not only opposition to but also violence waged against group homes, and the marginal existence that some former mental hospital patients lead living on the streets of our urban centers.

It may be that small, highly resourced PRFs will be a necessity for the foreseeable future. Small facilities serving under 100 of the most seriously medically and behaviorally handicapped clients may be essential until communities can be made ready to receive these most debilitated clients. Such PRFs should be staffed by highly skilled professionals and direct-care personnel who can not only serve the clients of their facilities but also function as consultants to community residential and day training programs. Is this alternative really worse than discharging difficult to handle clients to nursing homes that house hundreds of persons, where habilitative programming is inadequate, and where staff are poorly trained and their turnover is high?

As suggested earlier, one of the political drawbacks of large scale deinstitutionalization is the potentially negative impact it could have on the staff of PRFs. A solution could be found that eliminates this problem. For example, there could be an administrative mechanism for public employees to transfer from PRFs to community facilities and maintain their state jobs with all employment benefits. If the community facilities are part of the state mental disability service system, there should be little problem. If the community residential options are privately owned, as they frequently are, then PRF employee rights may be jeopardized. Such is the case in Pennsylvania, where Pennhurst is in the process of closing and its clients are being transferred to community residential programs. The experienced Pennhurst state employees would have to take, on average, a $6000 salary cut and a substantially less lucrative fringe benefit package to work in community living facilities (Conroy, 1984). In order for state mental disability service systems to minimize this internecine conflict, they may want to expand their role in establishing community residential alternatives or provide economic benefits for employees who must be terminated.

As suggested by the many illustrations cited, the rights of mentally handicapped people are brokered through the political process. As we progress through an era of fiscal conservatism in the 1980s, client rights may be jeopardized even further and the political process intensified. Past political activity may have served as a baptism of fire to initiate special interest groups and other players in the political arena to new heights of activism. There is preliminary but still inconclusive evidence, however, that the tax payers revolt may be running its course (Shribman, 1984). In the 1984 general election, all four major state referenda to roll back taxes or make it more difficult to raise taxes were defeated. The primary scene of political action in the 1980s may be in the legislative and executive branches of government rather than the judiciary. The 1970s may have been the decade of winning rights for mentally disabled persons in the courts, and the 1980s and 1990s may be the time for ensuring that those rights are implemented by providing quality service.

REFERENCES

Akerley, M. S. (1979). The politics of definitions. *Journal of Autism and Developmental Disabilities, 9,* 222–231.

Bates, P., & Wehman, P. (1977). Behavior management with the mentally retarded: An empirical analysis of the research. *Mental Retardation, 15,* 9–12.

Breen, P., & Richman, G. (1979). Evolution of the developmental disabilities concept. In R. Wiegerink, & J. W. Pelosi (Eds.), *Developmental Disabilities (pp 3–6).* Baltimore: Paul Brookes.

Briggs, M. (1980, June 12). Who should conduct PKU tests? *Southern Illinoisan,* p. 8.

Chafee, J. H. (1984, November 8). Speech to the Association for Persons with Severe Handicaps, Chicago.

Conroy, J. (1984, November 8–10). *Final results of the 5-year Pennhurst longitudinal study.* Presentation made at the Association for Persons with Severe Handicaps, Chicago.

Cullari, S. (1984). Everybody is talking about the new institution. *Mental Retardation, 22,* 28–29.

Cullari, S., & Ferguson, D. G. (1981). Individual behavior change: Problems with programming in institutions for mentally retarded persons. *Mental Retardation, 19,* 267–270.

Davis, E. M. (1981, November 23). Southern Illinois' prosperity is dependent on state jobs. *Southern Illinoisan,* p. 3.

Dold, R. B. (1984, October 22). Private Percy spends half-million. *Chicago Tribune,* p. 7.

Dowling, J., & Strong, W. C. (1984, November 25). The third house. *Southern Illinoisan,* p. 25.

Everitt, D. (1984). The ARC view of the Chaffee Bill. *Mental Retardation Systems, 1,* 46–52.

Fremouw, W. J. (1976). A new right to treatment. In S. Golann & W. J. Fremouw, (Eds.), *The right to treatment for mental patients* (pp. 7–28). New York: Irvington.

Frohboese, R., & Sales, B. D. (1980). Parental opposition to deinstitutionalization: A challenge in need of attention and resolution. *Law and Human Behavior, 4,* 1–87.

Gettings, R., & Howse, J. L. (1984). The federal government's role in expanding community based services: An alternative to the Chaffee Bill. *Mental Retardation Systems, 1,* 35–45.

Greenblat, M. (1978). *Psychopolitics.* New York: Grune & Stratton.

Halderman v. Pennhurst, 446 F. Supp. 1295 (E.D.P.A. 1977).

Holmes, O. W. (1963). *The common law* (M. D. Howe, Ed.). Boston: Harvard University Press. (Originally published 1881)

Kauffman, J. M. (Ed.). (1981). Are all children educable? (Special issue). *Analysis and Intervention in Developmental Disabilities, 1*(1).

Kelly v. Pennsylvania, 466 A.2d 1143 (Pa. Comm. W. Ct. 1983).

Koplowitz, H. B. (1980a, December 22). Patronage . . . "referrals" in 59th based on loyalty to Winchester. *Southern Illinoisan,* pp. 1, 3.

Koplowitz, H. B. (1980b, December 23). Williamson county caught in middle of patronage feud. *Southern Illinoisan*, p. 3.

Koplowitz, H. B. (1980c, December 24) Winchester: Patronage part of my job description. *Southern Illinoisan*, p. 3.

Landis, T. (1984a, May 9). Suit charges Winchester cost opponent Bowen job. *Southern Illinoisan*, p. 3.

Landis, T. (1984b, December 2). Winchester ponders possible roles in regional politics. *Southern Illinoisan*, p. 26.

Landis, T. (1985, July 11). Winchester cleared in federal probe of job-selling. *Southern Illinoisan*, p. 1.

Laski, F. (1980). Right to services in the community: Implications of the *Pennhurst* case. In R. J. Flynn & K. E. Nitsch (Eds.), *Normalization, social integration, and community services* (pp. 167–175). Baltimore: University Park Press.

Lottman, M. S. (1976). Enforcement of judicial decrees: Now comes the hard part. *Mental Disability Law Reporter, 1*, 69–76.

MacEachron, A. E. (1981). *Ideology, symbol, and action: An organizational field experiment.* Unpublished manuscript, Brandeis University.

McKnight, J. (1978). Professionalized service and disabling help. In I. Illich, I. K. Zola, J. McKnight, J. Caplan, & H. Shaiken (Eds.), *Disabling professions* (pp. 69–91). Boston: Marlon Boyars.

New York State ARC v. Rockefeller, 357 F. Supp. 752 (E.D. N.Y. 1973).

Ornstein, N. J., & Elder, S. (1978). *Interest groups, lobbying and policy making.* Washington: Congressional Quarterly Press.

Pennhurst v. Halderman, 451 US 1 (1981).

Randall, M. (1984). With disabilities undisguised. *Disabled USA, 3,* 1–7.

Reppucci, N. D., & Saunders, J. T. (1974). Social psychology of behavior modification problems of implementation in natural settings. *American Psychologist, 29,* 649–660.

Richardson, H. L. (1978). *What makes you think we read the bills?* Ottawa, IL: Caroline House.

Rosen, M., Clark, G. R., & Kivitz, M. S. (Eds.). (1976). *The history of mental retardation* (Vol. 1). Baltimore: University Park Press.

Scheerenberger, R. C. (1983). *A history of mental retardation.* Baltimore: Paul Brookes.

Sevener, D. (1982, August 25). ''Whistle-blowers'' to get legal protection. *Southern Illinoisan*, p. 20.

Sheldon, C., Johnson, K., & Walsh, K. T. (1984, December 3). ''To the barricades!'' Interest groups fight back. *U.S. News and World Report.*

Shribman, D. (1984, November 27). Is the U.S. tax revolt ending? *The Wall Street Journal*, p. 64.

Staff (1982a, February–March). Legislation needed for continuation of screening program. *D.D. Directions,* p. 3.

Staff (1982b, Fall). ARC/Illinois recognizes Governor Thompson. *D.D. Directions,* p. 2.

Staff (1984, Fall) SB 2053. *ARC/Illinois News*, p. 6.

Stickney, S. S. (1976). *Wyatt v. Stickney:* Background and postscript. In S. Golann & W. J. Fremouw (Eds.), *The right to treatment for mental patients* (pp. 29–46). New York: Irvington.

Syrett, H. C. (Ed.). (1970). *American historical documents.* New York: Barnes & Noble.

Talbot, J. A. (1978). *State mental hospitals: Problems and potentials.* New York: Human Sciences Press.

Taylor, S. J., & Biklen, D. (1980). *Understanding the law.* Syracuse, NY: D D Rights Center of the Mental Health Law Project and the Center on Human Policy.

Toffler, A. (1971). *Future shock.* New York: Bantam.

Toffler, A. (1975). *The eco-spasm report.* New York: Bantam.

Willems, E. P. (1974). Behavioral technology and behavioral ecology. *Journal of Applied Behavior Analysis, 7,* 151–165.

Wolfensberger, W. (1969).   The origin and nature of our institutional models. In R. B. Kugel &
W. Wolfensberger (Eds.), *Changing patterns in residential services for the mentally retarded*
(pp. 58–171b). Washington: President's Committee on Mental Retardation.
Wuori v. Zitnay, No. 75-80-SD (D. Maine, July 14, 1978).
Wyatt v. Ireland, No. 3195-N, (M.D. Ala, October 25, 1979).
Wyatt v. Stickney, 325 F. Supp. 781 (M.D. Ala. 1971).
Youngberg v. Romeo, 50 U.S. Law Week 4681 (1982).

6 Policy and the Perspective of State Government

Gareth D. Thorne, M.A.
Jack Thaw, Ph.D.

ON GOVERNMENT AND HUMAN SERVICE

History, at least in this country, has assigned the conditions of mental handicap principally to the custody of government (Deutsch, 1949; Wolfensberger, 1969). In a recent survey, Scheerenberger (1982) found that for just one population, institutionalized mentally retarded individuals, there were 282 public residential facilities in the United States serving over 125,000 clients with operating budgets totaling over three billion dollars. The role of government in the organization and delivery of human services is enormous, a fact unlikely to change in the coming decades. Innovating any dimension of human services to mentally handicapped persons will require a clear sense of how governments behave in this role. The intent of this discussion is to describe some of the major factors that affect government systems of service. The principal unit of analysis is state government, since so much of the service implementing responsibility lies at this level.

Understanding the problems of public systems of service in transition is the theme of this volume. Earlier chapters have examined the dynamics of administrative, professional, and line levels of the residential facility. The present discussion, in considering the perspective of the state system, emphasizes the function of policy, which is for most states the conceptual and procedural reference point for transitions at all levels.

Government by the People

Unlike a corporation, government must exist in one form or another. A corporation that does not succeed may simply dissolve. A government that does not

229

govern adequately may change form but may not cease to exist; therefore, it exerts a unique influence in the lives of each of us as though it were as fundamental to the persistence of life as the air we breathe. It is indeed difficult to conceptualize humanity without at the same time casting it into some political mold (i.e., governmental system). There seems no escape from this reality. The continuing challenge is to make government work to the best interests of all. The reality checks that must be raised at the outset simply are these: What you want may not be what I want; what you believe may not be what I believe; what you value may not be what I value. The government for the individual is in reality the government of compromise.

The majority rules. Or does it? The organized movement, the vested interest—do these direct the activity of government? And what of moral principle? Eunice Kennedy Shriver (1976) eloquently addressed this issue with the following statement: "It is the obligation of each of us to value and nurture above all the moral principles which teach us that all human beings are equal in law; that those who have the most gifts have the greatest responsibility, that indeed, those with the least must be entitled to the most in a compassionate society, and that every human being must count as one whole person" (p. xxi).

In context of such considerations, change in governmental activity is both inevitable and necessary. Government, indeed, must be a system in flux, striving to sustain its core of stability through a process of adapting to the vagaries of the constituency it serves and represents at any given time and place. Statutes, regulations, policies, directives, and procedures are the functional core elements that governmental systems use to bring about the orderly and predictable outcomes through which the changing needs of citizens are recognized and resolved.

The fundamental fact remains, however, that the governed are individuals, as are those who govern. Each is motivated and driven by political persuasions and moral and personal convictions. Many innovators entering governmental arenas seem not to appreciate that government is terribly "human." The actions of government are the actions of people in government. The reactions of government to the acceptance or rejection of its actions are the reactions of people in government. The defenses of government in response to its actions are the defenses of people in government.

We all have heard the term "civil servant" used to describe the government employee. Experience tells us that very few government employees regard themselves as passive servants to some fixed missions of government. There is, of course, a job to do in organizing, managing, protecting, and enabling the social structure of the public. This is the task of government, and this is the task of workers in governmental services. However, the same reality problems of varying wants, beliefs, and values affect the government employees as much as they do the constituent citizens.

There is probably no agency of government that does not confront powerful consequences in its operation from this human factor. This is especially so in governmental services to mentally handicapped people because the technological basis of service is far from perfected. Perhaps the point of departure for anyone who wishes to understand governmental human service is that what is done, as well as what is proposed, will be subject to disputes of preference, belief, and value.

Government by the Law

One of the greatest problems facing administrators of state agencies, as well as employees within the agency functioning as innovators of change, is the conflict that arises from invoking what law intends versus what is perceived to be appropriate to the needs of the people being served.

To illustrate, a state may choose to incorporate the Intermediate Care Facilities program for the Mentally Retarded (ICF/MR) under Title XIX of the Social Security Act for its institutions (U.S. Dept. of Health, Education, and Welfare, 1974). If the state chooses Title XIX as a course of action, certain critical decisions must be made that relate directly to the types of programs and environments available for clients. The regulations contain provisions which require facilities to standardize practices if they are to receive federal funds under Title XIX (Crosby, 1976). These standards may not be the most appropriate program for many mentally handicapped persons, particularly those whose medical and habilitative programming needs are minimal and not more than that of the average population. There is, however, no halfway Title XIX provision. If a living unit is designed as an Intermedicate Care Facility, then it must meet the program, staffing, and environmental standards specified by federal regulation in order to be certified. The state agency is locked into these requirements for all units certified under Title XIX. In many instances this imposes constraints or lack of flexibility on procedural and policy decisions that might otherwise be more beneficial to the clients of the certified unit.

If the state agency decides that the programs offered are contrary to those needed by the resident, then it must make a decision to abandon the Title XIX approach with subsequent loss of dollar benefits to the state. It is not easy to convince the financial elements of state government to make this adjustment, particularly if the federal funds are anticipated as revenue to the state and are incorporated as part of long range revenue projections. Gettings (1977) has described the difficulty of utilizing generic service funds without compromising programmatic principles that is often faced by administrators of mental retardation agencies. He points out that political and fiscal realities often require these administrators to make extensive use of federal and state generic funding sources. The problem occurs because, for many of these funding programs, service to retarded persons is only a secondary objective. The operating policies may not always be congruent with the goals of the agency. Thus, Gettings observes, the agency program administrator is faced with the dilemma of either loosely interpreting bureaucratic rules (and risking subsequent audits and possible disqualifications) or compromising the agency's programmatic mission to obtain generic support. This same dilemma can be experienced at the exact point of client service where the clinician is required to view the client through the lens of regulatory obligations, which, for that client, may not programmatically fit.

A second, and different, problem occurs because many federal and state laws that directly affect services to mentally handicapped persons designate responsibility for implementation to agencies that are ill-prepared philosophically or operationally to carry out the intent and mandate of the law (e.g., Ross, 1980). Mentally handicapped clients are served by many agencies of government, and there is a great unevenness in their capability to respond to federal and state mandated programs. In response to this, some states, such as South Carolina and Connecticut, have created separate departments of mental retardation to reduce the overlap. Welfare, health, and education agencies in these states have the option to contract federal and state mandated programs through these mental retardation departments that serve as the principle implementation agencies.

The ability to implement what law and regulation mandates is a source of constant frustration to chief administrators as well as agency staff in public systems of human service. In many cases, failure to carry out mandate is directly related to lack of funds. For example, individualized programs of habilitation for each client cannot occur if staff-to-client ratios are too thin. Solutions here rest with the state's economy and priority determinations, which are public matters resolvable only through the legislative and executive branches of government at the highest level. More recently, these problems have been subjected to the judicial process.

Other problems in carrying out legal mandates are rooted in the very acceleration of mandated change itself. Legal requisites affecting labor relations, occupational safety, affirmative action, education of clients under 21 years of age, human rights, due process procedures, nature of client physical environments, record keeping, and new staff competencies, to name but a few, have been imposed on the service system in the past decade or so. As suggested in Chapter 1 of this volume, these changes came suddenly after decades of nonchange. They also came in a most uncoordinated manner and with little lead time for preparation. Thus, for example, individualized education plans for profoundly retarded (but now school-eligible) clients cannot be carried out because the facility's teachers were trained to teach only higher functioning clients, and the local universities have barely begun to develop teacher training programs for this level of client handicap. In these areas, problems of compliance with individual mandates reflect more systemic troubles of coping with a volume of change that is outpacing the system's capacity to respond. The changes and mandates are for the most part desirable, but they must be planned so they can be managed. This is not occurring.

A third domain of difficulty in executing the intent of the law concerns those laws and regulations that require no funding or special resources but which impose cumbersome, if not impossible, procedural terms on the state agency and its facilities. For example, if the law requires protection of the rights of handicapped persons in public residential facilities through assurance of informed consent and due process, the procedural impact on an agency to implement such a requirement in behalf of its severely and profoundly retarded clients can become staggering. There may not be a single facility anywhere in which every decision affecting severely and profoundly retarded clients is made with the client's informed consent. The experience of moment-to-moment decision making that occurs when servicing noncommunicating persons may well permit a condition of total informed consent only at the risk of the service itself. This is a matter of great concern that often divides clinicians and lawyers.

Clinically practical and responsible alternatives to the choking constraints of blackletter law would seem to reside in concepts such as least restrictive residential environment (Chambers, 1976), normalization (Wolfensberger, 1972), and individualized programming (Crosby, 1976). Although there are disputes about how some of these concepts translate to methods (e.g., Throne, 1975) as well as imposing questions of interpretation, implementation, and accountability, they appear to hold potential as reliable safeguards of basic rights of clients.

At issue is the larger question of procedural guidelines and clinically responsible programming that would permit a state government agency to conduct its human service responsibilities *by the law* without hopelessly disabling the services *in the name of the law*. There are serious differences about the specifications of such procedures and programs some of which are in court (Harvard Law Review, 1977).

Government for the People

Citizens often are confused and overwhelmed by bureaucratic governmental systems that are so complex they seem to have no beginning or end. Its inertia seems circular, and Citizen Jones finds himself circling forever, particularly if he depends on government to provide for his welfare. When government acts as though it were insensitive and disrespectful of the dignity of the citizen, then problems are certain to ensue. For example, handicapped people routinely are povertized so that they can qualify for the governmental services they need. They must remain at the poverty level if they are to continue to be eligible to receive appropriate services. Government assesses the individual for all resources above the poverty level and then spends tens of thousands of dollars to care for a now totally dependent person.

At one time, institutionalized handicapped persons were encouraged to save their money and build a little nestegg to help in the rehabilitation process in the community while looking forward to the day of their release. Today, it is a common occurrence to make certain that the handicapped person saves nothing beyond what is allowable under the Social Security and Welfare maximum. Parents are urged not to provide for the handicapped child in their wills with full realization that such funds would be confiscated for back payments of services. Under such circumstances, seeds of distrust in the true concern of government for the handicapped are planted and flourish.

Currently, there is a vast movement toward getting people out of institutions and into residential programs in the community. Many parents are frightened by these plans because their child may be forced to leave the protection of the institution, which through the years, as part of publicly supported administrative policy, nurtured dependency on it. So great did this dependency become in certain places that inhumane conditions existed for years; yet, parents and others were afraid to speak up, or perhaps did not realize that services and programs could be better. The parents' fear to speak up was reinforced by an even greater fear that they might be required to take their child back home. The torturous decision to place the child in the institution had been made with the realization that without supportive community programs, they could not sustain their child at home.

The physical isolation of most institutions kept them effectively out of sight of a general public that was at various periods unconcerned with, frightened by, and resolved to extinguish the mentally handicapped person. Over the years, staff of many institutions became complacent about conditions they could not change. Old buildings and crowded, open dormitories became unassailed obstacles to any hope of effective programming. This history is well known and there is overwhelming documentation (e.g., Wolfensberger, 1969) that this type of government service "for the people" was for many years the type preferred by public officials, professionals, communities, and parents alike.

The post-World War II years marked the beginning of the great civil rights movement in the United States. All over this land the rights and needs of minority groups became the subject of open forum. Groups representing all kinds of minorities began to emerge from the general social turmoil of the 50s and 60s as effective forces demanding recognition of minority rights. Laws asserting fundamental rights and guaranteeing numerous protections (e.g., The Civil Rights Act of 1964) were passed by the federal and state governments. The groundswell came to include the mentally handicapped in the 1970s with the passage of significant legislation such as the Education for All Handicapped Children Act of 1975 (P.L. 94-142), the Developmentally Disabled Assistance and Bill of Rights Act of 1975 (P.L. 94-103), and the Rehabilitation Act of 1973.

Clearly, the nature of belief about government "for the people" concerning the mentally handicapped citizen has changed. More precisely, the change has been in fundamental principle and in concept. The basic rights of these persons have been retrieved from oblivion, an historical occasion of monumental importance. However, after more than a half century of neglect, the translation of rights into workable and valid service procedures may not occur either quickly or with simplicity. The public school desegregation struggle of the past quarter century is witness to this in a general context. There are examples closer to home. One can observe local school systems agonizing over the implementation of P.L. 94-142 (e.g., Sarason & Doris, 1979) or residential facility service professionals so oversensitized about clients' due process rights that they hesitate to teach clients responsibilities lest their instruction be interpreted as infringing those rights.

The rights of mentally handicapped individuals, therefore, are not yet fully secured in empirically validated systems of service (e.g., MacMillan & Borthwick, 1980; Mesibov, 1976). Even in specific areas such as the rights to treatment and to refuse treatment in civil commitment, both the law and its service implications are by no means at a criterion state of confidence (Civil Commitment, 1977). There are important implications here for government services. If there is consensus on principle but not methods, then the methods can be argued and what the government is actually doing (in terms of methods of services) for the people can be negotiated. If this is the case, and it appears to be, then the very security of the rights themselves may be yet in question. This matter is discussed at length in Chapter 5 of this volume.

For the present discussion, it is necessary to point out that the large, complex, and often cumbersome process of government can be expected to have difficulty with the unresolved translation of rights and principles to services. What government agencies construe as the translation may not correspond to what parents construe, nor to what advocacy groups will accept, nor to what the taxpayers will endorse. For example, parents of children in the same residential facility have highly divergent views about programmatic and service decisions affecting their children's future. Some maintain that they will sue the government if it attempts to place their child elsewhere. Others threaten suit if their child is *not* placed elsewhere. Some wish the institution to be rebuilt; others would have it eliminated entirely. The emotions and rhetoric that stir around these two issues alone presents the executive and legislative branches of state government with difficult choices. There is often an excruciating sense of impasse between positions (e.g., Ellis et al., 1981; Menolascino & McGee, 1981).

If what government ultimately decides to do on these and other questions is to stand longer term tests of valid human service rather than shorter term tests of emotional reaction, then the requirements of government agencies would appear to be intelligent planning, an acute sense of their own history, an obsessive regard to excellence in services and in service providers, and a commitment to self-evaluation. Former U.S. Secretary of State Henry Kissinger (1979) has written that policy occurs when concept encounters opportunity. For government services to mentally handicapped people, we suggest that programs of policy that protect and implement rights will occur when already available concepts encounter deliberate and prudently developed procedures of service. Bringing these to maturity with the strident and conflicting demands that today surround the government agencies designated to provide the services may well challenge and stress the system to its very foundations.

The Governmental Process and Innovation

Government is a process, although the events and products that punctuate it often have more visibility than the process itself. The general public may be affected by a new law or may utilize a specific government program at a certain point in time without appreciation of the complex and longitudinal proceedings through which the law or program was conceived, developed, funded, implemented, evaluated, and perhaps refined or corrected. Government programs and services to mentally handicapped people, along with their contemporary problems noted earlier, similarly are filtered through this process. It follows that innovators of such programs and services should be skilled in the working principles that affect the governmental process.

The implementation of law tends to occur in a process that extends from statute to regulation, to policy, to directive, and finally to procedure. The law enables the regulation establishing the rules and conditions under which policies are formulated. Directives provide specific instructions and constraints within the scope of policy, and procedures are the blueprints of action.

One of the first issues for those who would innovate the service system is determining the level (statute, policy, etc.) at which to intervene. Broad-based systemic changes logically would be targeted at higher levels of policy, working with participants such as commissioners of state agencies, planning and advisory councils, or perhaps facility directors. More circumscribed interventions, such as staff development programs in behavior training, might best be piloted at the direct service or action level. It is more often the case, however, that innovations have extended implications beyond the focal point of impact. For example, the psychologist changing direct-care roles through a staff training project may require resources that involve decision making at higher administrative levels. If the staff training project yields demonstrable results in the piloted residential units, it may generate interest, even direction, at policy levels.

For most innovator involvement, the point of greatest probable impact in a government service system is at the direct service or action level, at the point of laying on the hands, so to speak. Where the individual innovator is a service practitioner (e.g., psychologist, social worker, educator), this is especially so, because he or she normally will possess a more usable working knowledge of the service level variables than of the higher administrative situation. Indeed, there is evidence that the mental health field in general is filled with clinicians poorly versed in the essentials of administration (Hinkle & Burns, 1978). Some service innovators experience a sense of powerlessness with change introduced at this lowest point in the governmental hierarchy. They feel that the span of their involvement must have upward reach. This may be true although service practitioners' access to higher levels of administration will vary from state system to state system. Nonetheless, if true accountability for any innovation occurs at the point of client service outcome, as it should, then, at least theoretically, there is power for those proficient at that level.

It has to be considered, however, that at the action level, the change process is also likely to be highly subjective. Indeed, the degree of subjectivity in the governmental process seems to increase as the implementation of law moves from statute to procedure. Almost paradoxically, variations in interpretation concerning what the law intends appears to decrease as one moves from statute, to regulation, to policy, to directives, to procedures. This may be due in part to a kind of filtering process that occurs in the application of law. More likely, the closer one comes to the result of applying the law, the more one is convinced (though subjectively) about what the law really intended. To illustrate, if a statute provides for the habilitation of handicapped clients, what this means to the public or parent groups or even legislators may be subject to great variations of interpretation. However, when the statute is applied in a service action that affects handicapped individuals directly, the interpretation of the law seems quite clear to the practitioners, although it is *their* interpretation.

It is in circumstances where variation in interpretation of the law is greatest that barriers to implementation are most formidable and complex. Sarason and Doris (1979) provide clear testimony to this in their discussion of public school systems' interpretations of the Education for All Handicapped Children Act (P.L. 94-142). They describe, among other things, the intrusion of budgetary considerations, professional rivalries, and longstanding opposition to main-streaming as interests acting on the interpretation of 94-142 provisions (such as least restrictive alternatives) and 94-142 concepts (such as mainstreaming). They cite some urban school systems' mainstreaming interpretation as having handi-capped children sharing the gymnasium, lunch, and music with nonhandicapped children, but not the classrooms. Similar illustrations can be drawn from in-terpretive battles in other areas of legal mandate, such as barrier-free environ-ments (e.g., Schalter, 1978). It seems that where interpretation has more leeway, there is a greater probability of no action, delayed action, or restrictive action. "Between intent and performance is a wide area mined by obstacles that often destroy the intent" (Sarason & Doris, 1979, pp. 379–380).

It is reasonable to question whether the premise that increased and complex barriers correlate with increased variation of interpretation is also conversely valid, that is, where interpretive variation is least, implementation is more likely to occur without obstruction. To some degree this is probably so. Where there is consensus about intent, even if that consensus is highly subjective, one can expect greater likelihood of shared, collaborative action. It is probably the case that this condition is more likely to occur closer to the procedure or client service level of the governmental process. Consensus on intent here will not preclude differences about methods or procedures, but these obstacles may be more ob-vious to the innovator. What's more, they will probably be more clinical (as opposed to political or administrative) in resolution. These clinical and procedural issues are discussed in Chapter 3 of this volume.

An initial implication for innovating in the governmental process can now be drawn: That part of the process which is operationally closest to the point of service delivery is accessed more easily by innovators, especially clinically trained innovators. This seems to be so for three reasons:

1. Innovators trained in the mental health service professions are likely to have more expertise at this level of government than at political or administrative levels.

2. This part of the governmental process is more apt to be subjectively applied by agency staff. There is thus a norm of sorts that the process itself can be legitimately questioned, a condition suitable for the intervention of changes by professionals tied to the more autonomous values of their training.

3. The interpretation of the law or the mandated mission of the government system is likely to be less variable at the service level with the consequence of more methodological or clinical obstacles rather than overarching barriers of fundamental concept or direction. The former, it is argued, tend to be more graspable and workable.

We have emphasized the advantages of *access* and *probable impact* for innovations occurring at the client service level of government. Change, of course, can be introduced at the statutory or regulation level as well as at the procedural level, although the nature of the change will be different. Similarly, change can be introduced through efforts at different stations in the government's organizational structure. A state agency or department for the mentally handicapped has some organized structure that typically includes such stations as a Commissioner and a central office, advisory council, regional districts with administrative directors, and an array of community and institutional facilities with their own administrations, usually headed by a superintendent. Across states, these organizational systems have varying degrees of centralized or decentralized emphasis. They also are strongly affected by geography. In large states, for example, professionals in one facility may seldom meet with their counterparts in other facilities hundreds of miles away. By contrast, in a small state like Connecticut, representatives of all service professions from each mental retardation facility meet monthly on matters of professional issues, policy, and innovation. Here Connecticut Department of Mental Retardation policy collaborates with a consenting geography to permit service professionals more extensive activity in higher levels of the governmental process.

In general, however, access and probable impact are less likely to occur at higher stations of government organization or higher levels of governmental process. These higher places also are more directly affected by the political cycles, which may mean that such players as appointed commissioners have innovation interests dogmatically oriented to 4-year life spans.

Even with delimited access, change interventions can and do take place at all *levels* of the governmental process (statute, policy, regulation, procedure) and at all *stations* (central agency office, residential facility, etc.) in the governmental organization by innovators both internal and external to the service system. Again, in Connecticut, a group of service professionals were centrally responsible for the development of a major statewide policy setting standards and guidelines for the use of behavior modification procedures in all Department of Mental Retardation facilities (Thaw, Thorne, & Benjamin, 1978). The enabling statute for that policy was itself drafted with substantial input by service level psychologists.

The discussion thus far prompts the conclusion that there are within the governmental process clear opportunities to innovate. This is probably so in most systems, but moving opportunity to outcome requires understanding the relationship between innovation and the governmental system of services to mentally handicapped individuals. This relationship often is both complicated and puzzling, and many a brilliant innovative idea has become ensnarled in it, to say nothing of the innovator. Some further thoughts on this relationship are necessary.

In a broad discussion on the relationship of organizations (including those of government) to change, Kaufman (1971) concludes that a host of factors will almost always act to ensure that changes introduced into large organizations occur within rather narrow limits and over time frames up to 30 years. These factors include such variables as limitations of resources, systemic aversion to unpredictability, necessary compromises to opponents of innovation, interorganizational commitments (such as labor contracts), and great bodies of public law, regulations, adjudications, and internal rules accumulated over many years. Kaufman argues that these and other factors bind organizations to familiar and traditional paths; where change is introduced, many of these factors tend to isolate, contain, or routinize it.

Such constraints on innovation seem to mount when one considers the dimensions that distinguish public human service systems from corporate systems (e.g., Maloof, 1975). For example, policy making in the former often involves increased participation by consumers, advocates, and volunteers. Corporate boards are generally free of these influences. Focusing more narrowly within the public service domain, the development and administration of mental health systems has not only become a specialty of its own (e.g., Feldman & Cahill, 1975; Yolles, 1975), but a process beset with special problems that appear to affect innovation. For example, formal programs of professional preparation for individuals who will manage at all stations in the public mental health system are seriously limited (Barton, 1977; Feldman, 1973), yet the Report of the National Task Force on Mental Health/Mental Retardation Administration (1979) describes the mental health system as expanding enormously in size and becoming increasingly complex.

The Task Force Report also indicates that some of the key personnel one might expect to effect meaningful innovation (e.g., psychiatrists, psychologists, social workers, even administrators) have been inadequately trained in understanding the mental health system and its governmental/political context. These problems are compounded by the existence of little empirical research on administrative systems in the mental health fields (Hinkle & Burns, 1978).

Additional problems affecting the innovation of public services to mentally handicapped people have to do with the very nature of the service and its clientele. Feldman (1975) has described several factors that seem to present such problems. He points out, for example, that the highly dependent nature of the client population presents extraordinary difficulties for administrators attempting to maintain responsive, accountable, and humane programs. Where this dependency is total, as it is for many profoundly retarded clients, the demand even for basic care may stress the governmental process to its resource limits. Feldman also cites the intangible nature of the mental health services product and the difficulty measuring degrees of success. The governmental system answers to taxpayers; numbers of highway miles constructed or public water systems tested or even elderly citizens vaccinated against influenza are all more quantifiable than most service outcomes to mentally handicapped clients. Feldman also sees the multidisciplinary, professional, and highly autonomous nature of staff in mental health organizations as a force that may compete with the administrative direction of the system. A final factor is the very transaction between the service provider and the client, which can be highly private, intimate, and bound by rigorous professional ethics. Feldman observes that it is very difficult for the administrative system to collaborate with or intrude in this process, even when it is warranted.

Thus, the basic governmental process that operates most citizen services by implementing statutes, regulations, directives, policies, and procedures is, in its obligations to the mentally handicapped citizen, layered with numerous other variables that render it more uncertain and difficult to innovate. In most states, and no doubt in most municipalities, what emerges is less a predictable and stable process than a shifting mix of administration, professional services, and politics. The players in this system appear not to have been prepared well either for the system or for one another. The system's fundamental mission, the diagnosis and treatment of mentally handicapped clients, is conducted with a technology that, at its best, may be in its formative stages (e.g., Baumeister, 1981). All this activity occurs in circumstances of high external demand (see Chapter 1) and rests upon an earlier history of inertia and neglect (e.g., Deutsch, 1949; Wolfensberger, 1969).

This profile, by itself, is not reason to despair for the prospect of innovation. Rather, it should caution change facilitators to observe certain guidelines when selecting a place to intervene in the governmental process. In general, these guidelines call for assessment, that is, evaluating the variables mentioned earlier against the requirements of the innovation. More specifically, we suggest the following principles:

1. *Level × innovation × time:* An innovation should be introduced at a level or station in the governmental process where it can be implemented within reasonable time. Unlike those in most corporate systems, important elements of government are time limited. Innovations that require or assume the continuance of a political power structure over extended time may be at risk. Further, political systems desire greatly to make accomplishments within their own time in power. Long-term changes likely to achieve maximum effectiveness in another political administration tend to be given very low priority or are discarded. This is particularly true at the higher or appointive stations of government and is less so at the operations level. Thus, rather than discount long range planning, innovators have to section long-term concepts into shorter pragmatic goals in step with the cycles of the political process.

2. *Make innovations visible and economic:* Change agents should innovate with impact. Changes that efficiently affect or potentially could affect large numbers of the target population are most desirable. Appropriation and finance elements of government are charged with the task of continuously evaluating the economics of government service programs. Their judgments can be the principal influence affecting the funding and growth of a program regardless of the program's intrinsic value to the client consumers. Often these cost judgments lead to standardized governmental services in pursuit of efficiency at the expense of creative change. Innovators must be mindful of this possibility and accept that government is often a competitor for finite public resources. At the same time, they must not let government's obsession with economy suppress possibilities of creative innovation. Rather, their proposed changes must have some appeal to the efficiency nerve endings of the fiscal controllers.

3. *Analyze historical and readiness factors:* Every agency, department, or unit of government operation has its own history with change and change agentry. That history must be understood by innovators. It may help to define the strategies for intervention and to predict probabilities for certain types of changes. In the same sense, a governmental organization's readiness for change must be assessed. Will this agency or this service program be able to tolerate the process and content of this innovation at this time? Is management oriented to accept new approaches, and are managers sufficiently skilled to handle the transitions to and maintenance of innovations? Are line and professional staff groups supportive and trained well enough to implement the innovation competently? These are only some of the readiness questions that must be subjected to diagnostic scrutiny.

4. *Acquire external resources:* Resource-limited systems tend to be responsive to ideas or concepts powered by independent funding. Many administrators are quite willing to look gift grants in the mouth. Innovative proposals that would

otherwise fall victim through budget surgery or competing priorities gain access to the governmental process when they pay their own way. This access, in most instances, really amounts to borrowed time. The concept has its own free pilot period during which it must produce enough impact and results to be retained and internalized when the soft funding terminates, as it typically does. Nevertheless, such things as merit being equivalent, innovations backed by external resources will compete more favorably than those at the mercy of the state's general fund.

5. *Evaluate outcomes of innovation:* In recent years, accountability has become a formidable theme in government human service programs, where it once barely mattered. Unfortunately, the science of program evaluation in human services is also recent and shows the practical and methodological problems of its age (Schulberg & Baker, 1979). Nevertheless, the advent of such powerful influences as cost efficiency criteria, judicially imposed quality standards, and informed organizations of citizen advocates have rendered systematic evaluation of results mandatory. Successfully innovating service programs at any level of government will increasingly require that intervention be tied to sound evaluations of outcome. This matter is developed further in Chapter 7.

Several chapters in this book address issues of change and innovation at line, professional, and administrative levels of public service. In the next section, we examine the role of innovation in policy formation, the planning and directing function of government activity in human services.

POLICY IN GOVERNMENT SERVICE

The complex relationship between innovation and the governmental system of services to mentally handicapped individuals is sharply illustrated in the domain of public policy. Many professionals schooled in academic disciplines find the whole notion of policy a constraint on their ideas if not their values. Perhaps fewer see it as a resource. Our experience suggests that a majority of innovation-minded service providers working at the residential facility level have difficulty coming to terms with the role of policy in human services. Nevertheless, for all innovators of public human services, policy will be an unavoidable factor of increasing significance in the years ahead. We examine it from several perspectives.

Earlier discussion in this chapter supports the conclusion that a fundamental outcome of the governmental process is action. Outcomes of delayed or restrictive action and even decisions for no action curiously often occur only after intense activity by those working the governmental process. Perhaps this is what has led some observers (e.g., Dye, 1976) to define public policy simply as *all* actions of governments—what they choose to do and not to do as distinct from their stated intentions.

This is a useful starting point. In human services, the composition of a government action is an important consideration. Most often, the action reflects an interaction among three factors: (a) a philosophy, idea, or concept; (b) an estimate of pragmatic result; and (c) a public mandate. In his study of the laws of power, Berle (1967) described the centrality of an idea system to every organization. No administrator heading any agency can be expected to hold it together without a core of ideas or a constituting philosophy. This is especially so in systems serving mentally handicapped individuals. Service concepts and technologies are in the early stages of development, as is the underlying body of research. There is no lock on the conclusive treatment, and thus there is enormous opportunity and room to work the idea system. Persons with conceptual innovations—and typically these are academic and clinical professionals—will find this element of policy development a fertile area for activity.

Estimating pragmatic results is for Berle (1967) an activity that frequently conflicts with the idea system or philosophy. Balancing the two defines a basic requirement of administration. Blending concept into a pragmatically sound outcome is a mark of high administrative expertise. It is also a component of good policy making, but we find that many of the same individuals who are rich in ideas and conceptual principles cannot grasp this administrative factor. Feldman (1980) suggests that these professionals may have trouble reconciling the autonomous values of their academic training with organizational rules and loyalties. Innovators with this problem are well advised to accept the tension that exists between pragmatic administration and the companion idea system. They are also wise to accept that both are required to produce workable service systems and policies. Berle insightfully describes this situation as the endless paradox of contest between power holders and thinkers: ''Victory of either over the other is self-destructive. The two forces must coexist. Each is essential to the other; neither can exercise both functions'' (p. 8).

At this point, a working definition of policy can be suggested as follows: a definite course or method of action selected from alternative concepts and in consideration of given pragmatic conditions to guide or determine present and future direction. In state governments, our frame of reference for this chapter, policy in human services is usually formulated at the agency level, that is, in the department or office charged with responsibility for designated groups of citizens such as mentally retarded or mentally ill persons. The department's policies are public statements of a governmental agency's general attitude and position on matters of program direction and emphasis. This is the highest point in the hierarchy of governmental operations that can be effectively influenced by innovators without resorting to the office of the state's chief executive or the legislative process. These higher stations are often more difficult places through which to work targeted service changes anyway.

Responsibility for policy formation is usually mandated by law. The responsibility is, at times, given to boards and commissions as well as to agency executives. What is important for the present discussion is that policy formulation at these levels of responsibility is a potent activity that can be expected to determine the course of the governmental ship of state for the client consumers and their service providers.

But it is the third component of government actions in human service, the public mandate, that gives the whole matter of policy its complexity. Currently, the domain of public mandate is turbulent, some would say raging, with events entering the service system at a frantic pace and often without meaningful or planned order. These are the circumstances of event-compressed change described in Chapter 1 of this volume as generally afflicting service systems for mentally handicapped individuals. The effects of this turbulence on the public mandate are important. Those who wish to develop innovative policy will have to read the events that signal the condition of the public mandate if they are to produce acceptable and usable products.

The public mandate for a government agency is really the collective expectation of the aggregate of groups and individuals serviced by, affected by, involved with, interested in, or opinionated about the activity of the agency. Berle (1967) calls this aggregate the "field of responsibility," and once again his thoughts are instructive. He maintains that power holders or policy makers must accept a continuous and running dialogue with those making up their field of responsibility. A local school superintendent, for example, must respond to student needs, board of education fiscal constraints, parental opinion, political necessities, and local emotion about everything from curriculum to busing. It is apparent from the events of the past quarter century that public school systems are active, highly charged fields of responsibility. Over the past decade or so, the field of responsibility for agencies serving mentally handicapped persons also has become stormy. Perhaps as important, it has become substantially larger, now involving such participants as the federal bureaucracy and the judicial system to degrees unimaginable just 20 years ago. We argue that turbulence and expanding size make policy formulation across the field of responsibility a more complicated endeavor.

Berle (1967) cautions that when any substantial body of opinion is not involved in the dialogue, danger exists. A tension will emerge between the players in the organized dialogue and the nonparticipating fringes. If the latter groups are not accommodated, in time they will organize outside the field, seek admission, or overthrow the administrative seat with a revised mandate. The recent and accelerated rush of litigation in federal courts initiated by groups (such as advocacy organizations) at odds with the agency about mentally handicapped persons is sober testimony to tension and instability in the field of responsibility. Other forces, such as organized labor and varieties of consumer and special interest groups, are contributing to similar effects. In states experiencing these dynamics, the public mandate, never a fixed item anyway, can be expected to fluctuate broadly.

As indicated, not all of these inputs are coordinated, nor do they necessarily embrace similar objectives. It is no longer uncommon to find a state agency beset by one parent organization demanding a policy of total deinstitutionalization of larger facilities, another group of parents refusing to permit their handicapped offspring to be placed in community settings, and a squad of town residents attempting to "zone out" community group homes in their municipality. That same state agency may also have to respond to human rights organizations calling for increased staffing in the residential units of its facilities as well as the state's fiscal manager requesting a 5% budget cut proposal. The taxpayer, the legislator, the union employee, the advocate, the community, the legal aide attorney, the service professional, and countless other players all have their own notions of emphasis, which often conflict and render the public mandate unclear.

The implications of all this for policy formulation and innovation are considerable. Since policy sets directions and legitimizes emphasis, the multiple forces at variance in the field of responsibility create pressure for the policy makers. It is experienced as a "do it our way now" kind of pressure. Describing a similar situation, Merton (1957) quotes from Robert Louis Stevenson: "This is no cabinet science, in which things are tested to a scruple; we theorize with a pistol to our head. . ." (p. 224). Many agency commissioners and facility superintendents have stayed up nights in recent years cramming everything from infection control to the role of chaplaincy into formal policy statements.

Under pressure, governmental service systems have tended to move with more pragmatic, more conservative, more defensive, and clearly less creative approaches to policy formulation. For example, service systems involved in class action litigations will carefully construct policy to withstand the vigorous test of legal interpretation. When an agency or individual facility expends most of its conceptual energy defensively drafting protocols to anticipate every conceivable constitutional contingency in the restraint of assaultive clients, it may surrender confidence in its clinical process and have little resource left to plan long-term therapeutic environments and programs to habilitate the assaultive behavior itself. This is not an argument to take lightly the important issue of constitutional protections for clients. These are fundamental and must be guaranteed. Rather, the point suggested is that policy developed in defensive reaction to adversary legal proceedings may be limited in vision. Perhaps innovative policy must wait to follow resolutions for securing basic constitutional guarantees. Time will tell, but one does sense a forced postponement of innovative policy formulation in systems caught in the grip of litigation.

More generally, the unclear, often turbulent status of the mandate itself has implications for the planning or "planninglessness" of future policy. Toffler's (1970) observations are useful in this regard. He warns that too much social planning has been myopic, addressing only those futures close at hand. The deeper futures go largely unanticipated, and thus the impact, not of an innovation but of a chain of innovations over time, is unmanaged. There is good reason to apply these cautions to the human service systems we are discussing. The "my change now" mentality that characterizes the diverse elements in the field of responsibility is, to borrow a Toffler description, "blindly biased toward next Monday." What is needed are gradual and evaluated changes punctuating a flexible but consensus plan reaching into the next few decades. In some states, what seems to be happening instead is a fierce competition for outcomes in the near future. When observed up close, the effect, in terms of planning, seems random. Those experiencing such a system on a daily basis will tend to feel a sense of continual, but undirected change.

Our working definition of policy required that it guide or determine future direction. We believe that the turbulent and often noncoordinated condition of the public mandate will tend to combine with the growing size of the field of responsibility to press policy formulation toward an overemphasis on short future planning. The 4-year political cycle further contributes to this result. Thus, for example, in the early 1970s, deinstitutionalization and community alternative were fast becoming the received opinion in the field and agency heads rushed to write and implement policies of community placement. Many residents of larger institutions were summarily placed into the community in one way or another. For some, the transition went well and probably could have been executed years before. Many others, however, were placed into, but not prepared for, various communities. Teaching requisite skills for managing community logistics, social pressure, and the sudden absence of a fully supportive, dependent environment was not part of the placement policy. Not surprisingly, numerous able clients with clear community potential became placement casualties and were returned to the institution. One of the authors recalls a client casualty who learned to manipulate the placement policy itself: "When it gets too tough out there," he would say, "I know what kind of behavior will get me sent back to the institution for a while."

Nor were the various communities prepared for the relocated clients. Dealing with the potential for community resistance was another reflection of the limited reach of the placement policy. Many harsh zoning confrontations over the legality of group homes might have avoided if the community placement policy had included study and anticipation of community response and had incorporated meaningful education initiatives where that response was judged unfavorable.

Thus, we are led to conclude that those individuals who will practice policy innovation in public service systems for mentally handicapped people must learn to balance and blend the factors of concept, pragmatic result, and public mandate without being controlled by any one of them. They will have to understand the field of responsibility for their system to enable them to respond to its needs without being misled by its demands. Finally, a program of policy innovation that prefers an organized, longitudinal plan to random initiatives will require an obsessive regard to the client consumers, their needs, and reliable models for their future, near and distant.

Types of Policy

Viewing policy as all actions of government provides a more representative perspective about the guiding and directive forces in a public human service system. For it is clearly the case that products of the concept/pragmatic result/public mandate interaction can be found in more places than an agency's formal policy book. Policy determining activity occurs throughout a service system. Outcomes of this activity can be formal or informal, with implications for a whole facility or one small unit. It has been our observation that individuals effective in producing responsible change typically are knowledgeable about policy activity in all corners of the system. They tend also to understand how accessible each forum of policy making is to intervention.

A few types of policy activity are briefly described in the following subsection. The types sampled probably exist in most state systems, though the selection is neither exhaustive nor necessarily representative. The intent is to provide a sense of the mix of people and situations that contribute to policy development.

Political Policy. Government's overall direction at any given time is reflective of the political posture of the chief executive and the legislature. Political parties develop policies that give substance and visibility to their point of view on issues of public concern. When a given political party comes into power, the course of government may change, and the change more often than not is predictable if one is knowledgeable about the policy positions adopted by the party. Policy at this level is usually negotiated within the political party. Policy innovation, for the most part, is also confined to the membership, and policy changes are biased toward the survival of the party. Human service workers may bridle at this emphasis, but it is important that they come to terms with it. The political party is a primary process through which the collective voice of a public is presented. This political process and its policy posture must be understood, because the public service system to handicapped clients will, at the very least, be examined through the prism of political policy. When, for example, the policy of a state agency serving mentally handicapped persons calls for the normalization of living environments through massive renovations and staff increases, the party that came to power on high visibility pledges to constrain agency spending will scrutinize agency normalization plans against its own fiscal policy.

Political parties hold certain beliefs to which they ascribe value. They select from among alternatives a definite course or method of action that guides decisions. Political policy is probably the most controversial of the types reviewed here, because its formulation evolves from a highly subjective base within the political system. Its development is left mostly to a chosen few, who, as circumstances warrant, shape policy in their own image and to suit their own interests.

Innovators of program concepts and methods for mentally handicapped persons will have limited, if any, access or input to the political policy process in most state governments. But, as noted earlier, they can ill afford to disregard it. They and the agencies they serve must continually sensitize themselves to the political power structure and its policy emphasis. Thus, policy formulation at the cabinet or agency level in state government must be carefully tuned to the political order in power if it is to enjoy the support of that order. This is harshly pragmatic counsel, and it is not uncommon to see conflict arise between policy positions generated by client service needs and positions developed from political priorities. Experienced agency administrators and program innovators who successfully manage this type of confrontation typically are skilled in the delicate art of instructing the political base on the political merits of their agency's goals.

Operational Policy. Those actions that relate to the management of a state agency or department servicing mentally handicapped clients can be called operational policy. Operative policy statements reflect how an agency perceives its mission and responsibility to the public it serves. This type of policy is really an expression of the interpretation of the agency's mandate of law. However, its formulation is still affected by conditions at a given time, and able observers will read in operational policy the attitude and knowledge of administrative leadership.

Operational policy is an area of increased activity in recent years, having expanded in the wake of developing fields of responsibility and demand impacting upon agencies and their network of facilities. It is also a fertile area for innovation. In contrast to political policy, operational policy usually offers easier and more numerous points of access for individuals with ideas, concepts, or methods for changing service programs. However, each state agency or facility must be individually assessed for its accessibility, as there may be considerable variance across programs.

Even a partial listing of substantive issues currently being committed to policy at agency or facility levels in many states reveals the potential opportunities for creative change. The list that follows, taken from a Connecticut Department of Mental Retardation facility policy book, addresses matters and content that represent either (a) new ideologies in the field of responsibility, (b) unresolved questions due to incomplete technologies, (c) constitutionally required considerations, or (d) disputes among elements of the public mandate. All four of these concerns require fresh ideas and approaches to policy development. These samples from the Connecticut policy list also must be considered as a narrow range of subjects for operational policy when viewed against the requirements of the future.

Administrative Policy:
   1. Parameters of the interdisciplinary process
   2. Supervision of interdisciplinary teams
   3. Admission procedures

4. Transfer procedures
5. Discharge procedures
6. Management and program audits

Policies Concerning Human Rights of Clients:
1. Bill of rights for clients
2. Establishment of Human Rights Committee
3. Research with client subjects
4. Restrictions on clients' movement, communication, or privileges
5. Temporary emergency intervention for behavioral disruption
6. Use of restraints with clients
7. Privacy of clients
8. Access to client records
9. Alleged abuse or mistreatment
10. Behavior and casualty reports
11. Sexuality

Policies Relating to Programming and Habilitation:
1. Standards for individual program plans
2. Designated responsibilities for care, treatment, and education
3. Independent program review committee
4. Standards for evaluation and review of habilitative services
5. Standards for use of behavior modification methods

Policies Relating to Health Services:
1. Drug administration
2. Medical service reviews
3. Injury investigations
4. Infection control
5. Storage of medication
6. Preventive health services
7. Determining dietary needs of clients
8. Handling and storage of food

Personnel and Labor Relations Policies:
1. Affirmative action standards
2. Employment regulations
3. Employee problem resolution
4. Protection of complainants

Functional Policy.   Earlier we discussed the more subjective application of law that occurs at the service or line levels of government. The decisions, interpretations, and practices at these stations in a government agency form identifiable patterns that can be described as functional policy. This type of policy is nonformal, localized, and can be either clinical or managerial in nature. Often the patterns that emerge are time limited as well, guiding operations through a temporary set of circumstances or problems. For example, the adjustments that direct-care staff have to make in the daily routines of clients during an outbreak of influenza may set standards for operations under conditions of other infectious diseases above and beyond the procedures required by the facility's formal operational policy. Similarly, a facility's psychology department may develop a format for psychological assessment of clients that permits it to stay in compliance with the stringent time frames of ICF/MR regulations. The format, for as long as it is needed, is really an element of functional policy.

Patterns of practice that emerge as functional policy tend to be sharply sensitive to the daily rhythms and individual needs both of the client population and the staff groups that service it. Consequently, functional policy often reflects attitudes, beliefs, values, even competencies of the particular staff group observing the policy.

Functional policy also tends to emerge from the high degree of autonomy involved in the delivery of professional services. Several authors (e.g., Feldman, 1980; Gettings, 1977) have described the loyalty conflicts professionals experience between the standards of their respective disciplines and the needs and goals of management. The resolution of these differences often produces rules, procedures, divisions of labor, assigned responsibilities, or nonformal (but strict) standards, all of which amounts to functional policy. To illustrate, in facilities with "unit" or interdisciplinary service delivery systems, psychologists, social workers, nurses, and other professionals often find their assignments, service ratings, promotions, and supervision in the hands of unit directors not formally trained in their specific discipline. To protect the integrity of the discipline, some professional departments establish strong collateral systems of professional supervision so that the technical elements of a psychologist's work, for example, are evaluated and supervised by senior professional psychologists. The professional supervision may be smoothly coordinated with the unit director's authority or operate in some parallel condition. More than likely, one will not find its existence committed to formal agency policy. It exists as functional policy.

The problem with various pockets of functional policy that develop throughout a service system is keeping it all coordinated with the established mission of the agency. An administration's response to what it feels has become runaway patterns of practice often may be new issues of written directives or operational policy to stabilize the implementation of services. Faced with many functional approaches to resolving differences between units, one facility we know issued an operational policy on "Conflict Resolution" to avoid confusion and resolve impasse. Because functional policy is activated so close to the points of service, and because it reflects staff attitudes and competencies, problems with meaningfully attaching functional practices to the agency mission inevitably become matters of proficient staff development.

The innovative potential at the functional policy level is considerable. The localized nature of the intervention, as well as the autonomy that exists here, contributes to this. At the same time, innovators face risks because localized changes introduced without sufficient attention to the larger concerns of need, goal, and practice in the agency may court the objection of the agency. Alert to this problem, more experienced practitioners frequently involve middle and higher administration in functional changes from the start. This reduces unwanted surprises, broadens the range of ownership of the change, and increases the chance of extending the sweep of the innovation if that is desired.

Reactive Policy. There are aggregate groups within a government agency's field of responsibility but outside its span of control that monitor, evaluate, judge, and persuade the activity of the agency. Frequently these groups are consumer and advocacy organizations. Their agenda amounts to a line of policy that can be termed "reactive," and, in a real sense, it can have great influence on policy formulation within government.

In recent years, program innovators have made increasing use of consumer and advocacy organizations as a forum for discussion of change and as a process through which change can be effected. As a result, these organizations have become highly sophisticated in their oversight operations. For example, they have become a principal force in the legislative process influencing passage of new laws that redirect emphasis of expenditure and revise responsibilities of state agencies.

Reactive policy positions are usually developed to challenge the status quo. These positions, virtually by definition, are proposals for innovation. They may be submitted to dialogue with government policy makers, usually at an agency level, in an effort to reach collaborative changes. They may also be negotiated with other external organizations. At times, the reactive policy agenda may be too discordant with agency policy to permit any dialogue. The result is an adversary proceeding, often intense and often umpired by state and federal judges. For example, a few years ago, the United States Supreme Court had before it the litigated dispute of whether the Developmental Disabilities Act must apply to all state programs serving persons identified as developmentally disabled. Even before a decision was handed down, it was clear the High Court's resolution would have far-reaching impact on policy formulations concerning public programs. Whether the resolutions that derive from such contests yield better policy gathered about more enlighted missions remains a question in need of more returns and more systematic evaluation.

To pursue an earlier point, where policy positions of reactive groups compete with one another or with agency policy in a zero-sum game (i.e., required "winners" and "losers"), the showdown may disable public services to mentally handicapped persons more than any single alternative can correct. Innovators, with their portfolios of ideas, philosophies, system designs, and methods for improved service to mentally handicapped citizens, should find easy access to reactive policy groups in many states. Their ability to develop and urge non-zero-sum solutions focused on gradual movement through an organized series of innovations directed toward a prudently planned future may be pivotal in protecting client consumers from strident and costly contests over short future solutions.

Policy Development: Problems and Perspectives

Like any instrument or vehicle for change, policy has both distinct possibilities and limitations. An acute sense of what may be possible and what may not work rests on an equally acute working knowledge of the governmental system that will receive the change and absorb its impact. This requires a reliable grasp of the governmental process, the stations in the bureaucratic structure relevant to the change, the external field of responsibility, and the key players working in each of these areas. It further requires a diagnostic sensitivity to the needs and readiness of the government agency for which the innovative policy is being considered. Some needs may or may not be recognized by an agency. Even if acknowledged as a priority, a need may or may not be serviceable through policy. Even if policy is an appropriate vehicle, the agency and its extended field of responsibility may or may not be ready either to implement or to maintain the intervention.

These concerns are relevant to issues addressed elsewhere in this volume. It is the final subject of consideration for our discussion of policy in state public service systems.

Fitting Policies to Problems.   Certain matters are more difficult to commit to statements of policy and procedures than others. Formal policy often evolves slowly, going through various checkpoints of review and approval before signature by an agency commissioner or director. Revision of outdated policy must go through the same process and may be equally cumbersome. Thus, issues that develop and change more rapidly will be extremely difficult to control or standardize through policy vehicles that may quickly become obsolete.

Nor can all occasions of events in human service be fit into guidelines or policy procedures. Although policies for reporting and investigating alleged abuse of clients probably can be committed to an orderly and reliable procedure, standards for placing self-abusive or assaultive clients in temporary safety restraints may have to be as variable as the individual differences presented by the flailing, biting, or scratching clients they are designed to protect. In this instance, a more prudent approach to policy might emphasize specific supervision requirements.

Nowhere is the dilemma of "policy fit" more evident than in the various efforts to standardize, regulate, or establish guidelines for the use of behavior modification procedures with mentally handicapped clients. In the early 1970s, a wave of criticism of behavior modification methods precipitated calls to regulate and monitor their use (see Roos, 1974; Stolz, Wienckowski, & Brown, 1975; Thaw, Thorne, & Benjamin, 1978, for more complete discussion). A survey conducted during this period (Phelan & Carley, 1978) revealed that 31 of 41 states responding had implemented some form of written rules or regulations governing the use of behavior modification methods. The considerable variation in regulatory procedures across the states and agencies surveyed indicates the difficulty of committing this area to policy.

Sajwaj (1977) and Stolz (1977) have addressed this difficulty in some detail. Sajwaj points out that incorporating guidelines into administrative policy could, as behavioral technology evolves and develops, find practitioners in conflict with their administrative superiors or with the law. If policy revision is postponed, the accumulation of new developments in the field would gradually bring the standards into opposition with prevailing practice. Stolz argues that the intervention process varies so widely across settings and populations that it is virtually impossible to write guidelines or regulations that adequately cover all possibilities. She further suggests that when the practitioner is paid by someone other than the client, or when the client is not competent to make decisions about the treatment, or when the client's ability to give informed consent is reasonably questionable, then the problem of developing adequate guidelines becomes even more unmanageable.

There are difficulties for administrators as well. In one state, a policy that addressed behavior modification regulation was drafted by a group of service professionals. An extremely comprehensive set of operational directives was attached to the policy. These directives enumerated sets of techniques and precise staff competencies required to use each technique. It specified for each technique the staff who could qualify to write behavioral programs, the level of staff who supervise implementation, and the staff who could conduct the actual procedures. It also set down training curricula and criteria for each staff level. The entire effort was thorough and reflected the most current thinking in the field. However, when the facility directors of the state agency were presented with the final draft, they rejected it outright. For many of them, the proposed policy and its directives were administrative nightmares. They had neither the resources nor the time to comply with the sophisticated guidelines, yet their staffs needed to use behavior methods with clients. The directors easily were more willing to be responsible for the use of informal or "unregulated" behavioral methods than they were to endorse or commit to a formal policy whose standards they would violate immediately and for some time to come. They clearly understood their liability in both cases.

The policy drafters in this illustration had been overly ambitious. The system was not organized, resourced, or prepared to tolerate the policy as proposed. Innovators must adjust their ambitions to these tolerance levels to be successful with policy formulation. Where the tolerance is low, the policy intervention may have to be introduced in stages over an extended time frame to permit the system to adapt to it.

The questions of fit thus prompt the caution the policy may not be the answer for all matters of innovation nor an appropriate intervention for many problems of contemporary public human service agencies. Instead, the task with policy development seems to be one of acquiring competency in the selection of problems suitable for policy vehicles, coupled with maintaining a reliable image of the present and future situations upon which the policy is intended to act.

Dialogue with the Field of Responsibility. The policy drafters in the foregoing example erred in restricting their contact with principal administrators during the development of the policy. Without this exchange, they drifted beyond the bounds of what was acceptable to facility directors. Although subsequent revisions of their work corrected for this exclusion, which was more inadvertent than intentional, almost 3 years of work had been lost. Berle (1967) describes the recognition of the field of responsibility through a running dialogue with it as an essential task of governments, schools, and democratic institutions in general. He predicts tension between participants in the organized dialogue and elements in the field of responsibility not participating, but affected by outcomes of the dialogue.

These observations also apply to the formulation and innovation of policy which we have described as actions of government. Thus, in public systems serving mentally handicapped persons, it is advisable to court a wide range of participation in policy work. Facility directors should include staff groups in policy determinations that will affect them. The agency's central office, typically more remote from the line and professional work force, has to be especially sensitive in this regard. One way to do this is to devise systems that will enable a representative process of policy formulation where possible. In one state, for example, it is a matter of standing policy that representative groups of professionals, management, direct service providers, and other staff levels from each unit of the state agency's network meet on a regular basis to share ideas, develop procedures, and work on problems that affect the overall direction of the agency's mission.

Some key executive staff or facility chief administrators may find such intra-agency meetings for ''non-top echelon'' personnel threatening, particularly when policy development is the agenda item. Nevertheless, the risks of not decentralizing input to policy formulation may well exceed the threat a few will experience from doing it. For what is at stake for the field of responsibility (and especially for the staff groups in that field) is some ownership of the determinant events and actions that will govern their futures. Promoting such ownership may require some changes in concepts and practices of management (e.g., Greiner, 1972). Achieving it, however, may contribute to preserving the system itself from the erosion of disunity, fragmentation, and isolation among participants.

It is hard to measure the amount and nature of dialogue required for a specific group to experience an adequate sense of ownership or not to experience a sense of exclusion. Precise criteria are not readily apparent. Ambitious administrations will submit these questions to evaluative research (see Chapter 7). For this discussion, an emphasis, rather than a set of criteria, can be posed: The system's commitment to participation and the percolation of input upwards, *as perceived by the constituent groups of the field,* will define the character of the dialogue and the experience of ownership. If it is sufficient, then the system will withstand certain tests of that character.

A few examples of such tests can be illustrated. Many issues affecting an agency can be expected to generate a constituency of staff groups supporting an idea or proposal action, a constituency opposing it, and other groups on a continuum between them. Assume a resolution either for or against the proposal occurs. If the defining character of the agency is such that the involved groups experienced having had a fair chance to input their views, then, even if the decision does not go their way, it is likely they will accept it in a reasonable, nonadversary manner. In one agency, a strict policy concerning absenteeism and tardiness was issued from the top without input from affected groups. Even though the level of absenteeism and tardiness was excessive, the policy was met with an almost bitter resentment by staff groups. This reaction festered for months and seemed to affect interactions on other matters. Clearly, participation and ownership were inadequate in this case, and the price the incident exacted was high.

Another test of the defining character of the dialogue occurs because many actions and policies legitimately must be designed and delivered from the top down without consultation. Legal directives or issues with time frames that disallow extended dialogue are examples. If affected groups in the field of responsibility experience or feel a sense of inclusion in general, then these instances of direct top-down actions will be understood and accepted without objection or protest. If not, then such actions will be resisted, or at least mistrusted.

In sum, an adequate dialogue with an agency's field of responsibility is seen as requisite for a stable process of policy formulation and innovation. The fundamental requirement is that the process itself be perceived to be in the system, not over the system, by those affected by its outcome.

Structures and Expectations: Cautions.   The whole notion of broader based participation and decentralized input has in recent years been incorporated into accreditation standards and many service delivery systems (Crosby, 1976; Sluyter, 1976). Philosophically, this is the received opinion in many state agencies organized into unit systems practicing the interdisciplinary approach which is theoretically a decentralized, high participation methodology requiring collaborative decision making (Crosby, 1976). These structures appear to facilitate norms of open dialogue across the field of responsibility and generate expectations of decentralized control when it comes to planning policy. Yet, even in service systems sporting interdisciplinary labels, and more certainly in those with traditionally centralized organizations, fluid dialogue is limited and policy innovation may not occur except in response to external legal pressure. What's more, many involved parties (e.g., staff groups) may find this stationary condition acceptable.

What is at work here is a paradox common to many public human service systems for mentally handicapped persons, especially those which have recently adopted decentralized ideologies. Mintzberg's work (1979, 1981) on organizational structure is useful in characterizing the paradox. He has found that many organizations fall into identifiable configurations, each a combination of certain elements of structure (e.g., degree of centralized control, standardization of procedures, job specialization, etc.) and of situation (e.g., age, size, environment complexity and stability, degree of external control of the organization). According to Mintzberg, specific configurations are suitable for some tasks and ideologies, but not for others. For example, in organizations he calls machine bureaucracies, the emphasis is on standardization of work, usually through low-skilled, highly specialized jobs in a bureaucratic hierarchy heavy in middle line management and central control. This kind of organization functions best in a stable environment and is poor both at adapting to change and creating it. By contrast, a professional bureaucracy emphasizes the skills of highly trained professional staff and grants them significant autonomy through a decentralized, democratic structure such as one would find in many universities and medical centers. Decentralize even further into highly fluid project structures, which fuse experts from many specialties into limited-term "matrix" teams, each addressing highly focused problem areas, and we have Mintzberg's adhocracy. This configuration, low in formal bureaucracy, is very effective at conducting change in complex, dynamic environments.

The paradox in many large human service agencies occurs because many parts of a system may, in reality, function through centralized bureaucratic units despite official labels and commitments to the contrary. Mintzberg (1981) is quick to point out that many organizations mix different configurations and feel the pulls that underlie these structures throughout their systems. This is often true in facilities for mentally handicapped individuals where different units, similar in official function, actually vary widely in their faithfulness to broader based staff participation, open dialogue, or decentralized decision making.

The paradox is, at times, inadvertently occasioned by rigid performance control systems (e.g., some applications of the Title XIX ICF/MR formula) encased in open dialogue ideologies (e.g., interdisciplinary concepts). Performance control is often measured against compliance with state or federal standards and is judged by external monitors. At stake may be large sums of federal funds. As Mintzberg (1981) has found, this mix of ingredients tends to centralize and bureaucratize the operation, as managers responsible for compliance, in order to achieve the results required of them, tighten the screws of control. What emerges in function in such cases will contradict the ideology that "formally" describes the system.

A final expression of the paradox occurs in facilities experiencing extreme external pressure (e.g., class action litigations) or hostility in their environments (e.g., adversary citizen action groups). Mintzberg (1981) observes that organizations in these straits tend to suspend more democratic or complex procedures and revert to tight centralized control. Earlier in this chapter and throughout this book, the extraordinary pressures of accelerated change and demand that characterize many facilities servicing mentally handicapped clients are described. The defensive administrative control that often results from these conditions can be detected in increased use of snap directives, nonnegotiable administrative decisions, and a conspicuous absence of creative change. All of this takes place as the facility continues its philosophical allegiance to decentralized, open-dialogued, interdisciplinary, and participatory principles.

The implication of these paradoxical operations is significant for questions of policy innovation. Where staff have expectancies for an open and decentralized organization of the work place but experience its contradiction on a daily basis, the resulting dissonance may well be demoralizing for them. This will be particularly true for professional staff and especially where the centralized administrative control is perceived to intrude upon their professional ethics and sense of autonomy. An administrator who wants some service to all clients in a unit may reach that point with the unit psychologist for whom some service to all clients is a compromise from ethically proper service to any individual client.

Unchecked, the dissonance of unmet expectancies will not only demoralize staff groups, but may cause them to mistrust the organization itself. A confused and mistrusting staff system cannot constructively innovate policy actions because the fundamental elements of policy will have been violated. Earlier we described policy as an interaction of three elements: (a) a philosophy or concept; (b) an estimate of pragmatic result; and (c) a public mandate, which was defined as the collective expectation of the aggregate of groups and individuals affected by the organization. Where the paradox of misfitted structure and expectancy exists, philosophies and concepts will tend to be viewed as counterfeit by many—labels rather than commitments. Estimates of outcome will become unreliable, and the collective expectation of the aggregate field of responsibility, at least within the organization, is unlikely to remain cohesive enough to provide direction.

These conditions threaten the possibility of a stable process of policy development, especially for operational and functional policy products. Only power policy, developed narrowly, implemented coercively, and maintained through vigilance, instead of through acceptance, can be expected to survive. And we suggest that such a solution necessarily can not respond to the needs of the clients nor the requirements of their service providers. In time, the highly active and visible constituency of citizen action groups that surround most public human service systems come to notice this.

Not all agencies and not all parts of any one agency will manifest the structure-expectancy paradox at an extreme. More probably, dissonance between ideology and operating structure will occur at some stage of development. The task thus reduces to evaluating both the extent of the dissonance and the direction of its movement. Once this is accomplished, the next step is to secure a frank recognition by all involved groups that the dissonant condition exists and is affecting the way individuals feel about their work unit or their organization. This shared recognition is not easy to achieve in many human service organizations (e.g., Argyris, 1982), because contradictions between accepted theory and actual practice are embarrassing to administrators and provide ammunition to their critics. Nevertheless, open recognition of dissonance is an act of sensible administration, because it often lessens the tension and frustration experienced by those caught in the contradiction. It can also prompt a commitment to correct the condition, even if this must be done in stages over an extended time frame. The discussion of relationship building in Chapter 3 of this volume is germane to the whole process of resolving and coping with structure-expectancy dissonance, and the reader is referred there for more information.

SUMMARY THOUGHTS

Thomas Jefferson maintained that ". . . the care of human life . . . is the first and only legitimate object of good government. . . ." The thought itself is righteously invincible. The ordeal is with method. For those of our citizens who suffer mental handicap, government remains the principal agent of care. We have addressed some of the dimensions of its discourse with that responsibility. For those who would contribute to or improve the exercise of the responsibility, there is reason to be encouraged but a need to understand how government behaves in its role as human service provider. Our concern has been with government's task of translating laws, rights, and principles into services, and with its response to innovation. Mindful of the complexity of the subject, we have recommended perspectives through which to diagnose the process and action of government and a few approaches for intervention. We hope the reader has sensed our regard for the reach of possibility in government service and our preference for thoughtful encounters with the limitations of government systems.

REFERENCES

Argyris, C. (1982).   *Reasoning, action, and learning.* San Francisco: Jossey-Bass.
Barton, W. E. (1977).   Vanishing Americans revisited. *Administration in Mental Health, 4,* 76–77.
Baumeister, A. A. (1981).   The right to habilitation: What does it mean? *Analysis and Intervention in Developmental Disabilities, 1,* 61–74.
Berle, A. A. (1967).   *Power.* New York: Harcourt, Brace & World.

Chambers, D. (1976). The principle of the least restrictive alternative: The constitutional issues. In M. Kindred, J. Cohen, D. Penrod, & T. Shaffer (Eds.), *The mentally retarded citizen and the law* (pp. 486–499). New York: Free Press.

Civil commitment. (1977). *Mental Disability Law Reporter, 2,* 77–126.

Crosby, K. G. (1976). Essentials of active programming. *Mental Retardation, 14,* 3–9.

Deutsch, A. (1949). *The mentally ill in America.* New York: Columbia University Press.

Dye, T. R. (1976). *Policy analysis.* University, AL: University of Alabama Press.

Ellis, N. R., Balla, D., Estes, O., Warren, S. A., Meyers, C. E., Hollis, J., Isaacson, R. L., Palk, B. E., & Siegel, P. S. (1981). Common sense in the habilitation of mentally retarded persons: A reply to Menolascino and McGee. *Mental Retardation, 19,* 221–225.

Feldman, S. (1973). Introduction. In S. Feldman (Ed.), *The administration of mental health services* (pp. xi–xxiv). Springfield, IL: Charles C. Thomas.

Feldman, S. (1975). Administration in mental health: Issues, problems, and prospects. *Bulletin of the Pan American Health Organization, 9*(3).

Feldman S. (1980). The middle management muddle. *Administration in Mental Health, 8,* 3–11.

Feldman, S., & Cahill, P. S. (1975). Educating the mental health administrator: A report. *Administration in Mental Health, 3,* 88–89.

Gettings, R. M. (1977). Administration: Public agencies. In J. Wortis (Ed.), *Mental retardation and developmental disabilities: An annual review* (Vol. 9) (pp. 234–248). New York: Brunner/Mazel.

Greiner, L. E. (1972, July–August). Evolution and revolution as organizations grow. *Harvard Business Review,* pp. 37–46.

Harvard Law Review. (1977). Mental health litigation: Implementing institutional reform. *Mental Disability Law Reporter, 2,* 220–233.

Hinkle, A., & Burns, M. (1978). The clinician-executive: A review. *Administration in Mental Health, 6,* 3–21.

Kaufman, H. (1971). *The limits of organizational change.* University, AL: University of Alabama Press.

Kissinger, H. (1979). *White house years.* Boston: Little, Brown.

MacMillan, D. L., & Borthwick, S. (1980). The new educable mentally retarded population: Can they be mainstreamed? *Mental Retardation, 18,* 155–158.

Maloof, B. A. (1975). Peculiarities of human service bureaucracies. *Administration in Mental Health, 3,* 21–26.

Menolascino, F. J., & McGee, J. J. (1981). The new institutions: Last ditch arguments. *Mental Retardation, 19,* 215–220.

Merton, R. K. (1957). *Social theory and social structure* (rev. ed.). New York: Free Press.

Mesibov, G. R. (1976). Alternatives to the principle of normalization. *Mental Retardation, 14,* 30–32.

Mintzberg, H. (1979). *The structuring of organizations.* Englewood Cliffs, NJ: Prentice-Hall.

Mintzberg, H. (1981, January–February). Organization design: Fashion or fit? *Harvard Business Review,* pp. 103–116.

Phelan, C., & Carley, J. (1978). *Administrative regulations of behavior therapy/modification: A national survey* (Research Report No. 27). Capital Station, Austin, TX: Texas Department of Mental Health and Mental Retardation.

Report of the National Task Force on Mental Health/Mental Retardation Administration. (1979). *Administration in Mental Health, 6,* 269–322.

Roos, P. (1974). Human rights and behavior modification. *Mental Retardation, 12,* 3–6.

Roos, E. C. (1980). Developing public policy for persons with disabilities: The case for a categorical approach. *Mental Retardation, 18,* 159–163.

Sarason, S. B., & Doris, J. (1979). *Educational handicap, public policy, and social history.* New York: Free Press.

Sajwaj, T. (1977). Issues and implications of establishing guidelines for the use of behavioral techniques. *Journal of Applied Behavior Analysis, 10,* 531–540.

Schalter, J. (1978). Removing the hidden barriers to accessibility. *Amicus, 3*(4), 43–48.

Scheerenberger, R. C. (1982). Public residential services, 1981: Status and trends. *Mental Retardation, 20,* 210–215.

Schulberg, H. C., & Baker, F. (Eds.). (1979). *Program evaluation in the health fields* (Vol. 2). New York: Human Sciences Press.

Shriver, E. (1976). Foreword. In M. Kindred, J. Cohen, D. Penrod, T. Shaffer (Eds.), *The mentally retarded citizen and the law* (pp. xix–xxi) New York: Free Press.

Sluyter, G. V. (1976). The unit management system: Anatomy of structural change. *Mental Retardation, 14,* 14–16.

Stolz, S. B. (1977). Why no guidelines for behavior modification? *Journal of Applied Behavior Analysis, 10,* 541–547.

Stolz, S. B., Wienckowski, L. A., & Brown, B. S. (1975). Behavior modification: A perspective on critical issues. *American Psychologist, 30,* 1027–1048.

Thaw, J., Thorne, G. D., & Benjamin, E. (1978). Human rights, behavior modification, and the development of state policy. *Administration in Mental Health, 5,* 112–119.

Toffler, A. (1970). *Future shock.* New York: Random House.

Throne, J. M. (1975). The normalization principle: Right ends, wrong means. *Mental Retardation, 13,* 23–25.

U.S. Department of Health, Education, and Welfare. (1974). Regulations for intermediate care facility services. *Federal Register, 39,* 2220–2235.

Wolfensberger, W. (1969). The origin and nature of our institutional models. In R. B. Kugel & W. Wolfensberger (Eds.), *Changing patterns in residential services for the mentally retarded* (pp. 59–171). Washington: President's Committee on Mental Retardation.

Wolfensberger, W. (1972). *The principle of normalization in human services.* Toronto: National Institute on Mental Retardation.

Yolles, S. F. (1975). The importance of administration in mental health. *Administration in Mental Health, 3,* 43–50.

7

Human Aspects of Evaluation in Institutional Settings: Political, Methodological, and Social Trade-Offs

George J. Allen, Ph.D.
Laurie Heatherington, Ph.D.
Michael Lah, Ph.D.

Institutions servicing mentally handicapped clients are struggling with forces of revision and renewal that arrive haphazardly and are often beyond their resources to process. This circumstance is described in Chapter 1 of this volume and further developed in other chapters. This chapter centers on how to extract and evaluate meaningful questions about change in the turbulent setting of the contemporary institution. Although the evaluation process may seem to be a logical outgrowth of the recent emphasis on accountability, such is not the case. *Accountability* has become a fashionable term that describes a variety of procedures in the human service area. *Evaluation* remains a largely foreign process that imposes procedures and requirements that are generally seen by institutional personnel as confusing and unnecessary.

Unlike other contributors to this book, we are in positions external to habilitative institutional systems. Our perspective is that of outsiders hired to evaluate specific change programs within institutional settings. From this perspective, we analyze major issues surrounding evaluation in institutional settings. Following a discussion of three major perspectives from which to view institutions, we discuss issues pertaining to entering bureaucratic systems, conceptual and methodological issues of evaluation, and issues pertaining to implementation and utilization of program evaluations. Throughout our discussion we emphasize the difficulties and options that confront evaluators, and we suggest how these may be managed. Our own (sometimes painful) experiences as evaluators of a large-scale innovative staff training program within a facility for mentally handicapped persons illustrates these issues. Our goal is to provide insights and recommendations that will enhance the endeavors of those who design, administer, and evaluate innovative change programs.

CONTEXTUAL ASPECTS OF EVALUATION

Human service facilities are complex entities that may be viewed from three different perspectives—sociological, psychological, and ecological. Each vantage point originated from a unique discipline of knowledge, and each provides a useful but limited understanding of how such social systems operate. A multidimensional perspective may be gained by drawing conceptions from all three viewpoints. Our collective understanding of institutional functioning originated with a sociological focus. Within this perspective, (e.g., Blau, 1956; Goffman, 1961), emphasis was on delineating the structural and functional aspects of bureaucracies. The operation of institutions was conceptualized in terms of forces and vectors of power, authority, and status.

From the sociological perspective, five elements characterize the residential facility as a complex bureaucracy. First, there exists a *specialization of function.* Each individual staff member is expected to perform very specific tasks within an orderly routine. In a modern facility, no one person is totally responsible for the well being of any particular resident. Rather, it is assumed that if every staff member does his or her job, be it laundry, resident supervision, dietetics, or administrative paperwork, the needs of the residents as a group will be adequately provided for.

Second, a *hierarchy of authority* exists such that every person is, in theory, accountable to an immediate supervisor. In most residential facilities, staff members who work most closely with residents are at the lowest level of the hierarchy. Their activities are evaluated by others whose primary task is supervision rather than interacting with residents. These supervisors, in turn, are accountable to administrators on various levels, who have the task of ensuring that the entire bureaucracy functions smoothly. Administrators are concerned with developing work schedules, negotiating with unions, lobbying for funds from state legislators, writing grants for federal aid, and planning long-term goals of the institution. Thus, the higher in the hierarchy people are, the less personal contact they have with resident clients. It is not uncommon for a superintendent to have only a superficial familiarity with what actually takes place on any unit, even though in theory the administrator is responsible for everything that occurs in the entire facility.

A third characteristic of a bureaucracy is the existence of *numerous rules and regulations.* Rules represent generalizations that describe how to deal with potentially problematic situations. New rules are constantly being made to cover ambiguous situations, and probably no one person in any facility is familiar with all existing rules. Because typically so many rules exist, the same ones are not uniformly applied across situations. Instead, specific rules are often used to justify actions that are in the best immediate interests of various staff members within the organization.

The fourth characteristic of a bureaucracy is *impersonality*. Tradition and routine tend to be the hallmarks of well-functioning bureaucracies. People are treated as "cases" about which decisions are made on the basis of general rules. Primary emphasis is given to fitting clientele smoothly into the ongoing operation of the system. Despite occasional public protests to the contrary, traditional residential facilities generally operate on a cost-per-unit philosophy. This system has as its goal the "processing" of the greatest number of people with the least overhead. Both private industry and public health care facilities operate on this basis. Competitive pressures of a free enterprise market, however, force industries to achieve greater efficiency without substantially lowering the quality of product. Unfortunately, because health care systems have not been subject to competitive pressure, reasons for providing better services have been limited to self-initiative with minimal resources. Recent trends of citizen advocacy, mandated accountability, and judicial intervention have clearly increased at least the pressure to improve. Nonetheless, attending to the wide variety of personal needs that clients and staff have in a human service bureaucracy violates the cost-per-unit principle and would make the day-to-day operation of the facility much less efficient.

The final characteristic of a bureaucracy could be termed *resilient sluggishness*. Notwithstanding the rapid rates of change they are experiencing, there is a curious sameness to many total treatment institutions. For example, they possess relatively closed and impermeable boundaries that separate them from the larger community (Reppucci & Saunders, 1983). Similarly, despite alarmingly rapid turnover of staff at such facilities, the roles and functions of participants remain unaltered. Like a great blob of premolded plastic, the bureaucracy may be temporarily twisted out of shape by internal or external forces, but returns to roughly its original shape when the pressure has subsided. Those who work within the blob soon learn that rewards come to the patient plodders and not to the eager, the talented, the most hard working, or the upstart hotshot. The blob can be prodded to move in specified directions through the application of powerful social forces (e.g., federal mandates, litigation, etc.), but its progress is slow and its basic form remains stable.

The sociological perspective enables evaluators to analyze the formal properties of institutions. Emerging insights about power and authority often provide valuable guidelines for planning change interventions. Institutions, however, are run by people whose behavior transcends analysis of role functions, status, and other structural components. This viewpoint does not contain the constructs necessary to conceptualize important psychological ramifications of institutional life.

The psychological perspective contains many of the frameworks found in sociological perspectives, but gives them a uniquely different vantage point. The importance of individuals' perceptions and awareness of existing conditions is emphasized over their structural values as determined from the vantage point of an external observer. The psychological determination of status, for example, involves much more than placing one in a particular occupational role (e.g., unit supervisor). Rather, it is judged from many subjective evaluations people make about the abilities of one another to persuade, support, and influence.

Within this framework, change is viewed as having important psychic consequences. The rapid pace of change mandated for many public residential facilities can jeopardize the self-esteem of innovators, undermine the power of administrators, and threaten the perceived ability of line staff. Psychological influences point to five major impediments that constrain almost every level of staff.

Perceived staff overload is the first problem. Feelings of being overwhelmed develop as ever more tasks are imposed upon staff, who must discharge them without corresponding increases in resources or adaptive alterations in the service delivery system. Other factors tend to exacerbate this problem. For example, even when imbued with modern habilitative philosophy, most large human service facilities have deeply entrenched traditional bureaucratic structures that are unsuited to managing rapid turnover of clientele.

In addition, many institutions are currently under external scrutiny by courts, monitors, funding agency inspectors, and citizen action groups. Such scrutiny tends to be adversarial in practice, thus making it risky for institution officials to acknowledge, let alone address, problems developing from excessive rates of change. Within this context, the legitimacy of the difficulty is immaterial; acknowledging its existence is frequently construed as an admission of administrative incompetence by these external parties. Thus, administrators' survival often rests upon their ability to respond to multiple demands for reform while simultaneously resisting having to acknowledge the existence or seriousness of the presenting problems that initially created the organizational stress. This paradoxical condition translates downward into multiple, often conflicting tasks and pressures for middle management, professionals, and line staff.

One illustration of staff overload is provided by recently developed state policy in Connecticut that required all facilities serving mentally handicapped clients to comply with a set of operational guidelines for standardized behavior modification interventions. There are 115 pages of standards covering 12 major areas of intervention. Over 150 items of information (e.g., definitions, procedural requirements, etc.) cover the use of time-out interventions alone. Such a policy of innovation, which is cumbersome by itself, sets in motion other events that further multiply overload across staff. Since many employees are not competent with regard to the policy's many administrative and technical aspects, new training programs must be instituted. Under the new policy, many of the behavioral procedures require various human rights and administrative review. This calls for the establishment of new committees and new, often additional, assignments for existing staff.

Such events create a "multiplier effect," each contributing to the acceleration of the rate of change. This process presents increasingly serious problems for the adaptation of staff members as individuals and as groups. Institutional overload creates serious dilemmas for the evaluator. The very process of evaluating, almost by definition, adds an additional burden to an already overstrained system: more paperwork, more meetings, more people asking questions or observing behavior, and more disruption of routine. Because overload creates emotional as well as intellectual turmoil, any presentation of the importance of the evaluation must address both levels if it is to gain acceptance.

Conflict and confusion about institutional priorities create a second obstacle. Staff members at various levels possess stable attitudinal differences about the value of specific occupational tasks (Schmidmeyr & Weld, 1971), and the acceptability of specific tasks is related to their "visibility." Ullmann (1967) has noted that many staff activities that are directly related to client rehabilitation provide less clearly documentable justification for how staff members spend their working time. Those who engage in highly visible activities (e.g., report writing, housekeeping, socializing with superiors, etc.), however, are more likely to be rewarded by superiors. The resentment and disillusionment experienced at discovering this hidden limitation on rehabilitation efforts is a major contributor to staff turnover and burnout (Allen, Chinsky, & Veit, 1974).

In addition to finding conflicts between priorities, the evaluator will encounter confusion over which needs must be met at any particular time. Staff members at practically every level fail to recognize the importance of the tasks performed by remote personnel and view the demands placed on others unsympathetically. It is not unusual to find large segments of staff to be completely unaware of what roles and functions other employees have. Given the chaos and confusion that can exist within such an environment, evaluators must realize that their role will be fuzzily perceived (but likely to be viewed as self-serving). In addition, their functions may well be seen as having little relevance for either job security or the day-to-day demands imposed on staff.

Diffusion of responsibility is a third impediment that is frequently encountered. From the sociological perspective, traditional bureaucracies were viewed as having clearly defined hierarchies of authority and responsibility. Even within strictly autocratic hierarchies, however, it was often difficult to pinpoint who had responsibility for what. In part, this is due to increasing specialization of function that occurs as bureaucracies mature. As service demands on a facility multiply, individual staff find themselves being held responsible for participating in a greater array of activities, which grow increasingly remote from the primary goals of the institution.

Many facilities have converted to interdisciplinary team forms of service delivery, which rely heavily on consensus and shared power in decision making and program development. These more participatory formats have essentially "layered over" the traditional hierarchies of authority. Again, a paradox is encountered in that many staff are assigned functions (often in an autocratic manner) in interdisciplinary groups without adequate preparation. Thus, they are likely to perpetuate traditional bureaucratic behavior within the innovative structure. In addition, parallel structures are often created, so that direct-care staff are subordinated to multiple supervisors within traditional care units and interdisciplinary teams. Since superiors in these differing positions often have antagonistic goals, this condition further blurs lines of responsibility and creates trust and loyalty dilemmas for many staff groupings.

Diffusion of responsibility is often reflected in breakdowns in channels of communication. Meetings are scheduled, but no one shows up because an unspecified "someone" forgot to inform those who were supposed to attend. Attempts to pinpoint responsibility (especially for blameworthy events) are passively stonewalled or simply shrugged off. A more important consequence of this condition is that it becomes difficult to sort out staff busywork from essential activities. At the beginning of our evaluation, we found a number of program participants who were invariably too busy to talk with us. Our role as suspiciously regarded guests made it difficult for us to question the justifications that were sometimes offered (e.g., "Can't talk now. I'm expecting a fight to develop between these two guys.") for what appeared to be unimportant busywork.

Negative scanning is a fourth impediment. For most direct-care staff, the preferred level of functioning within a residential institution is stable, unvarying routine. Crises and emergencies tend to increase the work load of those who must resolve them, and can create bad public relations. Often, supervisory reaction to emergencies is to terminate the situation as quickly as possible and assign responsibility. The response may be punitive and involve attempts to reprimand or punish the culprits deemed responsible. In contrast, positive feedback from supervisors typically is not provided when routine is running smoothly because this is considered normative functioning. The fact that most feedback loops within residential facilities are negative breeds passive resistance to innovation on the part of the staff. Negative scanning also promotes suspiciousness about the motives of others, so that those who attempt innovations will often be viewed as doing so for self-serving reasons. Without there being strong reason to act otherwise, negative scanning by staff at all levels is clearly adaptive behavior.

Given the existence of negative scanning, evaluators enter the bureaucratic system with two strikes against them. Because they are usually recruited from outside the institution, they are justifiably viewed as not necessarily having the best interests of the staff at heart. They are also associated with some innovative change that threatens cherished routine and requires extra work from the staff. Evaluators are often forced to run a gauntlet of trust tests that are sometimes incredibly subtle. Failing even one of these tests can create meaty gossip for the institutional grapevine and invariably evokes resistance to the evaluative effort.

The final impediment is *fear of systematic evaluation*. In health care bureaucracies, traditional routine provides protection against most negative scanning for culprits. This protection receives able assistance from the general diffusion of responsibility. As noted earlier, the usual accountability system tends to be nonspecific and fuzzy. This ambiguity serves the purposes of maintaining the status quo and providing workers with a sense of comfort. Evaluations usually contain some formal system of assessing staff performance that is based on criteria that are unknown to the participants (Neigher & Schulberg, 1982). Implementation of criterion-based accountability systems has proven to be very threatening to participating staff. Employees are often so accustomed to working under a system of negative scanning that they almost automatically assume that any evaluative information will be used against them. Formal evaluation for the assessment and improvement of service frequently is a process alien both to their experience and to the history of the facility.

One investigation illustrates how staff cope with evaluative apprehensions. Spencer, Corcoran, Allen, Chinsky, & Veit (1974) collected observations by means of a videotape camera that was prominently displayed in one section of a client dormitory. Live observers made behavior ratings in this and two adjacent settings for a 2-week baseline period while the camera was present, and for 2 weeks after the camera's removal. They found that direct-care staff who worked within camera range engaged in significantly more formal training and socialization activities with mentally retarded children, while routine housekeeping chores and negative affect toward the residents dropped sharply. These changes, however, did not generalize into adjacent settings, nor were they maintained once the camera was removed. Interestingly, the source of change appeared to be a rumor that the videotape was being monitored by the superintendent, who was known to be a staunch advocate of client training. Thus, the staff appeared to be playing it safe, but the behavior they exhibited was atypical and transient.

The third organizing perspective for viewing health care facilities has an *ecological* focus. This perspective expands the utility of many elements found in the sociological and psychological viewpoints by conceptualizing a bureaucracy as an *ecosystem,* or a complex network of self-regulating feedback loops. Although a full explication of this epistemology is beyond the scope of this chapter, (see Keeney, 1983; Palazzoli, Cecchin, Prata, & Boscolo, 1978 for representative positions), emphasis is given to transactional relationships as a basic element of analysis.

The bureaucracy is viewed as an ever-changing organization of patterns of action and reaction regulated by both positive and negative feedback loops. When applied to institutional functioning, an ecological perspective yields numerous contradictions and paradoxes. Evaluators must be prepared to encounter (a) an overloaded system where the staff at every level is overworked and too busy, yet not seemingly busy enough from the viewpoint of employees in other positions; (b) staff who feel accountable to too many others who have vague functions and who exist under an ambiguous accountability system that diffuses responsibility; (c) staff conflicted about balancing institutional, supervisors,' clients,' and their own priorities, while clinging fiercely to traditional routine; and (d) employees burdened by rules and regulations, yet directed to act spontaneously and show initiative.

The ecological perspective can help sensitize evaluators to the fact that their efforts will create perturbations throughout the system. As outsiders, evaluators never can move within the institutional system like inside staff members. Evaluative activities thus will reverberate throughout the institution in unpredictable ways. Evaluators can expect to be viewed as "threatening," to be put through many *trust tests,* and to experience "passive hostility." They also have the resources to "empower" staff members. These are transactional patterns that will vary incredibly in the way they unfold. Adopting an ecological stance can heighten evaluators' awareness that their efforts involve processes that will transact with other complex processes in ways that will transform both sets of operations (Repucci & Saunders, 1983). Ensuring the success of our evaluation meant dealing with diverse groups, attempting to increase their knowledge of evaluative processes, and teaching them over time that we were concerned, competent, and trustworthy.

ISSUES PERTAINING TO ENTERING THE BUREAUCRATIC ECOSYSTEM

Our multifaceted analysis suggests that the typical institutional ecosystem contains many pitfalls for the unwary. Evaluation disrupts the social system and requires a balancing of conflicting priorities along with the development of trust among a large number of people. In one sense, we were fortunate in that the senior evaluator possessed a fairly thorough understanding of the host institution as a result of his participation in a research project that had been conducted several years earlier (Allen, Chinsky, & Veit, 1980). This project resulted in the development of an Interaction Recording System (Veit, Allen, & Chinsky, 1976) that provided reliable observations of encounters between retarded residents and direct-care staff.

The purposes of these earlier investigations were to gather systematic data about such encounters and to ascertain the major determinants of their frequency and quality. The descriptive pattern that emerged suggested a training environment where an overworked and undermanned staff simply did not have enough resources to meet the habilitative needs of severely and profoundly retarded residents. A large majority of staff-initiated interactions (68%) occurred in the contexts of housekeeping, directing movement of groups of clients, and providing for their physical care. Considerably less interaction was noted within socialization and play contexts (23%), with formal training activities accounting for only 9% of the interactions.

Even more intriguing was the discovery of several systematic influences on the distribution of various interactions. Because of a large average ratio of residents to staff (12:1), only 4% of the waking day of the average resident was spent interacting with a direct-care provider. Certain of the 37 clients, however, received a disproportionate amount of attention, while others got almost none. In a subsequent investigation (Dailey, Allen, Chinsky, & Veit, 1974), this uneven distribution was found to be reliably related to staff members' ratings of the physical attractiveness of the clients. The least attractive quartile received only 10% of the interactions that conveyed positive affect from the staff, and only 9% of the total that occurred in a social-play context.

Another investigation (Harris, Veit, Allen, & Chinsky, 1974), indicated that direct-care personnel engaged in significantly less ward routine (housekeeping) activities, but provided more formal training and social-play activities, and exhibited more positive affect when a single staff member was responsible for overseeing fewer residents. Differences in staff-to-client ratios, however, did not change the quality of interaction when two or more staff members were present. This discrepancy was interpreted as an example of diffusion of responsibility in that simply adding more staff did not automatically guarantee a higher quality of interpersonal contact for clients.

An action-oriented consequence of this research project was to provide administrators of the institution with a detailed report of our findings along with 17 specific recommendations for training and placement of staff. For example, we urged that inservice training for new employees be expanded to include information about the destructive bias created by the physical blemishes of particular clients. We also suggested that individual staff members be assigned more formal responsibility for training and socializing with specific clients, and argued for the development of mini-wards within the large dormitory.

Our report appeared at a time when the facility was beginning to implement numerous and sweeping innovations. The state legislature provided funds for the construction of more homelike cottage environments to replace some of the larger wards. Many of the most skilled residents were being discharged to community living arrangements. The Chief of Psychological Services at the facility began a series of training programs for supervisory personnel and developed an organization of student volunteers who received both classroom and practicum training in techniques to improve the self-help and other skills of the more seriously impaired clients.

In the intervening time, staff training became an even greater administrative priority preparatory to transforming areas of the institution into Intermediate Care Facilities that would be eligible for federal funding under Title XIX of the U.S. Social Security Act. The regulations of this legislation mandated, among other items, creation of interdisciplinary planning teams, development of highly structured living environments, maintenance of low client-to-staff ratios, and specification of individualized training programs for each client. Somewhat later in this time frame, litigation was brought against the facility's superintendent in an effort to guarantee that the most impaired clients would receive habilitation in the least restrictive environment, especially in community settings. It was within this volatile and tradition-shattering setting that we were asked to evaluate a large-scale training program for direct-care staff.

The context of our evaluation was several units housing 25 to 30 severely and profoundly retarded men. The architecture of the units reflected the historical trend of custodial care that characterized treatment of mentally retarded individuals until recently. Each living unit was self-contained and was divided into a sleeping area with beds arranged in a series of rows, a bathroom containing toilets without partitioned stalls, a large, open day room, and a fenced in outdoor play area off the dayroom. A central nursing station was located between the three inside rooms, thus enabling a single staff member to observe the activities of all residents in the unit.

The program was funded through a federal Title XX grant administered through a nearby university and was built upon the training foundation that had been established within the psychology department of the institution. The project was quite an ambitious one, encompassing both in-house and extramural components. The goal of the program was to train direct-care staff and supervisory personnel in applied behavior analytic and behavior modification strategies so that these skills could be employed to teach severely and profoundly retarded clients basic self-help skills (e.g., toileting, dressing, feeding, etc.).

The primary training vehicle was a series of videotaped presentations developed by the grant staff. The videotapes contained practical information about how to analyze and systematically alter behavior. Topics included how to go about selecting a changeworthy behavior; methods of measuring and graphing behavior; reinforcement, shaping, and fading strategies useful for promoting development of adaptive self-care skills; and procedures for dealing with maladaptive behavior. Each tape was designed to facilitate audience involvement by incorporating task-relevant exercises that assessed participants' knowledge of lecture material. These presentations were bounded by tapes that provided more general information (history of treatments for mentally retarded people, ethics and accountability, etc.) and were provided in the context of a series of 2-hour workshops conducted by one of the grant staff. All tapes were produced with the multiplier idea that they could be utilized at other facilities throughout the state and region.

A second central training component involved creation of a pool of proctors who would work individually with each participating trainee. These proctors also were drawn initially from the grant staff but later were selected from the ranks of trainees who had successfully completed the program. Proctors sought to develop mutually rewarding interpersonal relationships with the trainees and had the tasks of helping the latter with out-of-class training assignments, facilitating their understanding of videotape presentations, and consulting on the real-life behavior development projects each trainee conducted with a client.

These projects constituted a third integral training component. Each staff trainee was assigned to develop and implement an habilitative program for a single retarded client. The scope of the behavior change effort was individualized according to the needs and abilities of both trainer and client. Besides normalizing the lives of clients, *in vivo* training was designed to enhance the meaningfulness of videotaped presentations by enlisting the active involvement of the trainee. Proctors met with their trainees to help the latter create a practical application of whatever content had been presented previously. For example, trainees worked in conjunction with their proctors to select a changeworthy behavior in accord with specific guidelines to which they had been exposed during a prior videotape workshop. Staff would subsequently learn several alternative methods of charting behavior; they were then expected to select an appropriate one for the target behavior they had selected.

In addition to these three central components, the grant addressed a number of other objectives. An attempt was made to create a smooth interface between the unit staff and college student volunteers who worked in the unit teaching clients toileting, showering, and washing skills. A curriculum library containing timely and relevant reading material on client training procedures was also developed and implemented. A series of miniworkshops for various specialists (e.g., speech and hearing personnel) and on specialized topics (e.g., staff burnout) was conducted. Finally a maintenance system was developed to sustain improvements in client programs and to problem solve areas of difficulty.

We were hired under contract with Title XX and the program administrator to determine the value of these activities and began our evaluative endeavor in an advantageous position. We were somewhat familiar with the institution and its operation and had a good professional working relationship with the grant director and staff. In addition, we had been invited to participate by administratively powerful members of the host organization, and this backing facilitated our movement within the system.

Despite these advantages, we did not take our admission to the institution for granted. Rather, we paid careful heed to a growing literature (e.g., Allen, Chinsky, Larcen, Lochman, & Selinger, 1976; Malott, 1974; Murrell, 1973; Repucci & Saunders, 1983; Twain, 1975) that describes useful strategies for gaining entry into social systems. The guidelines appear to revolve around two basic themes: (a) the value of building a truly collaborative endeavor; and (b) the necessity of delineating the roles, functions, rights, and responsibilities of all involved participants.

Building a Collaborative Effort

True collaboration has three advantages over having a program imposed on staff by administrators (Allen, Chinsky, Larcen, Lochman, & Selinger, 1976). First, staff members are more likely to provide useful information about topics they understand if they believe that their input will have meaningful impact on planning and policy decisions. Second, staff are more likely to invest greater behavioral effort into a project that they have helped design. Third, collaboration fosters a stronger emphasis on task-oriented interactions and reduces feelings of passivity and helplessness.

In any ecosystem, a truly collaborative orientation is slow to develop, particularly in institutions that contain direct-care staff who have survived by passively clinging to routine. It can be fostered, however, if a consultant adheres to several guidelines. One particularly useful strategy is to designate members of participating groups as having expert knowledge about particular aspects of the program. During initial planning meetings, we presented detailed proposals of what we intended to evaluate, a prospective timetable, and an overview of the measures we hoped to employ. We sought concrete feedback from participants about whether these plans would mesh comfortably with the reality of their work routine. More importantly, we took seriously every suggestion staff made regarding how we could improve the evaluation. We respected their role as experts about both the operating characteristics of the unit environment and the clients who resided there. Whenever we implemented a suggested improvement into our evaluative format, we acknowledged the contribution of the staff member. We also provided our reasons for not including those suggestions that proved unfeasible.

A second important strategy involves having evaluators be active and visible in the settings they operate in. It is obvious that verbal statements about the importance of the project become more credible when backed by the active involvement and presence of administrators. Conversely, evaluators who preach about the importance of complying with the investigative effort but who do not spend appreciable amounts of time interacting with participants are not likely to be taken seriously. The wise evaluator will plan on "wasting" time socializing with staff and getting to know each participant personally. In most cases, this represents time that is well spent, as it can facilitate the development of mutual understanding and trust.

A third useful orientation is to emphasize a positive approach. As we noted earlier, praise for quality performance is typically lacking in bureaucratic settings. Personnel at all levels experience interactions that are biased toward the negative. After the superintendent of the institution in which we were involved attended a meeting to address staff members' concerns about personnel shortages, we suggested that he be sent a "thank you" note from the participants. His response to having the staff express their appreciation was to thank the participants for thanking him. He mentioned that this was the first time in 5 years that he had received a message of gratitude from any staff member. This incident began a positive loop of appreciation that continued to function (albeit sporadically) for 2 years. It also had the effect of increasing communicants' collective awareness about their respective functions and contributions. A positive atmosphere also can be developed by emphasizing that mistakes are an integral part of any learning process.

In the final analysis, development of true collaboration is promoted by gestures that indicate the evaluator indeed respects the integrity and expertise of staff members. The evaluator's area of expert knowledge centers on the assessment of attitudes, beliefs, and behaviors. Such assessment, however, cannot be conducted in a vacuum. Staff expertise resides in their knowledge of their working environment. The pooling of these complementary skill areas enhances the success of the evaluative effort.

This perspective also requires that the evaluator be skilled interpersonally and politically. In addition, our experience advises that more than a surface understanding of the history, norms, and rules that transact in a large organization will be required for success. With this counsel to the evaluator, we echo general recommendations that several authors in this volume have made to the program innovator and manager. This is not coincidental, as formal evaluation of programmatic change in an institution for the mentally handicapped is itself a complex change process.

Clarifying Roles, Functions, Rights, and Responsibilities

True collaboration is built on a foundation of mutual trust and respect. This atmosphere is almost impossible to establish until the roles and functions of the evaluators are clarified in relation to those of other participants. Evaluators normally have two basic functions, which center on the collection and presentation of data. Each of these tasks brings the evaluator into contact with different segments of the population of the institution. Data collection typically is aimed at service staff (e.g., direct service providers) or the clientele of the facility, whereas data presentation usually is negotiated with administrative personnel such as program managers.

Trust issues are particularly salient in dealing with the people who are being assessed, because those people possess the least amount of formal power. As individuals, however, they possess subtle but formidable veto power, which can take the form of passive-aggressive opposition. Members of these groups are understandably concerned with two important issues that center on (a) to whom is the evaluator loyal? and (b) who has access to what sorts of evaluative information?

Because evaluators are present as guests of an administrator, they are likely to be viewed as agents of the administration by direct-care staff and clientele. This view often is reinforced by the fact that administrators and evaluators engage in extensive negotiations about the program before making any contact with lower level staff. The logical extension of this perception is to equate the aims of the evaluator with those of the administration. Thus, at the residential unit level, the role of an independent evaluator all too easily may be transformed into that of agent, even ''spy,'' for the power elite.

The first and most obvious method of dealing with this potential misperception is to have evaluators frankly and honestly outline their roles and functions within the program. This sort of clarification is likely to be met with polite skepticism followed by a series of trust tests. These can take many forms. Among the two most common are attempting to enlist the evaluator's aid in a power struggle with a co-worker or supervisor and providing the evaluator with seemingly sensitive information and probing to determine if it was transmitted to the "wrong" parties.

In response to the first ploy, the wise evaluator will maintain a sympathetic but neutral stance toward the antagonists. It is particularly helpful for the evaluator to suggest that each disputing party direct complaints toward the other rather than gossip to an essentially powerless "outsider." The second form of trust test is probably more common and certainly more difficult to pass. Again, the most appropriate response is to discuss with the communicator any potential restrictions on transmitting the information further (e.g., Do I have your permission to discuss this with your supervisor? With my colleagues?).

We have already mentioned that in institutions knowledge is power. Those who are first to communicate hot news are typically viewed as having access to the inner sanctums of power, whereas those who are the last to know tend to be seen as powerless or, even worse, uncaring, uninvolved, or incompetent. Any evaluation generates knowledge that can be utilized for purposes other than that for which it was intended. For example, providing a supervisor with access to behavioral observations of the occupational activities of individual direct-care providers creates the possibility that these data could be used selectively to judge job performance.

The fact that it is impossible not to communicate evaluative information on some level makes it difficult for the evaluator to pass all the trust tests involving communication. For example, we instituted the practice of sending thank you notes to participating staff who had made themselves accessible for data collection. Over time, it turned out that failure to receive such acknowledgement was interpreted by one supervisor as indicating willful obstructionism on the part of particular staff members. After investigating several complaints about our practice, we substituted a single note of appreciation to larger subgroups. The intention behind our original procedure was to break the pattern of negative scanning we had encountered. Our attempts to create an atmosphere of safety, however, were subverted in a way that actually increased negativity.

Throughout the data collection phases, we maintained very tight control over the flow of evaluative information. We began laying the foundation for control when negotiating our evaluation contract, as is described shortly. We received an agreement that no administrator or supervisor (from the superintendent on down) would be provided with any data obtained from a single individual. Feedback was provided in the form of group averages and similar summary statistics and only in response to written requests for information that was pertinent to particular questions.

Our evaluation of staff performance involved assessment through both self-report questionnaires, and behavioral observation. We assured the staff that all information we collected would be kept confidential. We also struck a compromise on the costs and benefits of collecting data from anonymous sources. Information from such sources is less likely to be distorted systematically by various response biases such as social desirability (Nunnally & Durham, 1975; Nunnally & Wilson, 1975; Weiss, 1975). On the other hand, it is impossible to accurately link repeated observations made on the same informants if they are truly anonymous. Our compromise was to ask each staff member to choose a code name to use when providing questionnaire data. We were the only ones who knew the actual identity of each informant. Our system of behavioral observation identified participating staff by using their initials. Thus, we were able to link repeated behavioral assessments to the questionnaire responses while safeguarding individual confidentiality.

An additional safeguard was imposed by employing multiple observers who were systematically rotated through staff members. We also carefully instructed our observers in the etiquette required by their role as guests within the institution. They were expected to fit into the daily routine as unobtrusively as possible and were instructed to pass any requests for feedback made by supervisors or the participants themselves onto us. We would then contact the interested individual to deal with the request. Some of our observers tended to be so unobtrusive that their silent presence made the staff nervous. These individuals were then asked to observe basic social niceties such as greeting staff and making small talk with them.

We reduced the potential for interpersonal friction between the direct-care workers and observers even further by pointing out to the staff that the observers had as much apprehension about being on the unit as the staff had about being observed. One valuable offshoot of this strategy was to validate the expert power of staff members by asking their help in "taking care" of the observers. These safeguards facilitated data collection, helped create a relaxed atmosphere of trust, and enhanced the validity of resulting information. Where data are to be collected in naturalistic settings, these preparations are no small matter. Treating them superficially could easily disable any evaluative effort.

The second major aspect of collaboration involves negotiating with administrative personnel about the scope and format of the evaluation. The agenda of the program manager is by nature radically different from the concerns of subordinate staff. Most program managers are dedicated to providing and expanding services to clientele. For them, evaluative efforts serve a vested interest in demonstrating that a particular service is effective. The evaluation then can be used to justify continuation or expansion of the service.

Unfortunately, most program managers are unacquainted with the costly complexities that adequate evaluation entails. In addition, most grants for which program managers apply are designed to emphasize service components. Although the necessity of evaluation is mentioned, evaluation requirements are typically vague. In negotiating specific evaluative operations within this context, the evaluator is likely to encounter a "baseball statistician's mentality" (Edwards, Guttentag, & Snapper, 1975). This involves collecting as much information about as many facets of the program under study as possible. From the viewpoint of the program manager, this approach increases the likelihood that some redeeming features of the service will be revealed.

This approach, however, has a number of drawbacks from the evaluator's point of view. First, it can jeopardize the methodological quality of the evaluation by favoring haphazard collection of data that pertain to a large number of tangentially related activities within the service program. Second, it can impose a serious overload on the human resources to which the evaluator has access. In our negotiations with program managers, they provided a number of sound and even creative strategies of evaluation that simply were too costly for us to implement. A final disadvantage of this approach is that it can lead to the collection of such an abundance of data that it cannot be used effectively. When consulting at an institution where data collection had become a functionally autonomous activity, the senior author was asked his opinion about which of two training methods would be most appropriate for a client. When he asked to see data relevant to the issue, a staff member pointed to 12 boxes filled with graphs. The staff member said that they had been so busy collecting information over the past 2 years that no one had found time to sort it out, much less analyze it.

These issues with administrators and program managers are not only real and frequent, they are also extremely sensitive. We know of one administrator who would often begin meetings on evaluation services with, "What I want to be able to say about the project is this. . . ." He would then present the arguments and "facts" he wished to have when he went before the legislature for more funds. We find here still another circumstance where the evaluator must risk being blurred into the role of internal change agent. Evaluators must assist the facility, its administrators, and service professionals in preparing for meaningful evaluation. This may well require the initiative of tactful leadership in defining goals, identifying researchable questions, and generally safeguarding the entire evaluative product from overload and inextricable confounding. It may also require clarification of purposes and agendas so that they can be candidly negotiated. Here, evaluators may need to clarify the rules and neutrality posture under which they will operate.

An antidote to such difficulties exists in the form of a specific evaluation contract. A good evaluation contract delineates the rights and responsibilities of both program manager and evaluator; it represents, as fully as possible, their varying interests and defines constraints imposed by the institutional setting. The ideal contract contains specifications pertaining to two interlocking areas—the roles and functions of the negotiating parties, and the content and methodology of the evaluation itself. These can be seen in the seven characteristics of an evaluation contract as proposed by Deming (1975) and Twain (1975):

1. Clear specification of division of labor (i.e., who is responsible for what and when)

2. Some guarantee of financial security for the evaluative effort (e.g., certification that funds will not be cut off before completion of the project)

3. Full description of termination plans (e.g., stating an end point for data collection; determining deadlines for quarterly and final report)

4. Statements about goals for utilization of evaluative findings (e.g., to whom will what information be disseminated)

5. Specification of meaningful, objective measures indicative of success and/or failure of the program

6. Description of the experimental operations to be employed (e.g., random assignment, control groups, etc.)

7. Description of possible methods for reduction, analysis, interpretation, and presentation of data

An example of an evaluation contract that fits most of these criteria is provided in Table 7.1. This contract contains a number of additional features worth noting. First, it reflects an attempt to specify clearly contingencies that surround vaguely worded phrases. For example, an evaluator and a program manager might agree that a particular procedure will be implemented "whenever possible." The vagueness of this understanding can create interpersonal friction should either party announce that implementation is "simply impossible." Providing examples of institutional constraints on specific procedures can help avoid much of the unpleasantness that can result from misinterpreting vague agreements.

Second, the contract specifies that proposed program changes be negotiated. This feature not only lessens the likelihood that such alterations will be abruptly imposed, but also provides the evaluator with an opportunity to provide input about them. Finally, the contract attempts to strike a balance between the formal requirements of the evaluation and the expertise of the evaluator. It provides major program goals in the form of specific questions that must be addressed and also specifies broad requirements about data collection and methodology. Within these broad constraints, however, the evaluator is free to select the most appropriate investigative measures and methods.

The evaluation contract is obviously not a panacea for all the difficulties created by sudden shifts in institutional priorities and operations. Rather, it represents a method of codifying the good faith that must exist between program manager and evaluator. The contract cannot cover all possible contingencies that might arise during the course of the evaluation, but it does provide specific guidelines for dealing with such situations. In fact, many contractual negotiations tend to be verbal and informal, given the complex interplay of forces that operate within the bureaucracy. We strongly advocate, however, the development of a written contract that specifies the rights and responsibilities of the involved participants. Such an agreement not only provides a blueprint for infor-

TABLE 7.1
Extracts from a Sample Evaluation Contract

I. GENERAL CONSIDERATIONS:
1. This contract represents an agreement between PM, program manager, PE, program evaluator, and FA, funding agent.
2. The program described below was developed by PM, with funding provided by FA. Program is to be initiated on (date), with termination scheduled for (date). All parties agree that refunding through (date) is possible, contingent upon (specification of conditions).
3. The following program components require evaluation:
Component A: (brief description of program procedure and anticipated goal).
Component B: (brief description . . .)
II. SCOPE AND METHODS OF EVALUATION
1. The effectiveness of Component A will be determined by (statement of experimental operation and description of data to be collected).
e.g., a. changes in criterion test scores obtained before and after training from participants and a randomly selected control group.
b. daily "spot checking" of staff performance through use of a behavioral observation measure.
2. The impact of Component B will be determined by . . .
III. ROLES, RESPONSIBILITIES, RIGHTS, AND CONSTRAINTS:
1. PM will be responsible for (specify tasks).
e.g., a. selection and training of grant staff, preparation of specified training materials and operations.
b. determining composition of training and relevant control groups by random assignment whenever possible. (Specify particular constraints to randomization.)
2. PE agrees to perform the following tasks (specify details).
e.g., a. collect baseline data from experimental and control participants by (date).
b. prepare quarterly progress reports by (dates).
c. provide a final report including information about measurement operations, experimental designs, statistical analysis, and interpretation of outcomes by (date).
3. It is agreed that the final report shall be considered the (joint) property of (specify ownership, constraints over reproduction, copyright, etc.).
4. It is agreed that no member of the institutional staff shall have access to evaluative data collected on any participant. Evaluative feedback shall be in the form of group summaries, with the identities of the informants kept confidential.
5. FA agrees to pay PE $_____ for conducting evaluation, with payment distributed as follows: (specify amounts and dates). In addition, PM agrees to provide $_____ for (specify particular costs of evaluation).
6. PM agrees to inform PE of any major changes in program format and/or implementation timetable as soon as possible after they are necessitated. Similarly, PE will inform PM of necessary changes and adjustments in evaluative operations as soon as they become apparent.
7. The outcome of any negotiated changes shall be specified in writing and appended to this agreement.

| Program Manager | Program Evaluator | Funding Agent |

mal negotiation, but also legitimates the power of the evaluator to implement certain necessary procedures by codifying the support of key administrative personnel.

Summary Guidelines for Facilitating Entry

We know of no evaluators who have been welcomed with open arms into any health care bureaucracy. The disruptive and apprehension-arousing nature of evaluation is likely to create, at best, a climate of passive resignation and, at worst, one of hostile obstructionism. We offer the following suggestions for enlisting staff trust and cooperation, for without these elements any evaluative effort is threatened before it begins.

1. Enter the system slowly. Plan on spending considerable time to learn about the needs, desires, concerns, and apprehensions of participating staff. We found that focusing on the human concerns of staff members yielded an immensely positive return in cooperation and willful participation.

2. Assume that you will be considered untrustworthy until you prove otherwise. An institution-wise staff has many reasons to fear outsiders who disrupt traditional routine. We were able to develop an acceptable level of trust among most staff members by a variety of methods. Our initial strategy was to verbalize this assumption to participants and to mention that we would do our best to pass whatever trust tests they needed to put us through. Other trust-building strategies are contained in the following guidelines.

3. Seek to develop a truly collaborative endeavor by defining the role of staff as experts in the operation of the institution. After explicitly defining this role, we validated it by seeking staff suggestions and incorporating feasible ones into our evaluative format.

4. Be frank and honest in describing your own duties and loyalties with regard to conducting the evaluation within the bureaucratic ecosystem. The evaluator can get painfully squeezed by the power struggles and loyalty conflicts that exist in institutional settings. Our basic stance toward these dilemmas was to be straightforward in describing the reasons for our choice of a particular course of action whenever we were forced away from a neutral position. We attempted to specify the potential helpful and harmful consequences for both immediate parties to any dispute as well as for more remote staff groupings. Although certain staff did not always agree with our position, we received feedback that they respected our frankness.

5. Seek to provide meaningful rewards for participation. Participants in the training program we evaluated were burdened by extra tasks. We acknowledged our appreciation of their efforts in a variety of ways. We took the time to write thank you notes to participating individuals and groups and communicated our praise to supervisory and administrative personnel. We also affirmed trainees'

accomplishments by attending graduation ceremonies held by the facility's administrators. Our presence was a sign of our interest in each staff member's growth as a person and proved to be a very heartwarming experience for us.

6. Maintain careful control over confidentiality and the dissemination of information. Nothing can destroy staff trust as quickly as leakage of sensitive information. We endeavored to provide clear guidelines about who would be given what information under which circumstances for what purposes. More important, we never violated our commitments.

7. Train evaluation personnel in the etiquette appropriate to the setting in which they will operate. Our observers were thoroughly briefed on the working conditions direct-care staff had to endure, their psychological outlook, and the constraints imposed upon them. We sought to clarify the roles and functions of both staff and observers in a way that would foster mutual respect. We also moved rapidly to resolve the few misunderstandings that occurred by arranging face-to-face encounters between the disputing individuals.

8. Clarify roles, rights, and responsibilities of various participating groups through a detailed, written evaluation contract. Our contract provided a basis for whatever good faith negotiations were necessitated by program changes and also served to aid us in determining evaluative priorities.

CONCEPTUAL AND METHODOLOGICAL ISSUES

The evaluator must operate in a complex, ever-changing social system that requires altering the generally accepted criteria of laboratory research. In contrast to the clearly specified univariate manipulations found in traditional laboratory research, innovative social-helping programs are ecological entities. They contain multiple interactive components that possess complex linkages to other groups, structures, and systems within the institution. An intervention at one point will have manifold consequences that reverberate throughout the entire system in subtle but powerful ways. Despite such contextual differences, however, the adequacy of both laboratory experiments and evaluation depend on the careful application of acknowledged methods of empirical inquiry. In addition, the ultimate goal of both activities is to demonstrate the existence of causal relationships between a manipulable intervention and measurable outcomes.

The grant program we evaluated possessed these transactional ecological properties. The program was not only designed to facilitate training of specific staff, but also to have ultimate impact on other treatment centers for mentally retarded individuals. Certain components were tied to training endeavors (e.g., a dining skills program conducted by a staff member from a separate department; toilet training provided by an autonomous group of college students, etc.) that were already operating independently. These were advantageous features from the program manager's viewpoint because they broadened the service potential of the grant and also increased the base of potential political support. The multifaceted nature of the intervention, however, made it extremely difficult to derive unambiguous causal relationships to outcomes.

Evaluation of such programs is necessarily based on the premise that any complex intervention will undoubtedly produce multiple outcomes on a variety of attitudinal, behavioral, and organizational levels. Evaluators must also assume that no one set of empirical operations will provide a definitive answer to the ultimate question "Is this particular intervention effective?" because the question itself represents an oversimplification of complex social reality. Thus, program evaluators are forced to make inferences about overall effectiveness by combining answers that are obtained about many more specific questions (e.g., Was program component A associated with hypothesized changes X, Y, and Z in a systematic manner?). Program evaluation, therefore, involves performing a series of miniexperiments, each of which involves as high a degree of control as can be achieved within the constraints imposed by the institutional context.

Ensuring that each miniexperiment will add logically to the overall coherence of the evaluation requires developing a model that provides accurate description of interactions between program components and outcomes. A model is a conceptual creation constructed from theoretical and empirical knowledge about both human change processes and the existing social system. A good model suggests specific areas that are likely to change as a result of the intervention, guides the selection of instruments that can document such changes, and, most important, provides a framework for analyzing the mechanisms of change.

Our evaluative effort was based on a "radiating effects" model that is typically employed by community psychologists (e.g., Allen et al., 1976; Kelly, 1971). This model assumes that a complex intervention will generate multiple outcomes. The initial impact of any outcome is presumed to be inversely related to the number of potentially operative treatment interferences. A treatment interference, for our evaluation, was defined as any institutional constraint that *systematically* inhibited the effect of staff training; that is, the magnitude and direction of its effect was fairly constant across affected individuals. Table 7.2 describes the radiating effects we expected to find as a result of the staff training program.

Given the didactic nature of staff training, it seemed logical to assume that the strongest program effects would be reflected on measures that assessed whether trainees had actually learned new terms, concepts, and skills. Even though a number of other possible impediments to learning could be suggested, only three systematic institutional inhibitors were likely to be operative. For example, failure of the trainees to manifest reliable improvement on tests assessing knowledge of behavior modification principles could logically be attributed to a variety of personal factors, such as not being motivated to learn, failure to attend training sessions, and so on. Across a group of people, however, such factors do not provide viable explanations because widespread individual differences in moti-

TABLE 7.2
A Radiating Effects Model of Program Evaluation

Magnitude of Initial Impact			
High			*Low*
Direct Learning of Material	*Changes in Staff Attitudes*	*Changes in Staff Behavior*	*Changes in Clients*

Sources of Interference			
Deficiencies in assessment methods	Deficiencies in assessment methods	Deficiencies in assessment methods	Deficiencies in assessment methods
Inadequate training materials	Inadequate training materials	Inadequate training materials	Inadequate training materials
Inadequate training presentation	Inadequate training presentation	Inadequate training presentation	Inadequate training presentation
	Passive, custodial attitudes	Passive, custodial attitudes	Passive, custodial attitudes
	Group support for maintaining the status quo	Group support for maintaining the status quo	Group support for maintaining the status quo
	Resentful demoralization	Resentful demoralization	Resentful demoralization
		Pressures for client care and housekeeping duties	Pressures for client care and housekeeping duties
		Supervisor priorities de-emphasizing training	Supervisor priorities de-emphasizing training
		Communication breakdowns	Communication breakdowns
			Large client-staff ratios
			Chronic, low-level resident population

vation and skill level exist. Such individual differences are construed as "error variance;" they are viewed as having nonsystematic effects that cancel themselves out when testing is conducted across people.

On the other hand, if the trainees as a group fail to demonstrate that they learned a significant amount of material after watching the videotapes, it is more likely to be the result of inadequacies in the training materials (e.g., presenting content at too high a level for the trainees as a whole), failure to present the materials effectively (e.g., having the group leader miss crucial workshops), or deficiencies in the way that learning was assessed (e.g., using a test that did not accurately reflect the content presented). Each of these institutional impediments is likely to affect each of the trainees in a roughly similar manner, thus making its effect systematic across people.

A second set of questions dealt with whether workshop participation produces changes in staff attitudes. If trainees viewed their training as rewarding and meaningful, more favorable attitudes ought to be generated about the adequacy of the work environment, the value of client training, and overall job satisfaction. In addition, successful trainees might reasonably be expected to manifest an increased awareness of the roles and functions of other staff members.

The model suggests, however, that accomplishing attitudinal change would be more difficult than increasing staff knowledge, because more impediments to attitude change exist. The existence of training inadequacies could create an attitudinal backlash among staff who may feel cheated if the videotaped presentations were too difficult. In addition, many staff members hold attitudes that reflect a custodial orientation toward their clients as well as a passive stance toward innovative notions. The interpersonal interactions among many staff tend to reinforce continually such preexisting attitudes, thus forming another institutional impediment.

At this point, it is important to note that the model can encompass a number of counterintuitive possibilities at each radiating level. For example, successful training could conceivably raise participants' level of aspiration with regard to conducting meaningful habilitation with clients. This initial optimism could ultimately foster a variety of negative staff attitudes. The trained participants might be viewed as deviants and trouble-makers by other staff, a perception that could be reflected in less favorable ratings of the occupational environment. Similarly, existing unit conditions (e.g., chronic understaffing, communication breakdowns, etc.) might combine to defeat any attempt at systematic client training. After having their hopes raised, staff trainees are likely to react to repeated frustration and failure by becoming more passive, alienated, and negative. This phenomenon is a variant of what Cook and Campbell (1979) call "resentful demoralization." Another form of resentful demoralization can be inferred if control group members report more negative attitudes while participants' attitudes do not change.

An even more distant radiating effect involves determining if training leads to reliable changes in staff behavior in the unit setting. If the training program is to be viewed as having a lasting pragmatic impact, then trainees must consistently perform what they have presumably learned. It could be reasonably expected that the trainees we evaluated would engage in more formal training with clients, seek to improve interstaff communication (particularly across shifts), keep more detailed records of clients' progress, be less frequently engaged in housework, and be more consistently positive in their interactions with clients.

It was also assumed that such behavioral changes are not likely to be as robust as shifts in direct learning or attitudinal measures. In addition to the impediments previously described, a number of other systematic sources of interference constrain the behavior of the direct-care staff. Direct-care staff find themselves under constant pressure to perform housekeeping and client care chores. These more custodial activities are often necessitated by the low level of functioning manifested by clients and also represent priorities established by the unit supervisor. They must also endure constant inter- and intrashift communication breakdowns that threaten to undermine consistent application of their training efforts.

A final question set centers on whether changes in staff attitude and behavior will eventually foster reliable improvement in the client population. This issue is obviously a most important consideration from the viewpoint of agencies interested in enhancing the potential of disabled individuals. Such a fourth level radiating effect, however, is by far the most difficult to accomplish, particularly in the short term. Even if it were documented that an intervention such as workshop training promotes adaptive changes in staff members' skill level, attitudes, and unit behavior, two additional sources of interference adversely affect the development of client skills.

Because many of the less impaired residents had been moved from the unit through programs of deinstitutionalization and community placement, those who remained were the most handicapped individuals, manifesting the most serious behavioral deficits and learning most slowly. The slow rate of progress such individuals make during the course of training can quickly become discouraging to the staff trainee. Resulting resignation is likely to be augmented by the large client-to-staff ratio that typically exists on the unit. This factor conceivably would dilute any initial training impact, because only a small proportion of existing staff can participate in any one training sequence.

In developing this model, we made one other important assumption. Despite literature suggesting that such training facilities have extremely high rates of staff turnover (e.g., Butterfield, 1967; Klaber, 1969), we assumed that every subsequent training cycle would substantially increase the proportion of trained staff-to-available participants on the unit. Thus, we expected that over a 2-year period four cycles of staff training would have a cumulative impact on the functioning of the client population. We made this assumption after receiving verbal assurances from high level administrators that the current staff would be maintained. Although we were a little skeptical of this promise, our acceptance was reinforced when we learned of a Title XX grant stipulation that required trainees to remain on the job for a period equivalent to the training time provided them. Despite these institutional assurances, we later discovered to our regret that we should have taken the literature more seriously. In general, however, the model did provide a coherent framework for arranging the outcomes we obtained.

Overview of Specific Evaluation Procedures

The evaluative strategies we employed were derived from our hypothetical model of change and reflected four methodological criteria that constitute a rigorous evaluation, as described in the next section. The major strategies, which are fully described by Heatherington and Allen (1978) and Lah and Allen (1979),

TABLE 7.3
Overview of Data Collection Procedures for Staff Training Evaluation

Procedure	Group	Cycle 1	Cycle 2	Cycle 3	Cycle 4	Follow-up
Knowledge Assessment	In-Training	X. . .X	X. . .X	X. . .X	X. . .X	
Staff Attitude Assessment	In-Training	X. . .X	X. . .X	X. . .X	X. . .X	
	Untrained	X. . .X	X. . .X	X. . .X	X. . .X	
	Post-trained	X. . .X	X. . .X	X. . .X	X. . .X	
Observation of Staff and	In-Training	—	—	—	—	
Client Behavior	Untrained	—	—	—	—	X. . .X
	Post-trained	—	—	—	—	X. . .X
Assessment of Specific	In-Training	—	—	—	—	
Client Skills	(Acquisition)					
	Post-trained				—	X. . .X
	(Maintenance)					

Note: Time-limited assessment periods are denoted by X; solid lines denote continuous assessment.

are highlighted in Table 7.3. Staff training was accomplished in four 5-month cycles over a 2-year period. Each subsequent training cycle replicated the first in an experimental design that used each subject as his or her own control as well as providing between-group comparisons between untrained participants, those currently in training, and those trained in a prior cycle (post-training).

Before and after each cycle, all staff members rated their job satisfaction and provided opinions about the value of client and staff training. All staff who participated in the workshop cycles were assessed on a 37-item knowledge test of behavioral techniques before and after training. Staff behavior in the unit environment was continually spot-checked through use of the Interaction Recording System (Veit, Allen, & Chinsky, 1976). This observational system analyzes encounters between a direct-care provider and clients in terms of staff members' affect, client response, consequent staff behavior, and, most importantly, the context of the interaction (e.g., client care, ward routine, housekeeping, formal training, etc.).

The ward activities of the mentally handicapped clients were also systematically observed throughout each training cycle by means of the Behavior Sampling System (Olsen, Lukeris, Billings, & Pritchard, 1975). This device contains 10 categories that order client behavior along a social adequacy dimension, ranging from self-abuse and isolated self-stimulation at one extreme, through activities such as playing alone or being trained, to interacting with a staff person or another client at the other extreme. Finally, assessment of the behavior-shaping projects staff conducted with their selected clients was made through inspection of data-based progress reports. During the final two training cycles, we made independent assessments of the skills clients had been taught 12 to 18 months earlier. This was accomplished by repeatedly prompting each client to display the previously trained skill on at least 10 separate occasions.

Methodological Guidelines for Evaluation

Generation of specific research questions and creation of a conceptual model can aid greatly the search for causal relationships. The documentation of causality requires that careful attention be paid to the methodology of the evaluation. In the most general sense, all strategies of empirical inquiry are aimed at protecting observations and inferences from possible errors. Causal inference involves reducing systematic errors (i.e., artifacts) by employing operations that (a) cancel out their systematic nature, (b) insulate observations from their effects, and (c) discount their direction and magnitude (Kaplan, 1964). The procedures employed to reduce systematic error relate to the validity of the evaluation.

Cook and Campbell (1979) provide the most comprehensive taxonomy of empirical control strategies in their discussion of four types of validity with which evaluators must concern themselves. *Statistical conclusion validity* refers to the adequacy of statistical evidence purporting to demonstrate systematic covariation between intervention and outcome. Establishment of covariation, however, does not necessarily imply causality unless plausible alternative possibilities can be ruled out. Attempts to clarify the direction of causal influence by discounting plausible third-variable explanations of a treatment-outcome relationship constitute the domain of *internal validity*. Ensuring that the specific treatment procedures employed in a program are representative of basic behavioral processes and that the outcome measures are an adequate, theory-relevant sample of the hypothetical construct being investigated are the operations that relate to *construct validity*. Finally, attempts to demonstrate that whatever causal relationships have been postulated can be generalized across people, settings, and time define the domain of *external validity*.

Conceptually, these four types of validity are interrelated in complex ways. In general, inverted relationships exist between internal and external validity, and between construct and statistical conclusion validity. For example, providing training to a heterogeneous sample of direct-care staff makes it more difficult to document program effects because participants are likely to be less uniformly responsive to the intervention. Yet, the heterogeneous sample is more representative of the attendant culture than any group of participants who would be chosen on the basis of a particular attribute. Similarly, using multiple measures both within and across domains augments the construct validity of the evaluation (e.g., by demonstrating that a program fostered both subjective and performance changes), but also increases the likelihood that multiple statistical tests will yield spuriously reliable differences.

The minimal adequacy of the methodology contained in any program evaluation rests largely upon four fundamental empirical operations: (a) randomization,

(b) demonstration of reliability, (c) utilization of multiple methods of assessment, and (d) comprehensive sampling of data sources. These operations are aimed at breaking up any *systematic* effects of artifactual influences.

Randomization.   Random assignment (e.g., of people to treatments, of clients to trainees, etc.) is the most economical and powerful procedure that can be used to cancel out the directional influences of extraneous factors. This operation is designed to equate members of various groups *on the average*. All group members then receive treatment procedures that are identical in all respects except with regard to the variable(s) being manipulated. It is assumed that between-group differences are the result of the manipulation to the extent the groups do not systematically differ on other potentially relevant characteristics. Although individuals within each group certainly will vary in many ways (e.g., intelligence, motivation, susceptibility to life stress or illness, etc.), random assignment ensures that such differences will cancel themselves out when groups are treated as the basic units of analysis.

Although random assignment is a hallmark of traditional laboratory research, strong social norms mitigate against its use in action-helping endeavors. Typically, valuable resources are distributed on the basis of need, merit, opportunity, or political pressure. Program managers in institutional settings are particularly sensitive to how their various constituencies will react to having positive or negative resources distributed by chance. Thus, various bureaucratic forces often constrain true randomization in favor of avoiding political power struggles, maintaining staff harmony, and minimizing disruption to ongoing routine. The costs of compromising randomization can be high, especially in terms of jeopardizing the interpretability of obtained outcomes. Fortunately, adherence to the remaining three operations can cut this cost dramatically.

In our evaluation contract, we insisted that randomization be used whenever possible. This stipulation, however, created havoc with scheduling considerations. In addition, we belatedly discovered that the first group of trainees had been chosen primarily because they had expressed a desire to participate, were politically powerful within the direct-care groups, or both. This situation created a number of plausible alternatives to explain any positive program outcomes. We had better fortune when attempting to ensure that retarded clients were randomly assigned to attendant trainees. Some staff members had expressed a desire to work with ''the most trainable'' or ''my favorite client,'' but were receptive to the argument that the most ethically fair manner of distributing scarce training resources would be at random.

Reliability.   In the broadest sense, reliability refers to consistency. In classical psychometric test theory, reliability referred to three aspects of a measuring device—consistency across items on a test that purports to measure a single construct (called ''internal consistency''), consistency of test scores collected on the same individuals at different times (''test-retest'' or ''temporal stability,'' coefficients); and consistency in the reports of raters who simultaneously observe a sequence of events ("inter-judge" or "inter-rater" agreement). In program evaluation, reliability also refers to the consistency with which treatments are implemented across people, settings, and time.

Ensuring that assessment measures have adequate reliability is a necessary (but not sufficient) precursor to demonstrating acceptable validity. Reliable instruments provide standardized yardsticks for investigating change, and failure to employ such devices creates a host of possible interpretative errors. Evaluators can deal with this problem through a variety of procedures. First, it is important that measures with well-established psychometric properties be employed. This is preferable to having an evaluator develop a unique set of assessment instruments. Second, various nontreated, or placebo, control groups ought to be employed where administratively possible in order to enable assessment of the temporal stability of instruments to be made. Third, when direct behavioral observations are made, raters need to be trained carefully. A growing literature, (e.g., O'Leary & Kent, 1973; O'Leary, Kent, & Kanowitz, 1975; Reid, 1970; Romanczyk, Kent, Diament, & O'Leary, 1973) has documented that behavioral observation poses unique problems for reliability that are not found in traditional forms of testing. These investigations indicate that the assessment of reliability among even highly trained raters is a reactive phenomenon. Observers produce substantially higher rates of agreement when they are aware that reliability checks will be conducted. In the absence of such checks, reliability falls off. In addition, consistently assigning the same rating pairs to observe leads to criterion drift (i.e., divergence among the pairs over time) even when within-pair reliability is high. It is therefore very important that reliability checks be conducted throughout the course of the evaluation and that observers be randomly paired over time.

Multiple Methods of Assessment. Evaluators have found it convenient to divide assessment instruments into three classes: (a) self-reports of subjective perceptions (e.g., attitude surveys, questionnaires, interviews), (b) measures of overt performance (e.g., criterion test scores, work samples, behavioral observations), and (c) devices that tap covert physiological responses (e.g., heart rate, blood pressure). Each method of assessment encompasses a wide variety of more specific measurement devices. The multiple impact of complex social interventions is typically documented through measurements made within the first two domains.

In the evaluation of program change in institutional settings, multi-method measurement has three advantages over both univariate assessments and multivariate measurement operations conducted within a single domain. First, each method of measurement provides a unique, nonoverlapping source of information about the program. The only way that staff attitudes can be determined is by asking the participants for their subjective impressions, whereas behavioral observations of staff performance yield the most direct information about observable program impact. It thus becomes plausible to ''triangulate'' the effects of an intervention by examining consistencies and discrepancies between the two data sources. It is obvious that stronger inferences about such effects can be made if a particular program improves staff morale and work effectiveness than if it produces changes in only one of these areas.

Second, each measurement method possesses a unique set of methodological limitations that do not plague the other method. Self-report measures are typically transparent in that they provide cues about how to appropriately respond to them. This opens their interpretation to a variety of expectancy and halo influences, such as a tendency to provide socially desirable responses (Scheirer, 1978). Behavioral assessment methods generally are less open to distortion by such influences (Goldfried & Sprafkin, 1974). They are reactive, however, to a different set of influential biasing factors (e.g., sampling inadequacies, reliability anomalies) that do not distort self-report instruments.

Finally, outcome data from self-reported and behavioral sources tend to be statistically independent. Independence is a crucial feature in the triangulation process just described. The fact that each measurement method taps into nonoverlapping sources of variance considerably strengthens any causal linkages that are postulated. The use of converging measurement operations implies that no single data source is inherently superior to the other. The judicious use of instruments from both domains substantially increases the strength of the inferential statements about program effectiveness that can be made. Their combined use also can yield important information about the operation of possible distorting influences.

Comprehensive Date Sampling.   Conclusions from a program evaluation are made inferentially from samples drawn from particular target populations. It is assumed that these samples are reasonably representative of the functioning of people in larger real-life settings. Failure to achieve sampling adequacy can threaten all four types of validity, but is especially detrimental to external validity. Adequate sampling ensures that the program and its attendant evaluation are representative of other corresponding efforts. In order to achieve this goal, sampling must be made across people, settings, measures, and treatments.

Cook and Campbell (1979) describe three different sampling strategies. First, a random sampling can achieve a high degree of representativeness. This strategy typically is employed when people are the targets of interest (e.g., opinion polls, surveys, etc.), but it tends to be extremely costly in time and effort. Second, one may deliberately sample in order to increase the heretogenity of response. This strategy often is used when randomization is impossible to implement; it involves drawing data from as many diverse sources as possible. A third strategy involves selecting modal instances that represent the class to which one wishes to generalize.

Complex evaluative endeavors typically employ various combinations of these strategies, depending on the resources available to the evaluator and the constraints operative in the institutional setting. For example, the project we evaluated was conducted with participants who had a wide range of employment histories (3 months to 22 years), education (fifth grade to graduate school), and attitudes toward training mentally retarded people (custodial orientation to strong habilitative focus). They worked in a setting that in terms of architecture, chronicity of population, and large client to staff ratios was similar to many ward environments in both the institution and the state system. During the first phase of training, after we learned that the participants had not been randomly selected, we urged that the most heterogeneous sample be created. The high degree of diversity that resulted provided a stronger test for the program, because it could not be safely assumed that it would produce equivalent effects across people of widely differing ability levels. In using this strategy, we gained generality, but at the expense of statistical precision.

We employed the randomization strategy in obtaining our behavioral observations of staff and clients. We rotated observers through both days and time of day in such a way that a single rater would be coding the behavior of the same direct-care provider at the same time of day about once every 6 weeks. This sort of observation schedule can be "thinned" if necessitated by diminished resources. We did not have enough observers to monitor staff activities continuously and dealt with this problem by assigning raters to observe for about 2 hours daily. Over days, however, every half-hour time block during the waking day was targeted for observation. Combining these observations usually cancels out systematic biases due to specific scheduled activities (e.g., always observing at mealtime or during shift changes when the likelihood of formal training is low) or to consistent pairings of specific staff members and participating observers (which can produce halo effects from previous encounters).

We employed the modal instance strategy in answering certain research questions. We were particularly interested in determining whether trainees who had been transferred to other residential units following training engaged in more client training than resident staff members in their new placements. There were several formidable problems that required resolution before this issue could be addressed. Only five staff members had received transfers, and they were working in widely different environments (e.g., family-like cottages, a unit for blind residents). We decided to investigate this question by conducting a series of case study replications in which we observed each target staff member and a randomly selected control attendant on at least seven occasions. Each case study (i.e., comparison of the two direct-care staff) provided uncontrolled, impressionistic data about the question. If reliable differences that consistently favored the hypothesis had emerged across all five modal instances, however, this would constitute strong supportive evidence.

Evaluators must realize that these four empirical operations entail making trade-offs between a variety of conceptual and practical factors. The inference of causal relationships is by nature probabilistic. Causal linkages are rendered more probable to the extent that various threats to validity are ruled out. The most salient threats to validity are in large part determined by the aims of the evaluation and the choices and resources open to the evaluator.

We have presented some detail on these technical issues of evaluative research because they are commonly neglected in judging the effects of change in institutional systems. Program managers and chief administrators, facing demands to change almost all phases of their operation, have little patience for formal methods of empirical inquiry. Surface signs of success or failure are quicker to acquire and may be all that are necessary to fend off a court order or to persuade an appropriations committee. We believe, however, that change agents and program innovators who take the steps to subject their endeavors to the more rigorous methods of evaluation will recover more fundamentally sound service returns over the longer run. Another social-political function of the evaluator may be to help the institution's decision makers understand this.

ISSUES PERTAINING TO IMPLEMENTATION AND UTILIZATION

Careful conceptualization of the evaluation and attention to difficulties inherent in entering the social system can help circumvent many of the problems that arise in the course of the evaluative endeavor. Even the most scrupulous attention to these issues, however, will not guarantee a problem-free implementation, given the nature of bureaucratic settings. Our experience typified reports of other evaluators who operate in institutional contexts. We encountered a number of problems ranging from mild nuisances to potentially lethal threats. In this section, we touch on two issues that critically affect the implementation of an evaluation and two other issues that center on utilization of the resulting information.

The Shifting Environment

In previous sections, we discussed how health care bureaucracies typically are overstressed by a variety of internal forces and external factors that are likely to operate at cross-purposes. The real-life consequences of these influences make the evaluative setting an arena where multiple human dramas and confrontations are enacted against a constantly changing backdrop. Changes, even when planned, are seldom achieved rarely in a manner that considers the entire context of the system. In most cases, even planned and scheduled changes create considerable disruption to routine.

The evaluator must contend with the possibility that the evaluative setting will be disrupted as a result of many competing forces. Changes may occur in the physical environment or, more important, in the interpersonal atmosphere of the setting. Shifts in the former tend to be more obvious and generally easy to deal with. Most of the physical alterations we encountered had to do with unexpected changes in schedules and routines. For example, our observers would show up at the unit only to learn that all the clients had been taken on a day trip or that they had been assigned a new mealtime. In other instances, changes were made in a priori seating arrangements for clients in special settings (e.g., the dining hall), which made it difficult for the observers to code interactions accurately.

Changes in interpersonal climate are generally more difficult for outsiders to detect, comprehend, and manage. The attitudes and behavior of the unit supervisor exert an extremely important influence on unit atmosphere. The unit supervisor usually sets the functional (as contrasted to administratively stated) priorities for direct-care staff and possesses the reward and coercive power to enforce their realization. During the 2 years of our evaluation, the participants experienced four changes of supervisor. Each switch was accompanied by a tendency by the staff to retreat into traditional custodial activities until the supervisor's priorities were delineated clearly.

The consequences of investigating program changes in a stressed and changing human service environment are generally negative. Changes in physical layout or established routine can inconvenience evaluation staff and create unwanted "noise" in evaluative data. More serious disruptions (e.g., having an evaluation site closed because of highly contagious illness) can jeopardize the entire effort. Although such occurrences are unwelcome possibilities, we believe that interpersonal alterations represent more complex and potentially lethal threats. A worst case scenario can occur when the evaluator becomes even unwittingly involved in a power struggle between participating staff members and/or supervisors. If this should occur, formerly accessible staff suddenly disappear or become evasive; those who appear too sympathetic toward one faction (or the evaluators) may be ostracized; even relatively innocuous evaluative feedback may be subverted for blatant political manipulations. This sort of situation can evolve through what Twain (1975) calls a gradual "seduction of the researcher."

In dealing with a complex ecological system, we found it useful to build our evaluation around a series of miniexperiments that were designed to answer specific questions. This strategy fit well with the multifaceted program that was being put into operation and also enabled us to collect information within relatively brief time spans. When data collection required a longer time frame, we were careful to record obvious environmental changes (e.g., assignment of a new supervisor). We also realized that we would have to maintain a balance between the detachment required by our role as evaluators and the interpersonal involvement necessary to achieve rapport. To reduce the potential costs engendered by making compromises between these two positions, we set up weekly staff meetings that focused on these politically relevant issues. As noted previously, we refrained from taking sides in various power struggles by acting as sympathetic listeners and by being direct and straightforward in describing the compromises we chose.

Staff Turnover

One of our evaluative assumptions was that the effects of repeated cycles of staff training would produce a cumulative effect on the ward environment. As we noted earlier, despite negotiated safeguards against staff turnover on this unit, numerous pressures conspired to invalidate our assumption. On the administrative level, chronic understaffing throughout the institution led to the temporary relocation of direct-care personnel to other settings that enjoyed higher priority for full staffing quotas. Although these assignments typically were made for only short periods of time, they occurred frequently. Such movement not only disrupted the consistency of ongoing client training, but also made it difficult to obtain adequate observational samples of staff performance. Matters were further complicated by the fact that staff shifting worked both ways. Understaffing on the unit was remediated by supplying personnel who were unacquainted with the training program and unaware of the evaluation.

The rate of staff turnover was accelerated when several administrators decided that the training sequence was valuable. Rather than let the trained staff accumulate on the unit, there was a tendency to spread this valuable resource around. Although it was hoped that trained personnel would be instrumental in initiating client training in other settings, the actual effect was to dilute the impact of staff training in the target setting and to diminish the effectiveness of those trainees who were assigned to more "hostile," custodial-oriented units.

Table 7.4 depicts staff turnover rates during four cycles of staff training over a 2-year period. The data indicate that a cumulative effect of training could not be expected. Of the 27 staff members who completed the program, only 15 remained at the end of the grant period. In addition, the unit experienced over a

TABLE 7.4
Turnover Rates for Direct-Care Staff Who Participated in Four Cycles
of Staff Training

| | Cycle 1 | | Cycle 2 | | Cycle 3 | | Cycle 4 | | End |
Status	Begin	End	Begin	End	Begin	End	Begin	End	of Grant
Post-Training	0	0	6	3	6	5	13	11	15
In Training	6	6	6	5	9	8	9	8	—
No Training	23	23	17	20	11	16	5	8	13
New Aides	0	9	2	7	4	10	1	6	6
Transferred/Quit/Fired[a]	0/0	0/9	0/2	3/8	2/6	1/7	0/3	2/6	4/5

[a]First number refers to the aides who had completed training; second number denotes the total who were in transit during a cycle.

100% turnover during the evaluation period, with 45 new direct-care providers arriving and 46 leaving. While such a high turnover rate bodes ill for demonstrating reliable training effects, the actual situation was much worse. Four trained participants were absent for extensive periods of time (i.e., 1 to 3 months) as a result of injury and sickness.

There are no easy answers to the difficulties created by staff turnover. The many practical hassles (e.g., finding, *after* you arrive on the scene, that the care provider who was scheduled for observation has been transferred,) can be alleviated partly by establishing good lines of communication, but, in general, they simply must be endured. Fortunately, a number of methodological advances are providing evaluators with innovative strategies to combat the undesirable conceptual and empirical effects of staff turnover. At one level, randomization procedures have been proposed that can be applied to samples that are constantly changing (e.g., Conner, 1977; Goldman, 1977). Additionally, new methods for statistically analyzing data from "interrupted time-series quasi-experiments" have been developed (e.g., McCain & McClearly, 1979). On another level, evaluators are at long last moving away from purely quantitative assessment models and are placing greater emphasis on models that provide more qualitative case study information (Wilson, 1979).

The Consequences of "Small Effect"

Program administrators and participants have good reason to fear rigorous evaluation, especially when it is conducted by outsiders. Several reviews of the evaluation literature (e.g., Gilbert, Light, & Mosteller, 1975; Gordon & Morse, 1975) indicate that the likelihood of demonstrating program effectiveness is inversely related to the methodological quality of the evaluative effort. Both reviews concur in indicating that only about 20% of all rigorously evaluated programs are successful in meeting program goals. Much higher rates of "success," however, are found when the companion evaluation lacks methodological rigor and when it is conducted by investigators who were affiliated with the institutional program.

Within the many constraints imposed on us, we sought to subject the training program to as rigorous an evaluation as possible. Our effort, designed in accord with the model described earlier, incorporated assessment of both self-reported and behaviorally observed data domains. We employed highly reliable instruments, in-depth sampling of major data sources, and, whenever feasible, randomization. Although the major outcomes reported were lengthy and complex (Heatherington & Allen, 1978; Lah & Allen, 1979), they can be summarized briefly as follows:

Analysis of criterion tests indicated that the staff training seminars led to statistically reliable increases in participants' knowledge about behavior measurement and programming. This increase was significant despite widely divergent opinions expressed about the difficulty of the training sequence. Participants provided decidedly positive testimonials about the value of the program both for themselves and the benefits it presumably bestowed on clients. They were especially positive about the component that matched them with a training proctor who provided guidance and direction during their training efforts. In general, they indicated that the presence of the grant staff members had improved both morale and communication, with better cross-shift interactions being especially noteworthy.

Measures of attitude toward the job and ward life that were collected anonymously, however, revealed no reliable improvement over time. The few between-group differences that did emerge could be attributed to an increase in negative ratings by control subjects. This was viewed as indicative of "resentful demoralization" (Cook & Campbell, 1979) on the part of service providers who perceived themselves as receiving little attention from grant staff.

More importantly, analysis of observations of staff behavior failed to reveal any meaningful pattern of differences between trainees and control participants. For example, during the third training cycle, former trainees spent 33% of their time engaged in ward routine activities; current trainees spent 45% of their time engaged in this behavior; and untrained control staff devoted 44% of their time to ward routines. Time estimates for the three groups essentially were similar for all other categories (client care: 13%, 12%, and 17%; socializing with residents: 11%, 9%, and 9%; formal training 1%, 1%, and 1% for former trainees, current participants, and control subjects, respectively). The distribution of activities also is indicative of an environment that emphasized housekeeping, movement of clients, and meeting the physical needs of clients. Not surprisingly, failure to document more training activity was justifiably attributable to chronic staff shortages and turnover.

Analysis of changes in client behavior yielded mixed outcomes. Case study reports of each trainee's efforts to teach a client some adaptive skill were uniformly positive. Supportive data, however, were reported by the trainers themselves. In many cases, these data were extremely difficult to interpret because the relevant criteria had not been specified precisely. During the 2nd year of the evaluation, however, we did an independent assessment to determine whether the skills that reportedly were taught had been maintained. Of the 21 skill areas that had been targeted and trained in 15 clients, 10 had deteriorated at follow up, 9 had been maintained successfully, and 2 had improved. In addition, 60% of the clients had maintained at least some of the skills in which they had been trained 6 months to a year earlier.

Analysis of client behavior on the living unit, however, failed to indicate that the training of specific skills had any appreciable generalization to their overall level of functioning. Systematic observation of clients, conducted primarily in the day room and outdoor play areas, demonstrated that 90% of their waking day was spent in isolated self-stimulatory behavior. This figure did not decline during the course of the program, nor did reliable differences emerge between clients who had received individualized programming and those who did not.

In summary, we did find *some* behavioral evidence that the program met *some* of its stated objectives. Given the complexity of outcome, however, it is impossible to estimate the magnitude of effect without wrestling with yet another issue.

The Functional Autonomy of Evaluation

We have described some of the major outcomes of the project we evaluated and summarized them with a conclusion that is bound to make everyone unhappy. Did the program "work?" In attempting to answer this, we have come full circle to one of our original contentions that "making judgments about the value of a social helping endeavor involves making value judgments." Reactions to our reports ranged from cautious optimism on the part of some program managers to a statement by a middle-level administrator in the funding agency that "2 years of effort and a vast amount of tax money did not produce a damn thing."

Although interesting, those differences of opinion proved to be irrelevant to the continuation of the program. At the end of the grant period, the program suddenly ceased to exist, even though we had not submitted a final report. In fact, our evaluation proved to be totally nonfunctional with regard to affecting the existence of the program. It seemed as though a tacit understanding developed during the first year of the grant to the effect that it would be refunded for a second year but not longer, regardless of the outcome of the evaluation.

Curiously, the grant program itself created excellent public relations throughout the institution, for both project staff and direct-care staff. The confidence and morale of participants appeared to be uplifted by training and parleyed into an assertive advocacy for their unit. A new training position available to the facility was assigned on a nearly full-time basis to the target unit of the grant "to maintain the excellent work of the direct-care staff." The program maintenance format designed by the grant staff was adopted by the administration (with some modifications) and made mandatory for all units. Use of the grant's curriculum library was strongly urged by the administration, and the Inservice Training Department continued using grant products beyond the termination of the project.

The evaluation, however, was accorded much less recognition. Indeed, we received what is perhaps the unkindest slight that evaluators can experience—having our conclusions and recommendations ignored. They were not hailed, not disputed, not scornfully dismissed; they were simply assimilated into the mass of paperwork that characterizes any bureaucracy and ignored.

Our experience typifies that reported by many other evaluators. Cochran's (1978) contention that "we have learned little if anything about the utility of ongoing social policies" (p. 372) is representative of what Rossi, Wright, and Wright (1978) refer to as a "dismal aspect" of the current state of applied evaluation (p. 189). This situation has caused evaluators to wrestle with a fundamental dilemma about the overall meaning of their endeavors. What good is evaluation if it is not applied for the purposes for which it was intended?

The nonutilization of systematic evaluation also poses some serious consequences for change agents attempting to renovate the institution from within. The formidable problems confronting these individuals suggest there are clear risks to attempting programmatic organizational changes, especially of a systemic nature. Institutions experiencing accelerated change will be defensive and resistant to new innovations, which will seem at first to be creating more turmoil, clutter, confusion, and uncertainty. Innovators will have to choose their intervention avenues carefully. Systematic evaluative data represent a potentially imposing source of power. In places where judgments of program and administrative effectiveness are often a matter of conference table persuasion, formal evaluative data can provide no small leverage. Numbers can neutralize articulate but unsubstantiated opinion. Nonutilization of evaluative research becomes troubling in this context.

In partial response to this problem, evaluators have begun to pay increasing attention to the secondary effects of evaluative endeavors. These secondary effects derive from the primary purpose of any evaluation, which usually is codified through contractual negotiation. For example, evaluations aimed at facilitating program change (a) will yield knowledge about the surrounding system, (b) may have impact on program continuation, and (c) can potentially influence the development of ancillary non-targeted programs or activities. Judging the success of any complex evaluation solely on the basis of its stated primary objective can all too easily lead the evaluator to miss its potential impact in broader secondary areas. In the larger perspective of this book, it is not unreasonable to suggest that the importance of evaluation to the institution for the mentally handicapped may lie more in its ability to help filter and control both the rate and the quality of change than in the more narrow function of confirming or disconfirming primary interventions. This seems probable at least for the next decade or so.

Current literature on evaluation emphasizes two related areas of secondary impact—the generalization of knowledge and the use of evaluation as an instrument of social change. Both functions stem from the realization that the discovery of facts is a social process (Kaplan, 1964; Mahoney, 1976) or, as Cochran (1978) has noted, "data are both descriptions of events and events in their own right" (p. 364).

Cochran (1978) suggests that the knowledge generated by an evaluation can be exploited profitably to increase our collective understanding of not only social systems but also deeply rooted perceptual processes that affect the "corruption" of data. Analysis of the second area can facilitate understanding of people's strategies for maintaining power in complex social systems, as well as the external forces that constrain the evaluator. Abt (1978) provides a graphic example of this latter focus by detailing how inept government requirements can increase costs and reduce the effectiveness of evaluative endeavors. Much of what we have written can be viewed in a similar context.

Increases in knowledge about these parameters lead almost inescapably to the conclusion that the evaluation process itself can be used as an active instrument of social change. Accomplishing this, however, requires that the evaluator be willing to take explicit political and even moral stances toward the subject of evaluation. Many evaluators historically have been reluctant to do this because they view this stance as a repudiation of scientific "objectivity."

Fortunately, an increasing number of evaluators are coming to the realization that their efforts inherently involve judgments that stem from their conceptions about the existing social order. Sjoberg (1975) has described two major value orientations of social scientists—maintaining the existing structure versus supporting the disadvantaged—and has detailed how each stance influences the process of theory construction, problem selection, and choice of instrumentation. Cochran (1978) has called for evaluators to make greater efforts to measure what they value, and, in so doing, encourage those values.

Our own experience prompts a number of pragmatic recommendations to offset the impotence evaluative products currently manifest when employed to promote meaningful change in facilities for the mentally handicapped. Evaluators must engage the service system, particularly at administrative decision points. Rutman (1977) sees the separation of planning, management, and evaluation as a major factor in nonutilization. He advises that collaborative relationships be developed between evaluators and decision makers across these three processes. We strongly agree but suggest further that evaluators develop specific linkages with key service providers and administrators early on. Evaluators can assist the process of change if they have access to decision-making forums, and they can earn that access if they understand the workings of the institutional system. A regular feedback loop between the evaluator and chief administrator, for example, may yield information germane to a variety of matters facing both parties. We know one institution superintendent who found evaluative data reflecting a low percentage of direct-care staff time spent on formal training of clients extremely useful in deciding to assign high priority to strengthening the facility's inservice training program.

Once established, this relationship could have surprising utility. Evaluators are potentially valuable advisors to administrators and service professionals. They offer the prospect of quantitative input to managerial and programmatic decisions typically rendered through subjective opinion, instinct, or anecdotal information. Curiously, although accustomed to hard data in fiscal, budgetary, and personnel domains, management has accepted a more elusive standard for information in program organization and service areas. We would expect managers to make an easy adjustment to the utilization of evaluative data after a few trial experiences. Even the most power-conscious administrators seldom misunderstand the importance of making decisions on a solid knowledge base. The evaluators' moral and value systems may undergo some tests in the process, but if their value base is acceptably close to that of the facility, the relationship can work.

In strengthening the role of the evaluator, we would attend more closely to events *following* the completion of any given evaluation. The aftermath of most evaluations currently is far too passive for promoting change. As noted, it usually involves the submission of a report that is more likely to be filed than read. The evaluator, perhaps in concert with a supportive program manager or administrator, should personally present the evaluative outcomes at strategic meetings or special forums. Getting on the agenda of regular administrative or staff meetings is important. The presentations, especially at first, should be considered instructional. The evaluator may very well be auditioning for the future priority of those present. We also advise making multiple presentations and sharing evaluative feedback across staff groups at many levels of the institutional hierarchy.

We are arguing, in effect, that evaluators are information brokers who can service an institution with quantitative feedback about its operations. In facilities hell bent on change or choking under the uncoordinated external demands for change described in Chapter 1, the evaluator can supply vital information on the need for balance between the stability required for delivery of present services and the change needed for growth and response to demand. Broskowski and Driscoll (1978) have described this role for evaluators in some detail. They view the evaluative process as being a critical integrative and adaptive mechanism for the organization as a whole.

Specifically, evaluative data may more accurately indicate whether specific goals are too inflated given available resources (e.g., current levels of trained staff). Evaluators may be better able to tap the pulse of staff morale than managers soliciting feedback or rumors tracking through grapevine. Legal aid attorneys pressing for precipitous placement of clients in communities may be less adversary and arbitrary about their demands when confronted with evaluative information on the variables that affect successful adjustment to community settings. Indeed, perhaps in no other area may evaluation be more desperately needed than in the widespread and frequently antagonistic confrontation between the judicial system and the public human service system. These, and countless other matters, are appropriate topics for a system of evaluation.

FINAL WORDS

The main theme of this chapter is that evaluation is a highly complex *social* activity that is influenced by an incredibly large number of competing forces.

The key to successful program evaluation in bureaucratic systems is to achieve a balance between the political, methodological, and social necessities that affect the numerous participants who are involved on a variety of levels. Achieving such a balance is a delicate process that involves making numerous trade-offs that maintain respect for the integrity of participating staff without seriously compromising the integrity of the evaluator. Successful evaluation is best conducted in a context that emphasizes collaboration between evaluator and participants and thus fosters mutual respect and trust.

We have underscored that performing these functions requires evaluators to take political and moral stances. It also requires that evaluators learn how the institution and its various layers of bureaucracy and staff groups behave. Evaluators must know, for example, the unwritten norms of the direct-care staff, the existing conflicts or territorial disputes between professional groups or sub-units competing for resources, and the forces (e.g., collective bargaining, legal activity) that can and do affect priorities and operations almost on a daily basis. The task is a formidable and complex one that will tax our collective ingenuity during the coming years. The potential for socially beneficial pay-off, however, is immense and undoubtedly will be worth our best efforts.

REFERENCES

Abt, C. C. (1978).   The public good, the private good, and the evaluation of social programs. *Evaluation Quarterly, 2*, 620–630.

Allen, G. J., Chinsky, J. M., Larcen, S. W., Lochman, J. E., & Selinger, H. V. (1976). *Community psychology and the schools: A behaviorally-oriented, multilevel preventive approach.* Hillsdale, NJ: Lawrence Erlbaum Associates.

Allen, G. J., Chinsky, J. M., & Veit, S. W. (1974).   Pressures toward institutionalization within the aide culture: A behavioral-analytic case study. *Journal of Community Psychology, 2*, 67–70.

Allen, G. J., Chinsky, J. M., & Veit, S. W. (1980).   Conducting behavioral evaluations in residential facilities for retarded persons: Pit-falls and prospects. In R. H. Price & P. Polister (Eds.), *Evaluation and action in the community context* (pp. 107–123). New York: Academic Press.

Blau, T. M. (1956). *Bureaucracy in modern society.* New York: Random House.

Broskowski, A., & Driscoll, J. (1978).   The organizational context of program evaluation. In C. C. Attkisson, W. A. Hargreaves, & M. J. Horovitz (Eds.), *Evaluation of human service programs* (pp. 43–58). New York: Academic Press.

Butterfield, E. C. (1967).   The role of environmental factors in the treatment of institutionalized mental retardates. In A. A. Baumeister (Ed.), *Mental retardation: Appraisal, education, and rehabilitation* (pp. 120–137). Chicago: Aldine.

Cochran, N. (1978).   Grandma Moses and the "corruption" of data. *Evaluation Quarterly, 2*, 363–374.

Conner, R. F. (1977).   Selecting a control group. *Evaluation Quarterly, 1*, 195–244.

Cook, T. D., & Campbell, D. T. (1979).   *Quasi-experimentation: Design and analysis issues for field settings.* Chicago: Rand-McNally.

Dailey, W. F., Allen, G. J., Chinsky, J. M., & Veit, S. W. (1974).   Attendant behavior and attitudes toward institutionalized retarded children. *American Journal of Mental Deficiency, 78*, 586–591.

Deming, W. E. (1975). The logic of evaluation. In E. L. Struening & M. Guttentag (Eds.), *Handbook of evaluation research, Vol. 1* (pp. 53–70). Beverly Hills, CA: SAGE

Edwards, W., Guttentag, M., & Snapper, K. (1975). A decision-theoretic approach to evaluation research. In E. L. Struening & M. Guttentag (Eds.), *Handbook of evaluation research, Vol. 1.* (pp. 139–182). Beverly Hills, CA: SAGE.

Gilbert, J. P., Light, R. J., & Mosteller, F. (1975). Assessing social innovation: An empirical base for policy. In C. A. Bennett & A. A. Lumsdaine (Eds.), *Evaluation and experiment* (pp. 39–193). New York: Academic Press.

Goffman, E. (1961). *Asylums.* Garden City, NY: Doubleday-Anchor.

Goldfried, M., & Sprafkin, J. (1974). *Behavioral personality assessment.* Morristown, NJ: General Learning Press.

Goldman, J. (1977). A randomization procedure for "trickle-process" evaluations. *Evaluation Quarterly, 1,* 493–498.

Gordon, G., & Morse, E. V. (1975). Evaluation research. In A. Inkeles (Ed.), *Annual Review of Sociology I.* (pp. 339–361). Palo Alto, CA: Annual Reviews.

Harris, J. M., Veit, S. W., Allen, G. J., & Chinsky, J. M. (1974). Aide-resident ratio and ward population density as mediators of social interaction between retarded children and their aides. *American Journal of Mental Deficiency, 79,* 320–326.

Heatherington, L., & Allen, G. J. (1978). *An evaluation of the radiating effects of the Title XX Staff Training Program, 1977–1978.* (Technical Report). Storrs: University of Connecticut.

Kaplan, A. (1964). *The conduct of inquiry.* San Francisco: Chandler.

Keeney, B. P. (1983). *Asthethics of change.* New York: Guildford.

Klaber, M. M. (1969). *Retardates in residence: A study of institutions.* West Hartford, CT: University of Hartford Press.

Kelly, J. G. (1971). The quest for valid preventive interventions. In B. Rosenblum (Ed.), *Issues in community and preventive mental health* (pp. 109–139). New York: Behavioral Publications.

Lah, M., & Allen, G. J. (1979). *Component analysis of Project S.T.E.P. Title XX Staff Training Program, 1978–1979.* (Technical Report). Storrs: University of Connecticut.

Mahoney, M. (1976). *Scientist as subject.* Cambridge, MA: Ballinger.

Malott, R. W. (1974). A behavioral-systems approach to the design of human services. In D. Harshbarger & R. F. Maley (Eds.), *Behavior analysis and systems analysis: An integrative approach to mental health programs.* Kalamazoo, MI: Behaviordelia.

McCain, L. J., & McClearly, R. (1979). The statistical analysis of the simple interrupted time-series quasi-environment. In T. D. Cook, & D. T. Campbell (Eds.), *Quasi-experimentation: Design and analysis issues for field settings.* Chicago: Rand-McNally.

Murrell, S. A. (1973). *Community psychology and social systems: A conceptual framework and intervention guide.* New York: Behavioral Publications.

Neigher, W. D., & Schulberg, H. C. (1982). Evaluating the outcomes of human service programs: A reassessment. *Evaluation Review, 6,* 731–752.

Nunnally, J. C., & Durham, R. L. (1975). Validity, reliability, and special problems of measurement in evaluation research. In E. L. Struening & M. Guttentag (Eds.), *Handbook of evaluation research, Vol. 1.* (pp. 289–354). Beverly Hills, CA: SAGE.

Nunnally, J. C., & Wilson, W. H. (1975). Method and theory for developing measures in evaluation research. In E. L. Struening & M. Guttentag (Eds.), *Handbook of evaluation research, Vol. 1.* (pp. 227–288). Beverly Hills, CA: SAGE.

O'Leary, K. D., & Kent, R. N. (1973). Behavior modification for social action: Research tactics and problems. In L. A. Hamerlynk, L. C. Handy, & E. J. Mach (Eds.), *Behavior change: Methodology, concepts, and practice.* Champaign, IL: Research Press.

O'Leary, K. D., Kent, R. N., & Kanowitz, J. (1975). Shaping data collection congruent with experimental hypotheses. *Journal of Applied Behavior Analysis, 8,* 43–52.

Olsen, C., Lukeris, S., Billings, A., & Pritchard, M. (1975). *Behavior sampling system: Instruction manual.* Mansfield Depot, CT. Unpublished manuscript, Mansfield Training School.

Palazzoli, M. S., Cecchin, G., Prata, G., & Boscolo, L. (1978). *Paradox and counterparadox.* New York: Jason Aronson.

Reid, J. B. (1970). Reliability assessment of observation data: A possible methodological problem. *Child Development, 41,* 1143–1150.

Reppucci, N. D. & Saunders, J. T. (1983). Focal issues for institutional change. *Professional Psychology: Research and Practice, 14,* 514–528.

Romanczyk, R. G., Kent, R. N., Diament, C., & O'Leary, K. D. (1973). Measuring the reliability of observational data: A reactive process. *Journal of Applied Behavior Analysis, 6,* 175–184.

Rossi, P. H., Wright, J. D., & Wright, S. R. (1978). The theory and practice of applied social research. *Evaluation Quarterly, 2,* 171–192.

Rutman, L. (1977). Planning an evaluation study. In L. Rutman (Ed.), *Evaluation research methods: A basic guide.* Beverly Hills, CA: SAGE.

Scheirer, M. (1978). Program participants' positive perceptions: Psychological conflict of interest in social program evaluation. *Evaluation Quarterly, 2,* 53–70.

Schmidmeyr, B., and Weld, R. (1971). Attitudes of institution employees toward resident-oriented activities of aides. *American Journal of Mental Deficiency, 76,* 105.

Sjoberg, G. (1975). Politics, ethics, and evaluation research. In M. Guttentag & E. L. Struening (Eds.), *Handbook of evaluation research, Vol. 2.* (pp. 29–54). Beverly Hills, CA: SAGE.

Spencer, F. W., Corcoran, C. A., Allen, G. J., Chinsky, J. M., & Veit, S. W. (1974). Reliability and reactivity of the videotape technique on a ward for retarded children. *Journal of Community Psychology, 2,* 71–74.

Twain, D. (1975). Developing and implementing a research strategy. In E. L. Struening, & M. Guttentag (Eds.), *Handbook of evaluation research, Vol. 1.* (pp. 27–52). Beverly Hills, CA: SAGE.

Ullmann, L. P. (1967). *Institution and outcome.* New York: Pergamon.

Veit, S. W., Allen, G. J., & Chinsky, J. M. (1976). Interpersonal interactions between institutionalized retarded children and their attendants. *American Journal of Mental Deficiency, 80,* 535–542.

Weiss, C. (1975). Evaluation research in the political context. In E. L. Struening & M. Guttentag (Eds.), *Handbook of evaluation research, Vol. 1.* (pp. 13–26). Beverly Hills, CA: SAGE.

Wilson, S. (1979). Explorations of the usefulness of case study evaluations. *Evaluation Quarterly, 3,* 446–459.

Author Index

Subject Index